The Social History of Politics
Critical Perspectives in West German Historical Writing Since 1945

The Social History of Politics

Critical Perspectives in West German Historical
Writing Since 1945

Edited by Georg Iggers

ST. MARTIN'S PRESS
New York

© Copyright Berg Publishers 1985

First published in the United States of America in 1986

Printed in Great Britain

ISBN 0-312-73295-3

Library of Congress Cataloging-in-Publication Data
Main entry under title:

The Social history of politics.

Contents: From "Pöbel" to "proletariat" / Werner
Conze — The pseudo-democratization of the Junker class /
Hans Rosenberg — White-collar employees and industrial society in
Imperial Germany / Jürgen Kocka — [etc.]
   1. Social classes—Political aspects—Germany—Addresses, essays,
lectures.   2. Labor and laboring
classes—Germany—History—Addresses, essays, lectures.
3. Germany—History—1871–1918—Historiography—Addresses,
essays, lectures.   I. Iggers, Georg G.
HN460.S6S65   1985   306'.2'0943   85-22349
ISBN 0-312-73295-3

Contents

Introduction

The prestige of German historical studies in the twentieth century has been very different from that in the nineteenth. Then, German historical scholarship, identified with the name of Ranke, was accepted widely throughout the world as the model for historical research. As amateur traditions were replaced by the stress on history as a 'scientific' enterprise and a profession, German patterns of university education, specifically as they related to the training of the historian in critical methods, were imitated. Historical societies and journals were founded following the German example. Students flocked to Berlin to study with Ranke, Droysen, Sybel, and Schmoller.[1] All of this has changed since the First World War. German historiography has been largely ignored, and until relatively recently probably rightly so. An extremely narrow provincialism came to pervade historical thinking and historical writing

1. For a history in English of the conservative tradition of German historiography and historical thought, see Georg G. Iggers, *The German Conception of History. The National Tradition of Historical Thought from Herder to the Present*, Middletown, (Ct.) 1968, 2nd ed. rev., 1983; for two studies in German, see Heinrich von Srbik, *Geist und Geschichte vom deutschen Humanismus bis zur Gegenwart*, 2 vols., Munich, 1950, 1951 (by a conservative Austrian advocate of a Greater Germany), and Joachim Streisand (ed.), *Studien über die deutsche Geschichtswissenschaft*, 2 vols., Berlin/GDR, 1963, 1965 (from a Marxist–Leninist perspective). A very useful collection of brief studies of individual historians is contained in Hans-Ulrich Wehler (ed.), *Deutsche Historiker*, 9 vols., Göttingen, 1971–1982. See also Manfred Asendorf (ed.), *Aus der Aufklärung in die permanente Restauration. Geschichtswissenschaft in Deutschland*, Hamburg, 1974, particularly his Introduction, 'Deutsche Geschichtswissenschaft'; the thoughtful essays by Ernst Schulin, *Traditionskritik und Rekonstruktionsversuch*, Göttingen, 1979. On the influence of German scholarship in America, see Jurgen Herbst, *The German Historical School in American Scholarship*, Ithaca, NY, 1965; in France, see William R. Keylor, *Academy and*

at the universities, a preoccupation with German problems seen from a parochial political perspective. While historical studies internationally by the turn of the century, and with increasing rapidity since the two world wars, explored new methods and new themes, the majority of German university historians, and after 1945 of West German historians, held fast to historical and political notions which dated back to the period of German political unification in the nineteenth century.

The identification of the German historiographical tradition with Ranke is not entirely correct. Ranke's major contribution to historical scholarship in the nineteenth century was not the application of critical methods as such, which had a much longer history,[2] but the much greater consciousness about the rigorous use of these methods. Most important probably was the example which he provided for the training of historians. Ranke hardly fulfilled his own demand that the historian should avoid value judgments and let the documents speak for themselves. His definition of what constituted a historical source, with stress on documents of state, already involved a value commitment. Ranke assumed that the central institution in society, and therefore also the institution of central interest to the historian, was the state, but much more narrowly conceived than that of Hegel, for whom the state, as the embodiment of the ethical idea, encompassed culture and society. Ranke likened the state to an individual, possessing a personality of its own, an idea which guided its development and actions. The idea of the state expressed itself in the pursuit of the maintenance and growth of its power. The proper subject of history for Ranke was therefore the functioning of international relations, particularly the balance of power among the great states in the European community. Although the stress was on military and diplomatic matters,

---

Community: The Foundation of the French Historical Profession, Cambridge, Mass., 1975 and Martin Siegel, 'Science and the Historical Imagination in French Historiographical Thought 1866–1914', Ph.D. diss., Columbia, 1965; in Great Britain, Doris S. Goldstein, 'The Professionalization of History in Britain in the Late Nineteenth and Early Twentieth Centuries', *Storia della Storiografia*, no. 3, 1983, pp. 3–27.

2. See Peter H. Reill, *The German Enlightenment and the Rise of Historicism*, Berkeley, 1975; Andreas Kraus, *Vernunft und Geschichte: Die Bedeutung der deutschen Akademien für die Entwicklung der Geschichtswissenschaft im späten 18. Jahrhundert*; the volume by H. Bödeker, G. Iggers, J. Knudsen and P. Reill, *Aufklärung und Geschichte. Studien zur deutschen Geschtswissenschaft in der zweiten Hälfte des 18 Jahrhunderts*, Göttingen, 1985; Georg G. Iggers, 'The University of Göttingen 1760 and 1800 and the Transformation of Historical Scholarship', in *Storia della Storiografia*, no. 2, 1982, pp. 11–37.

religion and to a lesser extent literature played a role in determining the character and strength of a state. Nevertheless all considerations of domestic politics were to be subordinated to the exigencies of foreign policy.[3] Ranke, for example, could thus write the history of England in the seventeenth century as the story of the religious conflicts seen in the context of international politics with almost no reference to the great economic and social changes which were taking place. This stress on power relations, generally deprived of the religious and cultural concerns which humanised Ranke's historical narrative, was adopted by a broad segment of nineteenth-century historical scholarship in Germany and abroad. This conception of the state fitted better into the age of absolutism which formed the theme of the major part of Ranke's work than into nineteenth-century, post-revolutionary Europe to which it was applied by many of Ranke's admirers.

This approach to political history was closely associated in Ranke's thought with a theory of historical knowledge and a conception of what constituted the 'scientific' character of historical studies, 'scientific' in the sense of the German word 'Wissenschaft'. For Ranke there was a fundamental difference between history and philosophy, a distinction which later German historians and philosophers such as Droysen and Dilthey made between the cultural and the natural sciences. As Ranke stated repeatedly and emphatically, history dealt with the particular, philosophy with the general. History sought understanding, philosophy explanation. Historical science dealt with the conscious, voluntary actions of great individuals, although it also took into account the great tendencies at work in history. The historian therefore told a story; he did not analyse. 'There are forces, indeed spiritual, life-giving, creative forces, nay life itself, and there are moral energies, whose development we see,' Ranke noted. 'They cannot be defined or put into abstract terms, but one can behold them and observe them. One can develop a sympathy for their existence.'[4] The scientific character of history lay in the 'impartial' immersion into the sources, which almost always meant documents, the reconstruction of the intentions of the actors and the course of events and the intuitive perception of the larger historical context. Narration was the only

---

3. See Ranke's two essays, 'The Great Powers' in Georg G. Iggers and Konrad von Moltke (eds.), *Leopold von Ranke. The Theory and Practice of History*, Indianapolis, 1973, pp. 65–101 and 'The Political Dialogue', ibid., pp. 102–130.
4. Idem, 'The Great Powers', ibid., p. 100.

form of historical discourse. The actors were to be taken at their word. The procedure was critical only in so far as it attempted to establish the genuineness of the sources (external criticism) and the truthfulness of the statements they contained (internal criticism) without examining the motives and interests which underlay these assertions. Objectivity thus involved a highly uncritical note, the acceptance of the existing order as a manifestation of a moral order. Analysis, the introduction of 'abstract terms' into historical discourse, represented a denial of the vitality of human life and thus contradicted the demands of a science suited to the understanding of human affairs.

But Ranke's influence on nineteenth-century historical studies has generally been overstated. Ranke represented developments in historical studies, for example in the renewed critical interest in sources, which were shared by broad segments of scholarship in Germany and abroad. Typical for a broad sector of academic historical writing was the event-orientated and person-centred narrative history which Ranke exemplified. But in France, Great Britain, the United States and elsewhere, very different concerns, reflecting the greater democratisation of these societies which expressed itself in a much greater interest in domestic issues, scholarly history took on different forms.[5] But in Germany too Ranke was out of step with the times. He represented a consciously conservative outlook which championed the values of an older European order. Although he recognised the emergence of nationalism as a powerful force in the aftermath of the French Revolution, he continued to view the conception of a unified German state created in defiance of the European system of states with distrust and feared the move toward constitutionalism and limited parliamentarism which the German liberals favoured.

Much more important for the formation of German academic historiography were the historians associated with the 'Prussian School', Droysen, Sybel and, perhaps most of all, Treitschke. These historians came from a liberal orientation which underwent fundamental changes in the course of the nineteenth century. All were critical of Ranke, of his political conservatism, his professed objectivity, and his narrow conception of politics. In their view, the

5. See Keylor, *Academy and Community*; Siegel, 'Historical Imagination', Goldstein, 'History in Britain'; Herbst, *German Historical School*; as well as John Higham, Felix Gilbert and Leonard Krieger, *History. The Development of Historical Studies in the United States*, Englewood Cliffs NJ, 1965.

middle classes of property and education were to be active participants in a constitutional monarchy which guaranteed basic civil
liberties, particularly those of intellectual expression, and provided
for representative institutions. They favored the political and economic unification of a Germany under the leadership of a liberalised
Prussia excluding Austria. The transformation which took place in
the political and historical outlook of these historians between the
failed Revolution of 1848 and Bismarck's forcible unification of
Germany, a unification which amounted basically to the annexation
of Germany into Prussia, reflects closely what has been described as
the crisis of German liberalism.[6]

The thesis that Germany's political, social, and intellectual history in the second half of the nineteenth and the first half of the
twentieth century differed fundamentally from that of other economically developed societies in Europe and the English-speaking
world has been sharply challenged in recent years as we shall see
later in this essay. Nevertheless without this thesis it is difficult to
understand the hold maintained over German scholarship into the
second half of the twentieth century, through two world wars and
the experience of Nazism, by the political and historical conceptions which originated with the Prussian School. The history of
German academic scholarship in the nineteenth century is closely
bound up with the transformation of German liberalism. The
historians in the period of German unification who identified
themselves with the Prussian cause, such as Dahlmann, Droysen,
Sybel and even the somewhat younger Treitschke, conceived of
themselves as liberals in political, social and economic terms. They
championed Prussia because they viewed Prussia as a potentially
modern, progressive society. Before 1848 all called for constitutional reforms. Both Dahlmann and Droysen wrote histories of the
age of revolution in modern Europe.[7] Yet they all, including Gervinus, not unlike liberals elsewhere in Europe in this period, feared
the rise of democracy, were committed to monarchy, and stressed
the need for a strong national state. The defeat of the Revolution of
1848 represented a critical turn for these historians. Gervinus alone
lost his illusions about the ability of the Prussian state to lead the

---

6. On German liberalism, see James Sheehan, *German Liberalism in the Nineteenth Century*, Chicago, 1978; F. C. Sell, *Die Tragödie des deutschen Liberalis-
mus*, Stuttgart, 1953.
7. Dahlmann, *Geschichte der englischen Revolution*, 1844, and *Geschichte der
französischen Revolution*, 1845; Droysen, *Vorlesungen über die Freiheitskriege*,
Kiel, 1846.

way to a society responsive to public opinion and in the 1850s became an open critic of the established order and an advocate of political democracy. As a historian, he now moved away from a narrow focus on the national state to a broad comparative approach to the literature and culture of the modern world. His was one of the few voices to see the military events of 1870 which led to the unification of Germany under Prussian dominance 'as pregnant with incalculable dangers, because they lead us on a path which runs completely counter to the character of our people, and what is even worse, counter to the character of the whole epoch'.[8]

Despite their original opposition to Bismarck's successful effort in the Prussian constitutional conflict of the 1860s to ignore the desires of the Prussian diet in the conflict about the reorganisation of the army, the rest all, including for the time being Theodor Mommsen who later became a critic of Bismarck's policies,[9] shifted their support to Bismarck after the victories over Denmark and Austria. Droysen had said in 1866 that once Germany became unified, the process of liberalisation would begin.[10] Yet by 1871 this seemed to have been forgotten. The position of the historians, who now dominated the chairs of history at the German universities not only in Prussia but also elsewhere — Sybel became professor in Munich in 1856 — closely paralleled that of the German state. The new state provided the ground for the rapid development of modern industry and corporate capitalism. The introduction of universal suffrage by Bismarck for the lower house first of the North German Confederation in 1867, then of the German Empire in 1871, provided the appearance of popular representation, but of a parliament which while not without moral force had little power not only in matters of foreign policy and military control but of domestic legislation. The limited powers of the Reichstag were further limited not only by an upper house dominated by the Prussian monarchy but by a suffrage in the various German states which favoured the possessing classes. The extent to which the German pattern of political and social development differed from that of other European, particularly West European societies, has been questioned in recent years by historians who argued that Germany too saw the

---

8. 'Vorwort', *Geschichte der deutschen Dichtung*, 5th ed., Leipzig, 1871, vol. 1, p. vii.
9. See Alfred Heuss, *Theodor Mommsen und das 19. Jahrhundert*, Kiel, 1956.
10. See Iggers, *The German Conception*, p. 121.

triumph of a modern bourgeois society and culture.[11] Arnold
Mayer has recently tried to demonstrate the hold of aristocratic
classes over European politics and society generally in Europe until
the First World War.[12] Nevertheless there appears to be a difference
in the political development in Germany in the period between
Bismarck's wars and the defeat of the German Empire in the First
World War, a difference which was reflected in the intellectual
sphere, including historical scholarship.

The political, and as we shall see intellectual, compromise between the *Bürgertum* of property and education and the aristocratic
classes went much further in Germany than in the countries of
Western and Northern Europe. In Germany, as incidentally also in
the Habsburg Monarchy, the process of parliamentarisation was not
completed. Aristocratic influences remained dominant in a bureaucracy and a military establishment which functioned immune from
direct parliamentary control. A majority of Germans who considered themselves liberals, the core of the National Liberal Party who
had broken from the liberal Progress Party when the latter after the
war with Austria refused to absolve Bismarck of the blame of
having violated the Prussian constitution, supported the constitutional compromise.

The rapid industrialisation of Germany, accompanied by the
emergence of a growing, restless working class organised in the
Social Democratic Party, led the Prussian historians to an increasing
social conservatism. What remained of their liberal credo was their
support in the name of secularism and free thought of Bismarck's
campaign against the Catholic Church in the *Kulturkampf* of the
1870s. All except Mommsen supported Bismarck's break with his
liberal allies in 1878 with the introduction of protective tariffs
favouring the large East Elbian agrarian interests and the legislation
outlawing the Social Democratic Party. Sybel and Treitschke concentrated their efforts in the 1870s not only on combating Marxist
socialism but also the reformism of the *Kathedersozialisten* (Socialists of the Chair) around the *Verein für Sozialpolitik*, founded in
1872, which sought to reconcile the industrial workers to the
monarchical state. Treitschke's *Deutsche Geschichte*, begun in the
1870s and covering the years from the French Revolution to the
Revolution of 1848, represented perhaps the most important work

11. E.g., David Blackbourn and Geoff Eley, *The Peculiarities of German History.
Bourgeois Society and Politics in Nineteenth-Century Germany*, Oxford, 1984.
12. *The Persistence of the Old Regime. Europe to the Great War*, New York. 1981.

of both scholarly and popular history of the period. Here the main positions of the new historiography became clearly apparent. In the place of Ranke's professed detachment, Treitschke called for the political engagement of the historian and the scholar. Even more so than in other Western countries, historical scholarship in Germany became an instrument of political education and propaganda. Left of Treitschke's liberalism was his attempt to link the national cause with a broad consensus among the German middle classes, his rejection of the tradition of monarchical absolutism for the Bismarckian solution which integrated the middle classes of property and education into the monarchical order. In the place of Ranke's conception of the balance of powers, Treitschke viewed international relations as a battle field for the survival of the strongest. Treitschke advocated an aggressive German foreign policy directed against England which included the construction of a battle fleet and the establishment of colonies. Social Darwinism in this form was not restricted to Germany. Nor were the racial and antisemitic overtones which Treitschke introduced into his analysis of the modern world. Yet distinct was his radical rejection of the liberal principles he had once championed, his subordination of domestic considerations to the exigencies of military power, and his defence of the political and social status quo in Germany.[13]

Treitschke's *Deutsche Geschichte* still included a broad treatment of literary and cultural history seen within the context of politics. There also developed a rich literature in economic and social history, represented by the so-called Younger Historical School of National Economy, by economists such as Gustav Schmoller but also historians including Otto Hintze and Kurt Breysig. The new school of economic history saw economics as a historical discipline, avoiding the generalising approach of classical political economy and adapting the chronological, particularistic method of the political historians. Schmoller and Hintze accepted the national paradigm of the latter and concentrated on the relationship of state and economy in the Prussian monarchy with its paternalistic bureaucracy. Although more cognisant of the economic and social problems created by industrialisation and open to social reforms within the system, the historical economists nevertheless affirmed the political

13. See Heinrich Treitschke, 'Der Sozialismus und seine Gönner' (1874) in his *Aufsätze, Reden und Briefe*, vol. 4, Meersburg, 1929, pp. 122, 221. On Treitschke, see Andreas Dorpalen, *Heinrich von Treitschke*, New Haven, 1957; Hans Schleier, *Sybel und Treitschke*, Berlin/GDR, 1965.

order created by Bismarck and stressed the superiority of the
Prusso-German constitutional system to that of the Western parliamentary states. The awareness of the social dislocations created
by rapid industrialisation nevertheless called forth an intense interest in social history and in what was called the social question not
only within the German public but also at the universities.[14]
It is at this point that the first volume of Karl Lamprecht's
Deutsche Geschichte appeared in 1891. Lamprecht too concentrated
on the German national community. In two important ways, however, his approach to German history differed from that of his
colleagues. Lamprecht combined a concern with the political development of Germany since the Middle Ages with an interest in
economics, social conditions, and culture. He differed from the
cultural historians of the mid- and late-nineteenth century, such as
Riehl and Gothein, by relating culture and politics; he differed from
his colleagues in the discipline by expanding the scope of national
history to include many aspects of society and culture. But methodologically too he went in a different direction by combining a
narrative and chronological approach with the attempt to formulate
theses regarding Germany's historical development. This attempt to
formulate laws of historical development based on a romantic
psychology of the national soul was hardly convincing but raised
the question as to whether history like other areas of social enquiry
needed to go beyond the narration of events to the analysis of social
conditions.[15] Lamprecht was not alone in raising these concerns.
Throughout the international community of historical scholarship
the Rankean model of studying and writing history was questioned
on at least two grounds.[16] History it was believed should be more
comprehensive in its scope, including many aspects of economic,
social, and cultural life. Moreover, a narrative, event-orientated
approach concentrating on personalities in positions of power
should be supplemented by the analysis of the social structures in

14. See Gerhard Oestreich, 'Die Fachhistorie und die Anfänge der sozialgeschichtli-
chen Forschung in Deutschland', *Historische Zeitschrift*, 208, 1969, pp. 320–63.
15. There are several recent treatments of Lamprecht; see Luise Schorn-Schütte,
Karl Lamprecht. Kulturgeschichte, Wissenschaft und Politik, Göttingen, 1984;
Karl-Heinz Metz, *Grundformen historiographischen Denkens. Wissenschafts-
geschichte als Methodologie. Dargestellt an Ranke, Treitschke und Lamprecht*,
Munich, 1980; Matti Viikari, *Die Krise der 'historistischen' Geschichtsschreibung
und die Geschichtsmethodologie Karl Lamprechts*, Helsinki, 1977; and a recent
Ph. diss., University of Chicago, December 1984, by Susan Schultz.
16. See Georg G. Iggers, 'The "Methodenstreit" in International Perspective. The
Reorientation of Historical Studies at the Turn from the Nineteenth to the
Twentieth Century', *Storia della Storiografia*, no. 6, 1984, pp. 21–32.

which these events occurred and these personalities functioned. There took place an international debate on the nature of historical knowledge, involving philosophers, sociologists, and historians. Among these, scholars like Emile Durkheim, Paul Lacombe and François Simiand in France and Karl Lamprecht and Kurt Breysig in Germany argued that history was a social science which examined social processes and social structures with the aid of explicit theories; theories, however, which differed from those in the natural sciences by taking into account the unique context in which these processes occurred. Others, particularly the German neo-Kantian philosophers, Wilhelm Windelband and Heinrich Rickert, but also Alexander Xénopol who was active in France and Romania, argued that history as a cultural science required a logic of enquiry totally different from that of other sciences, one which stressed the unique, qualitative character of historical events which could not be subsumed into larger explanatory generalisations. The German academic historians understood the argument as a defence of their narrative, event-orientated approach to political history. This was an extreme position dominant in the German historical profession. Most historians elsewhere occupied an intermediate position, agreeing with Wilhelm Dilthey, Max Weber, and Henri Berr that all history requires conceptual constructs which nevertheless have to take into account the historicity of social phenomena.

The question of the proper subject of historical study and the methods best suited to it were discussed in the literature throughout the Western world, in the German- and French-speaking countries particularly, but also in the United States, Italy, Romania, Scandinavia and elsewhere. The New Historians in the United States, Henri Berr in France, Henri Pirenne in Belgium, and Karl Lamprecht and Kurt Breysig in Germany, called for the inclusion of social and economic factors into a comprehensive account of the past. They sought to establish a link between history and the social sciences without sacrificing the autonomy of history. Two major journals became forums for the international search for new approaches in history, the *Zeitschrift für Wirthschafts- und Socialgeschichte*, founded in 1893 by a group of Marxist historians in Austria but published in Germany, with articles in several European languages, and including contributions by historians from very different ideological orientations[17] — after 1900 it became the *Vierteljahrschrift*

17. Including also the very conservative Georg von Below.

für Wirtschafts- und Sozialgeschichte — and the more theoretically orientated *Revue de synthèse historique* founded by Henri Berr in Paris in 1900.[18] Yet the discussion in Germany was much more bitter than that elsewhere. The attack against Karl Lamprecht by important spokesmen of the German academic establishment took on strong ideological and political overtones which the methodological discussion lacked elsewhere. The *Historische Zeitschrift*, the central journal in the profession, became the vehicle for the often vitriolic polemics against Lamprecht, who was suspected not only of positivism but of Marxism. The outcome of the debate was the firm establishment of the traditional mode of national political history as the paradigm of historical scholarship.

In an important sense the German historical profession after the Lamprecht controversy drifted into isolation. Traditional patterns of a nation- and event-orientated political history maintained themselves elsewhere too until well after the Second World War. But there was a greater openness to questions of social history and to the methods and concepts of various social scientific approaches. Lamprecht's work was taken seriously abroad. He was invited to lecture in Paris and in the United States. German history increasingly turned to a defence of the German status quo. The revival of interest in Ranke at the turn of the century expressed itself in an application of Ranke's concept of the European balance of power to the world scene with the insistence on Germany's proper role both overseas and on the seas.[19] The emphasis on scholarly objectivity by the neo-Rankean historians merely hid their profound chauvinistic and anti-democratic prejudices. There no longer was any fundamental distinction in outlook and method between their historical work and that of the heirs of the Prussian school, the neo-Treitschkeans. The method of recruitment at the German universities, reinforced by the famous Lex Aron legislation in 1896 which barred Social Democrats from university positions, enforced ideological conformity. This conformity was intensified in the First World War when the professoriate generally sought to formulate an ideology which justified the German war effort against the Western Allies.[20]

18. See Keylor, *Academy and Community*; Siegel, 'Historical Imagination'; Luciano Allegra and Angelo Torre, *La Nascita della Storia Sociale in Francia. Dalla Commune alle 'Annales'*, Turin, 1977.
19. See Ludwig Dehio, 'Ranke and German Imperialism' in his *Germany and World Politics in the Twentieth Century*, New York, 1967, pp. 38–71; Hans-Heinz Krill, *Die Rankerenaissance*, Berlin, 1962.
20. See Klaus Schwabe, *Wissenschaft und Kriegsmoral*, Göttingen, 1969; also the

A moderately divergent position did in fact develop among German university intellectuals in the early twentieth century. Here again scholarship was closely interwoven with politics. Politically this position, best represented by Friedrich Meinecke among the historians, agreed with the conservative historical establishment in most major points, the soundness of the Prusso-German constitutional order, its superiority over the parliamentary democracies of the West, and the justification of Germany's naval and imperial ambitions. Meinecke, like Max Weber[21] and Pastor Friedrich Naumann, wished, however, to counteract the growing strength of Social Democracy by integrating the workers into imperial society through social reforms without basically modifying the monarchical structure. Meinecke, as editor of the *Historische Zeitschrift*, was in the foreground in the late 1890s in the campaign against Karl Lamprecht. At the same time, he sought to break the narrowness of a diplomatic-military approach to history by examining the role of political idea. His *Weltbürgertum und Nationalstaat* (1907) celebrated the unique fusion of power politics and culture which characterised the unification of Germany under Prussia and established its superiority over Western nationalisms. Meinecke reaffirmed Droysen and Dilthey's call for a specific methodological approach to history which concentrated on the particular; in Meinecke's case, the great personalities who combined political leadership with philosophic insight, and who could be understood only through an intuitive immersion into their writings. Politically, Meinecke in the First World War, like Naumann, Troeltsch, and Weber, supported the war effort including annexations but called for a greater realism regarding the limits of German strength and for the need of limited concessions to political democracy. These men became the opponents of the ultranationalism of the Pan-Germans during the war and the supporters of the new republic in November 1918, less out of enthusiasm than from a sense of the inevitability of events.

The aftermath of the defeat of 1918 led to a further hardening of the historiographical lines. The profession was unanimous in rejecting the war guilt thesis propounded in Article 231 of the Treaty of Versailles. German public opinion from the right to the left,

---

wartime essays, *Deutschland und der Weltkrieg*, Berlin, 1915, ed. by Otto Hintze, Friedrich Meinecke, Hermann Oncken, and Hermann Schumacher.
21. See Wolfgang J. Mommsen, *Max Weber and German Politics 1890–1920*, Chicago, 1985.

including the Communist, agreed on the injustice of the charge that Germany was solely or primarily responsible for the outbreak of the war.[22] Academic historians however went beyond this to the almost unanimous assertion that Germany alone was guiltless among the powers. At best, the powers 'slid' into war. Again historiographical and political positions were closely interwoven. Not only the main orientation of conservative historians but also moderates like Meinecke, Delbrück, and Oncken asserted the basic soundness of Bismarck's solution of the German question. Although they recognised tactical mistakes in the foreign policy decisions of Bismarck's successors during the rule of Wilhelm II, they, unlike certain socialist critics outside academe, such as Karl Kautsky and Kurt Eisner, emphatically rejected the notion that there was any connection between the structure of German state and society and an aggressive policy. Conservatives and moderates alike excluded a critical examination of social factors from historical interpretation. An older generation of conservative historians such as Georg von Below, Dietrich Schäfer, Ernst Marcks, Max Lenz, Otto von Westphal and Adelbert Wahl, as well as younger historians like Gerhard Ritter, Hans Rothfels, and Hans Herzfeld, combined their political rejection of the Weimar Republic with a reassertion of the traditional emphasis on national power as the central theme in historical scholarship.[23] There was as little room for dissidents at the universities as there had been during the Empire. Otto Hintze, who shared the intense attachment to Prussian traditions of the nationalistically orientated historians, constituted an exception in his attempt to apply theoretical constructs of society, akin in some ways to those of Max Weber, in his comparative study of the emergence of modern political society.[24]

Nevertheless important, even if isolated in terms of influence, voices of dissent were heard in the Weimar Republic. From very different approaches, Johannes Ziekursch, Veit Valentin — who had been purged from university teaching during the First World War

22. On the public debate within and outside academe on war guilt, see Wolfgang Jäger, *Historische Forschung und politische Kultur in Deutschland. Die Debatte 1914–1980 über den Ausbruch des Ersten Weltkrieges*, Göttingen, 1984.
23. On the historians in the Weimar Republic, see Hans Schleier, *Die bürgerliche Geschichtsschreibung der Weimarer Republik*, Berlin/GDR, 1975; Bernd Faulenbach, *Ideologie des deutschen Weges: Die deutsche Geschichte in der Historiographie zwischen Kaiserreich und Nationalsozialismus*, Munich, 1980.
24. For an English collection, see Felix Gilbert (ed.), *The Historical Essays of Otto Hintze*, New York, 1975.

— and the Catholic historian Franz Schnabel critically reassessed the failure of democracy in nineteenth-century Germany. Schnabel began a broadly conceived history of early-nineteenth-century Germany which integrated politics and political ideas with cultural, legal, and social developments. Yet with the exception of Ziekursch, who held a university chair and who like Schnabel was to be forcibly retired by the Nazis, the critics of the nationalistic mode of historiography were all outsiders to the discipline. Arthur Rosenberg was a *Dozent* for Roman history at Berlin, without a chair; others such as Eckart Kehr and Hans Rosenberg, students of Friedrich Meinecke, who encouraged a diversity of opinion in his seminars, were at the very beginning of their careers. Politics and methodology were intertwined in the writings of the young dissidents. The roots of German policy leading to the outbreak of the First World War and to Germany's defeat, they argued, were to be found in the inner tensions of the political system forged by Bismarck which in turn had to be explained in terms of the contradictions of German society in the Imperial period. In their view a narrative history of political events had thus to be supplemented by the analysis of social conflict. Arthur Rosenberg, who had been a spokesman for the German Communist Party in the Reichstag until he broke with the party in 1926 as it turned to Stalinism, used Marxian concepts of class struggle in his *Die Entstehung der Deutschen Republik* (1928).[25] He argued that from its very foundation Bismarck's Empire was doomed as a result of an untenable alliance against the threat of democratisation by two social groups with conflicting interests, the old aristocratic classes which dominated the government and the new industrial capitalistic interests. George W. F. Hallgarten examined the political and social character of pre-1914 economic imperialism as a source of the war in a work[26] which could no longer be published in Germany. Marxist notions of class were joined in Hallgarten's, in Eckart Kehr's and in Hans Rosenberg's work, with concepts of social analysis derived from Max Weber. Max Weber himself had emphasised the basic contradiction between the political structure and the social and economic realities in Imperial Germany. Weber was no democrat; he was committed to a vigorous and expansionist German foreign policy; he believed that this policy required a strong executive. Neverthe-

25. Transl. as, *The Birth of the German Republic 1871–1918*, New York, 1931.
26. *Vorkriegs-Imperialismus: Die soziologischen Grundlagen der Aussenpolitik der europäischen Grossmächte vor dem ersten Weltkrieg*, 2 vols., Munich, 1951.

less he saw in the social and political prerogatives which the Bismarckian system gave to an outdated agrarian Junker class a reason for Germany's inability to develop the full economic strength required by the exigencies of the world situation. Aware of the irresponsibilities of Wilhelminian policy, Weber recognised the superiority of a system like that found in Great Britain and (particularly) in the United States, which gave political parties an important share of political power and made the political leadership responsible to the parties. Kehr in his study of party politics and the construction of the German battle fleet at the beginning of the twentieth century[27] carried Weber's critique further in a democratic direction. In his view it was the fear of the potential power of the emergent working classes which drove the new corporate capitalism into an alliance with an agrarian aristocracy artificially kept afloat by protectionist legislation. But the interests of modern industry in the long run were irreconcilable with those of the aristocratic agrarian sector. In order to maintain social stability, the industrial and agrarian interest groups pursued a policy of imperialism and navalism which required that full mobilisation of the population possible only in a democracy, but it is this which they desperately attempted to prevent. The contradictions of Imperial society and politics thus paved the way to both the First World War and the Revolution. For Arthur Rosenberg, Hallgarten and Kehr history no longer revolved around a narrative but involved a set of problems which required the utilisation of analytical concepts.

These new beginnings of a critical social history of politics not only had little influence in a historical profession characterised by a conservative nationalistic consensus; they were also forcibly excluded from German academic life after the Nazi seizure of power. The latter marked not only the emigration of the critical historians — Kehr, who had encountered serious difficulties in his career even before 1933, died in that year in Washington, DC — but the end of an active academic role for almost all the scholars who had supported the Weimar Republic. Meinecke was forced to resign as editor of the *Historische Zeitschrift*, a position he had held since Treitschke's death in 1896; Oncken was hounded into retirement, as

---

27. *Schlachtflottenbau und Parteipolitik 1894–1901*, Berlin, 1930 (repub. 1965); English transl., *Battleship Building and Party Politics in Germany 1894–1901*, now available on microfilm from the University of Chicago Press. Kehr's essays have been translated into English as *Economic Interest, Militarism, and Foreign Policy. Essays on German History*, Berkeley, 1977.

were other liberals such as Johannes Ziekursch and Walter Goetz. Franz Schnabel lost his position. Veit Valentin, Gustav Mayer (the historian of Social Democracy), Arthur Rosenberg, George W. F. Hallgarten, Hajo Holborn, and many of Meinecke's promising students were forced into emigration.[28] The structure of the German educational system and in particular of the universities[29] explains in part why the historical profession did not reflect public opinion. After all a large segment in the Empire and in the Weimar Republic reflected democratic attitudes. Yet the Social Democratic viewpoint was almost unrepresented at the universities, even in the Weimar Republic. The system of secondary education virtually restricted university admission to the sons of the educated classes, the *Bildungsbürgertum*. This, as Fritz Ringer has shown,[30] was also the case in other European countries. But the relationship of the educated middle classes to parliamentary democracy was a very different one in Great Britain or France. The political ethos at the *École Normale* in Paris, which was a chief recruiting ground for the French historical profession, was positive to France's republican traditions. The procedure of recruiting future holders of chairs (*Ordinarien*) in Germany, the dependence of a scholar approaching middle age on a chair holder for whom he wrote a second dissertation (*Habilitation*), the procedure by which the chair holders could by a simple secret vote block a candidate's admission into the profession, all served to ensure that the profession remained uniform in ideological orientation and political background. It also assured that the professoriate in the Weimar Republic, with the few exceptions of moderates like Meinecke or Delbrück who embraced the republic not out of a sense of conviction but from a recognition of its inevitability after the collapse of 1918, was impassionedly opposed to the Republic.

28. On Nazi control over the German historical profession, see Helmut Heiber, *Walter Frank und sein Reichsinstitut für Geschichte des neuen Deutschlands*, Stuttgart, 1966; on the historians in emigration, see Georg G. Iggers, 'Die deutschen Historiker in der Emigration' in Bernd Faulenbach (ed.), *Geschichtswissenschaft in Deutschland*, Munich, 1974; and the chapter on the historians in Lewis Coser, *Refugee Scholars in America*, New Haven, 1984.
29. On the German universities, see Fritz Ringer, *The Decline of the German Mandarins: The German Academic Community 1890–1933*, Cambridge, Mass., 1969; Charles E. McClelland, *State, Society, and University in Germany, 1700–1914*, Cambridge, 1980. On the social origin of the German historians since the beginning of the nineteenth century, see Wolfgang Weber, *Priester der Klio. Historisch-sozialwissenschaftliche Studien zur Herkunft und Karriere deutscher Historiker und zur Geschichte der Geschichtswissenschaft 1800–1970*, Frankfurt, 1984.
30. *Education and Society in Modern Europe*, Bloomington, 1979.

The Nazi dictatorship did not effectively break the domination of the conservative nationalistic orientation. As we saw, the few historians who in the Weimar Republic had called for a critical reassessment of German political traditions were forced into exile or into retirement. The moderate voices such as Meinecke or Oncken who had supported the Republic were neutralised or, in isolated cases such as Wilhelm Mommsen, reversed their position and supported the Nazis. The attempt of the Nazis to coordinate the profession proved inconclusive. There were both points of agreement and of divergence between the historical ideology of the Nazis and that of the conservative establishment. Many of the historians were antisemites; many thought in *völkisch* terms of race; but they nevertheless continued to see history as a struggle of states. In contrast to Nazi notions of a Greater Germany, they were committed to Bismarck's *kleindeutsch* solution which placed Prussia in the centre of the German state system. They continued to distinguish between scholarship and propaganda although failing to acknowledge the strong ideological bias which guided and distorted their view of history. Elitist in outlook, they mistrusted the Nazi appeal to the masses and the romanticisation of the peasant; yet they welcomed the end of the Weimar Republic, the abolition of parties, and above all the assertive new foreign policy. The attempts of the Nazis to coordinate historical scholarship and teaching by means of the *Reichsinstitut für die Geschichte des Neuen Deutschlands*,[31] headed by Walter Frank, turned out to be successful only to a very limited degree despite the fact that a number of prestigious historians of the Weimar Republic, Erich Marcks, Fritz Hartung, Karl Alexander von Müller, who assumed the editorship of the *Historische Zeitschrift* and introduced its section on the Jewish problem, and the Austrian Pan-German Heinrich von Srbik served on its advisory board. The majority of German historians, however, went their merry way with little interference from the Nazis. Interference was not necessary because on very fundamental questions they were close to the Nazi position. The medievalists particularly accepted Nazi interpretations of the Germanic past.[32] The consensus on foreign policy, the revision of Versailles, the annexation of Austria and the Sudetenland, the campaign against France but also the war in Russia included almost the entire spectrum of German historians,

---

31. See Heiber, *Walter Frank.*
32. See Karl Ferdinand Werner, *Das NS-Geschichtsbild und die deutsche Geschichtswissenschaft*, Stuttgart, 1967.

including those like Meinecke who felt uncomfortable with Nazi domestic regimentation.[33] Few historians thus rethought their position. The Nazi orientation nevertheless led interestingly enough to a new concern with aspects of social history among isolated historians. Ideologically at least Nazi doctrine was less orientated towards the state than towards the mystical *Volk*. Nazi fixations on racial ancestry and purity led to the first important attempts at family reconstitution, carried out, of course, from a very different perspective than that of the French and British historical demographers of the post-Second World War period. Particularly in the area of the old regime of pre-industrial Europe two very important studies appeared which pointed in new directions. Otto Brunner's *Land und Herrschaft* (1939) in its concern with the interrelation of political, social, and attitudinal structures led away from the older narrative, narrowly state- and person-orientated approach to medieval and early modern history. There was also Wilhelm Abel's remarkable study of agricultural history from the Middle Ages to the Industrial Revolution. The latter, a pathbreaking work neglected in Germany until the 1960s but taken very seriously in post-war France and Eastern Europe, freed the history of agriculture from its romantic fixation on the peasant and on national culture and undertook a broadly comparative international study of the effect of fluctuations in food production, demography, prices and wages on the agricultural population.

Outside Germany, in emigration, German scholarship raised the question of the rise of Nazism which inevitably involved a critical reevaluation of the German past. Leaving aside for the moment the work of Kehr, the two Rosenbergs, to whom we shall return, and Hallgarten, the German historians in exile concentrated on ideology rather than on factors arising from tensions in the social and political structure. One noticeable exception was the attempt by the political scientist Franz Neumann, *Behemoth*, to analyse Nazi terror and dictatorship in terms of Marxist categories of the crisis of modern capitalism. Within the tradition of a *kleindeutsch* liberalism, Erich Eyck in British exile analysed the inadequacies of Bismarck's domestic and foreign policies which led to the 'personal regime' of Wilhelm II with its disastrous consequences for Germany internationally.[34] The key interest however resided in the history of

33. See Iggers, *The German Conception*, p. 223.
34. Erich Eyck, *Bismarck. Leben und Werk*, 3 vols., Zürich, 1941–1944; transl. as,

ideas. Hajo Holborn in a seminal article published in Germany in 1952 examined the social significance of the German concept of *Bildung* for the political development of nineteenth-century Germany.[35] Influenced by Friedrich Meinecke's *Ideengeschichte*, a large number of students of Germany's fateful development in the twentieth century, particularly in the United States, took up the theme of the intellectual and cultural divergence of Germany from the West, only this divergence was now seen as a source of tragedy for Germany rather than as an achievement of the German spirit. Since the French Revolution Germany's development had diverged from that of the West. George Mosse,[36] Fritz Stern[37] and to some extent I in my book on German historicism[38] sought basic roots for the failure of democracy in Germany in anti-democratic ideologies and anti-modernism. Fritz Ringer, in his masterful analysis of the German professoriate,[39] made a contribution to the social setting within which this divergence from the main tradition of European liberalism took place.

This ideological critique of the failure of liberal democracy and the heritage of the West European Enlightenment in Germany played an important role in the writings of two Communist analysts of the rise of fascism — Alexander Abusch in what was to become the German Democratic Republic and Georg Lukács[40] in Hungary; the latter's thesis of the fateful 'misery' (*Misere*) of Germany's political development was soon repudiated by historians in the GDR who stressed the 'lawfulness' of a progressive road to socialism. In West Germany after 1945 two early attempts to examine critically Germany's political development remained relatively ignored. These were F. C. Sell's book on the 'tragedy' of German liberalism and Heinrich Heffters's study of German self-administration in the nineteenth century;[41] both scholars were outside the discipline proper. The historical profession in what became the

Bismarck and the German Empire, London, 1950; also his *Das persöliche Regiment Wilhelms II.*, Zürich, 1948.

35. 'Der deutsche Idealismus in sozialgeschichtlicher Bedeutung', *Historische Zeitschrift*, 174, 1952, pp. 359–84; transl. as, 'German Idealism in the Light of Social History', in Holborn, *Germany and Europe*, Garden City, NY, 1971, pp. 1–23.
36. *The Crisis of German Ideology*, New York, 1964.
37. *The Politics of Cultural Despair*, Berkeley, 1963; *The Failure of Illiberalism: Essays on the Political Culture of Modern Germany*, New York, 1972.
38. *The German Conception*.
39. Ringer, *The Decline of the German Mandarins*.
40. Particularly Georg Lukács, *Die Zerstörung der Vernunft*, Berlin/GDR, 1954.
41. *Deutsche Selbstverwaltung im 19. Jahrhundert*, Stuttgart, 1950.

Federal Republic remained relatively unaffected by the collapse of
the Nazi regime in 1945. Walter Frank, who had already lost all
influence, committed suicide on the eve of the capitulation. A very few
of the historians, who had been particularly involved in propagating
Nazi racial ideas, Günther Franz, Erwin Hölzle and Adolf Rein, lost
their positions without losing their ability to participate actively in
the journals, publications and congresses of the profession. Others
as deeply involved as Karl Alexander von Müller and Walther
Hubatsch, who had few qualms about their past, were reintegrated
into the profession, as were Hermann Heimpel and Reinhard Wit-
tram, both of whom confessed their errors and in the latter's case
returned to a conservative national, religiously tinged, ideology.
What was left in 1945 was essentially the profession of 1933 purged
of its more liberal, critical elements. Of the historians who had
emigrated only two returned permanently: Hans Rothfels, the
spokesman in Königsberg before 1933 of a German mission in
Eastern Europe, who despite his Jewish ancestry attempted desperately to remain in Nazi Germany,[42] and the equally conservative
Hans-Joachim Schoeps. The tone of the postwar discussion was set
by the octogenarian Friedrich Meinecke's examination of the im-
port of Nazism in his *Die deutsche Katastrophe* published in 1946.
In speaking of the 'negative and disintegrating influence' of the
Jews[43], even a man who had been open to the Weimar Republic, and
incidentally supportive of Jewish students, revealed how little he
understood the enormity of what had happened in Germany.
Meinecke expressed an outlook which was to be widely repeated in
West German historical writing in the late 1940s and 1950s that the
explanation for the Nazi rise to power was not to be found in
German political traditions but in forces common to Western
Europe and basically foreign to Germany. 30 January 1933 was
basically an accident in German history. As Gerhard Ritter suggested, Germany turned to Nazism not because it was insufficiently
democratic but because it was too democratic. The intellectual
ancestors of Hitler were not Frederick the Great and Bismarck but
Robespierre and Lenin.[44] Ritter now forgot conveniently that in

---

42. See Rothfels' collection of essays and lectures, *Ostraum, Preussentum und
    Reichsgedanke*, still published in Leipzig in 1935; Clarence Pate, 'The Historical
    Writings of Hans Rothfels', Ph. D. diss., SUNY/Buffalo, 1973.
43. *Die deutsche Katastrophe*, Wiesbaden, 1946, p. 29; transl. as *The German
    Catastrophe*, Cambridge, Mass., 1950, p. 15.
44. See 'The Fault of Mass Democracy', in John L. Snell (ed.), *The Nazi Revolution.
    Germany's Guilt or Germany's Fate?*, New York, 1959, p. 81; *Carl Goerdeler*

1936 in the introduction to his biography of Frederick he had asserted this line of continuity.[45] Just as Meinecke had reasserted the soundness and superiority of Germany's cultural traditions so Ritter reasserted that of Germany's political heritage. The latter view was crucial to interpretations of the German resistance against Nazism. Both Ritter and Rothfels[46] saw the main heroes of the resistance in the conservative coalition of Prussian aristocrats and military men, profoundly Christian, who organised the assassination attempt of 20 July 1944. The Social Democratic and Communist resistance was ignored and its adherents, in so far as they interfered with the war effort, condemned as traitors worthy of execution.[47]

Nazism now was condemned. German responsibility for the outbreak of the Second World War was recognised but largely ascribed to Hitler himself. However, no special responsibility was accepted for the outbreak of the First World War. In an age of reconciliation with the Western allies, West German historians agreed with French historians in a joint statement on school-book revision that the war was the tragic outcome of the entanglement of alliances. The war was not provoked; Europe 'slid' into it.[48] The Treitschkean tradition which had dominated the historical profession in the Weimar Republic was now repudiated for one more akin to the moderate position represented by Meinecke, which asserted the basic soundness of Bismarck's work but saw critically the foreign policy manoeuvering of his successors. The conservative young historians of the Weimar period, Ritter, Rothfels, and Herzfeld, who became in the Federal Republic the most powerful individuals within the profession, identified themselves with this more moderate position. This was also the orientation of the influential Institute for Contemporary History (founded in Munich in 1950 with the active participation of Hans Rothfels) and its journal, the *Vierteljahrhefte für Zeitgeschichte*. In terms of methodology, the senior spokesmen for the profession, particularly Gerhard Ritter,[49]

und die deutsche Widerstandsbewegung, Stuttgart, 1955 (edition cited here, Munich, 1964, p. 97.)
45. *Friedrich der Grosse. Ein historisches Profil*, Leipzig, 1936.
46. *The German Opposition to Hitler. An Appraisal*, Hinsdale, 1948; in German, *Die deutsche Opposition gegen Hitler. Eine Würdigung*, Krefeld, 1949.
47. Cf. Ritter, *Carl Goerdeler*, p. 103. Ritter approves of the execution of the members of the Rote Kapelle by the Nazis.
48. See Jäger, *Historische Forschung*.
49. E.g., 'Scientific History, Contemporary History and Political Science', *History and Theory*, I (1961), pp. 261–79.

remained outspokenly critical of new approaches to political history, not only of the new social history of the French *Annales*, which Ritter condemned most vigorously, but also, even if less strongly, of the attempts, such as in Karl Dietrich Bracher's masterful study of the dissolution of the Weimar Republic,[50] to apply analytical concepts drawn from political science to the examination of political processes. The sharp division which had existed between the historians in the discipline proper and the historically-minded sociologists, such as Ralf Dahrendorf, and political scientists such as Ernst Frankel and Ossip Flechtheim, who examined the advent of Nazism in terms of social categories[51], remained.

A remarkable consensus dominated the historical profession of the Federal Republic at the end of the 1950s. The key professorial positions were still held by men who had been trained in Imperial Germany and begun their careers in the Weimar period — Gerhard Ritter, Hans Herzfeld, Hans Rothfels. The middle generation consisted of men like Werner Conze, Otto Brunner and Theodor Schieder who had trained in the late days of the Weimar Republic and attained chairs during the Nazi period. Totally lacking were those critical peers in their generation who had left Germany after January 1933 never to return. Except for a few unreconstructed apologists of the main lines of Nazi foreign and military policy such as Hubatsch[52], almost all historians now assigned Germany a crucial part of the responsibility for the outbreak of the Second World War, a responsibility which they, however, identified largely with the personal decisions of Hitler. The debate which became acute in the 1970s over the character of the Nazi regime, between those who sought to explain both the advent of the regime and its subsequent course in the context of the structure of German society and those who saw in it the dictatorship of a man,[53] did not even emerge. The insistence on a separate road of German history, the rejection of the Western European political and intellectual heritage which had been central to the credo of both extreme and moderate nationalistic

50. *Die Auflösung der Weimarer Republik*, Villingen, 1955.
51. See Ralf Dahrendorf, *Gesellschaft und Demokratie in Deutschland*, Munich, 1965, transl. as, *Society and Democracy in Germany*, Garden City, NY, 1967.
52. See Walther Hubatsch, *Weserübung. Die deutsche Besetzung von Dänemark und Norwegen 1940*, Göttingen, 1960.
53. See the exchange of views at a conference sponsored by the German Historical Institute, London, in 1979, Gerhard Hirschfeld and Lothar Kettenacker (eds.), *Der 'Führerstaat': Mythos und Realität. Studien zur Struktur und Politik des Dritten Reiches — The 'Führer State': Myth and Reality. Studies on the Structure and Politics of the Third Reich*, Stuttgart, 1981.

historians was muted in an age in which West Germany saw its fate inseparably intertwined with that of its NATO allies. In reviewing the course of events of the First World War, the historians now almost unanimously identified themselves with the supposedly moderate position, championed at the time by Weber, Meinecke, Troeltsch, and Hans Delbrück[54] and repudiated the aggressive policies and aims of the Pan-Germans. But this assumed that the Imperial government in fact followed a moderate policy, that Bethmann Hollweg honestly attempted to avoid war in the summer of 1914, that he pursued flexible and realistic war aims, and that his moderation, which reflected the views of a broad segment of Germany's cultured public, contrasted with that of Ludendorff and the Pan-German extremists who finally toppled him.

Fritz Fischer's *Der Griff nach der Weltmacht*,[55] published in 1961, came as a direct challenge to the assumptions about the German past which governed this consensus. It is important to note that Fischer himself, a professor (Ordinarius), was not an outsider, but very much a member of the professional historical community. Like other colleagues in his generation — he was born in 1908 — he had as a historian and as a recipient of grants from Frank's *Reichsinstitut*, cooperated with the Nazis, at the time probably out of conviction, and like his colleagues had repudiated this earlier position in his thinking after 1945. In the topics on which he worked, in political and religious history — he had been trained as an Evangelical minister — he followed the conventional methodological procedures. His book on Germany's war aims too was essentially traditional in its reliance on documents of states and the papers of statemen. Fischer's theses appear to have emerged, as he suggested to his own surprise,[56] from the reading of the sources in the East German archives relating to the crisis of July 1914 which had previously not been fully explored. Fischer came to two controversial conclusions. In supporting Austrian plans in the July crisis the Imperial government consciously followed a policy which took the risk of war. The notion that the war was forced on a reluctant Germany or that the European powers unwillingly 'slid' into the war, as had been maintained by his colleagues, had to be replaced by

54. On Delbrück, see Annelise Thimme, *Hans Delbrück als Kritiker der Wilhelminischen Epoche*, Düsseldorf, 1955; Arden Bucholz, *Hans Delbrück and the German Military Establishment*, Iowa City, 1985.
55. Shortened English version, *German War Aims in the First World War*, New York, 1967.
56. Cf. Jäger, *Historische Forschung*, p. 138.

the recognition that Germany played an active role in the outbreak of the war. This thesis was not entirely new. It had been maintained in the 1940s by the Italian historian, Luigi Albertini, but not seriously addressed in Germany. An even more serious challenge to the prevailing consensus was contained in Fischer's second important conclusion, namely that annexationist war aims, which foresaw German hegemony over Eastern and Western Europe, the replacement of Great Britain and Russia as the major powers in the Middle East and Persia, and the expansion of Germany's colonial empire in Africa and the Pacific, were not restricted to the Pan-Germans but were actively supported by the so-called moderates in the Imperial government under the leadership of Bethmann Hollweg. These aims did not evolve in the course of the war but were clearly formulated at the beginning. They possessed an uncanny similarity to the aims of the Nazis, for example in their plans for the expulsion of Slavic peoples from their lands. In the place of an extremist political opinion, which could be repudiated, and a moderate position, represented by Bethmann-Hollweg, which reflected civilised behaviour on the political and military plane, Fischer argued that there existed a unity in outlook which encompassed almost all of German opinion from the far right to the Majority Social Democrats.

Fischer's conclusions raised critical questions regarding the German past but also regarding the ways in which German historians had traditionally approached history. Going beyond the outbreak of the First World War, the book suggested that there existed a continuity between Germany then and Germany in the Third Reich. Hitler's accession to power in 1933 was not an accident, as Meinecke had suggested in 1945,[57] with no roots in the German past but a development which had to be understood within the context of German conditions. This explains in part the impassioned, in some cases (Gerhard Ritter) vitriolic and almost hysterical, reaction of a part of the German professoriate to Fischer's book.[58] The

---

57. Meinecke uses the term 'Zufall'. See *Deutsche Katastrophe*, chap. VIII, 'Der Zufall und das Allgemeine', pp. 87–104, transl. as, 'Chance and General Tendencies', *German Catastrophe*, pp. 56–70.
58. Cf. 'Eine neue Kriegsschuldthese?' in E. W. Graf Lynar (ed.), *Deutsche Kriegsziele 1914–1918*, Frankfurt, 1964, pp. 121–44 and elsewhere. Ritter's *Staatskunst und Kriegshandwerk. Das Problem des "Militarismus" in Deutschland*, 4 vols., Munich, 1959–1968, begun before the publication of Fischer's book, became an answer to Fischer. A good deal has been written on the Fischer controversy. See esp., Volker Berghahn, 'Die Fischer–Kontroverse — 15 Jahre danach', *Geschichte und Gesellschaft*, 6, 1980, pp. 403–19; John A. Moses, *The Politics of Illusion. The Fischer Controversy in German Historiography*, London, 1975.

conservative picture of the basic soundness of German society as it was forged by Bismarck was at stake. Yet the conventional methods of text criticism employed by Fischer did not suffice to answer the questions which his own research raised. The idea of the continuity of German policy in two wars had been raised in the late 1940s and the 1950s by Ludwig Dehio.[59] But Dehio saw German aggressiveness in terms of a notion, reminiscent of Ranke, of the play of the great powers, in which Germany, after the decline of France, saw herself exposed to the dangers of a hegemonical power. In the two introductory chapters of the book, however, Fischer saw the sources of German expansionism not in Germany's position internationally but in her political, social, and economic structure. The book thus raised questions about the causes of what it clearly saw as the catastrophic development of Germany in the twentieth century which it could not answer by conventional means of narrative historical scholarship.

At the 1964 Congress of the West German historians in Berlin Fischer's theses were at least taken seriously. There could, of course, be differences of opinion on his interpretation of Bethmann Hollweg's plans. There could be little argument about the specific actions of the Imperial government in the July crisis. Traditionalists like Egmont Zechlin and Karl Dietrich Erdmann continued to insist on the basically defensive character of German policy in the summer of 1914. Andreas Hillgruber argued that the Imperial government did not want war but out of defensive considerations thought it had to pursue a 'calculated risk'.[60] This conception of the 'calculated risk' was also entertained by Wolfgang J. Mommsen, who felt that Fischer had not proved his point, but did agree that considerations of domestic as well as foreign policy, the attempt to escape from the dilemmas of internal conflict and international isolation, led the government to enter the risk which led to war.[61] Two clear lines were emerging in West German historiography. On the one hand there was the traditional position, also maintained by younger historians like Hillgruber, that German policies in this crucial

59. See *Gleichgewicht oder Hegemonie*, Krefeld, 1948, transl. as *The Precarious Balance. Four Centuries of European Power Struggle*, New York, 1962, and *Deutschland und die Weltpolitik im 20. Jahrhundert*, Munich, 1955, transl. as *Germany and World Politics in the Twentieth Century*, New York, 1960.
60. See, e.g., *Die gescheiterte Grossmacht. Eine Skizze des Deutschen Reiches 1871–1945*, Düsseldorf, 1980, p. 49.
61. See 'Domestic Factors in German Foreign Policy Before 1914', *Central European History*, 6, 1973, pp. 3–43.

period were to be understood primarily in terms of the exigencies of the international scene. Methodologically this essentially meant a commitment to conventional methods of documentary research. The second position involved the conception that decisions of international policy were deeply intertwined with domestic considerations. The study of this relationship involved an examination of social, economic, and intellectual factors which did not immediately become apparent in the narrative reconstructed from the documents. What both orientations had in common and what distinguished them from the new currents of social history abroad was their continued concentration on national history, and essentially on the political history of the Prusso-German nation state as it had been created by Bismarck. They were primarily interested in seeking an explanation for the fateful course of German history in the twentieth century.

The critical reexamination of the German past was largely undertaken by a younger generation of historians who had been educated in the post-Nazi period. They were free of the emotional attachment to conservative German values. They were more open to the social science discussion outside Germany, particularly in the English-speaking world. Many studied in the United States and to a lesser extent Great Britain and thus were able to escape the narrow parochialism which marked their elders. Yet they were open not only to the Anglo-American social science orientations but also to German traditions of social science, to Marx, without being Marxists, and to Max Weber. They were very much aware of the critical approach to German history which the emigrés had brought to the United States. But they were less influenced by the examination of German intellectual currents, undertaken by George Mosse and Fritz Stern, or by the liberal political and cultural history of Hajo Holborn[62] than by those historians, Eckart Kehr, Hans Rosenberg, and to a lesser extent Arthur Rosenberg, who already in the Weimar Republic had applied methods of social analysis to the critique of the German past. Kehr's work, which was largely unknown, was republished by Hans-Ulrich Wehler in the mid-1960s. Wehler's introduction to the volume of Kehr's essays in 1966 outlined the basic concepts of the new critical orientation.[63] The historians of this new orientation did not constitute a school. They had studied

62. *A History of Modern Germany*, 3 vols., New York, 1959–1969.
63. Wehler's biographical Introduction to Eckart Kehr, *Der Primat der Innenpolitik*, Berlin, 1965.

under various mentors, not only Fritz Fischer but also two historians, Werner Conze and Theodor Schieder, who became increasingly
interested in social questions but themselves were essentially
committed to the traditional national outlook, and a younger social
historian of politics, Gerhard A. Ritter (not to be confused with
Gerhard Ritter), who was interested in the history of labour and in
the comparative study of parliamentary institutions in Europe. The
younger critical scholars shared the conception of the belated and
uneven modernisation of Germany which had been developed by
Kehr in his work on the battle fleet, but not only by him but by
various social theorists during and before the Weimar period.
Elements of this idea were contained in Marx and Engels' analyses
of German conditions and in a more explicit form in Weber's
writing. Thorstein Veblen formulated it clearly during the First
World War.[64] What distinguished the new generation of critical
historians from Marx and also from Weber was their unqualified
attachment to a liberal, social democracy.

This belief in a liberal, social democracy is crucial to the critical
'social history of politics' as defined below. In this sense the new
orientation is as political as the traditional nationalistic historians
whom they combat. They basically accept the traditional notion of
the divergent development of Germany from the main course of
Western democracy, but reverse the valuation. It is not Germany
but Western Europe and America which offer the model for normal
political development. This notion is summed up in the selections in
this volume from Hans-Ulrich Wehler's *Das Deutsche Kaiserreich
1871–1918*. Industrialisation was not accompanied in Germany by
the processes of political, or for that matter social modernisation,
which corresponded to it. In Marx's words of 1843, Germany in the
absence of a successful bourgeois revolution constituted an
'anachronism'. The process of economic modernisation took place
within a society in which the old social structures and power
relations were still in place and in which an aristocratic class of
agricultural capitalists continued to occupy positions of social prestige and political influence. In the face of the rise of a militant
industrial working class, the German bourgeois classes turned to the
autocratic state to prevent the democratisation which would have
given the workers a voice in government. The fear of socialism led
not only to an alliance between large industry and large agriculture

64. *Imperial Germany and the Industrial Revolution*, New York, 1915.

but also to the solidarity of preindustrial lower classes, artisans, small farmers, shopkeepers, and petty bureaucrats with the established order. This coalition of forces who wished to maintain their status in the face of changing conditions by all possible means led to a system of protective legislation which artificially kept alive economic sectors no longer viable and to the institution of whole systems of control in schools, church and army which ensured the maintenance of the class system. The tension between the authoritarian social order which was thus preserved by repressive means and the new forces generated by industrialisation produced increasing pressure to escape domestic conflict through foreign expansion, not only in search of new markets but as a means of preserving a national cohesion from which the industrial working classes were effectively excluded. As Kehr had maintained, the policy to enter a naval arms race was determined not by the exigencies of foreign policy but by the concern to maintain social stability.

What did this critical approach to German history signify for historical methodology? A number of things. First of all a shift of focus from a primarily narrative account of the decisions of leading political persons to an examination of the broader political and social contexts in which these decisions are made. This examination could follow relatively traditional approaches to the documents. Hans-Jürgen Puhle's book on the Agrarian League (*Bund der Landwirte*) published in 1966 narrated the activities of agrarian interest groups in Wilhelmine Germany on the basis of the papers of these groups to demonstrate the emergence of what he called 'pre-fascist' attitudes.[65] For the most part, however, the new historians turned from narrative to social analysis. The new critical historians, e.g. Wehler and Kocka, spoke of the necessity of history to utilise the systematic social sciences,[66] but, as they well recognised, there was no unified social science and the historian thus had to proceed eclectically in his application of methods and concepts. The new historical orientation is unthinkable without Marx, but it is not Marxist. In contrast to what we might call the consensus theory of the nationalist school, which recognised status groups but rejected the concept of class conflict, the critical historians proceeded

65. *Agrarische Interessenpolitik und preussischer Konservatismus im Wilhelminischen Reich 1893–1916*, Hanover, 1966.
66. Cf. H.-U. Wehler, *Geschichte als Historische Sozialwissenschaft*, Frankfurt, 1973, and *Historische Sozialwissenschaft und Geschichtsschreibung*, Göttingen, 1980; Jürgen Kocka, *Sozialgeschichte: Begriff, Entwicklung, Probleme*, Göttingen, 1977.

from the notion that society is marked by conflict. But like Marx, and unlike many later Marxists, including E. P. Thompson, they did not see this conflict almost exclusively in terms of the confrontation of capitalists and proletarians. They recognised the complex inter-action and diversity of classes, as Marx himself had done in the *Eighteenth Brumaire of Louis Bonaparte*, and were interested not only in class conflict but also in class collaboration. Their relation to Marxist social analysis is perhaps best developed in Jürgen Kocka's searching study of class society during the First World War,[67] which completely abandons narration for an analytical approach, supported by statistical data, to test the Marxist thesis of class conflict, here presented as an ideal-type in the Weberian sense to be compared with actual empirical evidence. In Kocka's book the complexity of modern industrial society becomes apparent. The economic class relations posited by Marx are modified by a variety of other factors, religion, ethnicity, status in a very variegated working class. State and labour unions, highly bureaucratised at this point, possess an autonomy of their own which does not corre-spond to Marx's concepts. These ideas are also developed elsewhere in the literature of the critical orientation. In the place of the Leninist concept of monopoly capitalism, the critical historians take up Rudolf Hilferding's idea, advanced early in the century, of an 'organised capitalism'[68] in which a high concentration of capital indeed has taken place but class conflicts are mitigated by state intervention, the integration of capital and labour into the political process, imperialism abroad and reform at home. It is questionable, however, whether this concept fits the situation well in any devel-oped industrial nation in the pre-1914 period. Conditions were very different in each of these countries. British capitalism had not experienced the degree of concentration of German or American capital; on the other hand the integration of organised labour into the state decision making process did not occur in Germany until the First World War and then only very partially.[69] What the critical historians shared with Marxists despite their repeated affirmation of empirical social science was their hesitation to use quantitative approaches. In the final analysis, they agreed with Max Weber, that

67. *Klassengesellschaft im Krieg 1914–1918*, Göttingen, 1973, transl. as *Facing Total War. German Society 1914–1918*, Leamington Spa, 1985.
68. See the discussions in H. A. Winkler (ed.), *Organisierter Kapitalismus. Voraus-setzungen und Anfänge*, Göttingen, 1974.
69. See Dieter Groh, *Negative Integration und revolutionärer Attentismus. Die deutsche Sozialdemokratie am Vorabend des 1. Weltkrieges*, Frankfurt, 1973.

all social reality reflects meaning and this meaning requires a conceptual understanding which cannot be reduced to mathematical relationships. What separated them from Marxism was, of course, not only their rejection of the world historical scheme of Marxism as simplistic but their commitment to a socially enlightened parliamentary democracy with its guarantee of individual freedoms. Several works are important for the development of the critical orientation. We have already mentioned the revival of Kehr's work in the 1960s. Very important for the crystallisation of the critical theory of the new social historians of politics was the work of Hans Rosenberg, who remained in the United States, but held several seminars in West Germany in the early years after the war which had a significant influence on a number of then young historians. Hans Rosenberg's classic study of the emergence of bureaucratic absolutism in Prussia, *Bureaucracy, Aristocracy and Autocracy: The Prussian Experience, 1640–1815*, published in English in 1958, provided a historical and theoretical foundation for the critical studies of the failure of democracy in nineteenth-century Germany, this notwithstanding the fact that the book, in part due to the intervention of Gerhard Ritter, did not appear in Germany.[70] As Wehler has suggested, Rosenberg's work was particularly significant for West German scholars because the older historical tradition of economics, represented by Schmoller but also Hintze, had died out and sociology, which once was highly historically orientated, had, in following Anglo-American models, become increasingly ahistorical.[71] In his studies of bureaucracy and monarchy in Prussia Rosenberg in a sense continued the work of Schmoller and particularly of Hintze, but now with a much more critical perspective which saw in the Prussian state not the servant of the people but an autocratic instrument for the preservation of the domination over Prussian and German society of the older aristocratic classes and the new industrial elite. In a subsequent book, *Grosse Depression und Bismarck-zeit*, published in 1967, Rosenberg developed ideas, which he had explored in essays since the 1930s, on the impact of recurrent business cycles, with their disruptions of economic growth, on politics. The stress was now less on events and personalities than on

70. Regarding Ritter's intervention see H.-U. Wehler, 'Geschichtswissenschaft heute', in Jürgen Habermas, *Stichworte zur 'Geistigen Situation der Zeit'*, Frankfurt, 1979, vol. 2, p. 721. In connection with Rosenberg's work, the important book by Alexander Gerschenkron, *Bread and Democracy in Germany*, Berkeley, 1943, should be mentioned here.
71. See Wehler's comment in 'Geschichtswissenschaft heute', p. 721, n. 16.

socio-political and economic structures. The effect of the depression of 1873 was different in Germany and Austria–Hungary, where parliamentarisation and democratisation had been thwarted and where the traditional classes felt their status to be threatened, to its result on the Western countries. The fear of the inevitability of modern social conditions and of democracy led to the emergence after the dislocations of 1873 of a complex of political attitudes which foreshadowed in their antisemitism, their stress on authority and order and their sense of a national community which transcended class lines many of the aspects of fascism. What distinguishes this approach to the triumph of illiberalism from older narrative studies of the failure of democracy, e.g. Erich Eyck's studies of Bismarck and Wilhelm II written in exile,[72] is the movement from a history which sees this process primarily in terms of conflicting personalities and ideas as they are revealed in the documents to one which analyses political conflict in the context of the social conflicts occasioned by industrialisation.

What this adds up to is the conception basic to the younger critical historians: that the events of 1933 can only be understood within the context of Germany's history since 1848, as the failure of democratic nationalism in a period of industrialisation, and that this failure, as Kehr and Rosenberg argued, must be understood in terms of the development of bureaucratic absolutism in Prussia. Kehr's and Rosenberg's ideas were developed further in two seminal but very different works by Hans-Ulrich Wehler, *Bismarck und der Imperialismus* (1969) and *Das Deutsche Kaiserreich 1871–1918* (1973).[73] In the first of these books, Wehler seeks to examine Bismarck's turn to colonialism within the context of the social and political dislocations caused by industrialisation in a society which was as unevenly modernised as Germany, less as a search for markets than as an instrument for national integration and stabilisation. A theoretical first part, in which the conception of the uneven development of Germany is developed, is followed by a second part which narrates the course of German colonial policy. The second work dispenses with chronological development almost entirely. Wehler examines the Empire as a politico-social system: he examines two simultaneous economic transformations, an industrial revolution which is accompanied by what Wehler labels an 'agri-

72. Eyck, *Bismarck*.
73. Transl. as *The German Empire, 1871–1918*, Leamington Spa, 1985.

cultural revolution' which strengthened the large aristocratic landlords, who as Rosenberg and Kehr had already demonstrated,
constituted a capitalistic class. Wehler then proceeds to portray the
alliance between these two classes which resulted in Bismarck's
'revolution from above'; the impotence of the political parties; the
role of interest groups in the political system; the mobilisation of
the traditional classes threatened by economic modernisation
against the socialists; the irreconcilable conflicts of interests among
the elements in this coalition, education, family, military, church,
and courts as the means both of social control and the preservation
of the class system; finally, the escape into antisemitism, integral
nationalism, imperialism, and war in the face of the insoluble
conflicts of a system which desperately sought to prevent democratisation.

Wehler's synthesis was preceded and followed by a host of
studies which attempted to provide a careful documentary basis to
this critical interpretation of modern German history. In 1960
Immanuel Geiss, a student of Fischer, published a study on German
war aims in Poland.[74] Helmut Böhme, another student of Fischer,
integrated the conception of the unequal modernisation of Germany into a study of the unification of Germany in which Bismarck's role was subordinated to that of the struggle of Prussia for
commercial superiority.[75] A number of studies by Hans Jaeger,[76]
Hartmut Kaelble[77] and Hans-Jürgen Puhle[78] examined the role of
economic pressure groups in German politics. Heinrich August
Winkler dealt with the political outlook of artisans and small
retailers.[79] Again the emergence of anti-democratic, often antisemitic attitudes were central to these studies. Dirk Stegmann followed
the course of the *Sammlungspolitik*, the attempt to create a broad
conservative coalition around the fear of socialism.[80] Peter Christian
Witt in his careful examination of the attempt at tax reform between

74. *Der polnische Grenzstreifen 1914–1918. Ein Beitrag zur deutschen Kriegszielpo-
    litik im Ersten Weltkrieg*, Lübeck, 1960.
75. *Deutschlands Weg zur Grossmacht: Studien zum Verhältnis von Wirtschaft und
    Staat während der Reichsgründerzeit*, Cologne, 1966.
76. *Unternehmer in der deutschen Politik, 1890–1918*, Bonn, 1967.
77. *Industrielle Interessenpolitik in der Wilhelminischen Gesellschaft. Der Zen-
    tralverband Deutscher Industrieller 1895–1914*, Berlin, 1967.
78. *Agrarische Interressenpolitik.*
79. E.g., 'Der rückversicherte Mittelstand. Die Interessenverbände von Handwerk
    und Kleinhandel im deutschen Kaiserreich', in Walter Ruegg and Otto Neuloh
    (eds.), *Zur sozialen Theorie und Analyse des 19. Jahrhunderts*, Göttingen, 1971.
80. *Die Erben Bismarcks: Parteien und Verbände in der Spätphase des Wilhelmini-
    schen Deutschlands: Sammlungspolitik 1897–1918*, Cologne, 1970.

1903 and 1912 pointed clearly to the social foundations of the political system, strongly influenced by the agrarian propertied classes, which doomed any reforms which would have weakened the privileged economic and social position of these classes.[81] In 1952 Otto Büsch had probed into the impact of Prussian militarism on Prussian society[82]. Volker Berghahn carried Kehr's work on the roots of navalism in German domestic politics into the twentieth century and focused more specifically on the causes of the First World War and on the problem of militarism in modern history.[83] Also important was the reassessment of the November Revolution of 1918 and its aftermath in the studies of the workers' councils movements and the Independent Social Democrats which finally challenged the assumption that there existed no alternative to the choice between the conservative, unreformed Weimar Republic on the one hand and Communism on the other.[84] In addition there existed a broad spectrum of historians who did not acknowledge the influence of Kehr and Hans Rosenberg on their thinking but nevertheless operated with the notion of the uneven modernisation of Germany in one form or another, such as Karl-Dietrich Bracher, Gerhard A. Ritter, Wolfgang J. Mommsen, and Hans Mommsen.

By the early 1970s the atmosphere at the universities in the Federal Republic had finally changed. A change of guard had taken place in the 1960s with the retirement of the historians, trained in the Wilhelmine period, who had dominated the profession until then, Gerhard Ritter, Hans Rothfels and Hans Herzfeld. The student movement contributed to the beginnings of a long overdue reform of the universities in the course of which the power of the *Ordinarien* was diminished. The monopoly of the conservative nationalistic orientation was broken. The political hold of the Christian Democrats was ended on the national level. The *Ostpolitik* initiated by the Social Democratic–Liberal coalition reflected a more critical and realistic attitude towards Germany's recent past

81. *Die Finanzpolitik des Deutschen Reiches von 1903 bis 1913: Eine Studie zur Innenpolitik des Wilhelminischen Deutschland*, Lübeck, 1970.
82. *Militärsystem und Sozialleben im Alten Preussen*, Berlin, 1962.
83. *Der Tirpitz-Plan. Genesis und Verfall einer innenpolitischen Krisenstrategie unter Wilhelm II*, Düsseldorf, 1971; but also extensive writings on the problem of militarism in modern society.
84. See Eberhard Kolb, *Die Arbeiterräte in der deutschen Innenpolitik 1918–1919*, Düsseldorf, 1962; Peter von Oertzen, *Betriebsräate in der Novemberrevolution*, Düsseldorf, 1963; Reinhard Rürup (ed.), *Arbeiter- und Soldatenräte im rheinisch-westfälischen Industriegebiet*, Wuppertal, 1975.

and its implications for German policy. New universities and new chairs of history were created. A majority of the younger generation of critical historians, born in the 1930s and 1940s, now found employment. The new critical orientation created its publication outlets. In 1972 the series *Kritische Studien zur Geschichtswissenschaft*, edited by Hans-Ulrich Wehler, Jürgen Kocka, Helmut Berding and Hans-Christoph Schröder, was launched. In 1975 the journal, *Geschichte und Gesellschaft (History and Society)*, subtitled *A Journal for Historical Social Science*, was founded under a collective editorship which included several of the young critical historians, including Wehler and Kocka, but also Wolfgang J. Mommsen, who, as we already saw, was much more qualified in his acceptance of the basic theses of the uneven modernisation of modern Germany.

Geschichte und Gesellschaft has sometimes been compared to the French *Annales* because of its openness to the social sciences. Yet this comparison is misleading. In contrast to the *Annales*, which consciously neglected politics and concentrated on the economic, social, and mental structures of pre-industrial societies, *Geschichte und Gesellschaft* was concerned primarily with the problem of change in modern industrial societies seen in the broad sense, as the 'Preface' to the first issue stated, of a 'history of social, political, economic, socio-cultural and industrial phenomena'.[85] Far from turning away from political to social history, 'with the politics left out', the new orientation proceeded from political concerns, largely related to the fateful course of German history since Bismarck's unification, and sought to examine these within the context of the social, cultural, and to an extent the intellectual structure of modern Germany.

Critics of the new orientation have pointed out that in many ways it continued to maintain many of the basic conceptions and methodological approaches of the traditional nationally orientated historiography. James Sheehan has spoken of the persistence of a 'national paradigm'.[86] For the critical historians shared the view that the integration of Germany into the Prussian monarchy under Bismarck was crucial for an understanding of later German history.

---

85. Vol. 1, no. 1, 1975.
86. Paper delivered at the American Historical Association, Chicago, Ill., December 1984; see also his 'What Is German History? Reflections on the Role of the *Nation* in German History and Historiography', *Journal of Modern History*, 53, 1981, pp. 1–23.

Their focus too was on Germany's political history. The difference was that this history was now seen critically and that it was examined in a socio-economic context. In an important sense, the critical history was as much the history of elites as the traditionalist history. It must be stressed, however, that almost from the beginning a comparative note was introduced into the works of the critical historians which compared the German development with that in other countries.[87] Nevertheless even the studies of special interest groups, of agrarians, artisans, lower level white-collar workers or large-scale business were primarily concerned with the impact of these groups on national politics. The primary sources were the papers of government, of the organised special interests groups, and of leading personalities or functionaries associated with them. Only after the middle of the 1970s did there emerge a significant literature which explored the working and living conditions of ordinary men and women from a critical perspective.

The concern after 1945 with German social history began in the seminars of two historians, Werner Conze and Theodor Schieder, who themselves did not share the critical assessment of modern German history of many of their students. Werner Conze's Working Circle for Modern Social History in Heidelberg, founded shortly after the war, addressed itself to the impact of industrialisation on politics and society with a particular interest in the emerging working class. Conze, as we see in the essay 'From '*Pöbel*' to Proletariat' in this volume, de-emphasises the role of conflict and stresses the peaceful integration of the working class into the national state. Industrialisation continued to be studied by Conze and his Circle within the framework of the German states of the nineteenth century. An important theme of the works of the Heidelberg Circle was the integration of the Social Democratic worker into the German national state. The discussion of class conflicts was now avoided, reformist approaches stressed. Compared with the fundamental structural changes which society had undergone in an age of industrialisation, the events from 1933 to 1945, however much to be condemned, paled in importance on the world historical scale. For both Schieder and Conze, Bismarck's solution of the German problem was the only one which had been

---

87. Cf. Wehler and W. J. Mommsen's studies of imperialism, Kocka's studies of white-collar workers, Puhle's study of agrarian movements and Berghahn's studies of militarism, including *Militarism. The History of an International Debate 1861–1979*, Cambridge, 1981.

possible within the concrete setting of the time and despite the
shortcomings of an insufficiently democratic constitution an essentially sound one.

From the Heidelberg Circle there very soon, however, emerged a
more critical approach to German social history. Dieter Groh's
study of the political and cultural isolation of German Social
Democracy is a case in point.[88] Kocka's study of the transformation of
management–employee relationships in the Siemens electrical company in the years between 1847 and the outbreak of the First World
War appeared in 1969 in Conze's series, *Industrielle Gesellschaft*.[89]
Kocka's study is significant from several points of views. Much
more than other studies of the critical orientation, it brought
sociological categories, here those of bureaucratisation in private
industry, to bear on the analysis of industrial relations. But it saw
this process within the context of the uneven political and social
modernisation of Germany. Kocka was interested in the anti-
democratic attitudes of German white-collar workers in contrast to
those whom he examined in a subsequent work on the United
States.[90] Kocka's work thus constituted an important turn from a
primarily politically orientated history of Germany seen from a
critical social perspective to a social history of men and women at
the work-place seen in the context of political structures and attitudes.

Since the middle of the 1970s an increasing number of studies
have dealt with the conditions of everyday life seen within the
framework of the undemocratic character of German state and
society. Several of them are represented in this volume. What marks
these studies, however, and distinguishes them from anthropologically orientated studies on everyday life in the tradition of the
Annales, is the close relation which they establish between working
conditions, housing arrangements, education, leisure time, health,
mental illness and crime on the one hand and the relations of power
and subordination in German society on the other. Klaus Tenfelde
moves from the traditional history of labour with its stress on the
socialist and trade union movements to a concern with the workers

88. *Negative Integration*.
89. *Unternehmensverwaltung und Angestelltenschaft am Beispiel Siemens 1847–
    1914*, Stuttgart, 1969.
90. *Angestellte zwischen Faschismus und Demokratie: Zur politischen Sozialge-
    schichte der Angestellten: USA 1890–1914 im internationalen Vergleich*,
    Göttingen, 1977, transl. as *White-Collar Workers in America, 1890–1940: A
    Socio-Political History in International Perspective*, Beverly Hills, 1980.

themselves, in this case the coal miners in the Ruhr Valley,[91] the economic and social conditions under which they live, but also their associations, their festivals, their songs. The essay on the Herne riots of 1899 in this volume reconstructs vividly the atmosphere in which the strike by Polish ethnic miners isolated from their German colleagues took place. A similar move from politics on the national scale to the examination of how the conditions of life and the way of life manifested themselves in a specific local setting occurs in Brüggemeier and Niethammer's essay on housing and pubs among Ruhr miners. Karen Hausen in her essay on the social impact of the introduction of the sewing machine into the household places the history of women into the context of women's work and raises the critical question of the social cost of technological innovation under conditions of capitalism.

The critical history of German politics in a social context has thus moved from an earlier stage which concentrated on the national scene with a particular concern to revise the basic assumptions and valuations of the traditional nationalistic approach to a history, which consciously maintains this critical orientation, but gives greater attention to life and culture in a political context. Several aspects of the critical history have increasingly come under attack from ideologically very different directions, both from traditionalists who rejected the broad scope of the critique of the German past by the critical historians and by historians from the left who believed that the critical orientation was not sufficiently critical of the past and in both its conception of politics and methods preserved many of the presuppositions of traditional German historiography.

James Sheehan in 1976 suggested that the critical school represented a 'new orthodoxy' in German historiography,[92] a characterisation which failed to take into consideration not only the openness of the new direction but the extent to which many of the chairs of history and such central publications as the *Historische Zeitschrift* and the history teachers' journal, *Geschichte in Wissenschaft und*

---

91. *Sozialgeschichte der Bergarbeiterschaft an der Ruhr im 19. Jahrhundert*, Bonn, 1981; see such volumes as Jürgen Reulecke and Wolfhard Weber (eds.), *Fabrik — Familie — Feierabend. Beiträge zur Sozialgeschichte des Alltags*, Wuppertal, 1978; G. Huck (ed.), *Sozialgeschichte der Freizeit: Untersuchungen zum Wandel der Alltagskultur*, Wuppertal, 1981; Detlev Peukert and Jürgen Reulecke (eds.), *Die Reihen fast geschlossen. Beiträge zur Geschichte des Alltags unterm Nationalsozialismus*, Wuppertal, 1981.
92. *Journal of Modern History*, 48, 1976, p. 567.

Unterricht continued to reflect traditional attitudes. The journal, *Geschichtsdidaktik*, founded in 1976, represented an attempt to present a forum for a more liberal orientation among history teachers. Wehler's *Das Deutsche Kaiserreich* became the subject of a bitter debate immediately after its publication in 1973. This debate involved both Wehler's interpretation of the German past and his approach to history. In a number of articles published in the *Historische Zeitschrift*, Andreas Hillgruber,[93] Klaus Hildebrand[94], Lothar Gall[95] and Hans-Gunther Zmarzlik[96] led the attack on Wehler's thesis that foreign policy in important ways reflected considerations of domestic policy and social conflict. International relations, they maintained, preserved a large element of autonomy and could not be integrated into a history of society. Hildebrand stressed the role of individuals in political decision, a position which he had first applied to the Third Reich which in contrast to the critical historians he saw more profoundly shaped by the personality of Hitler than by a socio-political context.

More interesting and incisive was Thomas Nipperdey's critique which appeared, it is important to note, in the pages of *Geschichte und Gesellschaft*,[97] at the invitation of its editors. Nipperdey questioned the notion of a German development fundamentally different from that of West European countries. Wehler, he charged, was guilty of presentism in viewing Germany's modern past from the perspective of the events of 1933 to 1945. There were other continuities in German history as well. The democracy of the Bonn Republic too rested on German traditions. There was a liberal as well as an authoritarian tradition. The events of 1933 could not have been predicted in the German Empire. Antisemitism, Social Darwinism and ultra-nationalism were not only German phenomena but attitudes which were shared by other European societies as well. Nipperdey accused Wehler polemically of being a 'Treitschke redivivus', of giving up the detachment which befits the historian for the propagation of a political perspective, and called in a separate essay, reprinted in the *Kritische Studien* for a new 'historism' which

93. 'Politische Geschichte in moderner Sicht', *Historische Zeitschrift*, 216, 1973, pp. 529–52.
94. 'Geschichte oder "Gesellschaftsgeschichte". Die Notwendigkeit einer Politischen Geschichtsschreibung von den internationalen Beziehungen', ibid., 223, 1976, pp. 328–57.
95. 'Bismarck und der Bonapartismus', ibid., 222, 1976, pp. 618–37.
96. 'Das Kaiserreich in neuer Sicht', ibid., 222, 1976, pp. 105–26.
97. 'Wehlers Kaiserreich. Eine kritische Auseinandersetzung', *Geschichte und Gesellschaft*, 1, 1975, pp. 538–60.

approaches all historical epochs with the values of its time.[98] Nipperdey recognises the limitations of traditional historism, its idealistic assumptions, its stress on human intentions, its sometimes narrowly political approach to history but defends its basic belief in scholarly and scientific objectivity against the critical historians whose aim is political and social 'emancipation'. The question of the political and social context in which the historians wrote is irrelevant to Nipperdey; the crucial question is the scientific validity (*Geltung*)[99] of their historical work. Historism, he warned, must not be identified with a nineteenth-century tradition of conservative historical scholarship in Germany; it encompassed not only historical but humanistic and social studies generally at the time and not only in Germany. Its concept of individuality involved a recognition of structural contexts. Historism can thus be renewed. But its renewal involves a return to a value neutrality in scholarship which the critical historians have questioned but many of their critics have called for.[100]

A further criticism of the analytical approach of the critical social history of politics came from those historians, including Nipperdey, who argued that history cannot do without narrative. This new stress on 'the revival of narrative' fitted into an international discussion at the end of the 1970s and in the 1980s. As Lawrence Stone argued, narrative did not need to mean a return to a traditional political history from above.[101] Nor, as Jörn Rüsen maintained, did it mean the exclusion of theory from the historical account. A merger was possible between a history which took into account social context as well as the concrete actions of individuals.[102] The former was to emerge not so much from an explicit statement of the theoretical position of the author as from the narrative itself. To an extent this was attempted in Thomas Nipperdey's *Deutsche Geschichte 1800–1866* (1983) which Wehler acknowledged as a master

98. 'Historismus und Historismuskritik heute', in Nipperdey, *Gesammelte Aufsätze zur neueren Geschichte*, Göttingen, 1976, pp. 59–73.
99. Ibid., p. 67.
100. There has been a lively debate since the 1960s between those historians who have held that history has an 'emancipatory' function, e.g. Wehler and Groh, and their critics, generally conservative, who have argued for impartiality and value freedom, e.g. Faber and Nipperdey. For a debate on these issues, see R. Koselleck et al. (eds.), *Theorie der Geschichte*, 4 vols., Munich, 1977–1982, esp. vol. 1, *Objektivität und Parteilichkeit*.
101. See 'The Revival of Narrative: Reflections on a New Old History', *Past and Present*, no. 85, November 1979, pp. 3–24.
102. See *Für eine erneuerte Historik. Studien zur Theorie der Geschichtswissenschaft*, Bad Cannstadt, 1976; *Historische Vernunft*, vol. 1, Göttingen, 1983.

work of historical synthesis.[103]

The theme of the revival of narrative, of a return from the analysis of structures to the reconstruction of the lives of concrete human beings was also taken up by a group of historians who championed very different political and social values from those of the tradition-alists, namely the advocates of a 'history of everyday life' (*Alltags-geschichte*). Two different orientations were reflected in this ap-proach: one, represented in the selections by Brüggemeier and Niethammer, Tenfelde and Hausen in this volume, proceeded from the assumptions of the critical school regarding the uneven modern-isation of Imperial Germany and sought to examine the impact of authoritarian structures on the living conditions of working men and women; the other is represented by a group of historians, centred at but not restricted to the Max Planck Institute for History in Göttingen, who from the standpoint of an anthropological ap-proach to history sharply questioned the political and epistemologi-cal assumptions of the critical school. From the perspective of the latter group, the premises of the social history of politics were criticised on several counts. Hans Medick stated the objections of these anthropologically orientated historians against the social his-torians of politics succinctly in an article published in *Geschichte und Gesellschaft*.[104] From Kehr to Kocka, the social history of politics had continued to focus on the nation. They had studied history from the perspectives of decision-making elites. This is a critique which is also made by the British Marxists whom we shall discuss below. But more important, Medick questions the whole concept of a 'historical social science' which informed Wehler and Kocka. He views the attempts not only in West Germany but in the United States and to an extent France and Great Britain to trans-form history into a 'social science' as forms of objectivism, of 'fixation on socio-economic "circumstances" to the neglect of act-ing human beings'.[105] As Kocka has suggested,[106] Medick's critique contained a return to certain concerns of traditional historism, but it must be added from a radically different political and social per-

103. Wehler, in *Die Zeit*, 14 October 1983, p. 32.
104. "Missionare im Ruderboot?" Ethnologische Erkenntnisweisen als Herausfor-derung an die Sozialgeschichte', *Geschichte und Gesellschaft*, vol. 10, 1984, pp. 295–319; also the exchange of views in Hans Süssmuth (ed.), *Historische Anthropologie*, Göttingen, 1984.
105. 'Missionare', p. 296.
106. See 'Historisch-anthropologische Fragestellungen — ein Defizit der Histori-schen Sozialwissenschaft', in *Historische Anthropologie*, pp. 73–83.

spective. The focus was now on the everyday life of men, women, and children, not on impersonal social processes. Medick calls for an 'alternative perspective' which 'while recognising the historical effect of material and political (*herrschaftlicher*) constraints' is primarily concerned with 'the interrelation of experiences of oppression and possibilities of action among the traditionally neglected strata, groups, cultures and genders who have been pauperised, excluded (*ausgegrenzt*), and deprived of their rights'.[107] A radically new approach to history and culture is called for. In a collective volume, *Klassen und Kultur* (1982),[108] which emerged from a number of international conferences sponsored by the Max Planck Institut in Gottingen and the Maison des Sciences de l'Homme in Paris, the latter reflecting the view point of the French *Annales* circle, Medick and others argued for a new logic of enquiry. If social science had traditionally assumed the existence of objective sets of relationships, the need now was to study the social and cultural world from the perspective of the women, men and children who composed it. The social science best suited for this study was cultural anthropology, and specifically the kind of anthropology represented by Clifford Geertz in the United States for whom culture presented itself as 'an historically transmitted pattern of meanings embodied in symbols, a system of inherited conceptions expressed in symbolic form by which men communicate, perpetrate and develop their knowledge about attitudes towards life'. Medick agrees with Geertz that the 'proper object' for anthropology and anthropologically orientated history is to 'sort out structures of significance', to discover 'the informal logic of actual life'. For Medick, as for Geertz, this precludes the formulation of theories as the precondition of study; rather this 'logic' reveals itself through 'thick description', through the immersion into the actual life of the observed.[109] Hence the historian can again turn to a singular individual as Carlo Ginzburg did in his account of the miller Menocchio, because even an eccentric like Menocchio reveals the roots of popular culture.[110] Narration again becomes a vehicle of historical discourse.

107. 'Missionare', p. 302.
108. Robert Berdahl et al., *Klassen und Kultur. Sozialanthropologische Perspektiven in der Geschichtsschreibung*, Frankfurt, 1982, pp. 955–65; see Kocka's critique in *Merkur*, 36, 1982, pp. 955–65.
109. For Medick on Geertz and the 'informal logic of actual life', see 'Missionare'.
110. *The Cheese and the Worms. The Cosmos of a Seventeenth-Century Miller*, New York, 1980.

This new anthropological history as conceived by Hans Medick is both highly political and unpolitical. It is unpolitical in its retreat from the political scene proper. E. P. Thompson, with whom Medick feels close kinship, is nevertheless criticised because he deals with spectacular aspects of popular resistance as they are expressed in the food riots of the eighteenth century rather than in their silent form in everyday life. Class, the contributors to *Klassen und Kultur* agree with Thompson, is a 'relationship', an 'historical relationship', 'a cultural as much as an economic formation', 'defined by men as they live their own history'.[111] Culture is political in so far as it 'is a means for carrying out domination — but always also an arena of resistance'.[112] The domination can involve concrete forms of political oppression, as Alf Lüdtke showed in his study of the Prussian police, but it can also take forms of passive resistance in the work place. This does not mean a neglect of the conditions of 'production and reproduction' which form the context of resistance. A masterful attempt to combine an examination of economic transformation, changing family relationships and culture with the resistance which older pre-capitalist attitudes towards work and consumption offer to the work-discipline of an emergent capitalist order of production is contained in the study of proto-industrialisation in the country side, *Industrialisierung vor der Industrialisierung*, published in 1977 by Peter Kriedte, Hans Medick, and Jürgen Schlumbohm at the Max Planck Institute.[113] Yet Medick emphatically rejects any conception of development and modernisation which such a study may imply. Medick accuses the 'historical social science', represented by Wehler and Kocka, of having neglected the 'costs of modernisation and industrialisation'.[114] Finally, the conception that history is a science, or a social science, in the traditional senses of these terms is to be questioned. History must again be de-professionalised; brought closer to the people through cooperative work in 'history workshops', in which trained historians and amateurs work together on historical concerns arising from their everyday existence.

Kocka and Wehler have replied to Medick in a debate, partly

111. E. P. Thompson, *The Making of the English Working Class*, London, 1963, Preface, pages 9–14.
112. *Klassen und Kultur*, p. 12.
113. See *Gemeinwohl, Polizei und 'Festungspraxis'. Staatliche Gewaltsamkeit und innere Verwaltung in Preussen*, Göttingen, in press (1985); see his lecture, 'Cash, Coffee Breaks and Fooling Around. "Eigensinn" and Politics Among Nineteenth-Century German Factory Workers', SUNY/Buffalo, April 1982.
114. Transl. as *Industrialization Before Industrialization: Rural Industry in the Genesis of Capitalism*, Cambridge, 1981.

carried on in the pages of *Geschichte und Gesellschaft*, not without the bitterness on Wehler's and Medick's part which has accompanied so many German controversies. They accused Medick both of a romantic nostalgia for a pre-industrial society and of a historism, which like the old historism, sacrifices methods of rational control for a subjective intuitionism. Both recognised the need to widen the social history of politics to include broad aspects of the history of everyday life. Both stressed, however, that this history must be seen within the context of broader social and political movements. A history of everyday life, as proposed by Medick, they believe, cannot achieve synthesis. 'It can tell stories from everyday life but not write *the* history of German everyday life, let's say from 1870 to 1970'.[115] Medick would, of course, with considerable justification deny that *the* history of everyday life exists. Both stress, and I believe rightly so, that without explicit concepts no history is possible. The texts do not tell their own story as Geertz's notion of 'thick description' presupposes.

Yet the fundamental difference between the two positions goes beyond scientific strategies and involves basic attitudes towards modern Western society, an emphatic endorsement on the part of Wehler of the values of Enlightenment, a basic scepticism towards these values on the part of Medick, in some sense the contrast between a committed Social Democratic and a Green viewpoint. Wehler warns of Medick's idealisation of the masses. He points at the antisemitism, the xenophobia, the hostility to progress among large segments of the population in the German past as an example. 'Fortunately the losers, who among so many historians of every day life occupy the centre of the stage,' he comments, 'were not the historical victors.' It is true that the antisemites and the ultra-chauvinists are hardly the men and women whom the historians of everyday life, with their own democratic commitments, have in mind. Yet there is an element of justification in Wehler's warning regarding the romanticisation of the men and women of the 'people' and in his reassertion of the humane and rational values of Enlightenment.

A somewhat different criticism came from a group of young British social historians of politics who in 1978 had contributed to a volume of essays, *Society and Politics in Wilhelmine Germany*,

115. See Wehler, 'Geschichte — von unten gesehen. Wie bei der Suche nach dem Authentischen Engagement mit Methodik verwechselt wird', *Die Zeit*, no. 19, 10 May 1985, p. 20.

edited by Richard Evans. We shall discuss it here because the
positions developed by two of the contributors, Geoff Eley and
David Blackbourn, in a German paperback published in November
1980, *Mythen deutscher Geschichtsschreibung. Die gescheiterte
burgerliche Revolution von 1848*,[116] and developed further by both,
particularly by Eley in other writings, caused a vigorous controversy in the Federal Republic. A critique from a neo-Marxist
position of the theory of the German *Sonderweg*, as interpreted by
the critical historians from Kehr to Kocka, it was nevertheless
welcomed by German conservative historians, falsely I believe, as
an endorsement of their position. On two points the critique
developed by Evans, Eley, Blackbourn and their colleagues resembled that of Nipperdey. Like Nipperdey they questioned
whether Germany's development was as different from that of other
West European countries as the critical school had maintained and
hence whether a clear line of continuity could be drawn from the
supposed failure of the 1848 Revolution to the Nazi seizure of
power. Moreover they too rejected the attempt to read German
history in the light of the events of 1933 to 1945. They set themselves the task 'to rehabilitate Wilhelmine society as an object of
study in its own right, to demonstrate its diversity and to show
something of the wealth of political and social processes which were
taking place in it'.[117] Like Medick, Lüdtke and the anthro-
pologically-orientated historians, they criticised the critical school
for continuing in the footsteps of the traditional historians by
concentrating on elites and focusing on the national state. Evans
and Blackbourn stressed that Germany was not identical with
Prussia. More attention must be given to developments on the
regional and local level. Greater importance must be given to the
grass roots, to women, workers, and youth. The 'history from
above', they proclaimed, must be replaced by a 'history from
below'.[118] They questioned the thesis of the manipulation of the
non-proletarian masses by the industrial and agrarian elites. Eley in
his study of the Navy League[119] sought to demonstrate the extent to
which ultra-nationalism derived less from the ruling elites than from

116. A revised edition has since appeared in English, *The Peculiarities of the English*,
   Oxford, 1984.
117. See Richard Evans' Introduction to Evans (ed.), *Society and Politics in Wilhelmine Germany*, London, 1978, pp. 35–6.
118. Ibid., pp. 23–4.
119. See Geoff Eley, *Reshaping the German Right: Radical Nationalism and Political
   Change After Bismarck*, New Haven, 1980.

broader segments of the population. Thus the masses in one sense forced the government into an intensive armament and an aggressive foreign policy. Corporate capitalism too, particularly in the Weimar period, was much less beholden to agrarian interests than the critical school maintained. Eley's interpretation implied that all was not as well in the Federal Republic as Wehler believed, that the conditions which made for the rise of fascism in Germany had by no means been fully eradicated after 1945. Nevertheless, when closely examined, the revisionism of the young British historians, despite the bitter acrimony of the debate which ensued particularly between Eley and Wehler,[120] contains basic points of agreement with the fundamental assumptions of the historians against whom their criticism is directed. They, too, focus on the interrelation of society and politics; they too see continuities in German history even if these are more complex than those seen by the critical school; and they, too, are critical historians who write history from political and social commitment.

In many ways the British critics have offered less of a refutation of the fundamental positions of the critical school than a partial corrective to their interpretations. As Kocka acknowledged, they have challenged the critical school to review some of its basic assumptions.[121] One of these assumptions has involved the notion, which Wehler considered fundamental to his analysis of German history, that the 'progressive economic modernisation of German society should have been accompanied by a modernisation of social relations and politics', which he understood in terms of parliamentarisation and democracy. Great Britain, France, and the United States served for Wehler, as they did for Barrington Moore and Ralf Dahrendorf, as the norm for industrialising societies. Eley and Blackbourn are undoubtedly right in questioning the 'idealised picture' of the '"western" pattern' and the 'causal chain bourgeoisie–liberalism–parliamentarism–democracy'.[122] They are also right in questioning the extent to which a small elite manipulated the masses of the lower-middle class and peasantry and em-

---

120. See the debate in *Merkur*: H. U. Wehler, '"Deutscher Sonderweg" oder allgemeine Probleme des westlichen Kapitalismus? Zur Kritik an einigen "Mythen deutscher Geschichtsschreibung"', 35, May 1981, pp. 478–87; G. Eley, 'Hans Ulrich Wehler', 35, July 1981, pp. 757–9; Wehler, 'Rückantwort an Geoff Eley', ibid., p. 760; H.-U. Wehler, 'Der deutsche Sonderweg: Eine Nachlese', 35, August 1981, pp. 793–803.
121. See 'Der "deutsche Sonderweg" in der Diskussion', *German Studies Review*, 5, 1982, pp. 365–80.
122. *The Peculiarities* (above, n. 116), pp. 10, 16.

phasising the role which populist pressures from below played in the transformation of the political parties. They undoubtedly contribute to the discussion on the origins of fascism by stressing more strongly than the critical school the continuities of right-wing populism as a lower-class reaction against capitalism from the Imperial period but also the transformation and modernisation of capitalism in the Weimar period. They thus raise the question whether 1945 marks as decisive a break with the unfortunate aspects of the German past as the critical historians, from the Social Democratic perspective of the 1970s, assume. They are finally also right in emphasising the extent to which in economic, social, and cultural relations an 'authentically bourgeois society' unfolded.

All these factors have to be taken into consideration in an assessment of the course of German history. Yet on the other hand one ·cannot help believing that the critical school has a more correct understanding of the role of political power than do their British critics. Eley and Blackbourn criticise Wehler from what they consider to be a Marxist position, that what makes a bourgeois society are the conditions of production and that the bourgeoisie was able to carry through its interests without controlling the apparatus of power. They also tend to overstress the parliamentarisation of Wilhelmine Germany. Yet as Evans recognises, Eley and Blackbourn's 'claims that the term "bourgeois revolution" should refer solely to the triumph of the capitalist mode of production, is hardly compatible with Marx and Engels' conception' — which in this sense is closer to that of Wehler and the critical school — that the term '"bourgeois revolution" encompasses *both* the change in relations of production which brought the bourgeoisie to a position where it displaced the feudal aristocracy as the dominant owner of property and labour power, *and* the consequent political changes by which the bourgeoisie secured the adaptation of "superstructural" elements to conform more closely to its interests'.[123] These political changes, as the critical historians recognised, took place only very incompletely in Germany and maintained elements of the old order in state, society, and culture.

In conclusion, a few words to assess the significance of the critical orientation both for German historiography and for the international discussion. There is no question that the critical orientation

123. "The Myth of Germany's Missing Revolution," *New Left Review*, no. 149 (February, 1985), p. 78.

consciously fulfilled a political function. From Kehr in the Weimar period, to Hans Rosenberg in the intermediate years, to Berghahn, Wehler and Kocka in the late 1960s and 1970s, to the more recent attempts at a social history of labour, the critical historians have sought to confront Germany's undemocratic past with its disastrous consequences for international relations. It is an attempt to come honestly to terms with this past and to create a historical consciousness for a democratic Germany, or perhaps more specifically for a Federal Republic committed to the values of a social democracy. The attack on the critical orientation by scholars such as Nipperdey, not to mention Hildebrand and Conze, in the name of detached historical understanding, has had political connotations as has quite openly the critique by the young British scholars and by the anthropologically orientated historians whom we have discussed. In fact, as we have seen, the entire tradition of German historical writing since, and including, Ranke has proceeded from political value positions which have informed and guided its research and its interpretations of the German past. But political commitment does not exclude intellectual and scholarly honesty. In fact the commitment opens up perspectives which then require critical examination.

I believe, however, that the historians of the critical orientation have also made a contribution to historical studies in Germany as a scholarly enterprise. They have broken through the isolation which marked German scholarship since the Lamprecht controversy and reestablished communication with historical discussion at least in the West. In many ways, as has been pointed out, in their preoccupation with problem of Germany's development, seen essentially from the centre and from the top, the critical historians have moved along very traditional lines. Historians in the Federal Republic have been relatively slow in exploring the new dimensions of social history which have played such an important role elsewhere. The critical historians, however, have overcome the gulf which has existed in traditional historical writing between the academic discipline of history at the German universities and the great German tradition of historical sociology from Marx to Weber and Hintze. In some ways, the hesitation of West German historians to follow in the tradition of the French *Annales* has had not only a negative but also a positive side. The study of the everyday life of the German people, inspired more by E. P. Thompson than by the *Annales*, is still underdeveloped, although the last three selections in this collection and recent issues of *Geschichte und Gesellschaft* reflect the growing interest in a history which focuses on working people. The critical historians have avoided the flight from politics and from the realities of a modern industrial world which have marked much of *Annales* social history. They have taken a critical stance to both the objectivism of the quantitative social sciences[124] and to the subjectivism of much of cultural anthropology. Their recent critics of the last ten years have pointed to areas in which their positions and approaches require rethinking and further development. Nevertheless the critical historians have provided an example for an intellectually rigorous examination of the modern world from a democratic perspective which deserves to be better known in the English-speaking world.[125]

124. This Introduction should not close without mentioning an approach to a 'historical social science' different from that of the critical orientation but not necessarily in conflict with it, the quantitative approach of the Association for Quantification and Methods in Research in Historical Social Sciences formed in 1976 under the name *Quantum*. It has been publishing a bilingual journal in English and German since then, *Historical Social Research. Historische Sozialforschung*. Critical historians such as Jürgen Kocka have recognised the utility of this approach and collaborated with it although also seeing its limits. Two German-born historians who have sought to combine quantitative methods with conceptual approaches are Konrad Jarausch in the United States who has worked closely with the *Quantum* group and Michael Kater in Canada, the latter in *The Nazi Party: A Social Profile of Members and Leaders*, Cambridge, Mass. 1983, and presently in a study of the medical profession in the Third Reich.

125. In the last two years, five extensive evaluations of the controversy surrounding the 'critical school' have appeared, ranging from Roger Fletcher's basically positive assessment to Irmline Veit-Brause's relatively critical one; three were written by historians in English-speaking countries and only one was published in German. They are: Dieter Groh, 'Le "Sonderweg" de l'Histoire Allemande: Mythe ou Réalité', *Annales. Économies. Sociétés. Civilisations*, 38, 1983, 1166–87; Roger Fletcher, 'Recent Developments in West German Historiography: The Bielefeld School and Its Critics', *German Studies Review*, 7, 1984, pp. 451–80; Irmline Veit-Brause, 'Zur Kritik an der "Kritischen Geschichtswissenschaft"', *Geschichte in Wissenschaft und Unterricht*, 31, 1984, pp. 1–24; Robert G. Moeller, 'The Kaiserreich Recast? Continuity and Changes in Modern German Historiography', *Journal of Social History*, 17, 1983/4, pp. 655–83;

125. Richard Evans, 'The Myth of Germany's Missing Revolution', *New Left Review*, no. 149, 1985, pp. 67–93. See also Konrad Jarausch's thoughtful essay, 'Illiberalism and Beyond: German History in Search of a Paradigm', *Journal of Modern History*, 55, 1983, pp. 268–84. Two articles by Americans which question Wehler's interpretation of the Bismarck period are Margaret Lavinia Anderson and Kenneth Barckin, 'The Myth of the Putkammer Purge and the Reality of the *Kulturkampf*: Some Reflections on the Historiography of Imperial Germany', *Journal of Modern History*, vol. 54, 1982, pp. 647–86; Otto Pflanze, 'Bismarcks Herrschaftstechnik als Problem der gegenwärtigen Historiographie', *Historische Zeitschrift*, vol. 234, 1982, pp. 561–600.

WERNER CONZE

From 'Pöbel' to 'Proletariat'.

The Socio-Historical Preconditions of Socialism in Germany

As Rudolf Stadelman has stressed in his book on the Revolution of 1848, early socialism and communism did not find, at that time, a politically significant response among the German population.* This was very different from France where the French socialists gained their first, albeit short-lived, revolutionary successes which raised hopes for the future. On the other hand, it is clear that the popular movement of the 'crazy year' of 1848 in Germany amounted to much more than a 'bourgeois' revolution. The mass of the urban and rural populations which had been seized by 'pauperism' and had been turned into a 'proletariat' may, for a while, have gone along with the bourgeois revolutionaries and their demands for constitutional reform; but it was also keen to advance the 'social revolution' which had been the nightmare of political writers and of the attentive bureaucrats of the autocratic state in the 1840s. The first beginnings of such a revolution can be observed in all parts of Germany and might emerge even more fully and tangibly, if more detailed research were undertaken into this subject. This much is certain: what the 'social revolution' was lacking to achieve its breakthrough was the necessary interaction between leadership and mass following. There existed, as in the Peasants' War of 1525, individual charismatic leaders and demagogues; but there was no continuation of people or programmatic ideas. And in

*Publ. orig. in *Viertelsjahrschrift für Sozial-und Wirtschaftsgeschichte*, 41, 1954, pp. 333–64. The author would like to thank the publishers for permission to prepare and use this translation.

terms of a sociology of knowledge, the masses who belonged to the lower strata and were often in a revolutionary mood, were in their majority not yet sufficiently emancipated to be willing to assert themselves with enthusiasm and conviction and for the sake of the revolution against the authority of state, church and society; this the more so since they had almost no revolutionary training, discipline or organisation. Nevertheless and despite their immaturity to trigger a 'social' revolution, it can be said that the lower strata of German society experienced at no other time in the nineteenth century a similar level of unrest and rebelliousness than in 1848. In view of this it should be worthwhile to investigate the origins, size and peculiarities of these strata up to the middle of the century and to reconstruct the debate of this problem among contemporaries. This article does not provide firm conclusions on this topic, but is intended as an essay to stimulate further research.[1]

Whereas in Britain the Industrial Revolution had begun roughly between the American War of Independence and the first major crisis of the capitalist world economy in the 1820s, Germany was still very remote from an upheaval of similar magnitude. Nor was there any fundamental change in this respect during the 1830s and 1840s. It was only after 1850 that Germany was affected by a major wave of industrialisation which paved the way for the emergence of an industrial system and her rise to the leading industrial power of the Continent. Yet even for this period it is necessary to make qualifications, if one speaks of an 'industrial revolution' comparable to that in Britain;[2] for all its dynamism, its intoxicating effect and its profound change which occurred in all spheres of life and not just within the economy, the process of industrialisation lacked the ruthless radicalism which had been the hallmark of the British development. When industrialisation set in on a large scale around 1850, it did not do so with a bang. Rather it developed as a consequence of social and economic conditions which had unfolded over a long time-span. Thus it had already been the princes of the

1. This article is based on a lecture which was given in 1953 and published subsequently with minor changes.
2. In his article "Das Königreich Hannover an der Schwelle des Industriezeitalters", in *Neues Archiv für Niedersachsen*, 1951, pp. 413–43, Hans Linde rightly refutes the notion of a 'presumed or alleged general validity of the Industrial Revolution as the ideal-typical model of all industrialisation processes' and coins the concept of 'industrial expansion' (*industrieller Ausbau*). This concept matches the reality of the German case well up to the founder period of heavy industry and railways. Thenceforward the notion of 'industrial revolution' may, within limits, also be applied to Germany.

period of enlightened absolutism in the second half of the eighteenth century who had considerably increased the ability of their states to cope with industrialisation by promoting economic development through a putting-out system and through manufactures. It was at this time and through 'industrial extension' that an early industrialism had emerged in the traditional manufacturing regions like Bohemia, Silesia, Saxony and Rhineland-Westphalia with its pig-iron and textile enterprises. These industries were technologically backward, but though endangered in times of economic crisis, they witnessed a slow development in the first half of the nineteenth century. This process must be linked to a sensational demographic explosion. This explosion, it is true, did not affect all German states and varied greatly from region to region, depending on the degree to which communications had been improved, commerce had been officially encouraged, the agrarian system had been liberalised and a population policy adopted. It also depended on location and accessibility as well as a number of regionally specific factors.[3] Demographic growth had been the result of a decline in mortality rates and under certain conditions, such as those in the eastern parts of Prussia following the liberation of peasants from feudal servitude, rising marriage as well as birth rates.[4] Above all, the demographic expansion had led to an overpopulation which occurred slowly, almost imperceptibly in the older manufacturing regions and explosively in the less densely populated regions such as the eastern provinces. This overpopulation was partly reinforced by liberal agrarian reforms and by the abolition of restrictions in commerce, trade and industry (*Gewerbefreiheit*). It threatened to unleash a catastrophe when the precariously balanced under-capitalised German industries experienced difficulties and possible collapse in the face of cheap goods (above all, textiles and iron wares) with which British manufacturers flooded the German market. Up to the 1840s the imbalance between a surplus of labour and a limited number of jobs in commerce and industry became greater and greater. A decline in real wages and unemployment were the inevitable consequence. In town and country, people, unprotected as they were, fell victim to mass poverty, to 'pauperism', a widespread figure of

3. For population movements see the map in Helmut Haufe, *Die Bevölkerung Europas*, Berlin, 1935. Gunther Ipsen's work has demonstrated the importance of population sociology for the social history of industrial societies. See also Gerhard Mackenroth, *Bevölkerungslehre*, Berlin, 1953.
4. See also Gunther Ipsen, "Die preussische Bauernbefreiung als Landesausbau", in *Zeitschrift für Agrargeschichte und Agrarsoziologie*, 2/1954, pp. 29–54.

speech imported from Britain. In Germany this pauperism was much less a consequence of incipient industrialisation with its low wages than a result of the fact that industry was incapable of absorbing the growth in the labour force in a period of overpopulation. Pauperism exposed the plight of the lower classes that had grown disproportionately. It represented the mass misery of a period which contemporaries saw as a period of transition; a time when the traditional ties of the corporate society (*ständische Gesellschaft*) into estates were irretrievably lost but the new constitutional form of an embryonic industrial society had not yet been developed. Pauperism was seen with apprehension as a new phenomenon which was something quite different from the poverty question or the existence of the propertyless and labouring classes in the traditional sense. This difference which was perceived in Germany during the 1830s and 1840s became articulated at the time in the notion of 'proletariat'. This term replaced the older notion of '*Pöbel*' or at least resulted in the latter word being used less frequently and with a narrower application. Both terms ultimately encapsulate everything that can help to explain the evolution towards pauperism. Let us therefore first investigate what these two concepts implied.

The word *Pöbel* was taken over into Middle High German from the French *poble* (Lat. *populus*). It signifies much more than the notion of a group of common people in a pejorative sense. *Pöbel* were those below and outside the existing feudal and manorial order — those who were 'outside the honours of work' (W. H. Riehl). This was the extensive stratum beneath the land-owning peasants and guild-organised artisans. They were known as *ordo plebeius* or *Pöbelstand*[5] — a stratum outside the estates and yet one which had been captured and 'tamed' by it. This stratum was permanently threatened by harsh poverty because the number of positions open to them remained limited. It was due to its marginal existence also particularly susceptible to crises and catastrophes.

Nevertheless, this was not a dispensable stratum. The existing feudal and manorial order was dependent on it because services were required in all spheres of life. Even the peasant who had to render services himself could not do without day-labourers and domestic servants, unless, of course, he, as a smallholder, had

---

5. Kaspar Stieler, *Der Teutschen Sprache Stammbaum und Fortwachs oder Teutscher Sprachschatz*, 1691.

himself moved downwards into the vicinity of the *Pöbel*. Carl Friedrich von Benekendorf writes in his *Oeconomica Forensis*[6] that cottagers (*Häusler und Büdner*) were among the most useful inhabitants of a village because they represented an indispensable labour force. He added significantly that the landless labourers (*Einlieger*), whose status was even lower than the cottagers, were merely hired; they were also available for work, but they were 'mostly infirm persons and where they appear in larger numbers they represent a bunch of old women'.[7]

This statement by Benekendorf, who probably gained his insight from his experience in his home region of Neumark, is an accurate assessment of what was the general situation at the end of the eighteenth century. Above all it makes a fundamental point: members of the rural sub-stratum were 'useful' and obtained their 'livelihood' through a smallholding, a poorly-fed cow on the overgrazed common and occasional or regular wage labour. Beneath them lived those in abject poverty, whose life was even worse than the marginal existence of the cottager/day-labourer. They were without a family, whom they would have been unable to maintain. Life had reached a dead end here; it no longer propagated itself or did so only through illegitimacy, i.e. again in a stunted form. There was an absolute inexorability about this lower limit. The *Pöbel* groups of corporate society were restricted to a limited sphere of life and its chances of propagation were reduced.

The size of their families depended, just as that of the peasants, on the extent to which the village could support them and on how labour was organised in it. On the other hand, it is true that any expansion of job opportunities, however small, would benefit the rural substratum rather than the peasants whose number of farmsteads remained unchanged. Hence the expansion of these groups even when society was still a corporate one. The situation in the towns corresponded to that in the countryside. The population beneath the guild-organised artisans could set up a family only in so far as it was able to find its 'livelihood', however meagre. Enterprises which operated within the framework of a putting-out or manufacturing system assumed a job-creating role which, particularly for many journeymen who would not rise to the position of master, formed a basis for founding a family. These urban families,

6. Berlin, 1775–84.
7. August Skalweit, 'Benekendorfs Oeconomia Forensis', in *Zeitschrift für Agrargeschichte und Agrarsoziologie*, 1/1953, pp.53f.

too, lived on the margins of existence. Their often-mentioned pitifully low wages forced wife and children to help out. They did so under conditions which, in contrast with work on the family farms, were damaging to health and morale.

Towards the end of the eighteenth century the traditional rule that the substratum was restricted in its procreative capacity slowly lost its general validity. To be sure, there is no formula which may be applied to the whole of Germany. The decline in mortality does not suffice to explain the growth of the substratum as it affected all strata and the upper classes probably even more than the lower ones. Nor is it possible to adduce the change, except in a very few states — Prussia being the most prominent example — to the liberal agrarian reforms and the abolition of guild restrictions. The factory system emerged only in a few traditional manufacturing regions or in individual units. Nevertheless there was a tendency towards the emancipation of the *ordo plebeius* since the time of the Napoleonic occupation, even if this was also only one among many factors. Hegel was among those who observed this process of the 'generation of the *Pöbel*'.[8] It soon grew beyond what those tied into the existing social structure thought possible and tolerable. This was what Hegel had in mind when he spoke of the 'sinking of a large mass of people below the level of subsistence' which, he thought, led to a loss of a sense of honour and legality and made it impossible 'to maintain oneself through one's own occupation and labour'. Hegel also considered it inevitable that the excessive growth of the *Pöbel* amounted to something fundamentally new because the balance of the old estates society was being destroyed by it. And he believed that the rise of the *Pöbel* posed a menacing question to those in political power. According to him, it revealed that 'its great wealth notwithstanding, bourgeois society is not wealthy enough, i.e. does not itself have enough wealth at its disposal in order to influence the excess of poverty and hence the emergence of the *Pöbel*'. Consequently there would be injustice. The *Pöbel* which is no longer able to maintain itself through its own labour would demand its maintenance as a matter of right. If this were to happen, it would have an inciting effect in the sense of the French notion of the 'classes dangereuses'. For if this right could not be established within the framework of the traditional social and political order, was there any alternative to achieving it by means of a constitutional

---

8. *Grundlinien der Philosophie des Rechts*, §§ 244, 245.

change? The question of social revolution had thus been raised. The substratum, it is true, had rebelled before. This rebellion had even reached crisis point in the social conflicts of the late Middle Ages. Even during the more tranquil period since the middle of the sixteenth century it had never been forgotten that 'the *Pöbel* is never more reckless than when it knows itself to be feared' (Lohenstein). However, basically there had been nothing revolutionary about this. As a rule it was not geared to bringing about a fundamental change and it had always been possible to contain the threat. Now the situation was different in that the *Pöbel* broke out of its confines and threatened to blow to pieces a finely balanced social structure. Could it be contained or had it already burst the dams and had to be channelled by new methods into a new river-bed?

In view of these conditions, perhaps it was not surprising that many states — and this time without Prussia in the forefront — tried to erect dams by adopting social restorative policies. One remembered the restrictive population policies, which small communities were able to impose by banning unwelcome newcomers or marriages which were concluded on shaky economic foundations.[9] As the *Oberpräsident* of Westphalia, von Vincke, put it in 1848 in a memorandum concerning the fragmentation of landed property: 'The happiness of bourgeois society depends on the existence of many industrious, healthy, strong people who are both intellectually and morally educated. This happiness is contradicted by the existence of a numerous and poverty-stricken *Pöbel*. The principle of unrestricted population growth is therefore not necessarily one to be adopted by the legislator'.[10] The ageing Freiherr von Stein, speaking to the Westphalian provincial Diet shortly before his death, warned against the danger 'which arises for bourgeois society from the growing number and growing claims of the lower classes. In the towns this class consists of a restless and property-less *Pöbel*, in the rural areas it is made up of the mass of small cottagers, *Brinksitzer*, *Neubauer*, *Enlieger*, *Heuerlinge*; it nourishes and nurses its greed and avarice within its ranks'.[11] The physician Weinhold who was generally rejected at the time because of his drastic proposals on contraception, put his finger on the problem

---

9. On the significance of the Hanoverian *Domizilordnung* of 7 July 1827, see Linde, 'Das Königreich', p.434.
10. Quoted in Wilhelm Schulte, *Volk und Staat. Westfalen im Vormärz und in der Revolution 1848/49*, Münster, 1954, p.115. This study contains very rich materials.
11. In the Provincial Diet on 14 January 1831. See Schulte, *Volk und Staat*, p.499.

when, in his *On Overpopulation* (1827), he demanded, in the spirit
of the old order and against that of liberal emancipation, that the
following groups should be prevented from procreation: all beggars
and other people 'who live outside marriage and in utmost poverty';
individuals unable to work and sick persons who live on communal
charity; 'all male servants, journeymen and apprentices in town and
country', and they were not to be given permission to marry before
they are able to maintain, 'apart from themselves, wife and
children'.[12]
Figures and quotations dealing with this matter could be multi-
plied. Here we will only present the example of Lippe-Detmold, an
advanced rural region. Here the number of *Kolonate* (of farmers and
small- and medium-sized peasants) increased from 5,700 to 7,600
between 1784 and 1848 owing to a growth in smallholdings; during
this period the number of landless labourers rose from 3,500 to
8,000.[13] This is a particularly extreme example of growth among the
lower strata. It was not like this in all regions, but the general trend
was basically the same everywhere.

There is a report from the Brunswick region addressed to the
government and dated 1821, a time when the movement had by no
means reached its climax, which refers to early and unthinking
marriages. The 'poor children of the cottagers', the report went on,
were getting married 'before they have acquired through work as
servants a bed, decent clothes and the necessary household equipment or before they have had a decent training in crafts with which
they will be able to earn a living; they lapse into poverty. The
marriages are usually much more fertile than those of other states'.[14]

The traditional concept of *Pöbel* was bound to lose its meaning in
the face of this explosion. Up to now, lower-class marriages had had
fewer children than those 'honourably' concluded among the
bourgeoisie and the peasantry. The concept of *Pöbel* was moreover
synonymous with restriction, not with expansion. Thus the word
which had still proved useful by Hegel was employed less and less
in its old social meaning. From the 1830s onwards the word *Proletariat* came into use as a term for a *Pöbel* that was leaving its

12. C. A. Weinhold, *Von der Überbevölkerung in Mitteleuropa und deren Folgen
    auf die Staaten und deren Civilisation*, Halle, 1827, pp.45f.
13. Herbert Hitzemann, *Die Auswanderung aus dem Fürstentum Lippe*, PhD
    thesis, Münster, 1953, p.29.
14. Ernst Wolfgang Buchholz, *Die Bevölkerung des Raumes Braunschweig im 19.
    Jahrhundert*, PhD thesis, Göttingen, 1952, pp.8f.

traditional confines.

Strictly speaking, the term 'proletarian' is not a novel one either. In his history tracing the elaboration of this concept Briefs[15] has shown, in sufficient detail for our purposes, that the ancient Roman word *proletarius* had lost its original sociolegal meaning towards the end of the Roman Republic. But the word did not fall into oblivion in its more general meaning. It came into more frequent use again from the late Middle Ages, especially in England where it was most justified. But its subsequent reintroduction in France and Germany was based on the Latin word *proletarius*. It signifies in general those without property, people who live a hand-to-mouth existence. The word is documented for Germany as early as the seventeenth century. Thus Kaspar Stieler writes in 1691 that 'poor, skimping craftsmen' represented 'not infrequently the greatest nuisance for a community and a source of the worst proletariat'. Still, the use of the word remained infrequent throughout the eighteenth century because there was no real use for it. However, when in the first decades of the nineteenth century the 'excess' of the *Pöbel* became a burning issue, the word gained common acceptance — strongly inspired by the French term *prolétaire*, signifying those who proliferated from below. The new term corresponded with the novel phenomenon of a *Pöbel* bursting its bounds and thereby ceasing to be a '*Pöbel* estate'. The pointed use of the notion of 'proletarian' is also reflected in the fact that it is linked, even before Sismondi, with the idea of a two-class society.

Even before Lorenz von Stein and Karl Marx there existed in Germany a notion that a class dichotomy was both pernicious and dangerous. This feeling spread even before it was taken up by early socialist thought or was related to the rise of industrialism. Carl Bertram Stüve, for example, who was barely touched by the problems of industrialism wrote about the two classes in 1832: 'The one [is the class] which at all times lives upon its property and the fruits it bears; the other one is compelled to use its muscle against the former to provide as much of its material wealth as is necessary for the maintenance [of the second class]'.[16] Stüve, to be sure, did not yet think of industrial society but had late feudalism in mind, as he was trying to promote the emancipation of the peasants with a view

15. Goetz Briefs, 'Das gewerbliche Proletariat', in *Grundriss der Sozialökonomik*, IX, Tübingen, 1926, pp.162ff.
16. Carl Bertram Stüve, *Über die gegenwärtige Lage des Königreichs Hannover*, Jena, 1832, pp.16ff.

to sociopolitical reform. Nevertheless, he perceived the mounting social crisis of his time. The demands, he wrote, of the growing and needy 'labouring classes' were escalating all the time. Meanwhile the means for meeting these demands are diminishing in view of the inflexible attitude of the 'consuming class'. Thus it was not only economic deprivation that was increasing but also the consciousness of it. Stüve's analysis is remarkable for our purposes because it darts from the relationship between landlords and peasants as well as smallholders. He is thus concerned with the struggle against feudal-agrarian society which, following a general trend, was about to assume a class character.[17] Thus the 'nobility-dominated rural life' (Brunner) of ancient Europe protruded into an age which had already developed the notion of an 'industrial society' and in which agriculture came to be, in the words of Albrecht Thaer, an enterprise 'which pursues the aim of making a gain and money through the production (and occasionally also through the processing) of vegetables and animal produce'.[18] This was also the motivation behind the demand for the liberation of peasants from feudal servitude. In terms of liberal ideology it was the creation of the conditions for the development of 'rationalised agriculture'. In terms of social policy (as in the case of Stüve), emancipation was seen as the creation of a healthy peasant *Mittelstand* which was to overcome the threatening class dichotomy of rural society. More than once the fear was expressed that the inability of the traditional elites to cope with the new social problems would be replaced by the ruthless domination of capitalism, of the profit-seeking enterprise which had been set free and was ethically indifferent.[19] What would follow was the helplessness of the unprotected and prop-

---

17. According to Linde ('Das Königreich', p.440), 'industrial development takes place on the social and economic basis of an intact agrarian society'. I cannot agree with this view. In fact agrarian society was outmoded in large parts of Germany by the first half of the nineteenth century. On the other hand, liberal reforms and the emergence of a 'rationalised agriculture' notwithstanding, there was also no need for an 'agrarian revolution'; nor, indeed, did one take place.
18. Albrecht Thaer, *Grundsätze der rationellen Landwirtschaft*, 4 vols., 1809–1812, § 1.
19. An example of a far-sighted conservative critic is to be found in J. M. von Radowitz who wrote in 1826 (*Gesammelte Schriften*, 4 vols., Berlin, 1853, p.5): 'Whereas the medieval serf was protected by the obligations of the feudal lord, the master now takes from the proletarian the essentials of his body — his strength — for himself and with [an air of] bitter irony leaves the rest to him. This is because the correct understanding of service and work has been lost. [The notion of] service is rejected and only work is considered valid. The servant is subordinate to a person; the labourer to a thing. . . . This is merely one aspect of the big question, but it demonstrates sufficiently that the recent

ertyless and the 'orientation towards the boundless enjoyment of worldly goods' — a *practical* atheism'.[20] In these words warnings were given of social tensions. As Franz von Baader in his 1835 pamphlet on the proletarians put it, 'the culture (*Zivilisation*) of the few is maintained only because of the absence of culture (*Unzivilisation*), even the brutality, of the many'.

The problem of the proletarian assumed an increasing importance against the background of the economic crisis of the 1840s. As Joseph Maria von Radowitz argued in 1846: 'The proletariat looms like a giant, and with it pauperism, the festering wound of the age, is torn open'.[21] By this time this was no longer an unusual statement. Following Lorenz von Stein, Radowitz had prefaced it with the conviction that the next revolution would not be a political, but a social one. A further stage in this escalating process was that the new doctrines of socialism and communism from France began to exert an influence on Germany and were connected with the proletariat, even though the proletarians themselves remained suspicious of the demand that they should develop a proletarian consciousness. They either remained completely untouched by the revolutionary slogans or adopted them but superficially. And in some cases they even found the teachings of the socialist intelligentsia repellent. Nevertheless, pauperism in town and country was an increasing indictment of existing conditions. Was it not possible that the rebellions and strikes of the 1840s — with the uprising of the Silesian weavers forming a climax — might transform themselves from a bread riot into a revolution in the spirit of the socialist and communist propaganda? The spectre of communism of which the famous introductory sentences of the *Communist Manifesto* spoke was no doubt real. As Lorenz von Stein had put it six years before the publication of Marx's pamphlet, Communism is *ante portas*; it is 'a dark, threatening ghost whom no-one believes to be real and yet its existence is recognized and feared by everyone'.

With Lorenz von Stein having prepared the way, it was Karl Marx who developed *his* particular conception of the proletariat in this situation. And with it he pushed to its extreme conclusion what

process of liberation is frequently no more than a transition from a subjugation to persons to a subjugation to material things and money'.
20. Wilhelm Emanuel Freiherr von Ketteler, *Predigten*, vol. II, Mainz, 1878, pp.185, 187 (Ketteler's 4th sermon, 1848).
21. Quoted in *Zeitschrift für Religions- und Geistesgeschichte*, 1/1948, p.124.

had been triggered off by the emergence of the proletariat whose existence represented a denial of bourgeois-capitalist society. The proletariat as the most extreme case of man's alienation from himself was charged with transcending this alienation in a revolutionary act and to bring about reconciliation within the framework of a socialist society.

Marx saw this transformation not merely as a moral question, but as one which was necessary within the dialectical process of history. The formation of the proletariat would prepare the final and decisive emancipation in human history. To him the proletariat was 'a class in radical chains'; a 'class of bourgeois society which is at the same time not a class within bourgeois society' due to 'the injustice being committed purely and simply against that class'. According to Marx, the proletariat could 'no longer claim a *historical* title but only a *human* title'. The proletariat was for Marx the 'complete denial of man'; hence it could become itself again only through the 'complete reconquest of man'.[22] This implied that the existing society which was held together only by state compulsion would dissolve. The day of man's liberation had come. Marx's radical definition of proletariat was not derived from empirical observation, but was rooted in his philosophical endeavour and in his critique of Hegel's philosophy of law. But his aims transcended philosophy. He intended to stress the influence of philosophy 'as being will' against the 'empirical world'.[23] In putting philosophy into practice in this way, he hoped to achieve its extinction (*Aufhebung*) at the same time. It was in this sense that Marx tried to win the great revolution in Germany in 1848, and he failed. The nightmare of revolution soon lost its horror image.

It is remarkable that another voice than that of the communists proved much more effective in 1848 wherever it reached the 'labouring class'. This was the *Bienenkorb-Brief* (*Beehive Letter*), published by the entrepreneur Friedrich Harkort; it was addressed to workers and actually read and kept by them. Showing a keen intuitive grasp of the realities of the situation the author defined the 'proletariat' in popular fashion and without philosophical ballast as follows:

22. Karl Marx, 'Zur Kritik der Hegelschen Rechtsphilosophie', in S. Landshut, ed., *Die Frühschriften*, Stuttgart, 1953, pp.222f.
23. Marx's dissertation, ibid., p.17.

There is much talk of the proletarians without explaining the term. I call someone a proletarian who in his youth has been neglected by his parents; whom they did not wash and groom and whom they did not teach to be good or go to church and school. He will not have learned his trade, will have married breadless and will procreate children like himself; he is always ready to seize other people's property and he represents a cancer growth within the community.

To Harkort, proletarians were also those who were drunkards and brawlers who failed to integrate themselves into the existing order and to whom 'Blue Monday was more holy than Sunday.

These two types of proletarians formed the 'genuine auxiliaries of the agitators', of the rootless intelligentsia. In traditional fashion Harkort juxtaposed this definition to proven ability and loyalty to one's profession:

'I do not count among the proletarians the decent worker who has been endowed by God, through his manual skill and his common sense, with a capital which cannot be taken away from him except by illness or old age. . . . These honourable people must be given help by stimulating business, through credit banks, a good education for their children and safeguards against illness and invalidity'.[24]

All the indications are that, with the exception of those who had lost all confidence, this view of the proletariat was much more plausible to the German workers than Marx's definition. They could not follow the fascinating grandeur of his scheme intellectually; all they could do was to accept it as a miraculous faith. But they were not prepared to do this, even if they had little confidence in the consolations dispensed by Harkort the entrepreneur. The German workers preferred the prospective safeguarding of their existence and the 'salvaging of the proletarians from the shame and deprivation of the *Pöbeltum*'[25] to the communist revolution of the literati. Viewing the situation from this perspective, the young Wilhelm Heinrich Riehl was able to say that the literary or rather 'intellectual proletariat' (*Geistesproletariat*) constituted the actual basis of the 'fourth estate' and represented a subversion force in the struggle against the existing order; the 'proletariat of material labour' on the other hand was for Riehl no more than a 'derived'

24. Harkort's 9th Open Letter (end of May 1849) with the image of a beehive, repr. in Schulte, *Volk und Staat*, pp.319ff.
25. On Karl Heinrich Brüggemann, see Johanna Köster, *Der rheinische Frühliberalismus und die soziale Frage*, Berlin, 1938, p.44.

group of the fourth estate. The mutually exclusive definitions of the proletariat by Marx, on the one hand, and by Harkort on the other, must be borne in mind, as we shall have to come back to them towards the end. However, we must first turn to the question of what is the picture which can be gained for our purposes from an analysis of society prior to the middle of the nineteenth century. There are two dimensions to this question: (a) the sociographic aspect, so as to gain an objective basis of socioeconomic and societal conditions; (b) the apect of a sociology of consciousness, so as to gain an understanding of the attitudes of the contemporaries.

In terms of social statistics, the 'emergence of the *Pöbel*' and of the proletariat may best be demonstrated and elucidated by reference to small areas, that is, examples taken from towns and especially from villages. However, in order to avoid arbitrariness and singularity we have selected the overall figures for Prussia. This country would appear to be suited for our exercise in two respects. To begin with, Prussia experienced a particularly radical application of the liberal reforms after 1810; secondly a dynamic early industrialism had developed over the Rhine, in the principality of Mark, in Ravensberg and in Silesia, in a few cases also elsewhere. In terms of its progressiveness the Prussian example therefore stands out above the average in Germany.

According to calculations by the Prussian statistician Dieterici,[26] which are meticulous, even if they are not based on census figures of even quality, the total population rose from *ca* 10 million to *ca* 16 million between 1816 and 1846. Starting from 100 index points in 1816, the individual groups of 'dependent blue-collar workers' rose as follows: factory workers to 243; journeymen to 212; day labourers to 167; servants (mainly in agriculture) to 117 and 'labourers' overall to 158. Meanwhile the total population had risen from 100 to 156. This means that:

(1) The overall number of 'workers' appears to have risen just about in proportion to the rise in the total population. However, this picture requires rectifying. To begin with, it must be remembered that 1816 is a year when the above-average growth of the lower classes had already reached an advanced stage, assuming, of course, that Dieterici's estimates for that year are broadly correct. The remarkably low rise in the number of servants stems from the

26. *Mitteilungen des Statistischen Bureaus*, I, Berlin, 1848, pp.68ff.

fact that this group was reduced significantly following the Napoleonic Wars and the agricultural crisis which ensued. Put differently, servants returned to their families. This reduction remained more or less unchanged in the western regions of Prussia. In the eastern provinces, when the economy was more labour-intensive, the reduction in the west was not merely made good in the wake of the liberal reforms; the number of servants actually increased markedly over and above the level of 1816.[27] If, in order to exclude the one-off reduction of 1816 from our comparison with 1846, we take 1822 as our starting-point we arrive at a remarkable rise in Dieterici's category of 'workers' within the short time-span of a quarter century: in terms of the male population over fourteen years of age, it rose from 41 per cent to 45.5 per cent.[28]

But this is not the end of the story. In order to gain a genuinely reliable picture, we must also attempt a socio-statistical breakdown of those numerous people who were neither 'dependent labourers' nor day labourers (i.e. 'persons independently living from hand labour'). If this could be done, we would find, as many individual cases indicate, that small-holdings and one-man artisan workshops increased due to the liberal reforms, the growing domestic market and the strong demographic pressure. These nearly 'self-employed' (as they appear in the statistics) operated as a rule on such meagre economic foundations that they can be classified as 'middle class' (*mittelständisch*) only with reservations. More correctly they frequently belonged to the 'proletaroid' stratum as defined by Sombart.

(2) We saw that even the total number of those who were categorised as 'workers' amounted to 45.5 per cent of the total male population that was gainfully employed. This means that almost half the population was part of the 'proletariat' in contemporary terminology and this was so without industrialisation having made any marked impact. However, if the phenomenon of 'proletariat' and 'pauperism' during the 1840s is to be fully understood, we shall have to include the 'proletaroids'. On the other hand, any attempt to arrive at clear-cut numbers and percentages is bound to fail because the border-lines of stratification were so fluid. Nor would it

27. This point which emerges from Dieterici's figures is confirmed in J. G. Hoffmann, *Die Bevölkerung des preussischen Staats nach dem Ergebnisse der zu Ende des Jahres 1837 amtlich aufgenommenen Nachrichten in staatswirtschaftlicher, gewerblicher und sittlicher Beziehung*, Berlin,1839, pp.196ff.
28. *Jahrbuch für die amtliche Statistik des Preussischen Staates*, 2, 1867, pp.231ff.

appear to be possible to draw these lines in socio-economic or
social-psychological terms. But figures and calculations clearly
show that at least 50 to 60 per cent of the population did not live in
the comfort and the security of a middle-class farmer or townsman,
but on a tight budget, and in times of crisis they existed in misery
and danger of starvation. This figure is further confirmed by a mass
of contemporary accounts from all regions of Germany.

Meanwhile, between 1816 and 1846 there had been a remarkable
shift in percentages between individual categories within the stratum of 'workers' as defined by the Prussian statistical survey. If, for
the reasons mentioned above in connection with the figures for
servants, we take 1822 rather than 1816 as our starting point, the
following picture emerges:[29]

Males over 14 years of age in the category of 'labouring class'
(Handarbeitende Klasse) as a % of the total male population over 14
years of age

	1822	1846
Miners (coal and salt)	0.6	1.1
Factory workers	2.5	4.2
Assistants and apprentices	8.8	11.6
Industrial occupations	11.9	16.9
Servants (of whom 85% in agriculture)	12.6	11.4
Day labourers and *Handarbeiter* (*ca* half of them in agriculture, incl. railway and road workers, overwhelmingly agrarian lower-class)	16.5	17.2
Mainly agrarian lower-class working in agriculture and unskilled day labour	29.1	28.6
Total of 'workers'	41.0	45.5

These figures reflect the incipient process of industrialisation in
the sense of a growing 'industrial expansion'. It was a trend which
continued in the 1850s and 1860s when numbers in industrial
occupations rose even more sharply. However, in fact much more
was happening in the lower classes than these statistics give away.
The traditional *Pöbel*, tied into an order of estates as it was, had
transformed itself into a 'proletariat'. This was the group which
W. H. Riehl defined, together with the *Bürgertum*, as the estate of

29. Ibid., pp.231ff., esp. 236f., 261f.

'movement', juxtaposing it to the estates of persistence (*Stände des Beharrens*) represented by the aristocracy and peasantry.

However, in the 1840s this 'movement' of the over-expanding lower strata headed more than ever before straight into pauperism. Traditional sources of income and maintenance disappeared; new ones were not yet created in sufficient quantity. It proved catastrophic in many parts of Germany that the agrarian substratum in the villages had failed to obtain a share during the distribution of the commons. Its members thus lost the feeding grounds for their cow or pig which the common land had hitherto provided. Moreover there was the crisis of the cottage industries which heralded their ultimate collapse. It affected spinning and weaving in particular, and the gap was not yet filled by the factory system which spread but slowly. The narrow scope of the German national economy at this time must be given full weight, if we wish to evaluate correctly the social conditions of the pre- and early industrial phase. The non-agricultural sector suffered from an over-supply of labour, ineffective machinery and lack of capital. Scarce consumer goods were not sufficiently available to the growing lower stratum.

It is not necessary to pile description upon description of the misery which affected both the overpopulated countryside and the industrial proletariat. The number of published and even more of unpublished contemporary reports is large. It is true that large parts of the lower classes lived in 'Irish conditions', i.e. they lived primarily on potatoes[30] the 'proletarians' bread'.[31] It was due to such foodstuffs that it had become possible for agriculture to maintain a growing number of these classes. If the old term 'nutriment' had described the prerequisite of the family in the corporate society, the expression 'lack of nutriment' was coined as the hallmark of pauperism.[32]

And yet, despite the undoubted accuracy of all these figures and descriptions we must beware of the exaggerations and generalisations extrapolated from the most disastrous years immediately before the outbreak of the 1848 Revolution. The degree of overpopulation was not uniform and low wages basically took account of the fact that most people did not live on their wages alone. We are

30. Government report from the Münsterland, 1835, quoted in Schulte, *Volk und Staat*, p.114.
31. Friedrich Schmitthenner, *Über Pauperismus und Proletariat*, Frankfurt, 1848.
32. *Deutsche Vierteljahrsschrift*, no.3 (1844), p.315 ('Pauperism and the Struggle Against It').

not yet dealing with the phenomenon of family wages in the sense
that a family had to survive exclusively on the wage of the father.
Day-labourers tended to have their own plot and small domestic
animals. Moreover, their wage was not paid merely in cash, but also
in kind, such as food and clothing. This applied of course also to the
servants who were part of the household even where the tradition of
joint meals with the farmer had begun to lapse. The livelihood of
these servants was secured as long as the farmer himself was not hit
by crisis or catastrophies. This also applied to the miner in his small
cottage who was sufficiently provided for by his *Knappschaft*
(union) that he must be excluded for our discussion of the proletariat and of pauperism; and later again miners successfully resisted
their absorption into proletarian socialism. This was even true of the
land labourer possessing no land and receiving no payments in kind
as a basis of self-provision inasmuch as the labour of his wife and
children made up the family income to subsistence level. Certainly
this was at the cost of their health, their moral values and their
family life. Additional pence, food or other goods also came in as a
result of religious, communal or private charities; the children
would also go out begging or stealing. Thus the families of labourers
were able to survive modestly if they lived very frugally and worked
for twelve, fourteen or sixteen hours per day — and provided
alcohol did not ruin the household and thus family life. The industrial entrepreneurs, who were mostly small manufacturers still connected with the crafts, were moreover forced to depress wages in
order to secure their own survival.[33] It was only in the 1840s that
they were able to accumulate some capital behind the incipient, yet
by no means sufficient, protective tariff walls of the German *Zollverein*. Capital accumulation alone created the prerequisites of investments in machinery and hence of increased employment and special
work conditions. The prospect of improvements, which actually
occurred around 1850, opened up for the shrewd observers in the
years of deprivation and starvation prior to the 1848 Revolution.
This experience facilitated a more confident view of the future than

33. Various contemporary calculations invariably reached the conclusion that the
    take-home pay was insufficient for a family with several children with a
    minimum level of subsistence which had already been set at a very modest level.
    Instructive examples in *Zeitschrift des Vereins für deutsche Statistik*, 1/1847 and
    2/1848. See also Paul Mombert, 'Aus der Literatur über die soziale Frage und
    über die Arbeiterbewegung in Deutschland in der ersten Hälfte des 19. Jahrhun-
    derts', in *Archiv für die Geschichte des Sozialismus und der Arbeiterbewegung*,
    9/1921, p.174.

the one commonly held under the impression of pauperism. We have now reached the second question raised by us, i.e. that concerned with the consciousness of contemporaries. From all that has been said so far, it may be stated in general terms that the novelty of the far-reaching social process which we have called the transition from *Pöbel* to *proletariat* was widely recognised. This may also be said of the behaviour of those actually affected by pauperism. The lower classes, it is true, were still a far cry from adhering to the radical slogan coined by the demonstrating silk weavers of Lyon in 1831: 'Vivre libres en travaillant ou mourir en combattant'. But in so far as these two alternatives were not politicised and merely expressed a mood of despair of those who had come to the end of the road, the uprising of the Silesian weavers articulated the same ideas. Rudolf Stadelmann has refused to overestimate the importance of 'proletarian' unrest during the 1848 Revolution. This is certainly correct in the sense that he meant to signify the lack of a proletarian movement which was revolutionary in the political sense. However, we must take more seriously the increasing ferment in the rural and urban strata of the *proletariat*. Not that socialism or communism was taking root! These were indeed no more than a concern of intellectuals;[34] take, for example, Friedrich Engels in Barmen. Or they were a concern of German proletarians and itinerant journeymen who transmitted the ideas of early French socialism. At most, socialist or communist ideas, occasionally and in an ephemeral way, captured the moods of small groups or an excited crowd. In view of this, the following points would appear to be worth further consideration and investigation.

The proletarian strata were increasingly seized by a feeling of being excluded. This happened at a time when the traditional authorities were no longer quite as unshakeable not only in the eyes of the middle class burgher, but also in those of the proletarians. With the old order swaying the permanence of a life in poverty was no longer merely seen and accepted within a rapidly changing society. Both in the rural areas and in the industrial towns the Age

34. See also the wording of the manifesto of the 'Ausschuss zur vollständigen Verwirklichung der Volksrechte', which met at Bamberg on 4 March 1848. The manifesto initiated the action of 'Young Germany' in the city and is mentioned in Ludwig Zimmermann, *Die Einheits- und Freiheitsbewegung in Deutschland in der ersten Hälfte des 19. Jahrhunderts*, Würzburg, 1951, p.240. It talks of the 'dark figure of pauperism' moving closer: 'The Fourth Estate is on the door-step of the Estates House and demands entry into the assembly hall . . . . This Estate is the most powerful of all . . . . Until now Communism is a mere phantom'. But this phantom might be given 'soul and life'.

of Revolution was also affecting the lower orders. It was one of the
social peculiarities of the south-west — the old regions of the
Peasants' War of the sixteenth century, where the dividing-line
between smallholders and the agrarian substrata remained fluid —
that the latter joined in the demands for an abolition of economic
burdens. The situation was different in the rest of Germany where
there existed a division between those integrated into the structure
of communal rights and the poor who were outside it. In these parts
the insistence on a clear change of existing conditions appears to
have been stronger than has been assumed due to the insufficient
knowledge we have had up to now. There is some information on
this question as regards the eastern provinces of Prussia. There is
also a recent analysis of the Brunswick[35] region north of the Harz
Mountains where the peasants, tilling the fertile soil of the *Magde-
burger Börde*, had adopted more rational (and also rather more
anti-clerical) attitudes than was on average the case in the rest of
Germany. This study has shown that a sharp class distinction
emerged in the villages in the 1830s and 1840s. During the Restoration, sociopolitical legislation in Brunswick had tried not merely to
contain the hitherto encouraged growth of the agrarian substratum, but also to restrict its freedom of movement. This was
done by putting the decision about settlement and expulsion into
the hands of the communities, i.e. of the privileged peasants. Yet the
demographic pressure continued. The substratum began to realise
that it was inescapably dependent on a peasant stratum which was
economically and politically dominant. Having fully grasped the
situation, they demanded an improvement of conditions. Thus the
July Revolution of 1830 immediately affected the agrarian substratum. In many villages these people began to organise riotous assemblies and to voice their demands loudly. The peasants responded
by forming vigilante groups of their own. In 1848 these early
stirrings had turned into a torrent of unrest and petitions. Thus
some thirty-four communities sent a message to the Duke of
Brunswick, demanding 'a speedy arming of the land-owning people
in the villages as a pressing need': 'The proletariat, the mass of the
propertyless, is beginning to arouse concern, serious concern'. A
report by the local administration at Salder stated: 'At this moment

35. Buchholz, *Bevölkerung*, pp.13, 28. See also Zimmermann, *Die Einheits*, p.179,
    referring to Upper and Middle Franconia. On the socialist–communist agitation
    among Franconian small-holders and agricultural proletarians see ibid., p.360;
    on the consequences of this agitation see ibid., p.364.

people are striving preferably to acquire possessions. The reason for this would appear to lie primarily in the spread of popular enlightenment'. This latter concept, it seems to me, encapsulates the essence of the changing consciousness of the substratum. 'Enlightenment' would not have to mean education or insight, but it certainly implied that people were torn away from a social existence which they had not reflected upon. They were challenged to acquire a class consciousness — however vague — and they tried to grasp that the general process of movement provided them with *their* opportunity. It was the first stage in a process of politicisation. That this might be connected with vague notions and even with a belief in political miracles — and this was probably quite often the case — is not surprising. W. H. Riehl has described this situation with reference to the 1848 Revolution.

This kind of 'enlightenment' had taken root especially among people, like railway workers, who had already become semi-uprooted. It led to sporadic riots and strikes in the 1840s.[36] Much has been written about the consciousness of journeymen before and during the 1848 Revolution. With some qualifications we can agree with Stadelman, who on this question has argued that they aimed at integration and security in the corporative spirit, not at socialist revolution. Their movement must be seen to some extent in the context of the traditional journeymen conflicts, i.e. their rebellion *within* the given order; they did not rebel against this order *per se*. On the other hand, we must not overlook that this stratum, too, which stood between the traditional crafts and the new factory system were motivated by a dose of 'enlightenment' in the new popular sense of the word.

One thing weighed heavily in this situation in which the poor crashed through the old barriers and voiced their material demands like other strata: this was that they were no longer sufficiently integrated in either the repressive or the charitable sense. The patriarchal ties with the noble landlord, which, all frictions notwithstanding, had made for a visibly human relationship, were lost or slowly disappearing. The 1848 Revolution, which abolished the manorial jurisdiction, did away with these traditions. Communal care which, especially in the villages, had first and foremost been manifested by the existence of common land, vanished because the *human* ties within the village community fell victim to liberal

36. Schulte, *Volk und Staat*, p.521.

emancipation, rationalised methods of agriculture and sharper class distinctions. Finally there was the loosening of ties between the Churches and those who were now called proletarian. How often was the spiritual care of the minister replaced by that of alcohol! How often did the firm hold of established authority on the minister prevent him from finding a way of making contact with the proletariat 'from above'! The discipline of tradition had also reached a point at which, for lower-class individuals, it was a travesty of the traditional proprieties of the old corporate society. This decline also meant that *Christian* morals and the Christian faith ceased to have their powerful influence upon people's lives. This, to be sure, was a trend; it was not a process which had reached its terminal point. If we were to examine the lives of ordinary people in those times, we would find innumerable examples of alienation from the Christian churches coexisting with devout faith and moral values as a sheet-anchor in a period of material deprivation.

When the *Landrat* (regional administrator) of Beckum reported in 1844 that, led by a bleacher, around 1,000 men from the vicinity of Brackwede had 'incited a revolutionary movement' and had conspired 'not to recognise henceforth any religion and any God and to remove their administrators', this case was no doubt an extreme example of atheism let loose. Clerics, the report continued, were to receive food, clothing and shelter, but no money. The movement wanted to destroy those machines that were detrimental to the weavers; 'the poor were to be eligible to become officers just like the rich'.[37] Free-thinking agitators generally did not have much success with 'hammering Christianity' (*Freiligrath*). Where the emergence of the Pietist awakening (the so-called *Erweckungsbewegung*) or the beginnings of a Christian-social movement produced a particularly strong response from the ordinary people, a development might be unleashed which was similar to that of the free churches in England and which actually kept the socialists away. The Ravensberg region is a great example of this. But circumstances there were unusual and the general trend was in the direction of secularisation. This trend can be discovered among proletarians in the strict sense even in a town like Barmen with its lively Christian community life.[38] It must also be remembered that by the 1860s Barmen was already one of the early strongholds of socialism when

---

37. Ibid., p.508.
38. Based on information by Wolfgang Köllmann.

the free-thinking intelligentsia met with proletarians who rejected bourgeois Christendom and the church of the propertied.

The attitude of the peasant estate towards the problem of the proletariat can be put in a nutshell: where class divisions had not yet occurred (as in the case of Brunswick) it was possible to link up with the peasants along the progressive-revolutionary road for as long as the demand for the freeing of the peasants had not been fulfilled. Once emancipation had taken place, the peasant remained, as W. H. Riehl has put it, an 'estate wedded to tradition'. It halted before the thrones and became the strongest element of conservatism within a society which was in a state of constant change. Here, too, south-west Germany with its division of land-ownership (*Realteilung*) stands out to some extent. After the 1850s, peasants were less and less worried by the expanding agricultural substratum, once this substratum began to leave the countryside and, as a correlate of industrialisation, moved to the cities.

Worries about the proletariat, discussions of pauperism and proposals for the solution of the 'social question' were widespread among the middle strata of trade, commerce and the educated professionals. There was a huge flood of pamphlets and articles[39] by bourgeois philanthropists, liberals, conservatives and socialists in the decade prior to 1848. Many of them were touchingly naive; but others were remarkably far-sighted in their analysis and pragmatic as far as their proposals were concerned. It cannot be said that the German middle-class at that time closed their eyes and failed in the face of the important social tasks. In fact plenty of fruitful proposals were put forward by its members. Many ideas which betray a pragmatic adaptation to a changing society originated from bourgeois society rather than from the state, with the latter tending to employ the time-tested methods of 'police law' which were, however, no longer adequate.[40] Citizens began to go beyond organised charity and help in times of crisis and to establish associations and provident funds. Social insurance started as a result of bourgeois activity and initiative in the 1840s and proliferated long

---

39. Indications in the very detailed and valuable, though incomplete work by Mombert, 'Aus der Literatur'.
40. See the important examples in Joseph Hansen, 'Rheinische Briefe und Akten zur Geschichte des politischen Bewegung, 1830–1850', in *Publikationen der Gesellschaft für Rheinische Geschichtskunde*, 36, vol. I, Essen, 1919, and vol. II, Bonn, 1942. See also Schulte, *Volk und Staat*; Wolfgang Köllmann, 'Wirtschaft, Weltanschauung und Gesellschaft' in *Hilfe von Mensch zu Mensch. 100 Jahre Elberfelder Armenpflege-System*, 1853–1953, pp.5ff.

before Bismarck implemented his major pieces of social insurance legislation under the auspices of the state. Many places saw the beginning of support for the factory proletariat under bourgeois leadership and even the education of this proletariat, until the emergence of workers' educational associations in the 1850s and 1860s. To be sure, these associations with their notion of *Bildung* into which virtually all nineteenth-century ideologies had been absorbed, proved too weak to weather the second and successful onslaught of socialism. It may even be assumed that they indirectly promoted the rise of their enemy — proletarian socialism — through their 'enlightenment' activities, that is, the *unintended* politicisation of the worker.

Many people were mesmerised by the magic word 'association', which proliferated from its French origins and reflected their desire to provide the society which was disintegrating around them with a new structure. In connection with proposals to solve the 'social question' the term was used by corporatist conservatives, social liberals and socialist revolutionaries.[41] The Prussian state also intervened either to promote association or to hinder it. A Cabinet Order of 13 November 1843 decreed that 'children being neglected and lacking the necessary supervision, as well as poor people going short because of illness or other emergencies', should be looked after. Under this decree the *Oberpräsidenten* were advised to encourage the formation of associations in order 'to reduce and ward off the physical, social and moral decline which emanates increasingly from the pauperism or the moral crudity of the lower class'. On the occasion of the first trade exhibition of the *Zollverein* in the summer of 1844, a founding committee of the Central Association for the Welfare of the Labouring Classes was formed in Berlin. Regional and local organisations quickly followed. However, the 'social movement' could no longer be channelled by the estate or by loyal dignitaries who tried to organise a modern version of poor relief. More than once the liberal or socialist intelligentsia tried to turn these organisations into platforms for their own programmes.[42] More than that: in several places — such as in the Bielefeld and Gütersloh regions[43] — thousands of weavers, spinners and journey-

41. Examples for western Germany in Hans Stein, 'Pauperismus und Assoziation', in *International Review of Social History*, 1/1936, pp.1–120.
42. Ibid., pp.713ff. See also Köster, *Frühliberalismus*, pp.71ff. and, above all, Nora Stiebel, *Der 'Zentralverein für das Wohl der arbeitenden Klasse' im vormärzlichen Preussen*, PhD thesis, Heidelberg, 1922, pp.98ff.
43. Schulte, *Volk und Staat*, pp.236f.; Stiebel, pp.117ff.

men crowded into the associations' meetings. What had been a limited affair of respectable burghers threatened to become a popular movement. Such developments were quickly suppressed as the state had no interest in them.

One of the most important voices of the propertied bourgeoisie was Friedrich Harkort. His *Remarks on the Obstacles to the Civilisation and Emancipation of the Lower Classes*, published in 1844, probably summarised all serious proposals of the time which aimed at the integration rather than the care of the proletariat. This essay incorporated all other ideas and may be seen as a climax of bourgeois consciousness with its characteristic continuation of conservative and liberal elements. Harkort was close to what he was writing about and felt a direct concern. As a practising industrial entrepreneur he was as removed from unworldly well-meaning philanthropy as from radical principles and theories. He combined a realistic view of the condition of the 'labouring class' with an unbroken belief in the possibility of social progress through civilisation and a love which was rooted in moral responsibility. He believed in the integration of the proletariat into bourgeois society. This proletariat, ignored by those in power, threatened to become 'the grave-digger of states' under the destructively dangerous leadership of revolutionaries. Harkort hoped to turn them into a labouring estate which, as a result of various measures, would be fitted into the existing constitutional order in town and country. His proposals were comprehensive; but they all were within the realm of what was practically possible. They involved, firstly, the raising of the general level of education as a precondition of the labouring class deriving greater satisfaction from life. Above all, education was to form the basis for greater productivity and hence greater national wealth. Next, he demanded the introduction of workers' protection laws which banned child labour and laid down a maximum number of working hours per day — he thought that eleven to twelve hours were perfectly manageable! He also attached great importance to the housing question, which had become all the more urgent as soon as industrialisation led to a separation of work-place from domicile. The example of miners' cottages therefore seemed to him to be the ideal model. In other words, in the age of improved mass transport, the small rural house with a cultivatable garden and a few domestic animals were seen by Harkort as a distinct possibility also for those who worked in the towns. These commuters were to cover lengthy distances by means of either railways or horse-drawn trams which were to connect work-places with suburban settlements. Finally, Harkort realised the importance of associations with their manifold advantages and he not only promoted the theory of cooperatives, savings banks and sickness benefit funds, but also gave a specific example by reference to the statutes of the *Unterstützungsverein der Fabriken-, Spar- und Sterbekasse'* at Lüdenscheid.

All these proposals and practical beginnings indicated the basic direction in which a slowly evolving social policy would move only in subsequent decades down to the present time. The importance and influence of Harkort lay in the fact that he was a prototype among a minority of entrepreneurs who combined the purposeful development of technology, organisation and business with social responsibility, active involvement and a fraternal love which was inspired by Christian idealism.

This leads us to a question which is at the heart of our problem. There were thoughtful Christians in this period when the firm ground of faith had disappeared, so that the flame of moral conviction and religious principles had to be rekindled. They recognised that this crisis of Christianity had its roots in the coldly acquisitive instinct of the capitalists and a 'pathological proneness to revolution' (Franz von Baader, 1835) among the labouring class. Both tendencies appeared to be signs of an egoism which the new economic system had unleashed and of a decline of an effective love of one's neighbour. This is what Ketteler had in mind in 1848 when, in his first sermon on the major social questions of the time, he put the untrammelled boundlessness of property and wealth on the same moral level as the envy of the Communists; when he blamed on 'lack of faith and Godlessness' the fact that St Thomas's doctrines of property were disappearing and even completely evaporating as the moral basis of a just social order. Ketteler put the problem in the spirit of the incipient Christian-social movement: 'Our social deprivation does not lie in our material poverty but in our mental attitudes'. Long before Ketteler's appearance in Mainz, and stimulated by the English example, the idea had emerged both among German Catholics and Protestants that the Christian mission must be renewed. In his essay *On the Current Disproportion between the Propertyless or Proletarians and the Propertied Classes in Society*, Franz von Baader as early as 1835 had started from the assumption that the unhealthy division of society into two classes could be overcome if the proper consequences were drawn from the Christian faith in daily practice.[44]

> A Christian, be he a king or a high priest or the lowest proletarian cannot say "L'etat, l'eglise c'est moi!" or "These paupers are mine, I can employ them as wage labourers or make use of them on the barricades as I please" . . . God commands that without exception one should help one's neighbour; it is not just that one should not harm him as is usually said. As if one element of an organism would not begin to harm other elements as soon as it stops to function for the whole.

The clergy, von Baader believed, had 'declined into a social non-entity' because of the degrading of the 'spiritual'. He now wanted to turn the clergy into the rescuer by giving it the great task of a Christian mission which was built into the constitution. On the Protestant side Wichern[45] tried to develop the forces of a Christian socialism based on neighbourly love by extending the Lutheran doctrine of vocation and of a lay priesthood. In his case, too, the notion of a great Christian association led him well beyond the traditional scope of Christian charity. Thus we can discover among the two major denominations in Germany new and far-reaching beginnings which tried to take account of the changing times of the future industrial system. Yet, despite the many practical things that were being done, all these attempts foundered. Christian socialism posed doctrinal difficulties for the Lutherans at least, as became clear later in the teachings of Stoecker and Naumann. Nor was either church capable, given their close ties with the existing socio-political order in the mid-nineteenth century, of taking the lead in social questions, as Baader and Wichern suggested. Nevertheless their effect on generating a consciousness of social responsibility was great and certainly much greater than is reflected in the achievements of the organised efforts in the framework of the *Innere Mission* or the *Caritas*.

For even if this was an age of growing materialism, these organisations touched the conscience of entrepreneurs and responsible bourgeois notables. These people were called upon not merely to contribute to charities, but also to engage in social work. And yet, the impact of the churches notwithstanding, their effect was too

---

44. See Ernst Benz, 'Ernst von Baaders Gedanken über den Proletair', in *Zeitschrift für Religions- und Geistesgeschichte*, 1/1948, p.107.
45. See Martin Gerhardt, *Ein Jahrhundert Innere Mission*, vol. I, Gütersloh, 1948, pp.37ff; see also J. H. Wichern, *Die Innere Mission der deutschen evangelischen Kirche*, ed. by Martin Gerhardt, Gütersloh, 1948.

weak to be successful at penetrating state and society from the centre of the Christian faith. How smooth was the transition from the Christian faith to 'Christian ethics' and thence to a humanism which was a-Christian and moral. However this may be in detail, *one* connection was clearly visible: the 'relationship between *morals* and the steady rise of the bourgeoisie'. This is what W. H. Riehl regarded as the hard central core of the social question, which he deemed to be first and foremost 'ethical' with questions of economics coming second.[46] Anti-church sentiments and the alienation from Christian morals continued, and two decades later, the proletariat was captured by an anticlerical socialism, after it had been 'enlightened' through 'education' (*Bildung*) and had begun to fight for its rights from a sense of class-consciousness. It is significant that socialism gained its first major successes during the time of the founding of the German Empire (*Reich*), when the hopelessness of destitute pauperism, which had prevailed in the 1840s, had been overcome, when those looking for work found large numbers of vacancies and real wages were rising slowly.

This leads us on to a last reflection: prior to 1848 the nightmare of an immense social revolution during the 1840s had been a source of fear and horror to some, and to others of hope and faith in the future; but after the abortive Revolution of 1848 it lost its suggestive power and only regained it later on in a new way. Had the nightmare been driven back merely by the superior force of the victorious authoritarian state, before which the bourgeois movement also had to give way? Or were there forces which worked internally which removed from this danger the fearfulness of the unknown? The states defeated the Revolution and restored their constitutional orders. After their victory they did nothing of significance to overcome pauperism through a public social policy and to integrate the proletarians socially. But the crucial change now occurred at an economic level. As we have seen, the first beginnings of this change can be discerned in the 1840s. Men like Friedrich List, Mevissen or Harkort had seen it coming. 'The unfolding of the entire industrial power of society' is how Karl Heinrich Brüggemann had pinpointed the goal in 1847.[47] List had coined the term 'nationwide manufacturing powers' (*Nationamnufacturkraft*) as early as 1839.[48]

46. Wilhelm Heinrich Riehl, *Die bürgerliche Gesellschaft*, 6th ed., Stuttgart, 1861, p.448.
47. Köster, *Frühliberalismus*, p.45.
48. *Werke*, V, 1928.

The years of crisis and famine immediately preceding the 1848 Revolution must not distract us from the point that in many parts of Germany industrial and agrarian expansion had progressed and that, taken as a whole, wealth was slowly on the rise even before the middle of the century. 'As far as Germany is concerned, the illness is not a population distribution which has become too dense; nor, on the whole, is it the machines nor the ubiquitous industrial factories; rather it is the lack of those machines and factories which would provide *our* workers with work and money rather than British ones.' This was written by Peter Franz Reichensperger in 1847.[49] The formation of the *Zollverein* and increasing capital accumulation, thence a growing economic activity, a favourable upswing and, after the uncompleted revolution of 1848, a catching-up in the technological field all pointed in the same direction. As far as the economic and organisational aspects of the social question and its resolution were concerned, the way forward was not the destruction of the machine or of impeding its introduction, but rather the expansion of technology and of rationalisation both in the field of primary production and of manufacturing industry. The problem, as we have seen, had been rooted in the disproportion between economic strength and the rapid growth of the mass of the population; it had also been due to the inability to mitigate the much-bemoaned inequality of property-holding between capitalists and proletarians. The starvation level wages of the 1840s were caused not primarily by capitalist greed, but by the constraints of economic under-development. This had been the climax of a crisis of transition when a return to the old economic policies of mercantilism and of a guild-based 'stability of livelihood' was no longer possible and when everything depended on achieving the breakthrough forwards. Consciously or unconsciously German entrepreneurs acted according to these requirements. What of course their behaviour also contributed to was that this vigorous breakthrough was achieved to the detriment of the 'labouring classes'. However, it should not be forgotten that this class had already produced itself without industrialisation as a result of conditions which have been sketched above. Their emergence took place before the greater

---

49. *Die Agrarfrage aus dem Gesichtspunkte der Nationalökonomie, der Politik und des Rechts und in besonderem Hinblicke auf Preussen und die Rheinprovinz*, Trier, 1847, p.291. Frequent similar statements for the 1840s. Dieterici's optimism, derived from the statistical data, is confirmed by Friedrich Wilhelm von Reeden, *Erwerbs- und Verkaufsstatistik des Königsstaats Preussen in vergleichender Darstellung*, 3 vols., Darmstadt 1853/54.

viability of the economy facilitated its further growth as an 'industrial population' (Ipsen). Ultimately industry, despite its early ruthlessness, did not result in the destruction of these classes, but in their salvation. Prototypically speaking, in the mid-nineteenth century the threshing machine became victorious in agriculture and expelled superfluous labour from the countryside. But these day labourers were not left penniless; instead they became available for industry which averted from them the threat of 'foodlessness'. The social question, it is true, continued to smoulder, and was even exacerbated as cities and industrial settlements rapidly proliferated. But the most important thing had happened: jobs had been created and continued to be created; a relative material security was attained. Living conditions continued to be frugal and 'proletarian'; but they were above the levels of the pauperism of the 1830s and 1840s, and they saw further improvements in subsequent decades. The basic step towards the integration of the proletariat had been taken. Along with this change, the word 'pauperism' itself began to disappear.

In this situation the much-debated idea of 'association' gained a new meaning. In other words, as industrialisation progressed, it became more and more urgent to organise on a societal basis the mitigation of material need, in so far as this was caused by the atomisation of the workers. If one adhered to the view that the path to the future was to be found not through a revolutionary change of the constitution, but through an increase in the 'nation's manufacturing capability', the logical conclusion to be drawn from this was that this could not be achieved without planning; society was to be put in good shape again and the propertyless had to be helped through appropriate combinations of a cooperative kind. This is what Harkort had in mind, writing of the new situation of the 1850s in 1856: 'If we search for the sources of poverty, we find as permanent factors illness and disablement, scarcity, parsimony, ignorance and lethargy. Lack of work and inflation recur periodically . . . . Neither the Church nor private charity is capable of meeting such needs. The local communities are too weak. There is only one effective and safe means: "association" '.[50] And indeed the above-mentioned establishment of mutual insurance and benefit schemes was the path and along which the development continued. But the measures were insufficient and not initiated by the state.

50. *Über Armenwesen, Kranken- und Invalidenkassen*, Hagen, 1856, p.4.

In these circumstances the predictions of Franz von Baader came true. As early as 1835 he had warned, on the basis of experiences in Britain: 'How can you be surprised if these proletarians . . . finally hit upon the idea themselves to band together to their own advantage or, as they would put it, to associate?' This was the hour of the trade unions, not under bourgeois leadership, but in a strong alliance with the Social Democratic Party which rose in Germany in the decades after 1871 to the position of a mass party. This party was able to fill the vacuum in which the 'labouring classes' (who had become a proletariat and more and more professed to be proletarians) found themselves. Yet the age of revolutionary barricades had passed; quite simply, the German workers were not prepared to accept the risk of radical revolution. They supported the notion of class struggle only in so far as it promoted the improvement of their material life and helped them to achieve recognition for their work and their estate. For the benefit of the worker the aim of integration into the existing order and the penetration and change of existing society proved stronger in the history of the Social Democratic Party than the radical consequences to be drawn from a theory of revolution.

The solution which was at stake in the mid-century lay, therefore, neither in the idea of revolutionary upheaval, nor in the notion of mere prosperity in the liberal sense. The integration of the former proletariat during the course of the next hundred years was a result of the continuing interaction of several major factors. These were:

(1) the continuous growth in the ability of the system to support the population as a result of modern technology and economic growth. This facilitated not merely a further demographic increase, but also the continued improvement in living standards and real wages;

(2) the 'association' of the working class in trade unions and parties. Without this pressure the process would not have advanced as much as was actually the case;

(3) the social policy of the state from Bismarck's time onwards. This policy reflected the recognition by the state, standing above class interests as it was, that it had particular obligations. It made up for what it had not yet been able to do during the decades of pauperism and early industrialization;

(4) the private social policies of caring and farsighted entrepreneurs who had argued since Harkort that fellowship and cooperation between employer and employees was one of the central

constitutional problems of industrial societies;

(5) the notion of Christian responsibility which remained alive after Ketteler and Wichern. On the part of the Catholic Church and following the papal encyclical *Rerum Novarum* of 1891 it led to efforts which comprised the entire social order;

(6) finally, let us not forget one last aspect, which is that documents, pamphlets, or statistics cannot give a clear impression of what is nevertheless all-pervasive: the simple desire of human beings to live and to live not just as individuals but also as members of a family. The human beings of the so-called lower strata had barely been roused during the period of pauperism. They were in their traditional consciousness and not yet alienated from the old social order. Then 'enlightenment' set in, followed by politicisation with its faith in political doctrines of salvation. Today — a century after the publication of the *Communist Manifesto* — people have generally become tired of these issues, both among the former *Mittelstand* and the former proletariat. Man wants to be himself; he is inclined to withdraw from public affairs which have overtaxed him in the past. This simple fact, which raises such serious problems for the present day, must be given particular attention as providing the motive force of the former proletarian's willingness to integrate himself and to leave the proletariat behind him. The constitutional problem of industrial society is still with us as urgently as before, that is, the task to cast this society into a new form after 'class society' has been thrown into the 'melting pot' (T. Geiger). To tackle it, we need not merely private persons, but also those who take on public responsibilities.

HANS ROSENBERG

The Pseudo-Democratisation of the Junker Class

For more than 500 years the *Junker* — the class of eastern German large-scale estate owners[1] — have provided the backbone of the aristocratic-authoritarian ruling groups which shaped the style of domination in East Elbia until, in 1945, they were destroyed as a class, even if they were not physically extinguished.[*]

The rise of oligarchical domination goes back to the formation of seignorial autocracies based on the large-scale estates (*Gutsherrschaften*). The consolidation of this pattern of local rural rulership was the result of a string of closely interlocked structural changes: the expansion and commercialisation of these estates once they became orientated towards long-distance export trade; the decline of urban economic life and of burgher independence, the disfranchisement and impoverishment of the peasantry and the conquest of the political power of the territorial *Ständestaat* by the landed aristocracy in the age of the secular agricultural crisis of the fifteenth century, followed by the expansion of large-scale agricultural production in eastern Germany during the Price Revolution of the sixteenth century.[2] That the historical heirs of this landed aristoc-

---

[*] Publ. orig. in *Festchrift für Hans Herzfeld*, Duncker & Humblut, Berlin, 1958, pp. 459–86. The author would like to thank the publishers for permission to prepare and use this translation.
1. Within the context of this essay, *Junkerdom* (*Landjunkertum*) signifies a sociological category, and not a political slogan or a romantic myth.
2. See Hans Rosenberg, 'The Rise of the Junkers in Brandenburg-Prussia, 1410–1653', in *American Historical Review*, XLIX (1943/4), pp. 1–22, 228–42; F. L. Carsten, *The Origins of Prussia*, Oxford, 1954, pp. 89–178; Heinz von zur

racy were able to maintain a legally and politically privileged leadership position until the Revolution of 1918, i.e. well into the epoch of modern industrialism, is a fact which is as impressive as it is remarkable.

In comparison with 'Western' developments it is one of the peculiarities of modern German history that this agrarian elite was able to play an unusually influential rôle in the social, economic and political life of its compatriots even beyond the collapse of the conservative Hohenzollern monarchy. It did so on an authoritarian, if democratically dressed-up basis long after it had been put on the political defensive and after it had been forced to cede its dominant economic position to heavy industry and finance capital. For even after the founding of the Second Empire — the conquest of Germany by Prussia — had been achieved, the traditional ruling groups of the Hohenzollern state, i.e. the owners of the so-called *Rittergüter*, the army officer corps and the higher civil service, remained at the top of the social honor and prestige system and continued to be the bastions of authoritarian patterns of rulership.

The monopoly of domination had been lost long ago, however. As early as in the age of absolutism, occupationally the nobility, seen as a whole, had split up into agriculturists, military officers and higher civil servants, who continuously replenished their ranks, and a reserve army of noble *déclassés*. The social upheavals of the nineteenth century reinforced the trend by which influence, power, wealth and prestige did not remain restricted to social descent and inherited property, let alone to privileged nonentities; rather, it had to be shared with all sorts of *novi homines*, among them 'a new bureaucratic service nobility, plutocrats with or without recent ennoblement, wealthy Jews, whether baptised or not, and occasionally even kempt or unkempt scholars'.[3] The ruling class was hence composed of an old-established nobility by birth, a new status elite in state service, with or without noble title, an aristocracy of wealth and an aristocracy of the intellect. These were the elite of the nation, occupying the leading positions in society, the state, the economy and in cultural life.

Even at the moment of their obliteration, which they had brought

Mühlen, 'Kolonisation und Gutsherrschaft in Ostdeutschland', in *Geschichtliche Landeskunde und Universalgeschichte. Festgabe für Hermann Aubin*, Hamburg, 1950, pp. 83–95; Walter Kuhn, *Geschichte der Ostsiedlung in der Neuzeit*, I, Cologne/Graz, 1955, pp. 142–59.
3. Robert Michels, *Probleme der Sozialphilosophie*, Leipzig, 1914, p. 150.

upon themselves, the *Junker* agrarians had played an important, if essentially catastrophic role. During the Weimar period they acted as co-directors of the destruction of parliamentary democracy; they helped to restore authoritarian forms of government and to sanction a dictatorship; in the Third Reich they became beneficiaries, fellow-travellers, tools. Gradually, they were outmanoeuvred and in certain instances turned into persecuted people and heroic resistance fighters.

It should be obvious that the social, economic and political class character of the landed aristocracy which will be at the centre of our analysis underwent very marked changes in the wake of its unusual career as a social group. The 'East-Elbians' reacted to the levelling tendencies and to the trend towards integration and democratisation during the previous two hundred years with more than an attitude of hatred and rejection. The conflict with the newly emergent social forces did not simply take the form of rigid opposition, strict self-isolation, and they did not just hold on, in bull-necked fashion, to privileges and pretensions which had become obsolete. Rather they also demonstrated a capacity to compromise and to exploit opportunities which freshly presented themselves and to make, by means of daring offensives, 'moral conquests' in competition with the 'wishy-washy' Liberals. If, in this epoch of 'permanent revolution', the *Junker* had been mere reactionaries, and if they had not become also progressive and modern, they would not have managed to survive as a privileged ruling stratum into the twentieth century.

This article aims to provide a sketch of the basic group characteristics, the limits of those developmental elements in the contradictory history of the *Junker* agrarians which were part of this process of democratisation. Of course, the problem of this no more than partially successful modernisation was not limited merely to the *subjective* response to new constellations which threatened or destroyed traditional social positions and forced the *Junker* to change their mentality and their individual as well as their collective behaviour. The psychic, ideological and practical adaptation to the egalitarian currents of the times can be grasped only if it is linked with the *objective* processes of ferment and renewal which were reflected in the real changes of class function, class structure, class attributes and class situation.

I

In this struggle for self-preservation in the face of decline in which the *Junker* were engaged, the failure of the 'Old Prussian' system in 1806 presents a dramatic turning-point. All of a sudden the aristocratic-autocratic structure of domination, which had begun to crumble long before, had become extremely problematical, and so had the status hierarchies based on birth and the supremacy of the nobility. As Hardenberg put it in his forward-looking way: 'Democratic principles within the framework of a monarchical system — this would appear to me to be the appropriate form to match the spirit of this age'.[4] But conversely there is also the confession of a more typical representative of aristocratic status attitudes and class domination:

It should be self-evident that a man of high status is also a man of extraction. What is the meaning of the word 'to extract'? [It means] to stand out from the crowd; and who is 'extracted' more than the person that is elevated over all others by birth; who belongs to an Estate and who enjoys privileges which can be gained by others only through the greatest effort, through excellent connections or not at all. . . . We are therefore far from thinking of change. Rather we must use all our energies to leave everything as it was. There is only one point which I would like to recall on this occasion. Since the nobleman is the born master of the peasants and since the latter harbours a total feeling of subservience only towards the *noble* landowners whom they plainly honour as a higher and quasi-superhuman being, it would seem to be urgently necessary, in the interests of preserving law and order, henceforth to bring all concessions to non-nobles to a complete halt and to force all burgher landowners to sell their estates to noblemen. What good is it for such people to call themselves owners of *Rittergüter* if they never gain full rights, if they cannot appear in the district and provincial assemblies, if they cannot name after themselves the places where the courts of justice sit and if they cannot ask for prayers to be said for them in church! Of course, it is still open to them to enter the service of a nobleman — a course of action which is definitely closed to the latter.[5]

Writing a century later, Friedrich Naumann stressed with some satisfaction the change which had taken place since the eighteenth century:

---

4. Quoted in G. Winter, *Die Reorganisation des Preussischen Staates unter Stein und Hardenberg*, I, Leipzig, 1931, p. 306.
5. Hans Albert Freiherr von S——, *Apologie des Adels*, Berlin, 1807, pp. 21, 45f.

> The old stratum of noble masters, numbering some 24,000, is on the defensive and now uses all sorts of means in order to keep its head above water in an age which is becoming democratic. In trying to rally auxiliary forces, this stratum is becoming friendly towards the peasants and artisans and, from time to time, even towards the labourers. For the same reason it forges alliances with industrial capitalism and with the [Catholic] Centre Party. . . . An aristocracy engaging in agitation! This in itself is a success of the general democratic current.[6]

The exclusiveness of the *Junker* began to vanish and its dissolution as a caste-like social status group of hereditary nobles set in when its ownership monopoly of the *Rittergüter* started to collapse; it was gradually transformed into an *open* acquisitive class of professional agricultural entrepreneurs into which all and sundry could buy their way. Up to the modernising agrarian reforms after 1806 landowning *Junkerdom*, agrarian nobility, aristocracy of the soil and privileged possession of seignorial *Rittergüter* had in principle been identical. But in practice this identity had been called into question as early as during the course of the eighteenth century. Already under the *ancien regime* of a pre-industrial hierarchical status society, the landed *Junker* had no longer been capable of fulfilling the task assigned to them, i.e. to provide the members of noble families with an economic basis commensurate with this lofty legal social status. In fact, there emerged a rather numerous landless and mostly impoverished lesser nobility — despite the existence of the noble land-holding prerogatives, subsidies and tax concessions by the state, despite the monopoly claim to cheap agricultural credit and preferential treatment within the system of aristocratic patronage in the bureaucracy and the army. The bottom layers of this substratum within the first estate comprised employees on the estates, small farmers, destitute people, unemployed parasites and vagabonds.

Irrespective of these manifestations of decline within the nobility, the opportunities for upward mobility by the substantially increased number of men of talent, advanced education and ambition in the lower estates remained strictly limited. Some thoughtful people recognised this problem before 1806 and warned

> that sooner or later this must lead to an explosion, if nothing is done to deflect it. There is a bulge appearing here within the social pyramid of the state which poses a serious threat to its equilibrium. Because of limits

6. Friedrich Naumann, *Demokratie und Kaisertum*, Berlin, 1900, pp. 92f.

which are ever more strictly drawn it happens only very rarely that an individual rises into the Estate above him. On the other hand, the pressure from below is enormous. . . . In most places nothing much can be undertaken in commerce and manufacturing; the army does not offer any prospects for members of the burgher estate. The nobility even appropriates to itself increasingly the better posts in the civil service while giving more honorific titles to these positions. What is to be done therefore? the opportunity to engage in agriculture would provide a swift outlet.[7]

In effect the economic power base of the old-established *Junker* class had become definitely shaky by the end of the eighteenth century, and did so despite all the legal and social barriers which had been erected against the pressure from below. During the decades between 1763 and 1806 the *Rittergüter* typically became speculative trading objects and with it emerged the alliance of over-indebtness, frequent transfer of ownership among nobles, and the longing for windfall profits. But up to the agrarian reforms of the Prussian Government these practices had remained *de iure* an internal affair and a social status privilege of the noble estate. *De facto*, however, the noble agriculturists had run up considerable debts with non-nobles prior to 1806 in the course of the concurrent long-term boom of grain and land prices. Moreover, even the ownership of noble estates had come to be transferred to a noteworthy extent to burgher and peasant buyers or creditors. This 'alienation of the soil' occurred either through open purchase or through purchase with the help of straw-men of noble descent; it also happened by means of hereditary leases or ordinary long-term leases.[8] Still, around 1800 an average of not even 10 per cent of all *Rittergüter* — and most of them at the lower end of the scale — had commoners as owners.[9]

The Edict of October 1807 provided the legal basis for the general liberation of the land from earlier restrictions and hence put the trade in landed estates on a broader social basis. This move also initiated the integration of agriculture into a liberalised socio-economic system and put into motion the democratisation of competition. The severity of this competition was henceforth deter-

---

7. Albrecht Thaer, *Einleitung zur Kenntnis der englischen Landwirtschaft*, I, 2nd ed., Hanover, 1801, pp. 679f.
8. See Fritz Martiny, *Die Adelsfrage in Preussen vor 1806*, Stuttgart, 1938, pp. 9–46.
9. More precise statistical details for the main provinces of the Prussian monarchy in Leopold Krug, *Geschichte der staatswirtschaftlichen Gesetzgebung im preussischen Staate*, I, Berlin, 1808, pp. 33ff.

mined primarily by the ups and downs in the economy, personal ability and achievement and the financial muscle of the competitors. The bitterness of this struggle led to far-reaching changes in the personnel structure of landownership, particularly during the two great agricultural depressions of the nineteenth century, those of 1806 to 1837 and of 1875 to 1898.

The intrusion of egalitarian tendencies into the sphere of life of the traditional landowning aristocracy manifested itself very sharply in the massive rise of 'non-noble scum'[10] to the position of owners of *Rittergüter*. Before 1806 mobility of ownership personnel and changes in its qualitative entrepreneurial and managerial calibre had been restricted in the main to men of noble social status. By this usage, some estates had passed from 'the hands of swindlers and inefficient managers into those of solid and innovating agriculturists'.[11] But once the legal structure of the system of social and economic relations in the countryside had been revolutionised from above and the acceleration of economic fluctuations turned out to be increasingly hazardous to traditional feudal life styles, the nexus between the dynamics of estate ownership and the principle of managerial and entrepreneurial efficiency became consolidated. Thus in the course of the nineteenth century numerous over-indebted or bankrupt noblemen were replaced as owners not only by financially potent and often more circumspect social peers, but above all by a medley of rural and urban upstarts emerging from the middle and lower social orders. To a large extent, the ownership of private landed estates of the highly privileged *Rittergut* type henceforth performed a new social role: at least for well-to-do, financially liquid, entrepreneurially adaptive and socially ambitious commoners it provided desirable opportunities for prestigious and profitable career making and upward mobility in the social ranking scale. Conversely, for the nobility as a whole this reshuffle of the ownership personnel signified an intensified decline of *Rittergut* ownership as the principal source of bringing, directly or indirectly, material and social security to the first Estate of the absolutist state. The complex process of diluting the traditional economic superiority of the old-established *Junker* nobility in the social order ran its course, although not only the total acreage of the large estates,

10. This is how Frederick II called those elements who were working their way up from below. See *Acta Borussica. Behördenorganisation*, XIV, p. 452.
11. Christian Jacob Kraus, *Vermischte Schriften*, ed. Hans von Auerswald, II, Königsberg, 1808, pp. 33ff.

especially that of the *Rittergüter*, remarkably increased in the course of the first seven decades of the nineteenth century, but also as a rule the economic productivity of large-scale agricultural business enterprises.

Clearly, the social personnel composition and structural group characteristics of the rural ownership elite underwent momentous changes with the replacement of noble dropouts by erstwhile non-noble leaseholders of the state domain, managerial employees of dispossessed noble estate owners, rich peasant farmers, non-noble and neo-noble civil servants, army contractors, merchants, manufacturers, bankers, professionals with a university education and, in rare instances, Jewish businessmen. In principle and in reality, sheer monetary acquisition, irrespective of one's birth, occupational pursuits and status prestige in the traditional hierarchical order of social stratification, had become a sufficient legal prerequisite for gaining through the medium of the free market the ownership of a *Rittergut*. Thus the newcomers 'promoted' themselves to landed *Junker* and hence to membership in the east German squirearchy, for this was and remained thenceforth their newly-acquired *objective* social class position so long as they remained owners of *Rittergüter*. As such they were the holders of those historically deep-rooted seigniorial status privileges and locally powerful jurisdictional prerogatives which in preceding centuries had been the exclusive preserve of members of the nobility, rights which now continued to be automatically connected with the peculiar legal ownership pattern as epitomised by a *Rittergut*.

It was not merely the legislative enactments of the so-called Prussian Reform Era but, significantly enough, also that of the Restoration after 1817 which in effect devaluated the *hereditary* nobility by birth as well as the *landed* nobility *per se* by establishing equality before the law for all owners of *Rittergüter*, irrespective of their former social status. Accordingly, the possession of traditional rights of seignorial local jurisdictions and authoritarian police powers as well as the newly acquired supra-local political group privileges were no longer tied to the noble birth of the owners or their entry into the nobility by royal decree. Rather it was solely determined by the ownership of a *Rittergut*. As indicated above, for non-nobles ownership of capital, if invested in this semi-feudal type of rural real estate property, had become the stepping stone for the personalised acquisition of legitimated lofty public prerogatives and aristocratic status attributes in state and society. With the perpetuation of anti-modernistic social class insignia, the proprietors of *Rittergüter*, whether they were members of the old nobility, recently ennobled or non-noble parvenus, jointly constituted the corporative political status group of the *Ritterschaft* in the provincial diets which had been reestablished in 1823. In other words, they represented the highly privileged, yet opened-up first estate of the Old Regime. A more preferential treatment of estate-owners of *old* noble lineage ensued only when the Upper Chamber of the post-1848 Prussian parliament was converted into the *Herrenhaus* and when political privileges were redistributed in a reactionary way in the process.[12]

However, this development could not undo the fact that under the impact of the abolition of the social caste system in land transfers and of the pressures and opportunities generated by the structural agrarian crisis of the 1820s and 1830s the personnel composition and social class characteristics of the *Junker* had undergone a radical change. Landed *Junkerdom* as a close-knit hereditary noble status group (*Geburtsstand*) with exclusive rights had been transformed into an open mobile elite of owners of *Rittergüter*, which through the market could be transferred *ad libitum* to buyers of highly diverse social antecedents. Thus the ownership personnel was rejuvenated by the heavy influx of urban burgher elements and experienced rural businessmen. Complex personalised intra-group difficulties of assimilation and integration notwithstanding, in the reformed social order approaching the industrial age the reconstituted group of *Rittergut* proprietors, seen as a whole, formed in essence a mobile semi-feudal *economic* upper class of acquisitive capital investors, thoroughly commercialised agricultural estate-managing entrepreneurs and employers of formally liberated peasant serfs. To be sure, this remodelled class was, as a matter of principle, different from other economically active upper-class groups by symbolising quite clearly a symbiosis of the traditional and the modern in the structure of the social stratification system. Though modernised in personnel recruitment and in innovating activity in the liberalised agricultural economy, the *Junker* class remained at the same time, by virtue of the retention of certain seignorial privileges, an exclusive professional status group (*Berufsstand*). Moreover, under the political leadership of old-

---

12. See Conrad Bornhak, *Preussisches Staatsrecht*, I, Freiburg, 1880, pp. 373ff.; Ernst Rudolf Huber, *Deutsche Verfassungsgeschichte seit 1789*, III, Stuttgart, 1963, pp. 81–5.

established noble members many of the non-noble 'intruders' came
to embrace a backward-looking political mentality henkering after
the hierarchical estate system of the *ancien regime* or even after the
corporatist political preponderence of the landed aristocracy in the
pre-absolutist state, the so-called *Ständestaat.*

Similarly, the 'democratised' hierarchy of army officers and
higher civil servants succeeded in the nineteenth century in maintaining their status as an aristocratic social prestige group and as a
separate, specially privileged occupational estate. They did so although recruitment and career making were in principle determined
by the enlightened bourgeois concept of higher education, talent
and personal achievement rather than by social origin, nepotism and
patronage. In a similar fashion the reformed group of *Rittergut*
owners remained an estate of lords and squires who were privileged
in many different ways and were so regardless of the fact that they
had been recast into an open, partly noble, partly non-noble class of
large-scale landowners and agrarian capitalists. Within this elite it
was the non-noble *Junker*, so to speak the newly-established upstart
'gentry', who quickly gained in weight, at least in terms of numbers
and as pioneers of efficient economic management.

As early as 1856, a mere 7,023 of a total of 12,339 *Rittergüter* in
the Prussian state with an average size of around 500 hectares were
still in the hands of noble families, including those which had been
recently ennobled.[13] On the other hand, it is true that the nobility
did succeed better in maintaining its position at the top of the
agrarian ownership hierarchy. In 1885 as much as 32 per cent of the
land of the seven eastern provinces and 68 per cent of the larger-
scale estates, i.e. 4,393 out of 6,454 comprising no less than 1,000
hectares each, were owned by the old and new nobilities.[14] In
particular, no more than a few bourgeois succeeded in acquiring

13. See K. Fr. Rauer, *Hand-Matrikel der in sämtlichen Kreisen des Preussischen
Staats auf Kreis- und Landtagen vertretenen Rittergüter*, Berlin, 1857, p. 451; C.
F. W. Dieterici, *Handbuch der Statistik des preussischen Staats*, Berlin, 1861, pp.
319f.
14. J. Conrad, 'Agrarstatistische Untersuchungen', in *Jahrbücher für Nationalökonomie und Statistik, Neue Folge*, XVI, 1888, pp. 140, 146, 151. Large-scale
estates were counted in the Prussian statistics as from 600 *Morgen* (133 hectares)
upwards. In 1866, prior to the annexations after the Prusso-Austrian War, a
total of 18,197 estates of this size and above were listed in the Prussian state.
Some 12,150 of these had the status of *Rittergüter*. The class of *Rittergut* owners
and of owners of large-scale estates was therefore no longer identical under the
conditions of the nineteenth and twentieth centuries. See August Meitzen, *Der
Boden und die landwirtschaftlichen Verhältnisse des Preussischen Staates*, IV,
1869, pp. 498f.

land in the latifundia range of 5,000 hectares or more. As late as the beginning of the 1880s there were only 10 owners of bourgeois origin among the 159 owners of latifundia, mostly in the hands of the high aristocracy, in the seven eastern provinces of Prussia.[15] Among them was the *Landesökonomierat* Kennemann who had declined the 'von' prefix. Together with the recently ennobled banker Ferdinand von Hansemann and Major von Tiedemann he formed the trio of agrarian millionnaires who founded the Association for the Promotion of Germandom in the Eastern Marches in 1894.[16]

The process of defeudalisation which is the most decisive prerequisite of genuine democratisation evolved considerably more slowly than the embourgeoisement of *Junkerdom*. This was the process concerned with the removal and liquidation of aristocratic class privileges in general and hence with integration into the nation on the basis of civil equality. As is well known, patrimonial local jurisdiction and hunting rights survived until 1848. It was only the agrarian legislation of 1850 which finally cleared the way for the abolition of the seignorial landlord's claim to a whole range of compulsory services in kind and money which were still very important.[17] The county law of 1872 and the law of 1891 regulating the public status of the village communities removed the privileges of patrimonial police powers and of the personal representation of the owners of *Rittergüter* in the county diets; on the other hand, the *de facto* position as holders of authoritarian administrative powers on the local level remained essentially untouched. The democratisation of tax burdens, which began in 1861 with the abolition of exemption from ground-tax, was practically reversed by Miquel's financial reform. The elevated political position resulting from the Prussian three-class voting system and the preeminent collective position in the *Herrenhaus* were successfully defended until 1918. It was only in 1927 that the final destruction occurred of the remnants

15. Conrad, 'Agrarstatistische', pp. 155f.
16. See R. W. Tims, *Germanizing Prussian Poland*, New York, 1941, pp. 37, 217f.
17. It is characteristic that as late as the decade from 1850 to 1860 some 1,262,988 smallholdings were affected by conflicts over these obligations and ultimately 6,319, 352 *Spanndiensttage* and 23,444,396 *Handdiensttage* were abolished — of course against payment, for the Prussian *Junker* did not easily abandon something for nothing. See Georg von Viebahn, *Statistik des zollvereinten und nördlichen Deutschlands*, II, Berlin, 1862, p. 584. Nor did the agrarian legislation of 1811 and 1816 give anything free of charge to the peasants obliged to render services. They had to pay dearly for the lifting of obligations and services on their land and for the certification of their property rights.

of administrative lordly powers with the dissolution of the large-scale estates as independent communal and police districts (*Gutsbezirke*).

Thus it was only in the Weimar Republic that the big agrarians were deprived finally of their aristocratic privileges and symbols of exclusive domination. As far as their legal status was concerned they had now become an 'ordinary ' social stratum. Within the hierarchies of wealth, of income and of consumption levels the *Junkertum* as an economic group had found themselves declining even during the Imperial period. The really large-scale estate-owners of the old and the new nobility, it is true, succeeded in maintaining a leading position among the ranks of German millionaires, especially those who had invested in industry at the same time.[18] But most estate owners could no longer afford an aristocratic life-style, if compared with the affluence of the upper brackets of the economic bourgeoisie. Their net income was too low to live beyond the means of a glorified middle-class existence.

This process of genuine decline would have been more rapid and precipitous, if the *Junker* class, the differential social background of its members notwithstanding, had not succeeded in the late nineteenth century in welding itself together into a community which represented homogeneous agrarian-capitalist interests, developed a powerful fighting potential and firmly adhered to a feudal-conservative ethos and ideology. This community could count on being given preferential treatment by the state authorities also in a material-economic sense. It is one of the ironies of this entire development that the persistent claim to *standesgemäss* affluence and the pretensions to an especially elevated and socially distinguished position were accompanied by a simultaneous decline to the rank of an ordinary economic interest group. It was a democratisation of a kind that the 'needy' *Junker*, who had been dragged into the plebeian struggle for existence, slowly turned into a demagogue in the process.

II

Up to 1848, the levelling of intra-class distinctions remained largely confined to legal aspects and to growing similarity of

18. There were 856 nobles among those 3,074 Prussian tax-payers who had taxable

occupational activities as agriculturists. The theoretical equality of legally ascribed status position which bourgeois owners of *Rittergüter* achieved vis-à-vis the aristocratic *Junker* was rather meaningless in practice when it came to matters of social self-esteem and pride, conceptions of honour and social acceptability, patterns of personal interrelations and intercommunication, and political influence. The nobility preserved a firm hold over the corporatist organisations of the *Rittergut*-owners. Politically speaking, non-noble holders of such estates were condemned for the time being to serving as 'front-men' and 'window-dressers'. As for social companionship and personal friendship, they were mostly still considered to be beyond the pale! On the other hand, however, the newly-established parvenu squires did provide models in the transition to a modern market economy by acting as pioneers of agricultural progress and by emerging as coolly-calculating agrarian entrepreneurs. In this respect they fulfilled a similar function as those non-noble leaseholders and entrepreneurial managers of large estates which had been carved out of the state domain in the eighteenth century. Henceforth there was but one course open to the aristocratic landowner in the face of the ups and downs of a competitive capitalist market economy: to remain efficient and profitable. Neither seignorial privileges nor favours and subsidies extended by the government to the large-scale agricultural enterprises by means of monetary, fiscal, transport-political, commercial or administrative measures could overcome this basic fact.

The transition to rationalised agriculture was accelerated by the radical change of ownership and personnel during the agrarian depression of 1806–37. The landed nobility 'democratised' itself by developing into a class of productively operating large-scale estate owners whose economic behaviour was increasingly guided solely by considerations of business. It was no longer ground-rents or seignorial rights that now formed the basis of their income, but entrepreneurial profit. Except for the larger entailed holdings (*Fideikommiss*), self-management became the regular pattern in eastern Germany of the economic exploitation of landed estates, rather than

---

wealth of more than 2m marks in the years just before the First World War. Of the 747 tax-payers with assets of more than 5m marks, 319 were aristocrats, among them 49 dukes and barons and 77 counts. See Richard Lewinsohn, *Das Geld in der Politik*, Berlin, 1931, p. 23. For a list of names with precise data on wealth and income (albeit limited to Berlin), see Rudolf Martin, *Jahrbuch des Vermögens und Einkommens der Millionäre in Berlin*, Berlin, 1913.

the leasing of entire estates or even their break-up into smaller tenant units.[19] As early as the mid-nineteenth century the noble and non-noble *Junker* agriculturists constituted a unified stratum of entrepreneurs who far surpassed the old agrarian aristocracy in terms of their know-how, productivity and usefulness to the country as a whole. A generation later, in principle they were no longer essentially different from the mostly bourgeois industrial entrepreneurs as far as their business objectives and their basic socioeconomic attitudes toward the maximising of profit were concerned.[20] Nor did, above all, the truly wealthy among the noble estate owners haughtily stay aloof from bourgeois share-holding capitalism. Instead they also learned to exploit these blessings of the nineteenth century. They assumed a decisive leadership role as stock market speculators and highly-paid figure-heads, lending respectability to firms with their names and thus helping to democratise the capital markets. They did this just as, previously, they had become intimately involved in speculation in spirits and commodities in the Baltic area and had shown 'a very deplorable skill in the plebeian tournament of *Wechselreiterei*' (bill-jobbing).[21]

And yet, despite their highly developed sense of profit making, the *Junker* missed their chance to hitch themselves on as active organisers to the extraordinary industrial development of the Second Empire. The Silesian magnates, on whose land rich deposits in raw materials had been discovered, recognised early that coal and iron ore are faster money-makers than grain and potatoes. But they remained the exception. If few *Junker* ever found a place in industrial management or participated in industrial enterprises which had nothing to do with their landed properties, it was not their lack of entrepreneurial talent or a disinclination to earn more money that was responsible for this; rather it was their aristocratic social pride and their reluctance to be considered a *Koofmich* (money-grubber).

A humanisation of relations between employers and employees was one inevitable result of the gradual transformation of the

19. See August von Miaskowski, *Das Erbrecht und die Grundeigenthumsvertheilung im Deutschen Reiche*, I, Leipzig, 1882, pp. 6ff.
20. See Theodor Freiherr von der Goltz, *Geschichte der deutschen Landwirtschaft*, II, Stuttgart, 1903, p. 177; Robert Stein, *Die Umwandlung der Agrarverfassung Ostpreussens*, III, Königsberg, 1934, p. 324; Max Weber, *Gesammelte Aufsätze zur Sozial- und Wirtschaftsgeschichte*, Tübingen, 1924, pp. 473–7.
21. Albert Schäffle, *Gesammelte Aufsätze*, II, Tübingen, 1886, p. 41. See also Rudolph Meyer, *politische Gründer und die Corruption in Deutschland*, Leipzig, 1877, pp. 35, 65, 88ff., 96; Otto Glagau, *Der Börsen- und Gründungsschwindel in Deutschland*, Leipzig, 1877, pp. 497–519.

seignorial aristocracy into a modern entrepreneurial group of agricultural businessmen. Under the influence of Pietism and of the Enlightenment the enormous social distance between master and serf had begun to narrow in the eighteenth century. However, the decisive prerequisites of the much vaunted 'patriarchical relationship' between landowner and landlabourer developed in real life only in the decades after 1806:[22] by the abolition of serfdom and compulsory labor services; by the subsequent, more ramified legislative enactments pertaining to the long, bitter struggle over the terms of peasant emancipation and the redistribution of landed property rights; by the dynamics of the market conditions and, especially from the middle of the nineteenth century onwards, by industry's sharply increased competitive demand for workers.

The reorganised exploitation of the economic resources of the consolidated *Junker* estates usually entailed the operation of more or less large, highly centralised agricultural enterprises under the exacting personal control of the owner. However, the management of an estate's cultivated area was largely based on the 'prosper or perish' principle and on patriarchal relationships between the *Junker* entrepreneur and his labour cultivators, with the majority of the contractually-tied cottage labourers (*Insten*) actually enjoying greater material security, if not prosperity than even the better-paid workers in industry and commerce. But in the later part of the nineteenth century this kind of community of interest was gradually dissolved. It was 'rationalised' as a result of the proliferation of a cash-wage system, the large-scale employment of cheap, mostly foreign migratory seasonal labour, the disengagement of the more permanently employed farm workers from the estate's owner household and the replacement of the cottage labourer's flexible share in the gross product by fixed deliveries in kind (*Deputate*).[23]

Even in the age of personal liberty and freedom of movement the historically deeply engrained values, norms, and behaviour habits of unquestioning subordination and subservience to their 'social betters' continued to play an important role in the consciousness and deportment of the modernised rural labour force of eastern Germany for a long time. The mental adjustment of the *Junker* to the

22. This has also been forcefully stressed by such an excellent authority on this subject as Theodor Freiherr von der Goltz, *Die ländliche Arbeiterklasse und der preussische Staat*, Jena, 1893, pp. 190ff.
23. See Max Weber, *Die Verhältnisse der Landarbeiter im ostelbischen Deutschland*, Leipzig, 1892, pp. 19, 775–90.

transformation of the labour system and a more 'democratic' treatment of their employees was similarly a slow process.[24] But at the end of this process there emerged 'the master with democratic gloves' who had gradually replaced the swashbuckling agrarian autocrat of the *ancien regime* period — the commander of serf-subjects, who instilled fear and occasionally resorted to the cane and the whip. On the other hand, the weakening of the traditional sense of domination did not imply a disappearance of authoritarian and militaristic attitudes and habits. Even if he did not lag behind others as regards the 'average mixture of naive brutality and paternal kindness',[25] the prevailing type of modernised landed *Junker* mostly did not see himself as an ordinary employer, but as a 'superior' to his worker 'subjects', from whom he demanded a military discipline.

The far-reaching similarity of the basic economic interests of the noble estate owners and their bourgeois counterparts led to an early merger into a distinctive agrarian-capitalist stratum of producers who felt a strong sense of *economic* class solidarity. The Revolution of 1848, the political power aspirations of the rising liberal bourgeoisie (urban intelligentsia and well-to-do businessmen in

24. What was to be done, in practical terms, was expressed by Aloysius Biernacki at an early stage and with a clarity which leaves nothing to be desired: 'The servants are now to be treated as free persons and not as slaves who exist merely for ourselves; one has to look after their housing, food provision and care in case of illness just a bit more than was hitherto the case in most places; humiliating and hard punishments will of course have to be abolished altogether and one can be certain that infinitely more will be achieved with constant supervision, mild treatment and the occasional small admonition (*Belehrung*) than with beatings. The abolition of compulsory domestic service (*Gesindezwang*) would be very detrimental to the estate-owner who will not be moved to adhere to the principles put forward here; he will have no choice but to sell or lease his estate'. Quoted in Albrecht Thaer (ed.), *Annalen des Ackerbaus*, IV (1808), p. 367.
25. Max Weber, *Gesammelte Aufsätze zur Sozial- und Wirtschaftsgeschichte*, p. 474. See also the interesting confession by Elard von Oldenburg-Januschau (*Erinnerungen*, Leipzig, 1936, p. 44): 'I succeeded in creating on my estates a sedentary class of labourers (*Arbeiterstand*). At first I was forced to confront personally a number of disobedient and recalcitrant labourers and to enforce order and obedience with my fist. The useless labourers were got rid of in this way over the years and the good ones were attracted. The means I employed towards this goal was justice. I had learned as an officer what justice is made of. . . . I have always seen the secret to the solution of the employee question as lying in the principle of being a just superior and benevolent trustee (*Vertrauensmann*) of my labourers in all situations. . . . On the other hand I was never soft (*nachsichtig*), but saw to it that obedience remained the first priority on the estates. In this way there developed over the years on all my estates a relationship of trust between my employees and myself whose forms may seem peculiar to many Germans who do not come from the East'.

industry and trade) and finally the growing fear of the industrial proletariat and of socialism saw to it that they also developed common social and political bonds. Being engaged in a joint struggle for the preservation of their property, for the defence and strengthening of their class privileges and the consolidation of a collective political power position, there also crystallised a mutual rapprochement in respect of status consciousness, life-styles and notions of honour as well as of tactical behaviour in politics and of political ideology.

The melange of owners of *Rittergüter* experienced a levelling process both from the top and from the bottom. The progressive 'embourgeoisement' of personnel and economic activity as a class was compensated for by the gradual social integration of the non-noble *Junker* into the landed aristocracy and the 'aristocratisation' of their social consciousness and political attitudes. As it became easier to penetrate the old upper strata, the assertiveness, craving for prestige and vanity of bourgeois careerists could be satisfied. Their early representatives had frequently been proud that they had 'made it', although they were not of noble birth. It is only in the Second Empire that this retrogressive process of 'refeudalisation' became significant for the social history of Germany. The spectacular achievement of the founding of the Bismarckian Empire enabled the conservative hardcore of the descendants of the former seignorial aristocracy to assimilate intellectually and psychically the liberal-minded minority of the landed nobility as well as the non-noble estate owners who had once started off as liberals themselves. Moreover they succeeded in making considerable moral conquests among the captains of industry and urban intellectual and profes-sional elite groups.

The family histories of the Nathusius', Thaers, Scharnwebers, Wilckens, Hansemanns, Miquels, Kapps and many others may be cited as examples here of how bourgeois estate owners turned into arch-conservative haters of democrats. Often these people behaved more *Junker*-like than the Old-Prussian landed aristocracy itself. The time had come when almost the only difference between the old landed nobility and their non-noble or recently ennobled peers was their social origin and the pride in their ancestry, although nobles by birth often also stood out because of their more self-confident deportment, more polished manners, more influential connections and more detailed knowledge of the Almanach de Gotha, as well as a poorer preparation for the farming profession and more strongly marked spendthrift consumer habits.[26]

As the landed aristocracy, the officer corps and the higher civil service opened their ranks to wealthy or particularly gifted bourgeois upstarts und thus reinvigorated their own class, they withdrew potential leaders from the liberal and democratic movements whose vitality became weakened. Notions of aristocratic rank and hierarchy as well as authoritarian thinking and attitudes became 'democratised' as these newcomers, through acculturation, assimilation and more or less close social intercourse became absorbed. There was also the incorporation of aristocratic values into the upper strata in general via the system of exclusive student fraternities, the institution of the reserve officer and the generous handing-out of decorations and honorific titles. In this way a general democratisation of society and of public life was slowed down and blocked.

The strengthening of an aristocratic *esprit de corps* among the *Junker* manifested itself by an internal levelling process which promoted a narrowing of mental perspectives, a growing homogeneity of stereotyped social and political thinking and a decline of serious cultural and intellectual interests to a level which can only be called inferior in comparison with the concurrent upward mobility of sizable segments of the highly differentiated middle and working

26. See the comments of so knowledgeable an expert as the *Landesökonomierat* J. G. Koeppen (*Beiträge zur Beantwortung der Frage: sind grosse oder kleine Landgüter zweckmässiger für das allgemeine Beste?*, Berlin, 1847, pp. 73f.): 'Once a young man has gained the conviction after ten or fifteen years of military service that he will find it difficult to achieve promotion to the position of general, he decides to become a farmer (*Landwirt*). He will either take over a family estate or buy one. The capital resources at his disposal are as a rule small. He would now dissipate it on equipping his house and garden and on acquiring riding and carriage horses with accessories. Our farmer will have spent a year beforehand on a reputable estate, have studied the agricultural literature and perhaps even have been a member of an agricultural school for a while. If he is a capable and at the same time well-informed man, he will start running his estate with many high hopes. As a result of the above-mentioned preparations, he will also have learned enough to be able to recognise the faults from which the estate he has taken over is suffering. But there are so many of these faults that he does not know where to start in order to remedy them. Are new buildings more important, or is it the purchase of animals? Should the fields be surrounded by ditches or is it preferable to establish meadows? All this requires money, expertise and time. . . . As he wishes to move ahead, he will start many projects, will omit doing the correct things and will find himself in financial difficulties before realising it. The hoped-for yields fail to materialise and a certain expenditure is necessary to maintain the customary life-style'. Half a century later, in 1903, Professor Conrad found that 'the appropriate training of estate-owners is acquired in the saddle of the cavalry'. In these people were reared 'born-needy farmers who can only be maintained through state aid in these times and at the expense of the rest of the population'. See Curt Bürger, *Die Agrardemagogie in Deutschland*, Berlin, 1911, p. 6.

classes in the German Empire. However, this shrinkage of the social gap between 'aristocrats' and 'commoners' did not induce the *Junker* to think any the less of themselves. Impressive and unusual personalities as well as representatives of an intellectual elite could be found quite frequently among the conservative or liberal spokesmen of the agrarian nobility during the first two-thirds of the nineteenth century. Now they began to disappear slowly or fell into silence. They were replaced by a type whose intellectual horizons were limited by clichés and whose behaviour had become fixed in standardised status conventions. These were the people who draped their robust materialism with idealistic and nationalistic slogans and who insisted stubbornly on their privileged position. It all added up to 'a haughty arrogance and inner hollowness covered up by polished manners', this was 'bad *Junker*dom instead of genuine chivalry'.[27]

III

The social neo-feudalisation of the higher ranks in Imperial Germany was paralleled politically by a gradual hardening of antidemocratic attitudes among both the old and the new elites. There were important concessions to the masses, such as the paternalist social insurance laws of the 1880s which were based on the *Herr-im-Hause* principle. Nevertheless the ruling elites felt a growing *inner* aversion to the advance of these masses and to the growth in the number of *Reichsfeinde* (Reich enemies); they began to resent the shifts in the balance between the classes and the increasing political influence of the lower strata, including that of the industrial working class. This was what lay at the heart of their subjective reaction to the objective transition towards more democratic methods and forms of organisation which had now become inevitable. Meanwhile the facade became more democratic and they plunged into the arena of levelling political competition. But this was done merely in order to defend their oligarchical predominance against the political and economic pressure groups which kept pushing from below and which tried to gain a role in state and

27. Julius Stahl, *Die Philosophie des Rechts*, II/2, 3rd ed., Heidelberg, 1856, p. 112; also Rudolph Meyer, 'Adelsstand und Junkerklasse', in *Neue Deutsche Rundschau*, X (1899), pp. 1084ff; Harry Graf Kessler, *Walther Rathenau*, Berlin, 1928, p. 54; Kurt von Stutterheim, *Zwischen den Zeiten*, 1938, pp. 45ff.

society commensurate with their newly-won cultural and economic significance:

> The upper classes can no longer rule without institutions which make their activities public and permit the control of these activities. Every state must have the confidence of the great majority of the people and has to regain it successively. [No state] can exist merely on the basis of force. It is due to these major changes of the last two centuries that the need arises for our public institutions to be democratised.[28]

The first decisive step from isolationism into the arena of public opinion manipulation was taken when the old landed aristocracy set its face against the Stein-Hardenberg reforms which assailed the fundamentals of a hierarchically-structured status society. For once the preservation of privileges and of status prejudices was at stake, the *Junker* deigned 'to start a public row with the plebeians about the state of public affairs'.[29] Nor could they remain 'devoted horse-, hunting- and dog-lovers or, at most, scientific farmers, improvers of pasture, sheep breeders, brandy distillers or beer brewers'[30] during the Restoration, when they were threatened by an agricultural crisis and thrust into a radical structural change. The widespread survival of noble pretensions notwithstanding, it was already in this period that the pressing political need arose to defend the interests of the large-scale landowners with journalistic and propagandistic means against a jealous bureaucracy, the bourgeois intelligentsia and the industrial and commercial entrepreneurs in the urban centres. There was also the task of gaining the confidence of the freed peasant farmers and emancipated land labourers through constructive action. It was the particular achievement of Bülow-Cummerow, the best-known agrarian politician and propagandist of the pre-1848 East Elbian landed aristocracy, to have put this message across to his peers. Friedrich List called him 'the Marshal "Move-Forward" of the Pomeranian *Junker*'. And so indeed he was, also as president of the so-called *Junker* Parliament, the Association for the Preservation of the Interests of the Large Land-Owners and for the Promotion of the Wellbeing of all Labouring Classes. The lively agitation of this organisation had a considerable impact on large sections of the population and was, so to speak, a forerunner of the Agrarian League (*Bund der Landwirte*) of 1893.

28. Gustav Schmoller, *Charakterbilder*, Munich, 1913, p. 300.
29. Friderich List, *Schriften, Reden, Briefe*, VII, Berlin, 1931, p. 114.
30. Ibid., pp. 110f.

The Revolution of 1848 and its aftermath generated momentous changes in the determination and distribution of the rights of political citizenship and thereby also in the nature and the functioning of social inter-class relations in the remodelled political realm. For the Prussian *Junkertum* as a whole the time had come for them to adjust themselves to the use of novel, more 'modern' methods in seeking the preservation of their traditionally eminent position in the social, economic and political order. Hence the constantly renewed efforts to achieve popularity with the help of modern means of agitation and to woo for political support among the 'common people'. The large-scale *Rittergut*-owners recognized at an early stage that splendid political bargains could be struck with constitutional monarchies and parliamentarianism. As early as the spring of 1848 the *Junker* masqueraded as democrats in the United Prussian Diet by advocating suffrage rights to be granted to agricultural servants (*Gesinde*). There were only very few large landowners who voted against universal suffrage. Among them was Thadden-Trieglaff from Hinterpommern who confessed with crudely naive cheerfulness:

As is well-known, I am a conservative because it is written that he who has will be given; and as a genuine Prussian my understanding of the old maxim of my family, *Suum cuique*, is not merely that you should keep what you have got, but also that you should take what you can get, or more accurately: what you can gain in good conscience.[31]

Accordingly, hard-line Old Conservatives who refused to conclude a pact with 'Godless and lawless greed' could not be easily swayed even by Bismarck. As Ludwig von Gerlach said in 1866: 'The universal suffrage means political bankruptcy'.[32]

The *Kreuzzeitung* Party which had been founded in 1848 had made it its main task to defend the privileges and the political, economic and social power position of the large-scale landowners. Nevertheless it combined this mandate with a programme that was forward-looking. Hence the declaration to complement 'the struggle against the Revolution and its pernicious principles and consequences with a positive attitude towards the new order of things; only he will have command of the future who is able to

---

31. Quoted in Gerhard Schilfert, *Sieg und Niederlage des demokratischen Wahlrechts in der deutschen Revolution 1848/49*, Berlin, 1952, p. 70.
32. Quoted in Hans Rosenberg, *Die Nationalpolitische Publizistik Deutschlands*, II, Munich, 1935, p. 932.

respond positively to the ideas that move the present'.[33]

The major political change which we have been alluding to began with the great conservative counter-revolution of 1848 to 1879, that is, with the long-range transformation of a doctrinaire *counter-*revolution into a creative *anti-*revolution. Despite its modernisation which resulted from its adoption of the organisational forms of a political party and of an economic pressure group, the *Junker* basically never achieved more than an essentially superficial and opportunist adaptation of their political tactics, strategy and mentalities to the liberal, democratic and national trends in public life.

The founding of the Bismarckian Empire made it possible to re-educate the large majority of the East Elbians to the extent that they were prepared to make limited compromises with bourgeois-liberal notions of constitutional and parliamentary government. But this was achieved only after prolonged struggle and by means of a combination of old-fashioned cabinet politics with Napoleonic demagogy. What facilitated the laborious transition to a policy of concessions and cooperation was that the *Junker* class did not have to wrestle with serious economic problems in the decades up to the founding of the Empire. They enjoyed a most favourable agricultural boom and, at least relatively speaking, they achieved the historical pinnacle of their economic power as a stratum of wealth-producing and wealth-augmenting agricultural entrepreneurs.[34] It was also in this situation that it became possible to overcome the aversion of the particularist Prussian landed aristocracy against an audacious foreign policy, against the nightmare of the 'nationalities swindle' and the 'majority terrorism' of the articulate Liberals. Slowly the *Junker* was convinced that aristocratic status interests and the political power of the traditional ruling elites could be fostered to great advantage by the display of nationalism and by solving the national question through a revolution from above.

Bismarck represented the small conservative band of pioneering revolutionary agrarian aristocrats and feudal bureaucrats. It is significant that another group of aristocratic *Junker* renegades failed among their peers where Bismarck succeeded. These were those aristocrats who played a leading role in the liberal parties during the

---

33. Felix Salomon, ed., *Die Deutschen Parteiprogramme*, I, 3rd ed., Leipzig/Berlin 1924, p. 43.
34. See Gertrud Hermes, 'Statistische Studien zur wirtschaftlichen und gesellschaftlichen Struktur des zollvereinten Deutschlands', in *Archiv für Sozialwissenschaften und Sozialpolitik*, 63 (1930), pp. 121ff., 130–5.

1860s, and did so because of their personal qualities and inclinations, but very rarely, like Leopold von Hoverbeck and the Saucken family, as representatives of their class. Just as National Liberals soon became nationalist conservatives, Conservatives did not change into democrats, but turned into democratised reactionaries. The upper classes and in particular those conservative forces which were dominated by the landed aristocracy failed to make the link with democracy in the Second Empire and their failure was even more blatant later on.

Meanwhile in Britain an open, largely non-titled aristocracy created a new future for itself as the leadership of a liberal and democratic mass movement, by transforming itself into aristocratic patriots who were prepared to make sacrifices and to act as agents of the popular will. Consequently it was not just a theoretical possibility for former industrial workers in the twentieth century to rise even into the titled nobility. In the German Empire and the Weimar Republic the political democratisation of the rejuvenated landed aristocracy, with the exception of a few disparate individuals, remained confined to the wearing of a democratic mask and the use of democratic methods for undemocratic objectives, motivated by an anti-democratic mentality.

As far as day-to-day politics was concerned, the big agriculturists remained closely allied with the conservative parties from 1879, when the tariff alliance of 'rye and iron' was forged, until the rise of National Socialism. The *Deutsche Reichspartei* never really developed beyond the confines of a party of notables with an upper aristocratic flavour. Nevertheless the Silesian magnates, who led it and who were adherents of *Realpolitik*, saw to it that its connections with heavy industry and the high nobility (*Standesherren*) of south-west Germany were never ruptured.

In the last quarter of the nineteenth century the breakthrough of international competition on the grain markets precipitated a severe structural crisis of the agricultural economy.[35] No doubt it posed a serious long-term threat to the profitability and, possibly, even to the economic survival chances of the *Junker* sector of the national economy. Under these circumstances the *Deutsch-Konservative Partei* (DKP) moved toward practicable reorientation by develop-

---

35. See Hans Rosenberg, 'The Economic Impact of Imperial Germany: Agricultural Policy', in *Journal of Economic History (Supplement)*, III (1943), pp. 101–07; idem, 'Political and Social Consequences of the Great Depression of 1873–1896 in Central Europe', in *Economic History Review*, XIII (1943), pp. 61f., 64f., 68.

ing into a broadly conceived agrarian interest- and pressure-group organisation which aimed at the political mobilisation and indoctrination among the great mass of peasant producers. Revealingly enough, after 1893 the Agrarian League which was dominated by noble and non-noble *Rittergut*-owners began to call the tune within the DKP. The landed aristocracy had to make an extraordinary political, propagandistic and organisational effort in order to stay on top in the age of universal suffrage and at a time of menacing economic competition. Now the metamorphosis of an aristocratic conservatism into a plebeian one began in earnest. In grey daily life the formerly exclusive position of the *Junker* was quickly called into doubt. Allegedly 'unpolitical' military officers and ranking 'supra-party' civil servants who survived the purge of liberal privy councillors during the Puttkamer era found it easier to remain 'gentlemen'. With few exceptions, they were only indirectly involved in the transition to the age of mass agitation.

The 'master in democratic gloves' was forced to accept peasants and even land labourers as agricultural 'colleagues', as the lower orders were increasingly drawn into the processes of public opinion formation at state level. In contrast to the older regional credit organisations (*Landschaften*) which had been reserved for the large-scale *Rittergut*-owners, it now became unavoidable also to admit peasant owners as members. As a result, these originally aristocratic mortgage institutes were gradually transformed into general agricultural credit corporations.[36] It also seemed advisable to give petty-bourgeois voters a genially commiserating pat on the shoulder. This happened under the guise of *Mittelstandspolitik* and in close alliance with the Protestant Church which had become politicised during the Restoration period. There is a classic statement by Thadden-Trieglaff which puts it all neatly into a nutshell: the task is 'to serve one's neighbour in true love by maintaining the victorious habit of domination (*Herrschen*)'.[37] The patriarchal-corporatist relationship between the *Junker* employer and his labour force, which had begun to disintegrate in the late nineteenth century, now experienced its inexorable decline, and this was true not merely in the economic sphere, but also in local politics in which quite robust methods were being deployed. A decent Old Conservative like the ageing Herr von Kleist-Retzow, who had the

36. See Wilhelm von Brünneck, *Die Pfandbriefinstitute der preussischen Land-schaften*, Berlin, 1910, pp. 48ff.
37. Quoted in Kurt Feibelmann, *Rudolf Hermann Meyer*, Würzburg, 1933, p. 13.

welfare of the lower orders at heart, described the spirit and the ethos of this moribund 'feudal democracy' as follows: 'If we demand of our people that they should vote for us, it is incumbent upon us that we should look after them'.[38] By saying this he had much more in mind than the provision of free beer to the labourers on the estate when on special occasions in the manor house one could hear the sound of champagne corks popping.

Although the extremely influential political position of the *Junker* was not rooted primarily in parliamentary power and owed much more to the splendid connections that existed with the Court and with the authoritative government executive, and although the agrarians basically rejected parliamentarism, they did not lack the ability skilfully to exploit parliamentary institutions and to apply various instruments of pressure. These flexible tactics were accompanied by a rigid insistence upon the Prussian three-class voting system. Just as during the period of reaction after 1848, this system, from the 1880s onwards, proved its worth as a bulwark of the aristocratic Prussian *Obrigkeitsstaat*, with well-known repercussions upon the policies of the Reich government. This is why Minister Puttkamer, speaking in the Prussian Lower House on 5 December 1883, classified the three-class voting system as 'a precious good which the government has no intention of abandoning'.[39]

Public voting guaranteed 'safe' results in rural precincts under the officially-sanctioned control of the local *Rittergut*-owners. But even in the supposedly 'secret' Reichstag elections the local administrative authority of the *Junker* continued to be 'a reliable and indispensable pillar of state and society against the subversive objectives of the revolutionary party',[40] notwithstanding the growing influence of Social Democracy upon the lower strata in the countryside.[41]

Wherever patriarchal conditions survived, it did not happen infrequently that a closed column of farm-hands on an estate were marched directly and under the supervision of the inspector from the field to the polling station. There they would be issued with the 'correct' ballot paper which the landlord, who was at the same time

---

38. Carl Rodbertus-Jagetzow, *Neue Briefe über Grundrechte*, ed. R. Michels and E. Ackermann, Karlsruhe, 1926, p. 7.
39. See Hellmut von Gerlach, *Die Geschichte des preussischen Wahlrechts*, Berlin, 1908, p. 37.
40. Thus the view of Ernst Holtz, the conservative *Landrat* at the Kattowitz district. See *Jahrbuch für Gesetzgebung, Verwaltung und Volkswirtschaft*, XV (1819), p. 181.
41. See Rudolf Heberle, *From Democracy to Nazism*, Baton Rouge, 1945, p. 26.

the poll supervisor and administrative officer, would then graciously take back. Occasionally he would use an empty cigar-case or a soup bowl without a lid as a ballot box.[42]

Attempts to strengthen the political influence outside the *Gutsbezirke* were considerably more laborious and exhausting; above all, they tended to be more demoralising. Here the task was to win over other groups to agrarian concerns and to drive out unwelcome competitors. The *typical* estate owners were averse to political agitation among the 'masses'. They were status-conscious aristocrats, who as reserve officers or retired profesional officers, were used to giving orders and to reprimanding and disciplining people. They therefore found it difficult to 'recognize, even *pro forma*, the equality between master and servant which the universal suffrage stipulated'.[43] They were uncomfortable and it went against their inclinations, when they had to put themselves up as candidates, when they had to vie for the support of voters and when they were expected to act as 'representatives' of common people. Most of them moreover agreed with Oldenburg-Januschau's dictum: '*Vox populi, vox Rindvieh*' ('Voice of the people, voice of the mindless herd'); they regarded the Reichstag as an awkward 'talking-shop' (*Quasselbude*) whenever it did not toe the line. However, they could no longer afford to give vent to their reactionary sentiments when they were on the campaign trail. Nor could they appear before the public proclaiming Old Conservative slogans such as: 'Authority, not majority and that's it' or: 'Only soldiers are of any use *vis-à-vis* democrats' and 'freedom equals right [i.e., privilege], and freedom and right are the opposites of equality'.[44] It was also detrimental to both morals and character that the wild agrarian demagogy of the 1890s[45] resorted to the mysticism of a 'blood-and-soil' ideology which flourished thenceforth as well as to many

42. See Walter Koch, *Volk und Staatsführung vor dem Weltkriege*, Stuttgart, 1935, pp. 7, 11; Hellmut von Gerlach, *Von Rechts nach Links*, Zürich, 1937, p. 32f.
43. Lilly Braun, *Memoiren einer Sozialistin. Lehrjahre*, Munich, 1909, p. 233; also von Oldenburg-Januschau, *Erinnerungen*, p. 61.
44. *Denkwürdigkeiten aus dem Leben Leopold von Gerlachs*, II, Berlin, 1892, p. 752.
45. See also the sober statement by Gustav Schmoller (*Jahrbuch für Gesetzgebung, Verwaltung und Volkswirtschaft*, XIX, 1895, p. 624): 'Anybody who out of an income of 100,000 marks has temporarily lost 20,000 or even 50,000, does not require for this reason support by the state, even if he dresses himself up as a needy peasant'. Even more drastic the statement by the 'Junker traitor' von Gerlach (*Geschichte*, pp. 36f.): 'All Conservatives were convinced that it was the duty of the state to provide so much in the way of tariff protection and charitable gifts (*Liebesgaben*) that even the most incompetent landowners could survive on poor soil. As much as possible from the state, as little as possible to

other appeals to irrationalism, and that the noble and time-honoured principle of 'commonwealth above self-interest' was used as a facade behind which the chase after subsidies continued at full speed.

Thus it came about that 'the lie as a supplement of power' (F. Nietzsche) was added to the mass propaganda of the agrarians. The confusion and degeneration of political morals which arose from this led to objective dishonesty, empty phrase-making and crass cynicism. These became typical operative group characteristics which in real life often proved perfectly compatible with subjective honesty and personal decency.

The *Junker* of Imperial Germany did not succeed in transcending the antimony between progressivism and a reactionary militancy. Tenaciously and fossil-like they clung to their specific class privileges and power positions. They did not learn to reduce their immodest political, material and social claims; nor did they adapt to the change in the social and economic structure and to the decline of traditional values. They did not integrate themselves into society nor reconcile themselves to the humiliating realities of their shattered position as *Herren*. What accelerated their decline and led to their downfall was that they employed democratic political techniques, but abused them in a demagogic fashion behind the mask of patriotism; they made a mockery of these techniques ideologically and discredited them morally. In the same way it also proved self-defeating that the *Junker*, like the great majority of conservatives in Germany, merely posed as democrats and turned democratic rules into a travesty. Yet with regard to these skills, they were outmatched by the National Socialists.

IV

The dichotomy between the objective class situation of the *Junker* and their backward-looking status consciousness, their illusory attempt to cling to the bygone glories of social and political inequality and economic supremacy resulted in tensions and con-

---

the state! This was the watchword. They showed modesty only when it came to paying taxes. Expenditure for expensive horses, for their parks, their private teachers and nannies, for hunting etc. was counted as part of the necessary cost of living'. See also Pauline R. Anderson, *The Background to Anti-English Feeling in Germany, 1890*–1902, Washington, 1939, pp. 132–55.

flicts. It was these tensions and conflicts which prevented their integration into the Weimar Republic and their constructive participation in the consolidation of the improvised parliamentary democracy after the 1918 Revolution and even more so during the crisis years after 1929. In this way, the East Elbians missed their last great opportunity to secure a political leadership position within a liberalised and more egalitarian constitutional order, rather than to try and gain such a position *against* that order. This strategy would have required the final abandonment of traditional pretensions and privileges; it would also have necessitated the organisation of a conservative mass party which was prepared to cooperate constructively through selfless service for the people and by setting a positive example.[46]

The decline of the *Junker* class which had become clearly discernible in the last decades of the Empire continued even more precipitously after 1918. Similar signs of disintegration and of a feeling of insecurity among the ruling circles may be detected in the proposals to stage a *Staatsstreich (coup d'état)* which circulated in the decades before 1914. At that time reason triumphed over political blindness. The swash-buckling hardliners merely toyed with violent methods and the garrulous monarch confined himself to a few empty phrases. After 1918 the decline of the large-scale estate owners did not at first manifest itself in a deterioration of their economic class situation. Rather it was reflected in the loss of their political privileges, the reduction of their erratically fluctuating political influence, the weakening of their prestige as a group, the deflation of their sense of being the masters, a growth in intellectual poverty and an increasing scrupulousness.[47]

As a class of capitalist producers and owners, the agrarians demonstrated an astonishing tenacity and immobilism, a far-reaching differentiation in the distribution of property notwithstanding. It would be quite wrong to say that the old aristocracy

---

46. See also the verdict by Hermann Rauschning, *Die Revolution des Nihilismus*, 4th ed., Zurich, 1938, pp. 181, 184f.
47. In a superficial way this decline was also reflected in the social composition of the Reichstag. In 1871 103 of its members were estate-owners; in 1912 the figure had declined to 66 and to a mere 17 by 1930. The number of titled MPs was as follows: 1871 = 147 (40 per cent of all deputies), 1912 = 55, 1930 = 19. See Karl Demeter in *Vierteljahrsschrift für Sozial- und Wirtschaftsgeschichte*, XXXIX (1952), 16, 22. In 1913 as much as 21.89 per cent of the deputies in the Prussian Diet were owners of large estates. The percentage in the Prussian *Landesversammlung* of 1919 was a mere 0.74, and 2.44 in 1925. See W. Kamm, *Abgeordnetenberufe und Parlament*, Karlsruhe, 1927, p. 19.

became democratised through impoverishment — not even when Prussia became the citadel of Social Democracy in the Weimar Republic. The great agricultural depression of the late nineteenth century had been replaced by an extended, though by no means uninterrupted, Indian summer which lasted from 1898 to 1928. Prices for east German estates over 1,000 hectares[48] doubled and trebled in the first two decades of this period. Subsequently wartime production and war deliveries proved very lucrative. The inflation enabled the agrarians to rid themselves of most of their debts.[49] On the other hand, agricultural productivity declined from 1914 despite increased profitability, as gross produce yields were reduced while real net incomes rose.[50] Rising net yields provided no more than partial compensation after 1924 when dangers arose as a result of a rapidly rising renewed indebtedness and higher fixed costs as well as of the declining purchasing power of agricultural produce. Nor did it help much that agriculture was taken out of the free market economy and that protective tariffs rocketed sky-high. Protectionism finally went so far that by 1931 grain prices in Germany were up to 300 per cent above the levels on the world market.[51] As a consequence of the advanced formation of *Fideikommiss*[52] estates and generous subsidies from the government ownership of property was more secure and stable in the area of the large-scale estates than in the nineteenth century. This was so — despite the complaints about the 'bad times'[53] which had become stock-in-trade — thanks to the highly successful emergency cries to obtain state help. The situation on the eve of the Great Slump was still such that 'mere'

48. See *Deutsche Agrarpolitik* (Veröffentlichungen der Friedrich-List-Gesellschaft), V, Berlin, 1932, p. 409.
49. See Max Sering, *Deutsche Agrarpolitik*, Leipzig, 1934, p. 113; Constantino Bresciani-Turroni, *The Economics of Inflation*, London, 1937, pp. 299, 319.
50. See F. Beckmann, *Die weltwirtschaftlichen Beziehungen der deutschen Landwirtschaft und ihre wirtschaftliche Lage 1919–1926*, Berlin, 1926, pp. 4f.
51. See Wilhelm Röpke, *German Commercial Policy*, London, 1934, p. 59; J. B. Holt, *German Agricultural Policy 1918–1934*, Chapel Hill, 1936, pp. 101ff.; Karl Brandt, *The German Fat Plan and Its Economic Setting*, Stanford, 1938, pp. 155f., 302.
52. In 1917 there were 1,369 *Fideikommiss* estates with a total of 2.5 m. hectares (7.3 per cent of the total area of land). Some 90 per cent of these estates were in the hands of the nobility, many of them recently ennobled (the great majority of the *Fideikomisse* were created in the period 1850–1914). See Max Weber, *Gesammelte Aufsätze zur Soziologie und Sozialpolitik*, Tübingen, 1924, pp. 328f., 367; Walter Schiff in *Archiv für Sozialwissenschaft und Sozialpolitik*, 54 (1925), p. 109.
53. Even when the grain prices and the profit margins were particularly high complaints could be heard, as in 1873, that 'agriculture could no longer feed the farmer'. See Lujo Brentano, *Alte und neue Feudalität*, 2nd ed., Leipzig, 1924, p. 306.

industrial tycoons or wealthy merchants were represented in smaller numbers among those with very large fortunes than the magnates of the agrarian plutocracy[54] who, it must be added, were simultaneously involved in heavy industry or belonged to the financial aristocracy. On the other hand, there was a larger number of industrialists and merchants who had large fortunes.

In these circumstances the large-scale landowners continued to be a group with massive economic power. Their constant jeremiads notwithstanding, they were materially better off in the first decade of the Weimar Republic than in the first twenty-five years of the Empire. Moreover the *Junker*, often themselves authoritarian personalities and not just admirers and preachers of authoritarian ideologies and methods of government, were able to rely on the political support of relatives and friends in the *Reichswehr* and in the administrative and judicial bureaucracy. However, none of these advantages could compensate for the loss of popular confidence with which the agrarians saw themselves confronted after 1918 even in the agricultural regions of the Reich. In the new mass democracy of Weimar it was the ordinary voter who possessed the greater leverage. They found their political dispossession, which had become a sudden reality, all the more difficult to accept because their economic power was still intact and because they continued to feel a strong traditional urge to rule. But as parliamentary government had now been established, any struggle to regain old positions or to conquer new ones without a successful intensification of mass propaganda was condemned to being an outright failure.

Some representatives of the large-scale estate owners therefore always endeavoured to adapt to the new democratic order and 'to formulate, in the conception and definition of their political ideals and in their practical political work, . . . their own positive demands which are capable of carrying state and nation forward'.[55] Yet that small minority which was serious about its willingness to enter into the experiment in democracy or, at the least, was serious about its conservative *principles* found it impossible to assert itself.

Even the representatives of the intellectual and ethical elite of the *Junker* class, which were now very rarely to be found, moved on well-trodden paths when they were searching for new ways. In

54. This qualification has to be added to the statement by R. Michels, *Umschichtungen in der herrschenden Klasse nach dem Kriege*, Stuttgart, 1933, p. 108.
55. H. E. von Lindeiner-Wildau in Bernhard Harms (ed.), *Volk und Reich der Deutschen*, II, 1929, p. 41.

contrast to those elements among their peers who were becoming increasingly ruthless and who were inclined to give the Republic 'short shrift' with the help of *putsch* paramilitary organisations, they continued to combine a well-reflected faith in principles, ideals and romanticised historical legends with professional achievements, conservative interest politics and a disdainful contempt for the new plebeian rulers and the new ministers 'without landed property [*Ahr und Halm*] who are not being warmed by our sun and not wetted by our rain'. Yet even during the most stable and most hopeful Weimar days the typical spokesmen of this educated and monarchist elite never got beyond emotional arguments, self-satisfied apologias and sterile slogans.[56]

Pushed into a corner immediately after 1918 and left there to sulk, the East Elbians managed to stage their party-political comeback through their association with the German Nationalist People's Party. They even succeeded in winning over new followers in the constituencies of Western and South Germany, including some large urban districts which had been practically closed to them until now.[57] Although it was the result of a merger between DKP, *Reichspartei* and various splinter groups, the German Nationalist People's Party had a broader social base than its predecessors. That is also why it did not identify itself with the interests and ideas of the east German *Junker* entrepreneurs. It is significant that the agrarians were outdone by heavy industry after 1928 in the political leadership of this party.

The agrarians could not even maintain their influence in their own special sphere, i.e. in the countryside and in agriculture. They succeeded, it is true, in pervading 'the agrarian-corporatist associations with a *Junker* spirit';[58] they were also temporarily successful in bridging the conflicts of interest within agriculture by expanding the *Landbund* into the 'Green Front', whose policy — as Count Kalckreuth proudly stated — was up to 90 per cent the policy of the *Landbund*. But not only did the peasants despair politically of the role of the *Junkers* but the latter, split among themselves as they were, also began to despair of themselves when at the beginning of the Great Slump the *Reichslandbund* moved away from stubborn Hugenberg and thereby dissociated itself from the destructive op-

56. Ewald von Kleist, 'Adel und Preussentum', in *Süddeutsche Monatshefte*, XXIII, 1925/6, pp. 378–81.
57. See Ernst Hamburger, 'Parteienbewegungen und gesellschaftliche Umschichtung in Deutschland', in *Die Gesellschaft*, I, 1925, pp. 345ff.
58. Erwin Topf, *Die Grüne Front*, Berlin, 1933, p. 68.

position of the German Nationalists to the Weimar 'system'. Another contributing factor was that the *Landbund*, in pursuit of a nakedly opportunist material interest policy against 'agrarian bolshevism', pushed the moderate elements within its own ranks into the background and in the process was thrust into the great pseudo-democratic race against the Nationalist Socialists.

It must suffice to remind the reader that the political reorientation of the agrarian elite, which was used to wielding power, was experienced at, and hungry for, such power and which ultimately became a headless body, culminated in a terrible fiasco. If one looks at the deeds and their consequences rather than at expectations and high-flown words, we reach the final and historically decisive phase of their descent into the people. This phase was marked by a slithering into political radicalism, conspiratorial tactics and uninhibited demagogy; it was also marked by the march into political adventurism, the slide into the Third Reich, the capitulation of the *Reichslandbund*, the pact with naked force and the descent into moral nihilism. In this way and for a few years the aristocratic landowner became a *Volksgenosse* of a special kind; he became a 'great peasant' and, as a collective, he became the 'elder brother', the 'soil-rooted leader' within a 'front of farmers' in which large-scale landownership was elevated to the position of *Kulturträger der Volkheit*.[59] For a while the majority of the *Junker* succeeded in achieving a comfortable and profitable accommodation in the changed circumstances of the Third Reich. They were part of an 'improved democracy' under the aegis of the Nazi Party; in the Reich Food Estate (*Reichsnährstand*) they became the 'centre-piece of the great German *Volksgemeinschaft*' and the '*Führer*' of an enterprise'. They also succeeded in combining their political self-emasculation and enslavement with the reality of an economic elite position and the illusion of a social one. Yet the price which had to be paid in the miserable final episode of the history of a social class which in the course of centuries of change had occupied so important a position was both suicidal and horrific. This price was to have become accessories to the creation of the German catastrophe and, in the wake of this, to have to face historical destruction. Who can seriously believe that the East Elbian estate-owning class will be reborn, should Germany ever be reunited in a Western sense?

59. See Dr von Rohr (ed.), *Grossgrundbesitz im Umbruch der Zeit*, Berlin, 1935, pp. 29, 62, 147.

JÜRGEN KOCKA

White-Collar Employees and Industrial Society in Imperial Germany

White-collar employees in Germany developed a particular consciousness which took the civil servant as its model.* This
consciousness, which was a result of the peculiarities of German
industrialisation and cultural traditions,[1] was particularly marked
among those employees who found themselves in a work-place
situation where they dealt with blue-collar workers, so to speak, as
their 'subjects' (Untertanen). If we consider those who were employed by the large-scale enterprises of the turn of the century, it
might appear that their self-image as private civil servants was not
without justification. It was certainly better founded than it had
been in any enterprise during early industrialisation. Certainly there
were strong similarities between their position and that of civil
servants in a large government department. Around 1900 the principle of efficiency and drive (Leistungsprinzip) was losing its import-

---

* It should be explained that salaried (white-collar) employees in the private
  sector did not enjoy the status of civil servants (Beamtenstatus), which was
  restricted to those employed in the public sector; however, they saw themselves
  and were identified as 'private' civil servants (Privatbeamten). This idea was
  developed and substantiated in preceding chapters of the book from which this
  essay has been extracted: J. Kocka, Unternehmensverwaltung und Angestelltenschaft am Beispiel Siemens 1894–1914. Zum Verhältnis von Kapitalismus und
  Bürokratie in der deutsche Industrialisierung, Ernst Klett Verlag, Stuttgart,
  1969, pp. 523–44. The author would like to thank the publishers for permission
  to prepare and use this translation.
1. See D. Lockwood, The Blackcoated Worker, London 1958, pp. 29ff., who in his
  analysis of early British white-collar workers makes no reference to a self-image
  modelled upon the Civil Service; rather it appears that the early clerks took the
  ideal of the gentleman as their example. See also R. Lewis and A. Maude, The
  English Middle Classes, London, 1953.

113

ance in determining the salary levels of employees working for Siemens, the electrical engineering trust. Only the directors were the exception from this rule. The activities of the great majority of employees lost all those features which bear the marks of entrepreneurial dynamism, private-capitalist initiative, a willingness to take risks, to improvise and innovate. Instead they increasingly approximated the mere implementation of administrative acts based on rational planning and a division of labour. This was true even of those employees who worked on the marketing side of the company. Open competition as a primary determinant of entrepreneurial success was increasingly restricted by horizontal agreements between companies, and cartels and syndicates emerged in its place. All this led to a corresponding restriction of the room for manoeuvre available to the commercial and marketing side of the enterprise. The majority of these employees followed rulings from the top and administered a market which had been carved up among different companies. The 'victories' of the enterprise were no longer won in the jungle of the early-capitalist market. Rather they were won in the research and development departments which rationalised production methods and reduced unit costs; they were also achieved in negotiations and organisational innovations in which no more than a few people participated. Following the expansion of the educational system, qualifications gained outside the company played an increasing role, albeit not a dominant one. There were even the first signs of a respect, normally to be found in a bureaucracy, for claims based on civil service status (*Berechtigungen*). Outside influences to which companies were exposed as well as internal trends towards bureaucratisation were at the root of these developments.

However, these tendencies were less important than those which began to highlight the fact that white-collar workers were dependent employees in a private economy. They were increasingly dependent on a well-functioning labour market which determined their chances of finding employment and their salary levels. There was also the related problem of job security. The most vital interests of the white-collar employees were therefore subjected to the mechanisms of a private-capitalist economy, even if the impact of these mechanisms was cushioned in large-scale enterprises like Siemens & Halske (S & H) or Siemens-Schuckert-Werke (SSW).[2]

2. Flourishing and steadily expanding large-scale enterprises like Siemens & Halske

It was different in the public sector: here the principle of the free market was put out of action where the monopoly of the state (and the local authorities) in providing and creating civil service positions was concerned. This was the basis for of civil service claims to tenure, adequate material support and pension rights. In contrast, white-collar employees in the private sector usually did not enjoy contractually laid down privileges, even in large-scale enterprises such as Siemens. For them, salaries on the basis of seniority, holidays, job security and pension provisions were based on nothing more than concessions on the part of the employer. These concessions resulted from tradition, but could be revoked by the company board at any time. The position of public servants was regulated by laws which guaranteed stability and security. The position of white-collar workers in private industry was at best secured by three-to-five-year contracts and by the firm's service code (*Dienstordung*). Unlike public sector laws, both could be revised by the company board at any time. Promotion prospects in industrial enterprises were much more dependent than in the public service upon individual effort, and above all upon a personal assessment by a superior.[3] This assessment became the more crucial the more the immediate success of individual decisions became submerged within a huge enterprise based on the principle of a division of labour. There was largely a lack of any objective criteria as to whether someone deserved employment or promotion which were comparable to the *Berechtigungen* used in the public service. Even if the duties of many employees in large-scale enterprises came close to the activities of civil servants in the bureaucracy, the socio-economic situation of white-collar workers was still far removed from that of public servants. Basically, they were involved in a contractual relationship with their employers, even if it contained certain elements of a loyalty and duty nexus which were typical of civil servants, involving the individual *in toto*.[4] After the turn of the

and Siemens-Schuckert were not entirely representative as far as the question of job security was concerned. Being subject to greater profitability pressures, smaller entrepreneurs could not afford to guarantee their employees job security either in times of crisis or up to retirement age. According to an enquiry of the DTV, some 27 per cent of the technicians and engineers included in the sample had been unemployed in the five years up to 1903. See also R. Jaeckel, *Statistik über die Lage der technischen Privatbeamten in Gross-Berlin*, Jena, 1908, pp. 86, 94: of some 3,265 technical employees in Berlin polled in 1907 some 1,048 (=32.1 per cent) reported to have been unemployed at least once.
3. F. Marbach, *Theorie des Mittelstandes*, Berne, 1942.
4. See E. Lederer and J. Marschak, 'Der neue Mittelstand', in *Grundriss der*

century, a minority of industrial employees drew the conclusion from this difference between their own situation and that of public servants and abandoned the idea of modelling their self-image and their demands on the example of the civil servant; instead they perceived themselves as employees facing their employers and began to pursue a trade-union-inspired policy, without however wishing to give up their autonomy *vis-à-vis* the blue-collar workers.[5]

The majority of white-collar employees, on the other hand, responded to the problems which threatened their self-image as private civil servants by emphasising that image. It was now even possible to call the clerical assistants (*Handlungsgehilfen*) lower down the scale *Beamte*.[6] The public servant continued to be the figure with which they identified themselves. This identification now became the basis for collective action. From 1900 on, it was reflected in the agitation surrounding the Employee Insurance Act (*Angestelltenversicherungsgesetz* — AVG) of 1911, which was inspired by existing regulations for the Civil Service and gained a wide significance for the evolution of social policy. It is now necessary briefly to discuss a number of factors relating to changes in social prestige between the groups concerned in the period before the First World War. Only in this way will it be possible to recognise the importance of this self-image modelled on the Civil Service. It was an image which had been upheld for many decades and was now emerging in public outside the company sphere; it was also an image which we have explained, *inter alia*, in terms of the gap between the prestige enjoyed by public servants on the one hand and employees in industry, on the other.[7]

There can be no doubt that technology had witnessed a boost to

---

   Sozialökonomik, sect. 9, pt. I, Tübingen, 1926, p. 126, who found that there was a growing similarity between civil servants and white-collar employees in view of the fact that the relationship of loyalty and hierarchy which was typical of the Civil Service increasingly turned into a contractual relationship.

5. Thus the Butib, its name notwithstanding. See the summary of its demands in W. Mertens, 'Zur Bewegung der technischen Privatbeamten', in *Archiv für Sozialwissenschaft und Sozialpolitik*, vol. 26, 1908, pp. 649–713. In 1909 the Bund resolved not to collaborate with the Bund der Festbesoldeten because public service employees worked under conditions different from those of the private sector employees. See *Jahrbuch für die soziale Bewegung*, 1909, p. 336.

6. See W. Stiller, *Der Verein für Handlungs-Commis von 1858*, Jena, 1910, with the sub-title 'A Contribution to the History of the Movement of Private Civil Servants'.

7. See J. Kocka, *Unternehmensverwaltung und Angestelltenschaft*, Stuttgart, 1969, pp. 186ff.

its general prestige from the *Gründerzeit* around 1870 onwards. Reservations voiced by the educated middle classes against technology which was debunked as being utilitarian lost their former power. Quite often they had even given way to an admiration of technology which amounted almost to a progressive gospel and was particularly strong among the youth. Increasingly, sectors of the population turned their attention and enthusiasm to modern technology, influenced here by the role which military technology had played in the unification of Germany.[8] They were impressed by the books of Max Maria von Weber[9] and Max Eyth (*Hinter Pflug und Schraubstock*) which were widely read and stylised the creative progressiveness of the engineer. They were finally carried away by the great discoveries that followed the age of the steam engine, railway and telegraph, i.e., first that of electric light, then that of the motor-car and the races organised with its rise and later that of the first flying machines, of the Zeppelin and the cinematograph.[10]

The development of science-orientated secondary schools (*Realschulen*) and of technical universities also indicates that a non-humanist education was slowly overtaking that of the more classically-orientated grammar schools and older universities. This trend culminated in 1899/1900 when Emperor Wilhelm II gave the technical universities the right to award doctorates.[11] Frequent references to the prestige of 'German industry' abroad put the rise of technology into a national context. 'Made in Germany' had changed from a mark of negative discrimination to a sign of high quality. The successful upvaluing of technology, which had met with many obstacles, also found an expression in the varied technical interests of the Emperor, in his praise of, and support for, the technical universities. 'The best families', he proclaimed, 'who thus far, it appears, have distanced themselves now encourage their sons

---

8. It is no coincidence that the German Emperors paid frequent visits to Krupp's factories and in particular those involved in armaments production. Wilhelm I and his son, while Crown Prince, did so at least four times, Wilhelm II at least eight times.
9. See F. Schnabel, *Deutsche Geschichte im 19. Jahrhundert*, Freiburg, 1954, vol. III, pp. 450f.
10. See the chapter 'Wirtschaft und Technik' in G. Kotowski et al. (eds.), *Das Wilhelminische Deutschland. Stimmen der Zeitgenossen*, Frankfurt, 1965, pp. 109–24, with various materials documenting the positive reception of technological progress, but also including some sceptical statements.
11. See W. Treue, 'Das Verhältnis der Universitäten und technischen Hochschulen zueinander und ihre Bedeutung für die Wirtschaft', in F. Lütge (ed.), *Die wirtschaftliche Situation in Deutschland und Österreich um die Wende von 18. zum 19. Jahrhundert*, Stuttgart, 1964, pp. 234ff.

to turn to technological subjects and I hope that this trend will grow'.[12] The engineers above all were convinced of the epochal significance of technology: 'While there is absolutely no doubt that technology has become a significant cultural factor in our cultural life, its triumphant rise (*Siegeslauf*) has also conquered the hearts of all people'.[13] The growing importance of the applied sciences was also reflected in the increased self-confidence of many engineers.[14] Their claim that the non-technological spheres be 'engineericised' and that social and political life be shaped according to technological criteria was given limited support by the Emperor.[15] If they articulated their ideas at all, many engineers frequently reacted to these transformations not so much with naively formulated technocratic claims to leadership, but with an imprecise demand for more 'influence' or 'standing' (*Geltung*).

It was the economic upswing since the end of the Great Depression much more than technology itself that created the preconditions of the imperialistic ideas which gained greater importance in Wilhelmine society towards the end of the nineteenth century. This also applies to the hypothesis that Germany had become an *Industriestaat* which from 1900 was deployed to provide an ideological basis to the legislative demands of industry.[16] In this way, industry and commerce appeared in the public's consciousness as the foundation of German greatness. This was used by entrepreneurs and merchants to demonstrate how important they were to society, culture and to the German nation as a whole. Thus we read; 'Especially we Germans, who have made very rapid and much-envied economic strides, will need, at a time of increased potential for tensions, a stratum of merchants who possess a deep and all-round knowledge of business and the world, such as can only be provided by the best

12. Thus Wilhelm II on 19.10.1899, quoted in W. Schröder (ed.), *Das persönliche Regiment*, Munich, 1907, p. 150.
13. C. Weihe, *Die akademisch-technischen Berufe*, Berlin, 1904, p. 4.
14. See W. Franz, *Ingenieurstudium und Verwaltungsreform*, Berlin, 1909, p. 9: 'Just take a single link out of the great technical works and the intellectual life of the period will immediately experience the most difficult problems. What a massive and all-embracing power is encapsulated in technology! . . . And yet — what is the esteem enjoyed by the technologist in his national community?'
15. Thus the Kaiser proposed to 'move the technical universities into the foreground', arguing that they 'have to solve great tasks, and not just technical ones, but also big social tasks'. Count Arthur von Posadowsky-Wehner, the State Secretary in the Reich Office of the Interior, speaking on the occasion of the fiftieth anniversary of the Verein Deutscher Ingenieure in 1906 emphasised the task of the engineer as a social mediator.
16. See H. Kaelble, *Industrielle Interessenpolitik in der Wilhelminischen Gesellschaft*, Berlin, 1967, pp. 127f., 152.

education and real-life training'.[17] Georg Siemens, a banker whose
father, as a civil servant, never accepted his son's decision to become
a businessman, described the situation at the turn of the century as
follows:

> The activity of a businessman does not enjoy a special esteem among civil
> service circles as far as its usefulness is concerned. In my view [this is so]
> because the[se] gentlemen are still so full of the ideas of earlier centuries
> and simply cannot yet imagine the colossal change that has occurred
> during the past fifty years in the relationship between [different social]
> forces.[18]

Some ten years later, Walther Rathenau stated that the 'art of
business' enjoyed general high prestige and was frequently even
over-estimated. It was now directly competing with the traditional
virtues of the civil service and the military.[19]

It was a reflection of the growing esteem enjoyed by trade and
commerce that historical accounts glorified the 'German merchant'
of the Hanseatic League as well as the 'royal merchant' of the
eighteenth century.[20] At the turn of the century the notion of the
wealthy businessman carried with it clear nationalist overtones. In
after-dinner speeches even the employees were deemed always to
have adhered to 'a genuinely businesslike, Hanseatic spirit'
(Rostock).[21] One extolled the personality 'who was called upon to
give the German name the widest popularity and recognition,
especially abroad. The German merchant was and is this personality'. The 'foundations of our German fatherland, of our greatness
and our power-consciousness' were seen to rest primarily upon the
'estate of merchants'.[22] As *Deutsche Handelswacht*, the organ of the
Deutschnationale Handlungsgehilfen-Verband (DHV), put it,
'foreign nations were beginning to fear the German merchant as the
future ruler of the large empire of the world market'.[23] This notion
of the businessman who was widely travelled, cosmopolitan, urbane

17. L. Rothschild, *Taschenbuch für Kaufleute*, 20th ed., Leipzig, 1878; 53rd ed.,
     Leipzig, 1910.
18. K. Helfferich, *Georg von Siemens*, Berlin 1921–3, vol. III, p. 350.
19. W. Rathenau, *Zur Kritik der Zeit*, 17th ed., Berlin, 1919, pp. 210f.
20. See also R. Ehrenberg, 'Handelshochschulen II', in *Deutscher Verband für das
     kaufmännische Unterrichtswesen*, Braunschweig, 1897, p. 6.
21. Verein junger Kaufleute (ed.), *Festbuch zur Hundertjahrfeier der 'Union'*,
     Rostock, 1909, p. 36.
22. Ibid., pp. 38f. See also similar statements in G. Steinhausen, *Der Kaufmann in
     der deutschen Vergangenheit*, Jena, 1912, p. 131. This book was written for the
     Verband Deutscher Handlungsgehilfen at Leipzig.
23. *Deutsche Handels-Wacht*, vol. V, 1898, p. 427.

and at home with foreign languages, continued to appear in the
columns of the white-collar employee journals whose headlines
were embroidered by symbols of long-distance trade such as a
globe, heavily-laden ships and Mercury, the god of trade.[24]
    However, these changes in societal consciousness which occurred
during the Wilhelmine period did not lead to a tangible upvaluing of
the groups employed in commerce and industry; nor did they result
in a belated acceptance of capitalist-industrial modes of thought.
There can be no doubt that industrialists like Wilhelm von Siemens
were part of the Berlin Establishment, if public honours and social
contacts are to be taken as a guide. He had a large estate (*Rittergut*)
outside Berlin, was nominated Privy Councillor (*Geheimer Regierungsrat*) and awarded an honourary doctorate in engineering science. These were honours bestowed upon him by very different
spheres of public life. He mixed with top civil servants and invited
them to his hunting estates.[25] The Prussian Minister for Public
Works took a one-week holiday on Wilhelm von Siemens's estate at
Biesdorf.[26] However, the civil servant was no model for the owner
and director of the House of Siemens just as he probably did not
have the admiration of the firm's top employees. Rather, civil
servants were strongly drawn to taking up leading positions in the
private sector, not least for financial reasons. This is not only
demonstrated by the entry of Tonio Bödiker, the President of the
Reich Insurance Office, into the Siemens board of directors from
where he later moved to the Siemens & Halske supervisory board; it
is also evidenced by the employment, sometimes on a provisional
but often on a permanent basis, of technical civil servants (such as
Regierungsbaumeister) who, coming from the technical departments of central or local government, achieved higher positions in

24. Thus the cover of *Handelsstand*, the journal of the Verein für Handlungs-
    Commis von 1858, carried a globe, ships and the baton of Mercury. Similar
    symbols were used in the issues of October, November and December 1898 of
    Deutsche Handels-Wacht. The Kaiser undertook a trip to the Near East at this
    time.
25. Archiv des Werner-von-Siemens-Instituts, München (SAA), 4/Lf 775, diary of
    Wilhelm von Siemens, referring to his elevation to Geheimer Regierungsrat on
    1.1.1905. At the same time he became a member of the Akademie für Bauwesen.
    Dresden Technical University awarded him an honorary doctorate in engineer-
    ing science (Dr-Ing. e.h.). Wilhelm was also a member of several scientific
    societies, among them the Elektrotechnische Verein, the Deutsche Bunsen-
    gesellschaft and the Staatswissenschaftliche Gesellschaft at Göttingen which had
    some thirty members, most of them civil servants and professors. He was also a
    member of the Presidium (Vorstandsrat) of the Deutsche Museum at Munich.
26. See ibid., entry for 1.1.1906, referring to Budde's stay. Von Thielen, Budde's
    predecessor, also visited Gut Biesdorf.

the Siemens echelons. And Siemens was not an exception in this respect. The three Krupp directors, Jencke, Roetger and Hugenberg, were all former civil servants.[27] By 1912 this migration had become so widespread that the problem was debated in the German Parliament (*Reichstag*).[28] It is also unlikely that directors of the AEG electrical engineering trust, like the successful Felix Deutsch or even Emil Rathenau, looked up to the former Prussian minister, Herrfurth, or the former State Secretary for the Navy, Hollmann, who succeeded each other as well-paid figureheads on the AEG supervisory board and whose assets consisted of good connections with the spending departments of the government.[29] Senior managers, acting as they did as aides to the entrepreneur, enjoyed a prestige which the industrialists of the earlier period had lacked.

Yet, their greater social recognition notwithstanding, it would be wrong to speak of a public opinion that favoured industry. Large sections of the press as well as opinion-moulding social scientists did not take a kind view of 'large-scale capital'.[30] As the secretary of one industrial association (probably with slight exaggeration) put it: 'Nowhere in the world does the entrepreneur enjoy so little prestige and favour as in Germany . . . . [To the people] the large-scale industrialist is a less well-known figure than the large-scale land-owner'.[31] Thus the criticism of capitalism by socialists, *Mittelstand* and agrarians combined to influence a public which favoured economic concentration.[32] If Gustav Stresemann in 1905 sensed 'little enthusiasm for the value of an industrial society' (*Industries-*

---

27. See W. Fischer, 'Selbstverwaltung und Interessenverbände im Deutschen Reich, 18/1–1914', in C. Böhret and D. Grosser (eds.), *Interdependenzen von Politik und Wirtschaft*, Berlin 1967, p. 444.
28. See *Stenographische Berichte des Deutschen Reichstages*, vol. 283, pp. 561ff., 12.3.1912. The Reichstag discussed the problem of higher civil servants who had retired (frequently because of alleged incapacity — 'Dienstuntauglichkeit') and then supplemented their pensions with lucrative salaries paid by private companies. Those civil servants who joined industry waiving their pension rights were not mentioned.
29. This is how Liesching, a member of the Progressive Party, explained why the companies were interested in attracting former civil servants. See ibid., p. 564. See also F. Eulenburg, 'Die Aufsichtsräte der deutschen Aktiengesellschaften', in *Jahrbuch für Nationalökonomie und Statistik*, III series, vol. 32, 1906, pp. 100ff. Examples from the AEG trust may be found in F. Pinner, *Deutsche Wirtschaftsführer*, Charlottenburg, 1925, p. 399.
30. See Kocka, *Unternehmensverwaltung*, pp. 444ff., on the efforts by the companies to influence public opinion.
31. P. Steller, *Das Unternehmertum und die öffentlichen Zustände in Deutschland*, Berlin, 1911, p. 1. Steller was the General Secretary of the Verein der Industriellen des Regierungsbezirks Köln.
32. Ibid., p. 2.

taat) and saw the legislature and public opinion as 'retarding' factors hostile to industry, his views were in line with the contradictory approach to a social and economic policy which was taken in the German Empire[33] — a system which was strongly shaped by the forces of bureaucracy and agriculture.[34]

In this connection the feudalisation tendencies among the German *haute bourgeoisie*, which accelerated around the turn of the century and which Wilhelm von Siemens reflected, gained a new significance. This also applied to the militarism of the prewar decades which likewise became a force that moulded society. Both symbolised the relative social (and political) weakness of the industrial elite which had gained in economic strength. As has been shown above, the head of one of the country's largest companies (Siemens) found it quite possible to combine the notion of bourgeois-capitalist expansion on the world market and the demand for imperialistic great power politics with a critique of capitalism touted in agrarian or *Mittelstand* rhetoric and with anti-urban attitudes and life-styles. The Siemens-Schuckert director Alfred Berliner who, according to Sombart, as a Jew was largely instrumental in bringing about an organizational-commercial modernisation of Siemens in the wake of the 'commercialisation' of the electrical engineering industry after 1800, was likewise the owner of a *Rittergut*.[35] Just as the bourgeois-capitalist 'great power' policies of the German Empire were, in terms of domestic politics, permeated by authoritarian traditions and agrarian-feudal interests,[36] the rise of the industrial upper bourgeoisie in the age of imperialism similarly occurred against a background of a successive shedding of genuinely bourgeois attitudes and life-styles.[37]

33. See the criticisms which Max Weber advanced in his Inaugural Lecture at Freiburg University in 1895 from the perspective of a nationalism of the 'machtstaatlich-grossbürgerlich' variety. See also the criticism that the industrial policy of the Reich lacked a clear line made by the Left Liberal deputy and representative of the Werkmeister in *Schriften des Werkmeister-Verbandes*, vol. II, 1906, pp. 3f.

34. G. Stresemann, 'Die Stellung der Industrie zur Frage der Pensionierungs-Versicherung der Privatangestellten', in idem, *Wirtschaftspolitische Zeitfragen*, Dresden, 1910, p. 58; also Kocka, *Unternehmensverwaltung*, p. 369.

35. See SAA, *Biographische Sammlung zu ausgewählten Personen aus der Firmengeschichte (Berliner)*; W. Sombart, *Die Juden und das Wirtschaftsleben*, Leipzig, 1911, p. 132; for criticisms see Kocka, *Unternehmensverwaltung*, p. 369.

36. See E. Kehr, *Schlachtflottenbau und Parteipolitik, 1894–1901*, Berlin, 1930, pp. 430f., with the critical statements by Max Weber, Emil Rathenau and others cited there.

37. W. Zorn, 'Typen und Entwicklungskräfte deutschen Unternehmertums im 19. Jahrhundert', in *Vierteljahrsschrift für Sozial- und Wirtschaftsgeschichte*, vol. 44,

One aspect of this was that the pursuit of special commercial interests was only reluctantly admitted in public, unless 'national interests', relating to the world market and 'great power' politics, could be invoked. An attitude which began to take the bureaucratic model as its guide can also be discerned in the widely read *Rothschild*, the 'merchant's pocket-book'. It raised the questions, firstly, of why the 'commercial estate' had improved its position in economic terms, but hardly at all in terms of social prestige and, secondly, why it was held in lower esteem than the professions or the officer corps. The author of the article also provided the answer to this puzzle: 'The basic reason for the inferior standing of the commercial estate lies in the fact that the activities of the latter, in contrast with the above-mentioned [groups], are deemed to be independent (*selbständig*) and egotistical'. The soldier and the civil servant, on the other hand, were held in high esteem because they served the general public.[38] Even trade and commerce, whose original orientation was anti-bureaucratic, apparently developed a tendency formally to reject an essential feature of capitalism, i.e. the independent and unwavering pursuit of self-interest. They did so for accommodationist reasons and in the name of providing an (ideologically somewhat distorted) service to the whole nation.

The rise of trade and industry carried with it even less social upvaluing of commercial and technical white-collar employees. The crisis of the 1870s with the anti-industrial resentments generated by it reinforced the complaints of the engineers concerning their low social prestige.[39] As a professor at the (Berlin) Charlottenburg Technical University put it, probably with some exaggeration, production engineers (*Maschineningenieure*) were widely seen, even up to the 1880s, as 'superior lock-smiths' and the *Verein Deutscher Ingenieure* (VDI) was thought to be a 'club of machinists'.[40] In 1893

1957, p. 76; W. Hock, *Deutscher Antikapitalismus*, Frankfurt, 1960, pp. 18f., 74 (n. 14).

38. Rothschild, *Taschenbuch*, pp. 11ff. Patronage, a sense of duty towards the whole, a preparedness to sacrifice and a broad education were put forward as an antidote. Here are also to be found the roots of the striving for higher education among merchants.

39. See, e.g., the speech by the technical director of an iron-manufacturing enterprise at the general meeting of the Technische Verein für Eisenhüttenwesen in Düsseldorf (J. Schlink, *Über die sociale Stellung des deutschen Technikers*, Berlin, 1879) who complained about the differences in social prestige which he thought existed between civil servants, lawyers, teachers, doctors and clergymen on the one hand and engineers on the other.

40. A. Riedler, *Emil Rathenau und das Werden der Grosswirtschaft*, Berlin, 1916, p. 115.

Sinzheimer took the view that in Germany, in contrast with other countries, the low esteem of engineers and technologists should be compensated for by high salaries.[41] From the end of the century onwards, these complaints increased in volume. It is hardly justified to speak of a 'movement of engineers', which is supposed to have arisen from the gap between a sophisticated technical training and the low prestige of the engineering professions.[42] Nevertheless, there was a growing sense that these groups were socially underprivileged. A representative of the *Verein Deutscher Diplomingenieure* formulated this feeling as follows: 'At the moment [the papers] still report that the collaborators [of Count Zeppelin] are engineers. But once Zeppelin No. 5 has happily made a few journeys, you will no longer read about an *Oberingenieur*; the man then sitting in the cabin will be a qualified lawyer (*Assessor*). And thenceforth technical staff and machinists will merely be required for "technical" maintenance'.[43]

The prejudices of the educated middle class were the root cause of this persistent state of affairs, even if they were less strong than at the beginning of the industrial revolution.[44] The organisations and spokesmen of the engineers tried to circumvent this rejection by emphasising the need to obtain a general education. They warned against narrow specialisation, even though this was what was needed above all in the ranks of the middle management. And ultimately they were successful in linking up their technical universities, endowed with the right to award doctorates, with the highest levels of a *bildungsbürgerliche* educational system which, through many informal channels, allocated social and economic privileges.[45] As a former president of the VDI demanded: 'Every larger enterprise ... must in a certain way also constitute a small-scale cultural centre which may form a platform enabling broadly educated engineers and private civil servants' to participate, 'like their

41. L. Sinzheimer, *Über die Grenzen der Weiterbildung des fabrikmässigen Grossbetriebes in Deutschland*, Stuttgart, 1893, pp. 180ff., 186.
42. L. Bernhard, 'Die Stellung der Ingenieure in der heutigen Staatswissenschaft', in *Jahrbuch für Gesetzgebung, Verwaltung und Volkswirtschaft im Deutschen Reich*, vol. 28, 1904, p. 130f., who gives 1895 as the starting date of the 'movement of engineers'.
43. W. Franz, *Ingenieurstudium und Verwaltungsreform*, Berlin, 1909.
44. See Schlink, *Technikers*, pp. 4ff., where he gives as the main reason for the lower prestige of the engineers their lack of an obligatory classical education. Similarly, Sinzheimer, *Weiterbildung*, pp. 180f.; Bernhard, *Ingenieure*, pp. 128f.
45. See *Verein Deutscher Ingenieure, 1856–1926*, Berlin, 1926, p. 32, with references to the Association's efforts to establish the applied sciences in the educational system. See also J. Kollmann, 'Des Ingenieurs Erziehung', in *Der Ingenieur*, 20.

bosses', in public cultural life.[46] The ambiguous attitude of the engineers towards civil servants moreover continued to be informed by the struggle against the monopoly position occupied by the lawyers: 'The engineer has made the entrepreneur a wealthy, even a rich, man; it is the lawyer-dominated administration that prevents him from bringing wealth and happiness to his fatherland and his country (*Staat*)'.[47] Such complaints and grievances became more acute for two reasons which are inseparable from the rise of trade and industry.

To begin with, the engineers and scientists became more self-confident and put forward increased demands. But at the same time, the upswing was based precisely on the fact that the position of the individual white-collar employee became more restricted, less important, other-directed and partially even socially degraded.[48] There was a direct link between the industrial boom of the prewar decade, the rationalisation, concentration and bureaucratisation of the enterprises, the proliferation of technical training and, finally, the increased discipline imposed upon white-collar workers. The rise of German industry was tantamount to the rise of the industrial tycoon and a small stratum of top managers. This occurred not merely in terms of industry's profitability but also in terms of this minority's power and room for manoeuvre. Many engineers felt dissatisfied as far as their professional consciousness was concerned because the demands made upon them at their work-place no longer lived up to their ideas about the professionalism of the engineer and about their own expertise. They also were dissatisfied with their economic and social status which, so it seemed to many of them, could only be improved through collective organisation.[49]

On the other hand, the image of the public civil servant did exert a remarkable fascination, even if it had seen changes in detail since

46. Thus H. Oechelhäuser, 'Die "allgemeinbildenden Fächer" an den Technischen Hochschulen', in *Abhandlungen und Berichte über technisches Schulwesen*, vol. V, p. 70; ibid., pp. 70–2, the guidelines of a Committee, founded by the VDI, concerning the 'general department' in Technical Universities; ibid., pp. 72–9, a list of general educational lectures at Technical Universities at this time.
47. Bernhard, *Ingenieure*, p. 119. Almost all writers take a similarly combative attitude towards the domination of the lawyers. See Schlink, *Technikers*, pp. 4ff.; Riedler, *Rathenau*, p. 115; Franz, *Ingenieurstudium*, passim.
48. On this discrepancy see *Deutsche Industriebeamten-Zeitung*, vol. V, 1909, p. 435.
49. See L. Brinkmann, *Der Ingenieur*, Frankfurt, 1908; H. Klages and G. Hortleder, 'Gesellschaftsbild und soziales Selbstverständnis des Ingenieurs', in *Schmollers Jahrbuch*, vol. 85, 1965, pp. 670f. Butib saw insufficient remuneration as one main cause of the low social status of the engineer. See *Deutsche Industriebeamten-Zeitung*, vol. V, 1909, p. 436; Jaeckel, *Statistik*, 158.

the first phase of industrialisation. This was even true of foreign observers.[50] Writing at the beginning of the century, Otto Hintze praised the 'high virtues which the civil service estate had never been lacking'.[51] As is clearly evidenced by the programme of the Association of German Private Civil Servants or by the statements of white-collar representatives during the debate on the AVG, employees admired particularly, in a fashion that was quite alien to the capitalist ethic, the job security enjoyed by civil servants. Indeed, around 1900, just as during the crisis of the 1870s, the notion of civil service tenure gained in significance and attractiveness, given that employees in private industry continued to be exposed to the crisis proneness of a market economy.[52] Nor does it appear that the average current incomes of middle-ranking and lower white-collar employees rose much above the average of the equivalent civil service grades. They hardly provided compensation for the lack of job security obtaining in private industry.[53]

By the turn of the century, after the various crises of advanced capitalism, the trend towards a secure civil service position with pension rights had become a significant force in Germany. This is demonstrated, *inter alia*, by the arguments with which Stresemann, speaking before the League of Industrialists (BDI), justified the AVG. He pointed to the tendency of parents to direct their best qualified offspring towards a civil service career in order to guarantee them a 'secure future'. He continued: '... this tendency to favour the civil service does exist and, to some extent, we have to take into consideration the existing esteem for civil service status. These currents siphon off extremely valuable talents which industry needs at all cost in order to remain competitive'.[54] Heinz Potthoff, the secretary of the *Werkmeisterverband*, added another point: 'Certainly it is for the most part economic considerations, job security and the prospect of a pension which cause the private employee to strive for civil service-like positions; but in large part it

---

50. See, for example, S. Whitman, *Das Kaiserliche Deutschland*, Berlin, 1889, p. 85.
51. O. Hintze, 'Der Beamtenstand', in idem, *Soziologie und Geschichte*, Göttingen, 1964, p. 77. However, Hintze also mentions as civil service vices corruptibility, laziness and careerism.
52. See H. Rosenberg, *Grosse Depression und Bismarckzeit*, Berlin, 1967, p. 54, for the upvaluing which civil servants achieved during the Great Depression.
53. See the statement by the Centre Party deputy, M. Erzberger, in the Reichstag on 12.3.1912 in *Stenographische Berichte des Deutschen Reichstages*, vol. 283, p. 566.
54. Stresemann, *Industrie*, pp. 54f: this was in a speech he made before the Bund der Industriellen in 1906.

is also the striving for social recognition, [and] increased esteem which produce a longing among employees to achieve a civil service position'.[55]

Thus many German entrepreneurs took as their guide preindustrial ideals and life-styles which originated in agrarian feudalism at a time when German capitalism expanded and organised itself most vigorously; when Social Darwinist ideas and slogans of power politics were frequently to be heard. Meanwhile a constantly rising number of their employees looked towards civil service-like positions and bureaucratic models which, in Germany, were similarly preindustrial in origin.[56] The repercussions of several crises reinforced, within the framework of a capitalist economy, those large groups which refused to apply to themselves entrepreneurial values such as risk, initiative, efficiency, competition and free self-responsibility. The trend towards feudalisation among many German entrepreneurs corresponded to the trend towards achieving civil service-like positions among the white-collar employees.[57] In Germany, the beginnings of bureaucratisation were rooted in the genesis of the bourgeois society and in the conditions of industrialisation. Now, at the turn of the century, these beginnings combined with the historically unavoidable instabilities of a capitalist economy and both produced, in their midst, a *Mittelstand* which was anti-capitalist as far as its ideas and aspirations were concerned.[58]

This development, which went back as far as the early phases of industrialisation, now turned into an effective demand for a change in social policy. With its adoption the white-collar employees succeeded in fixing by law (the AVG) a special position for themselves within the welfare and insurance system. They achieved this success at the last moment, i.e. just before the actual economic

55. Thus H. Potthoff, *Die Organisation des Privatbeamtenstandes*, Berlin, 1904, p. 7. On Potthoff see also n. 33 above; he was secretary general (Syndikus) of the Werkmeisterverband.
56. However, it appears that this proclivity declined somewhat in the last years before the First World War.
57. J. Schumpeter (*Capitalism, Socialism and Democracy*, New York, 1942) and D. Landes (*Unbound Prometheus*, Cambridge, 1970) point to certain parallels with Britain. Against this, we would like to emphasise the specifically German traditions and pressures behind this orientation which took preindustrial models with their anti-capitalist and anti-bourgeois elements as its reference points and which can be traced forward into National Socialism in terms of its social and intellectual history. However, a comprehensive and detailed comparative study would be necessary in order to separate general repercussions of industrialisation from national peculiarities with sufficient clarity.
58. Marbach, *Mittelstandes*, pp. 140ff., identifies an anti-capitalist interest as the common feature of both the self-employed and the dependent Mittelstand.

rationale of the privileged position of 'private civil servants' evaporated, for the majority of these groups, in the anonymity of the office
with its division of labour. The result was a clear legal and semantic
separation of blue-collar workers (*Arbeiter*) from white-collar employees (*Angestellte*) which has continued into our own times, even
if it has become increasingly difficult to recognise its rationale.

In order to be successful, these separatist tendencies of the
Siemens employees required active reinforcement through the personnel policy of the employing company. This had been the case in
many large corporations during the nineteenth and early-twentieth
centuries. Consequently, there was already a clear division between
blue- and white-collar workers within these firms. In addition, the
striving for separateness and privilege among these employees,
which was rooted in their professional and civil service mentality,
could not have asserted itself had it not been for the support of
dominant groups in Imperial Germany. These were the financial
considerations of the Imperial government[59] and the aspirations of
the political parties that were competing for electoral groups which,
like the employees, were rapidly growing, but politically still
volatile.[60] But what also helped them were the *mittelständisch* and
anti-socialist intentions of influential circles.

If one follows their first statements which touched upon issues
beyond their firms and their professional concerns, the private civil
servants saw themselves as a 'broad *Mittelstand* stratum'.[61] The
1894/5 action programme of the DHV included the demand that the
Mittelstand had to be preserved.[62] The term '*Mittelstand*' frequently
appeared in the context of the fear that the employees might decline
to the level of blue-collar workers; or it was used in the context of a
rejection of Social Democracy. In both cases the term pointed to a
requirement that these *Mittelstand* groups needed support in order

---

59. An expansion of the existing system of social insurance would probably have
   implied that the Reich would have had to pay contributions also for those
   white-collar employees who would have to be insured anew. Contributions
   under the AVG were paid, on a 50:50 basis, by employers and employees alone.
   The Government bill of 20.5.1911 for the AVG argued that an expansion of
   workers' insurance would be too expensive.
60. Despite reservations on the part of the Social Democrats and the Progressives,
   the AVG was unanimously approved by the Reichstag. Both these parties would
   have preferred an expansion of the existing social insurance scheme. In 1907 the
   parties quarrelled over who had seized the initiative in proposing the AVG. See
   Stenographische Berichte des Deutschen Reichstages, vol. 227, pp. 470ff.
61. See *Privat-Beamten-Zeitung*, vol. V, 1889, p. 3.
62. See the action programme of the DHV in *Deutsche Handels-Wacht*, vol. I,
   1894/5, n.p.

to help to erect defences against the forces of revolution (*Umsturz*). In this way the slogan encapsulated on the one hand, the notion of a double demarcation (from those above and those below — *Abgrenzung*) and consequently a double threat; on the other hand, it emphasised the variety and the potential of this group which was worthy of encouragement and, finally, its great significance for the continued stability of state and society.[63]

Since the beginning of the 1890s, however, *Mittelstand* policies, as pursued by the government, concentrated on providing aid and concessions to peasants, retailers and small-scale businessmen. These measures were of little help to the white-collar employees. The interests of private civil servants and employees were not helped by the law against unfair competition, the 'small-scale supporting measures' (*Kleinen Mittel*) for agriculture, the funds for inner colonisation; nor were they served by the meat inspection law, the handicraft chambers, compulsory guild membership in certain conditions, the protection of the title of master craftsman, the regulation of apprenticeship, the restriction of door-to-door trading, the law on department stores and the stock exchange act. On the contrary. It was only possible to bracket as *Mittelstand* peasants, small-scale merchants, self-employed craftsmen, lower- and middle-ranking civil servants, white-collar employees and some members of the 'liberal' professions, if, following Schmoller, one used such superficial definitions as levels of wealth and income and ignored the actual interests of different groups.[64] After all, it had been precisely this latter factor which had led to the politicisation of the *Mittelstand* concept. By including better-paid workers, maintenance personnel and foremen (*Meister*) as well as the 'higher administrative personnel' and by extolling them as 'one of the most dynamic energetic elements with great prospects for the future', as the 'core of the newly forming *Mittelstand*', Schmoller was able optimistically to predict the growth of the *Mittelstand* and hence the reduction of social tensions.[65]

Politicians and employees referred to this speech by Schmoller

---

63. See H. Böttger, *Vom alten und neuen Mittelstand*, Berlin, 1901, pp. 5f., 9, 38ff.
64. In G. Schmoller's view ('Was verstehen wir unter dem Mittelstande?', in *Die Verhandlungen des 8. Evangelisch-sozialen Kongresses*, Göttingen, 1897, pp. 157f.) persons counting among the Mittelstand had to have an annual income of between 1,800 and 8,000 marks, on top of 'quite a bit' in assets (up to 10,000 marks). See also his definition of 'Mittelstand', ibid., pp. 134f.
65. Ibid., pp. 154, 160. He added, with reference to public service employees: 'Thus we have in front of us new strata of a Mittelstand which have a considerable weight'.

before the Evangelical-Social Congress when they spoke of the 'new *Mittelstand*' and actually had the 'dependently employed *Mittelstand*' in mind.[66] It was only after 1904 and after the first small successes of white-collar agitation that the concept was effectively taken on board by the discussion on social policy. It facilitated the adoption of the traditional corporate (*ständische*) connotations of the term *Mittelstand* at a time when these *ständische* structures were in fact crumbling and, simultaneously, it could imply a happy optimism about the future: 'If therefore the old *Mittelstand* is declining, a new *Mittelstand* is developing which replaces the former at least in financial terms'.[67] The concept made it possible even for proletaroid groups to set themselves apart from those who existed, in accordance with the assumed hierarchical image of society, beneath their own respective rank on the social scale. The talk about the *Mittelstand* always assumed the existence of at least three social strata: upper, middle and lower.

First indications that industrial white-collar workers were beginning to behave like trade unionists emerged in 1906,[68] one year after the founding of the *Bund der technisch-industriellen Beamten* (Butib) and after the white-collar organisations had influenced the 1907 election campaign.[69] Thenceforth *Reichstag* politicians took an interest in this growing stratum which all parties now saw as part of the *Mittelstand*.[70] The term was employed in particular by those parties which supported the idea of a special insurance scheme for white-collar employees.[71] For a National Liberal like Stresemann the task was 'to prevent by means of a special insurance scheme that, after the blue-collar workers, the new *Mittelstand* also becomes alienated from industry'.[72] The spokesman of the conservative

66. Similarly Böttger, *Mittelstand*, p. 8, who also more or less adopts Schmoller's financial criteria. Marbach, *Mittelstandes*, p. 193ff., believes that the identification of 'new' with 'dependent' is not quite correct, as employees such as book-keepers had existed for a long time. Conversely, he talks of a 'new self-employed Mittelstand', e.g. designers, garage owners.
67. Potthoff, *Organisation*, p. 6. He explicitly quotes Schmoller ('Mittelstand', p. 7).
68. See P. Lange, 'Der neue Mittelstand', in *Die Neue Zeit*, vol. 25/2, 1907, p. 364, and above all the references to the reports of the Breslau and Halberstadt Chambers of Commerce.
69. Thus Potthoff in the Reichstag on 14.3.1907. See *Stenographische Berichte des Deutschen Reichstages*, vol. 227, p. 474.
70. Ibid., p. 467, with a statement by the National Liberal deputy, von Heyl, relating to the 'new Mittelstand' which he saw as the 'core of the Mittelstand'. The SPD deputy, Heine, did not reject the term (ibid., p. 479). See also the statement by the Centre Party deputy, Trimborn, on 20.10.1911, ibid., vol. 268, p. 7439.
71. See also *Deutsche Industriebeamten-Zeitung*, vol. 7, 1911, pp. 340f.
72. Stresemann, *Industrie*, pp. 60, 49.

Reichspartei argued that the white-collar workers, as a group, acted as a 'link and bridge (*Mittel- und Bindeglied*) between divergent social classes, between workers and employers'. The middle-class parties would do well 'warmly to promote this estate as a pillar against Social Democracy'.[73] The Catholic Centre Party, finally, saw the AVG as an 'essential piece of *Mittelstand* policy'.[74]

The protagonists of a unitary insurance scheme, on the other hand, avoided the concept after a brief period of vacillation.[75] They pointed to the heterogeneity of the interests subsumed under the vague notion of *Mittelstand*; this all the more so, because the self-employed retailers and traders took a sceptical view of the AVG which was bound to impose higher costs upon them.[76] Just as prior to 1900 the 'private civil servants', the white-collar employees were not interested in a support of the 'old' *Mittelstand*, the latter took no interest in, or viewed with suspicion, a policy favouring the employees.[77] Common interests between the 'old' and the 'new' *Mittelstand* (or to be more precise; between self-employed and employees), which might have given force to the term in a more than superficial sense, probably existed only in their joint opposition to the working class and its organisations.[78] This opposition was also the common bond with the industrial entrepreneurs, whose interest in a special insurance scheme was openly articulated by Stresemann. Being opposed to the notion of class struggle, he explained, industry had spoken against an extension of a unitary insurance scheme, because such a scheme would, so to speak, give the seal of approval to the idea that all groups in dependent employ-

73. See the statement by Deputy Linz on 14.3.1907, *Stenographische Berichte des Deutschen Reichstages*, vol. 227, p. 481.
74. See also the Centre Party deputy, Trimborn, on 20.10.1911 (ibid., vol. 268, p. 7439): 'These groups represent, so to speak, the corps of leaders and sub-leaders, with whose help industry, commerce and agriculture have gained their victories in the economic field'.
75. On 20.10.1911 the Social Democrat deputy, Schmidt, spoke of the 'so-called Mittelstand' (ibid., p. 7444).
76. Ibid., with the assertion that a newly-founded 'Mittelstandsvereinigung' was refusing to accept 'Angestellte'. See also the statement by the Centre Party deputy, Irl, on 30.11.1911 (ibid., p. 8183), warning, in the name of the self-employed Mittelstand, against an excessive widening of the groups to be covered by the AVG.
77. T. Geiger, *Die soziale Schichtung des deutschen Volkes*, Stuttgart, 1932, pp. 128f. stresses the incompatibility of interests and 'mentalities' between the 'old' and the 'new' Mittelstand. On the attitude of the Centralverband der Deutschen Industrie see Kaelble, *Interessenpolitik*, p. 66.
78. However, it was not a completely united front, with Butib and the Werkmeister-Verband, among others, taking up a clear position against the SPD and the Free Trade Unions.

ment were engaged in a common class struggle.[79]

Thus it was on the one hand the desire to recruit better 'human material' for the industrial 'officer corps' and to strengthen the 'professional enthusiasm' and 'devotion' among the 'circle of mentally occupied and technical collaborators' which motivated organisations like the BDI; on the other hand, it was also a major consideration of the BDI to maintain the 'feeling of solidarity of the private civil servants with commerce and industry' which appeared threatened and, by making concessions, to block an emergent trade unionism. A related consideration was to present, with the help of these newly-won masses and within the context of a restricted public opinion, a greater power-factor than had been available hitherto against a tide of public opinion which had many reservations about industry.[80]

The establishment of the special insurance scheme (AVG) was motivated by the fear of a united front of all dependent workers and of a strengthening of Social Democracy. This scheme became the basis of a separate white-collar employee class, just as the granting of a privileged position to employees within the Siemens trust had done before.[81] The notion of the 'new' *Mittelstand* served as the ideological catch-word of a policy of social integration by explicitly differentiating large groups of employees from the proletariat and by constructing a community between these groups and the self-employed which, in reality, did not go beyond superficial and ideological criteria; the notion also promised, in a totally vague form, a mediation between oppositional forces within a class society and hence a stabilisation of that society. In the final analysis, this

79. On 20.11.1911. See *Stenographische Berichte des Deutschen Reichstages*, vol. 268, p. 7452; the attitude of the Centralverband der Deutschen Industrie, on the other hand, remained wavering and contradictory towards the AVG.
80. See Stresemann, *Industrie*, pp. 54f., 57–60. One reason why the Bund der Industriellen gave its support to the scheme more unambiguously was that the medium-sized enterprises which dominated the Bund could not afford company-run insurance schemes, even if these would have been better suited to realise the same objectives. Big business, on the other hand, which called the tune in the Centralverband, tended to see the AVG as competition to their own programmes. On these debates inside the Centralverband, see Kaelble, *Interessenpolitik*, pp. 66, 106. See ibid., concerning the link between AVG and 'liberal Sammlungspolitik (rallying policy)'.
81. The impact of this motive upon the government's decision to establish a separate scheme would require a special investigation. According to the *Schriften des Werkmeister-Verbandes* (vol. I, 1906, p. 19), Posadowsky spoke in favour of an expansion of the existing social insurance scheme as late as July 1906. When he submitted his first Denkschrift on the subject in 1907, he left a decision between the two solutions open. The second Denkschrift of 11.7.1908 opted for the setting up of a special Reich insurance office (Reichsanstalt).

was the function of the AVG which established a privileged position in the field of social insurance.[82]

Whatever the weighting between them, the reasons which led to the decision to grant social policy privileges to white-collar employees rather than to blue-collar workers are to be found in the developing separatist consciousness of the former, in financial calculations on the part of the government, in the vying of the parties for voters and, above all, in the *Mittelstand* policies of certain powerful groups. In view of these causes and actual motives, it was ultimately irrelevant where the line between white- and blue-collar workers was drawn. A political tug-of-war determined whether this or that group of employees was included in the circle of those covered by the AVG. The allies and opponents in this tug-of-war were the various occupational groups, trade organisations and employee lobbies, as well as the political parties and the state bureaucracy which was supposed to provide the legal know-how (*juristischen Sachverstand*). The definitions and descriptions of who was a 'private civil servant', a 'private white-collar worker', which were put forward during these debates, resembled ideological justifications rather more than they provided an objective (*sachbezogene*) basis for decision-making and legislative action. After all, their invariable purpose was to establish a demarcation line for a particular group of employees in such a way that it justified the superior provision of that group.[83]

The government finally admitted that it was futile to attempt to find a general definition[84] for white-collar employees to be covered by the special insurance scheme. It confined itself to drawing up a catalogue of occupational categories and to define the scope of the law by simple enumeration. It proved impossible to formulate a common concept under which the groups listed might be sub-

---

82. On the ideological substance of the catchword 'Mittelstand' see also H.-J. Puhle, *Agrarische Interessenpolitik und preussischer Konservatismus in Wilhelminischen Reich*, 1893–1914, Hanover, 1966, pp. 98ff.

83. See the criticisms which the Social Democrat deputy, Heine, advanced on 14.3.1907 against the notion that white-collar employees were engaged in 'primarily intellectual' work in *Stenographische Berichte des Deutschen Reichstages*, vol. 227, p. 479.

84. The impossibility of devising such a definition provided the supporters of a single insurance scheme with additional ammunition, as such a scheme made definitional exercises unnecessary. See *Schriften des Werkmeister-Verbandes*, V, 1907, p. 16; *Stenographische Berichte des Deutschen Reichstages*, vol. 227, p. 479 (statement by Heine on 14.3.1907); ibid., vol. 268, p. 8185 (statement by the Progressive deputy, Cuno, on 30.11.1911).

sumed.[85] For the occupational categories defined as 'white-collar employees' in this way the new insurance was to 'secure a higher measure of state support than can be offered to them through the workers' insurance'.[86] The government considered the following criteria, which justified their privileges, as common to white-collar employees: education, living conditions and social status.[87] These were the groups

> which, by comparison with workers occupy a socially and economically elevated position; [they are the] groups which stand between the owner and the worker within the company; [they are] on the one hand called upon to represent the principal and to support him in the running of the enterprise; on the other hand, they are also expected to hire workers, to advise and to lead them. These are persons who are of special importance to their respective company because of their particular expertise [and] special trustworthiness; persons who, owing to their training and the nature of their contract, have positions similar to those of civil servants . . . .[88]

Such descriptions likewise could do no more than to justify *ex-post facto* the selection of these groups and did not constitute the actual basis of that process. Their vagueness apart, they applied only to one part of those whom the government had selected for inclusion in the AVG. At least the large group of shop assistants who were not represented in the Association of Private Civil Servants and who in contemporary statistics were still counted among the blue-collar workers,[89] hardly fulfilled any of the criteria listed.[90] But even many technicians, foremen, agents and other employees did not meet the elitist description drawn up by the government. Rather that description must be taken as an ideological justification of a

85. On § 1 of the AVG see Kocka, *Unternehmensverwaltung*, p. 518. The government spokesman, Dr Caspar, admitted this on 30.11.1911. See *Stenographische Berichte des Deutschen Reichstages*, vol. 268, pp. 8184, 8187.
86. Government Bill of 20.5.1911. O. Bode, in *Die Invaliden- und Angestelltenversicherung in vergleichender Darstellung*, Berlin, 1913, provides a systematic comparison of the two schemes.
87. Government Bill of 20.5.1911, with a restriction of these criteria to the 'majority of the white-collar employees'.
88. Thus Clemens von Delbrück, the State Secretary in the Reich Office of the Interior, in his speech before the Reichstag on 10.10.1911, in *Stenographische Berichte des Deutschen Reichstages*, vol. 268, pp. 7432f.
89. See *Statistik des Deutschen Reiches*, Berlin, 1878 et seq., vol 111, p. 73; idem, vol. 202, p. 37; G. Hartfiel, *Angestellte und Angestelltengewerkschaften in Deutschland*, Berlin, 1961, p. 24.
90. The plight of the Handlungsgehilfen had been a topic of discussion since the early 1880s. Except for a minority charged with higher office duties they were probably hardly better off than the majority of the blue-collar workers.

legislative decision that had resulted from other considerations. This gap between actual reasons and proclaimed motives — between actual criteria of selection and the public justification of those criteria and of the privileged position of white-collar employees in general — is clearly demonstrated if one looks at what the ministerial bureaucracy admitted to be its procedure: as it was impossible to develop a sufficiently clear-cut division between blue-collar workers and white-collar employees, the catalogue in the government bill followed 'closely the text of the workers' insurance acts which had been elaborated upon by over thirty years of application by the Reich Insurance Office . . . . It is here that all these terms have been fully developed and specified through detailed court decisions'.[91] This meant that the criteria as to whether or not someone was a white-collar employee were taken from a completely disparate context.

In the 1880s and 1890s the government had, for public insurance purposes, put workers as well as white-collar employees of industrial firms, clerical assistants, agricultural workers and 'other employees', provided they had an income of less than 2,000 marks per annum, in the same category.[92] This had been done irrespective of the vocational differences and branches of the national economy which they belonged to. The common criterion was their 'social and economic position' and the motive had been to protect them,

91. Thus the Government spokesman, Dr Caspar, before the Reichstag on 30.11.1911, in *Stenographische Berichte des Deutschen Reichstages*, vol. 268, p. 8181. See also his statement, ibid., p. 8184. Caspar referred to the 'Guidelines of the Reich Insurance Office of 6.12.1905 Relating to the Circle of Persons insured under the Terms of the Invalidenversicherungsgesetz of 13.7.1988'. These 'Guidelines' were attached to the Government bill of 20.5.1911. It was on this basis that Parliament debated and ratified, prior to the AVG, the Reichsversicherungsordnung of 19.7.1911, esp. § 165.

92. This 2,000 mark limit which applied to white-collar workers only, *not* to blue-collar workers, was of the utmost importance. The Government Bill relating to the Accident Insurance Act of 1881 and which had seen no possibility of making a clear distinction between workers and 'Betriebsbeamte', had envisaged this limit to apply also to blue-collar workers; by a small amendment, the Reichstag had subsequently restricted it to the Betriebsbeamte. This confronted the courts, the legal commentators and the Reich Insurance Office with the task of deciding, when considering cases of employees who earned over 2,000 marks, whether the individual concerned was a blue-collar worker or a 'Betriebsbeamter'. Later, after the clause had been extended to other insurance schemes and occupational groups, they had to decide as to whether a person was a worker or an Angestellter. The criteria which had been developed in the process by long and meticulous legal practice were invoked by the Government in 1911. See Government Bill of the Accident Insurance Act of 8.3.1881 (= Appendix 41 in *Stenographische Berichte des Deutschen Reichstages*, vol. 65 pp. 222, 228, 237,) and the Report of the Reichstag Commission, ibid., vol. 66, p. 834. The Bill's § 1 was no longer made an issue in the subsequent discussions and served as the model of the other insurance laws.

together with the blue-collar workers, from economic hardship and to prevent their political radicalisation. At that time the government had seen no reason to identify clear social and economic differences between them. For both the above categories the crucial factor was 'the insecurity of a livelihood which was based exclusively on the use of a person's ability to work (*Verwertung der persönlichen Arbeitskraft*)'.[93] The results of these previous decisions — legal definitions and ordinances — were now taken over as the basis of the AVG. Of course, this created a paradoxical situation: groups of employees who had previously been combined irrespective of their professional and sectoral divisions because they were deemed to be in need of insurance cover and who were thus protected in the same way as blue-collar workers, were now — with the help of the same definitions — separated again from the latter in order to differentiate them economically and socially and to grant them privileges over the blue-collar workers.

These origins of the group and the particular concept of *Angestellte* explain why lawyers and social scientists later found it so difficult to provide a common basis and denominator for the term.[94] The classification of white-collar work as 'elevated' or 'similar to that of the civil service' and the privileges derived from this, which from the start applied only to a section of the employees, was made even more questionable when, in the 1920s, *all* office workers became included in it.[95] And this the more so because technological change constantly added new occupations which, based on an advanced division of labour as they were, happened to be routinised and required few skills. The meaning behind the legal and semantic separation of blue-collar workers from white-collar employees (*Arbeiter* from *Angestellte*) evaporated more and more, although not completely. Its meaning can only be understood historically and was distorted by ideology. Proposals were made to revise it.[96] But just as its origins and early legalisation were almost inextricably intertwined with social and political conflicts and compromises of interests, so powerful interests also block a revision, until the day when the differentiation loses its economic, social and cultural anchorage in reality completely.

93. Government Bill of the Accident Insurance Act of 8.3.1881. Similar again, the introduction to the Invalidenversicherungsgesetz of 19.1.1899.
94. See the survey of the scholarly and legal discussion of the 'Angestellter' concept in subsequent decades in Hartfiel, *Angestellte*, pp. 52–82.
95. See the AVG of 28.5.1924.
96. See Hartfiel, *Angestellte*, pp. 110ff.

PETER-CHRISTIAN WITT

The Prussian Landrat as Tax Official, 1891–1918

Some Observations on the Political and Social
Function of the German Civil Service during the
Wilhelmine Empire*

According to Otto Hintze, 'righteousness, a sense of
duty, unselfish diligence, a regard for the commonweal and simple
loyalty' were, apart from their expertise (which was taken for
granted), the outstanding qualities of the German professional civil
servant.[1] These qualities supposedly gave the *Beamten* as individuals and as a social group, a vast superiority over all other civil
services, above all those of countries with parliamentary-democratic
systems of government. If there was occasional criticism of the
German civil servants and in particular of those of their leaders who
were involved in top-level political decision-making, it was invariably concerned merely with their efficiency.[2] The essence of
Hintze's view remained untouched by this criticism: it was the
exceptional historical and political traditions of Prussia-Germany
which were assumed to have led to the emergence of a type of civil

* Publ. orig. in I. Geiss and B. J. Wendt (eds.), *Deutschland in der Weltpolitik des
   19. und 20. Jahrhunderts*, Verlagsgruppe Bertelsmann GmbH, Düsseldorf,
   1973, pp. 205–9. The author would like to thank the publishers for permission
   to prepare and use this translation.
1. O. Hintze, 'Der Beamtenstand', in idem, *Soziologie und Geschichte*, 2nd ed.,
   Göttingen, 1964, p. 77. The article was first published in 1911.
2. See the scathing criticism in Max Weber, 'Parlament und Regierung im neu-
   geordneten Deutschland', in *Gesammelte politische Schriften*, 2nd ed., Tübingen, 1958, pp. 365ff. The article was first published in 1917.

servant whose lodestars were expertise, adherence to the letter of
the law and absolute personal integrity and who was also measured
by these yardsticks in public. In many other countries by contrast
— and here Hintze particularly mentioned the United States and
France — civil service positions were distributed as spoils among
the followers of a politician who had just taken office. Consequently civil servants in such countries were bound by political
loyalties and by ties that were alien to an administration committed
to the *Rechtsstaat* and the rule of law.[3] It is undeniable that Hintze's
analysis of the German civil service was also designed to defend a
quasi-constitutional monarchical system of domination and to
highlight its advantage *vis-à-vis* parliamentary systems. This is why
it is all the more surprising that, quite independently of how the
Prusso-German monarchical system might be judged, Hintze's
assessment of the role of the civil servants operating this system has
survived almost unshattered to this day, at least wherever the civil
service as a social group is analysed in generalising terms. Unfortunately, nothing is to be gained from such stereotypical descriptions for an analysis of the official conduct of public administrators
that would help to illuminate the social and political conditions of a
state which civil servants can and do influence in a very direct
manner.

It is not even possible to uphold the first of Hintze's preconditions, i.e. that, in contrast with parliamentary-democratic systems, selection of German civil servants was guided exclusively by
expertise and talent.[4] Eckart Kehr[5] has provided an impressive
analysis of how, in the 1880s, concern over maximum homogeneity
influenced selection according to social background and within the
framework of specific training methods; he has also shown how the
loyalty of the civil service towards the existing political systems was
being tested — a system whose highest objective was the maintenance of an undisturbed societal equilibrium; and more particularly
of an equilibrium which guaranteed the preservation of rights that
were graded according to social origin, wealth and education. Only
that person could expect his permanent incorporation into the Civil
Service of Prussia and of the Reich with its many financial and social

3. Hinze, 'Beamtenstand', pp. 95, 97f.
4. See also J. C. G. Röhl, 'Higher Civil Servants in Germany, 1890–1900', in
   Journal of Contemporary History, 3/1967, pp. 101–21.
5. E. Kehr, 'Das soziale System der Reaktion in Preussen unter dem Ministerium
   Puttkamer', in idem, *Der Primat der Innenpolitik*, Berlin, 1965, pp. 64ff. (transl.
   as *Economic Interest, Militarism and Foreign Policy*, Berkeley, Calif., 1977).

privileges[6] who had demonstrated his unbroken loyalty to the existing political system, either as an unpaid *Referendar* and *Assessor* in the higher Civil Service or as so-called *Zivil-* or *Militaranwärter* in the middle and lower ranks. In contrast to their self-image and to what historians have been saying, it was this selection procedure which turned the German *Beamten* into a political civil servant. It was now one of his tasks to defend the monarchical system which guaranteed his membership of a privileged group. These realities will make it necessary to subject the 'virtually legendary precision of the Prussian administration'[7] and the 'unbending sense of justice' of the German Civil Service to a renewed test.

Not much progress has been made as far as systematic research into the German bureaucracy prior to 1918 is concerned. A few publications, such as those by Preradovich and Schärl or recent work on the top regional administrators (*Ober-* and *Regierungs-Präsidenten*) in some Prussian provinces, touch upon central problems of administrative activity only in a tangential way.[8] However important an investigation of the social background of civil servants may be, it should not, as in the case of Preradovich, be confined to establishing the percentages of bureaucrats with a noble or bourgeois background. Nor can a description of civil service training be a substitute for a precise analysis of administrative practice. Ernst Fraenkel's paradigmatic study of the application of the law by the judiciary[9] must be extended to comprise the entire civil service. Only in this way will it be possible to gain reliable insights into social reality which will then permit us to develop theoretical models of the conditions of the exercise of power in Imperial Germany and of how patterns of domination changed over time.[10]

6. It must be remembered here that the salaries of German civil servants were unusually high. In the years prior to 1914, even petty officials without special training generally received a higher salary than the highest-paid blue-collar workers, i.e. face-workers in the Ruhr mines. See G. Bry, *Wages in Germany, 1871–1945*, Princeton, 1960, pp. 230, 438.
7. N. von Preradovich, *Die Führungsschichte in Österreich und Preussen, 1804–1918*, Wiesbaden, 1955, p. 112.
8. Ibid. See also W. Schärl, *Die Zusammensetzung der bayerischen Beamtenschaft, 1806–1918*, Kallmünz, 1955; D. Wegmann, *Die leitenden staatlichen Verwaltungsbeamten der Provinz Westfalen, 1815–1918*, Münster, 1969; W. Runge, *Politik und Beamtentum im Parteienstaat*, Stuttgart, 1965.
9. E. Fraenkel, *Zur Soziologie der Klassenjustiz*, Berlin, 1927.
10. This as a general comment on theorisation irrespective of any empirical back-up and specifically against F. Ronneberger, 'Die Bedeutung der Verwaltung für den sozialen Wandel', in W. Rüegg and O. Neuloh (eds.), *Zur soziologischen Theorie und Analyse des 19. Jahrhunderts*, Göttingen, 1971, pp. 83–102.

In view of the special importance which the Prussian *Landrat* had within the bureaucracy, an analysis of administrative practice at this level may provide a starting-point for answering the questions which have been sketched out so far. To begin with, the *Landrat* was the hinge between the central government and the communal self-administration. This point emerges, if nothing else, from the way in which he was appointed: he was 'presented' by the Prussian Ministry of State and then confirmed by a vote in the district committee (*Kreisanschuss*). The *Landrat* combined in his office political leadership functions with direct administrative tasks, and there was between him and the ordinary member of the public no bureaucratic filter in the shape of a large civil service apparatus.[11] At the same time, his duties included policing tasks as well as fiscal administration, so that it was impossible for the average burgher to avoid encountering the *Landrat* in public life.[12] It should be evident that such comprehensive administrative powers endowed this office with influence which would mould the political, economic and social life of the district (*Kreis*) in a very direct way. It also explains why this post had a special attraction for the local nobility above all other positions in the bureaucracy. This tradition no doubt contributed to no small degree to the fact that, by comparison with other civil service categories, the *Landräte* displayed a remarkably high degree of social homogeneity.[13] Moreover, this office was regarded as a position for life which, in the self-image of its holders, did not require careerism nor a further definition of social status. Since the middle of the nineteenth century, the post of *Landrat* increasingly became the launching-pad for an administrative career which would propel the holder into the highest echelons of the ministerial bureaucracy charged with the actual task of governing.[14] The high

---

11. In 1905 some 454 of 484 Prussian Landkreise (rural districts) had one further state official, the Kreissekretär. A mere thirty districts with a high percentage of an industrial and commercial sector work-force had two of these secretaries. No more than fifty had additional petty officials and scribes (Bürohilfsarbeiter). See *Deutsches Zentralarchiv Merseburg (DZA II)*, Rep. 151 I C, no. 827, Prussian Ministry of the Interior to Prussian Ministry of Finance, 20.8.1905; ibid., Prussian Ministry of Finance to Prussian Ministry of the Interior, 27.10.1905.
12. See F. Gelpke, *Die geschichtliche Entwicklung des Landratsamts in der preussischen Monarchie unter besonderer Berücksichtigung der Provinzen Brandenburg, Pommern und Sachsen*, Berlin, 1902.
13. The share of aristocratic Landräte declined constantly up to 1918, but was still over 50% at that time. See von Preradovich, *Führungsschichten*, pp. 112f.; Archiv der sozialen Demokratie (Bonn), Severing Papers, M. 85, Amtlicher Preussischer Pressedients, 6.3.1925.
14. See O. von Bismarck, *Gedanken und Erinnerungen*, Stuttgart/Berlin, 1928, pp. 46ff.

proportion of former *Landräte* in the key ministries of Prussia —
such as the Ministries of State, of Internal Affairs, of Finance,
Agriculture and Commerce — and, well above the Prussian quota,
in the Reich ministries,[15] is not just a sign of the growing career
consciousness of the *Landräte*, as Bismarck interpreted it; it is also
an indication that this office — like that of state prosecutor in the
judiciary — had became an important staging-post in the procedures that were to test the political and social reliability of higher
civil servants.

This article tries to arrive at some conclusions concerning professional qualifications of the *Landräte* for their task and concerning their social and political role within the power-structure of the
Prussian state by investigating their activities as tax officials. The
Income Tax Act of 24 June 1891 had made the *Landrat* Chairman of
the local Tax Assessment Commission.[16] This, it is true, was only a
small aspect of his duties. On the other hand, this chairmanship can
hardly be overestimated in terms of the political, economic and
social significance of his office. Tax assessment, after all, was the
basis of the three-class voting system in the communities and at
state level; through it, it was possible to exert a very considerable
influence on the composition of the electorate in the three classes;[17]
more importantly, tax assessment formed the main statistical basis
for income distribution estimates and, via the supplementary tax
assessment, also for the wealth distribution estimates in the state of
Prussia. As a result of this, tax assessment occupied a key position in
the struggle for the preservation or loss of political and social power

15. These comments are based on a sample analysis covering the career of all higher
     civil servants in the ministries of Prussia and the Reich.
16. The Assessment Commission was made up partly of members nominated by the
     Prussian Ministry of State, partly elected by the Kreistag. The chair was taken
     by the Landrat, or by the mayor of towns which were independent of the Kreis.
     It was their task to examine the tax returns or, in the case of taxpayers who made
     no return, to make an estimate of their income and to fix the amount of tax
     payable. Appeals could be lodged with the Assessment Commission of the
     respective regional district (Regierungsbezirk) and with the Finance Ministry.
     After this appellants could turn to the administrative courts as far as the
     Preussische Oberverwaltungsgericht.
17. However irrational and unjust the three-class voting system may have been,
     what really perverted it was a stipulation that allocation to a particular voting
     class depended on the level of taxpayment in the constituency itself, not in
     Prussia as a whole; consequently the system was open to any kind of manipu-
     lation. In Berlin and Potsdam, for example, annual tax payments of 1,000 marks
     implied allocation to the second class during the elections of 1903, 1908 and
     1913. One-tenth of this level was sufficient in the Regierungsbezirk Allenstein
     in East Prussia to be allowed to vote in the first class. Calculated on the basis of
     the material in DZA II, Rep. 77, tit. 43, no. 89, vol. 8-11; ibid., Rep. 151 II, no.
     2229.

positions. The Conservatives, who held a solid majority in the Prussian House of Deputies,[18] had immediately recognised in 1891, when the existing class-based income tax was replaced by a progressive income tax, that, at least as far as the countryside was concerned, tax assessment was not to be put into the hands of tax inspectors under the authority of the Finance Ministry, as Miquel, the minister responsible, had demanded. Rather this was a task that was to remain with the *Landräte*, who were dependent on both the central government and the district assembly (*Kreistag*).[19] This was the only guarantee that the irrationality of historically-grown political and social conditions was not undermined by the cold rationality of a tax administration which was less interested in the permanent preservation of these conditions than in the fiscally lucrative implementation of tax legislation which already favoured agricultural incomes and properties.[20] Of course, there was a continued interest in taxing agrarian income as mildly as possible; but the leaders of the agrarian pressure groups soon came to recognise that tax assessment by the *Landrat* opened up many more far-reaching possibilities. And it did not make any difference whether the pressure group concerned was the small, but politically powerful Association of Tax and Economic Reformers or the numerically strong Agrarian League. In this latter group a relatively small stratum of large-scale estate-owners, led by '*Landjunker* demagogues and professional functionaries', had succeeded in winning the support of the majority of the peasants, who, in any case, were comparatively disadvantaged by the economic and fiscal policy aims of the East Elbian landowners.[21] The results of this system of tax assessment by the

18. The majorities of the conservative parties were rooted in the fact that the East Elbian provinces invariably sent more deputies to the Diet than was justified on the basis of tax yields and size of population. Thus East and West Prussia, Pomerania, Posen, Silesia and Brandenburg (except for Berlin and the Potsdam district) elected 192 deputies. However, if tax yields had been taken into consideration, these provinces could not have claimed more than 100 seats; if population had been the yardstick, some 161. The Western provinces (except for the districts of Arnsberg, Düsseldorf and Cologne) sent 169 deputies, although tax yields gave them a claim to a mere 158 and population size two seats less! By contrast, the districts of Berlin, Potsdam, Arnsberg, Düsseldorf and Cologne had a total of seventy-two deputies. They should have had 175 seats on the basis of their combined tax yields and 116 seats if calculated by population size. See *Kölnische Volkszeitung*, no. 914, 3.11.1904.
19. See H. Herzfeld, *Johannes von Miquel*, Detmold, 1938, vol. II, pp. 216ff.; A. Wagner, *Finanzwissenschaft*, II, 2nd ed., Leipzig, 1890, pp. 299ff., 523f.
20. This was, in a nutshell, what the Conservatives contributed to the 1891 reform debate. When after 1918 a centralised Reich fiscal administration was built up, agrarian pressure groups protested with the same old arguments.
21. H. Rosenberg, 'Zur sozialen Funktion der Agrarpolitik im Zweiten Reich', in

Landrat therefore soon came to form the permanent basis from which agriculture launched its demand for state support. This could take the form either of higher tariffs, as demanded at the time of the 1902 Tariff Bill, or of a further expansion of tax concessions which favoured agrarian side-lines like the distilling of spirits or the production of sugar;[22] it could also take the form of special methods of property assessment as enshrined in the Prussian supplementary tax or the Reich inheritance tax of 1906.[23] Finally, the results of tax assessment were ideally suited to agitate against any change in the distribution of fiscal powers between the Reich and the Federal States. This applied in particular to the agitation against the introduction of a Reich death duty or a Reich income tax which would have fallen within the legislative powers of the Reichstag.[24]

The assessment practices of the *Landräte* remained the object of permanent internal disputes between the Finance Ministry, which pressed for higher revenues, and the Ministry of the Interior, which was responsible for the *Landräte* and invoked overriding 'political' considerations.[25] However, the question of tax assessment became a matter of public concern when the Agrarian League, aided by the Conservatives, threatened to defeat Reich Chancellor Bülow's plan to extend, within the framework of the 1909 Finance Reform Bill, the death duty from distant relatives to the offspring and spouse of the deceased.[26] It was Professor Hans Delbrück, a rather more conservative follower of Bülow's, who opened a whole series of massive attacks against the assessment practices of the *Landräte*. He declared that the estate owners not only constantly committed tax frauds, but were actively supported in this by the *Landräte*.[27] Delbrück had based his first volley of shots on straightforward observations relating to the development of national wealth and of revenue from Prussian income tax which did not tally.[28] But soon

---

idem, *Probleme der deutschen Sozialgeschichte*, Frankfurt, 1969, pp. 65ff.
22. P. -C. Witt, *Die Finanzpolitik des Deutschen Reiches von 1903 bis 1913*, Lübeck/Hamburg, 1970, pp. 40ff.
23. Ibid., p. 125, n. 455.
24. Ibid., pp. 226ff.
25. See, on this point, *DZA* II, Rep. 151 II, no. 117, Memorandum of the Director General of the Administration for Direct Taxes in the Prussian Finance Ministry, Heinke, 5.11.1918.
26. P. -C. Witt, *Finanzpolitik*, pp. 263ff.
27. H. Delbrück, 'Die Finanzreform. Der Kampf um die Nachlaßsteuer', in *Preussische Jahrbücher*, vol. 135, 1909, pp. 559–65.
28. In a further article ('Volksvermögen und Steuerdeklaration', in ibid., vol. 136, 1909, pp. 166–87, esp. 180ff.) Delbrück corrected his calculations and reinforced his criticisms against the tax assessment activities of the Landräte.

he received information from all sections of the population[29] which showed, the noisy protests of the Agrarian League, the Conservative Party and its press organs notwithstanding,[30] that Delbrück's allegations had revealed the broad outlines of the system of political and social corruption which was rampant in the tax administration of the *Landräte*. On the other hand, it was not even the tip of the iceberg that had become visible for the public.

Against otherwise customary practice, the government did not prosecute Delbrück for having offended the Civil Service (*Beamtenbeleidigung*); instead it confined itself to refuting, without much vigour, the general charge of incompetence and of *Landrat* support for agrarian tax evasion.[31] No doubt there were also tactical considerations behind this response. At this point in the negotiations relating to the Finance Reform Bill, Bülow still welcomed all measures that might have induced the Conservatives to accept the death duty for offspring and spouses. But a more important explanation of the muted reaction by the government was that the Finance Ministry agreed with Delbrück's charges.[32] Having observed the assessment practices of the *Landräte* over a longer period, Rheinbaben, the Minister of Finance, had come to the conclusion that there existed a most elementary ignorance of the Income Tax Act and the executive directives issued by the Ministry[33] and that this had resulted in not insignificant losses to the Treasury.[34] Rheinbaben also believed to have discovered a lack of interest among the *Landräte* in matters relating to taxation. This had frequently gone so far as to result in total inactivity, especially in the case of those *Landräte* who, as members of the Prussian House of

29. See Bundesarchiv Koblenz, Delbrück Papers, No. 11, Karl Delbrück to his cousin Hans, 17.2.1909; ibid., 6.3.1909. Karl had gained experience as a member of one of the Assessment Commissions. This file also contains information from the tax secretaries (Steuersekretäre) who were directly involved in the practices of the Landräte. Many of the cases mentioned by them were used in Delbrück's second article (see n. 28 above). They also form the basis of F. Meisel, 'Moral und Technik bei der Veranlagung der preussischen Einkommenssteuer', in *Jahrbuch für Gesetzgebung, Verwaltung und Volkswirtschaft*, vol. 35, 1911, pp. 285–373; idem, 'Wahrheit und Fiskalismus bei der Veranlagung der modernen Einkommensteuer', in *Finanzarchiv*, vol. 31, 2/1914, 144–68.
30. See R. Ehrenberg, 'Einige Irrtümer der Reichsregierung', in *Der Tag*, no. 104, 5.5.1909.
31. See the statement by the Prussian Finance Minister von Rheinbaben in *Stenographische Berichte des Deutschen Reichstages*, vol. 237, pp. 868ff., 19.6.1909.
32. DZA II, Rep. 77 tit. 43, no. 89, vol. 9, Rheinbaben to Moltke, 28.7.1909, also for the following.
33. See the files relating to income tax assessment, ibid., Rep. 151 II, no. 1926 et seq.
34. An example of this ignorance may be found in ibid., no. 2275, Reports of the Regierung Merseburg, 17.2.1914 and 1.5.1914.

Deputies or of the Reichstag, had assumed duties as parliamentary representatives. Rheinbaben saw only one solution to this situation: to replace the *Landräte* by tax officials — a system which had meanwhile been adopted by all the south German states. The change was not even to occur throughout Prussia, but was to be introduced in a number of industrial districts in the provinces of Rhineland and Westphalia as well as a few rural districts in East Elbia which formed the hinterland of the cities of Königsberg, Danzig, Stettin, Frankfurt/Oder and Breslau.[35] The decisive consideration which guided Rheinbaben was his conviction that the Chairman of the Tax Assessment Commission, who was required by the letter of the law to scrutinise personally all income tax returns at all stages of the negotiations and to chair the Commission on Preliminary Assessment,[36] could not possibly undertake these tasks on top of the many other duties which the office carried with it.

The responsible civil servants in the Ministry of the Interior actually agreed with Rheinbaben's criticisms of the efficiency of the tax administration by the *Landräte*. They even declared explicitly that there was no doubt that the establishment of a special tax administration would result in considerably higher revenues.[37] Nevertheless the Minister of the Interior rejected the proposed replacement of the *Landräte* as chairmen of the Tax Assessment Commissions with the exception of the city districts of Essen, Dortmund-Hörde and Solingen-Lennep. He argued that any further measures would 'certainly be interpreted as a concession after the attacks by Professor Delbrück on the fiscal treatment of the agricultural population.' He added that the Prussian Royal Commission on Administrative Reform (which had been meeting since 1908) had spoken out against any change in the system of tax assessment.[38] His conservativism and well-proven pro-agrarian attitude notwithstanding,[39] Rheinbaben, faced with the public criticism and in view of the discussions in the Royal Commission, was not prepared to drop his proposals. He insisted, in letters which he sent over and over again, that tax assessment required a fundamental change. However, he never encountered more than a formal willingness to

35. Ibid., Rep. 77 tit. no. 89, vol. 9, Rheinbaben to Moltke, 28.7.1909.
36. See § 36–9 of the Income Tax Act of 24.6.1891.
37. *DZA* II, Rep. 77 tit. 43, no. 89, vol. 9, Note by Geheimer Regierungsrat von Ziller, 15.8.1909; ibid., Note by Geheimer Oberregierungsrat von Falkenhayn, 7.10.1909; ibid., Note by Undersecretary of State Holtz, 20.8.1909.
38. Ibid., Moltke to Rheinbaben, 15.10.1909.
39. Witt, *Finanzpolitik*, pp. 94ff., 172ff., 226ff.

cooperate on the part of his opponent, the Minister of the Interior Moltke.[40]

The latter was moreover always able to rely on a majority in the Prussian Ministry of State and to point to the constellation of parties in the House of Deputies which made impossible a general replacement of the *Landräte* in their position of tax assessors. Nor did Rheinbaben succeed in convincing those ministries which were not directly involved that numerous individual cases, which justified a criticism of the conduct of specific *Landräte*, amounted to a general incapacity of the *Landräte* to carry out their task. Neither could his colleagues be persuaded that the tax returns of the agrarians were treated intentionally in a dilatory fashion, as was being asserted in public.[41] His successor, August Lentze, who until then had been Mayor of Magdeburg, therefore finally decided that he needed reliable evidence against these accusations in order to be able to judge the performance of the tax administration by the *Landräte*. That was the reason why, in the autumn of 1910, he ordered the *Geheime Finanzräte* Dr Sander[42] and Henatsch[43] to undertake a review of all East Elbian administrative districts.

The reports by these two commissioners were devastating as far as the expertise and training of the *Landräte*, the conscientious fulfilment of their duties and their integrity as a group were concerned. Yet although his disputes with Dallwitz, the new Minister of the Interior, over the tax administration reached unprecedented levels of bitterness, Lentze could not bring himself to improve his own negotiating position in the Ministry of State by informing his colleagues and the Royal Commission on Administrative Reform of the results of the review. Instead he classified all the papers which had been accumulated and used them only in his debates with the Minister of the Interior, who was the disciplinary superior of the *Landräte*.[44] All detailed reviews in the districts[45] showed as a major

40. *DZA* II, Rep. 77 tit. 43, no. 89, vol. 9, Rheinbaben to Moltke, 25.10.1909; ibid., Rep. 87 ZB, no. 17004, Memorandum by Rheinbaben, 30.3.1910.
41. See, for example, ibid., Rep. 87 ZB, no. 17003, Prussian Minister of Agriculture von Arnim-Criewen to Elard von Oldenburg-Januschau, 24.3.1910.
42. He was born in 1859, working with the Administration for Direct Taxes, promoted Geheimer Finanzrat on 22.10.1909 and nominated President of the Landesfinanzamt Berlin-Brandenburg in October 1919.
43. He was born in 1860, promoted Geheimer Finanzrat in 1908 and Geheimer Oberfinanzrat in 1917. After 1918 he was Ministerialdirigent in the Prussian Finance Ministry and head of the First Tax Department.
44. *DZA* II, Rep. 77 tit. 43, no. 100, vol. 1, Special Note for Interior Minister relating to Memorandum by Lentze, 1.12.1911.
45. Copies of the Reports in the files of the Interior Ministry; the originals of the

deficiency that the *Landräte* generally did not develop an interest in their task as tax assessors, but left it almost entirely to the tax secretaries who worked under them. Yet these secretaries either did not have the necessary professional training for this job, or, if over the years they had acquired an expertise greater than that of their superiors, they did not possess the authority necessary to impose an adequate assessment — especially on the estate owners.[46] The *Landräte* displayed a reasonable degree of activity only in certain individual cases; these were when the secretaries advised that the returns of estate owners be queried and a detailed review of their incomes be undertaken. The *Landräte* then flatly prohibited any queries by their secretaries[47] or blocked any directive from the Chairman of the Income Tax Appeal Commission in the office of the superior *Regierungspräsident* that a review be initiated.[48] Taxpayers who kept accounts were 'virtually completely protected against scrutiny' because neither the secretaries nor the *Landräte* were qualified to go through the books.[49] Farmers and businessmen who did not keep accounts had to fear unpleasant inquiries only when the estimates of their incomes had fallen too drastically by comparison with the previous year. If the estimate was higher this, too, meant in practice that no further questions relating to the return would be asked.[50] It should be obvious that, where this system obtained, income tax was paid in full only by dependent

---

Finance Ministry must be deemed to be lost. As the reports for all districts raised the same criticisms against the assessment practices of the Landräte, the subsequent analysis is based essentially on two reports. The first is based on Dr Sander's investigations in the Regierungsbezirk Köslin, the other on Henatsch's findings in the Regierungsbezirk Frankfurt/Oder. See also the files from several Landrat offices in Brandenburg in Geheimes Staatsarchiv Berlin, Provinz Brandenburg, Rep. 6 B LR Westprignitz, nos. 19, 20, 28, 32, 159. These documents give impressive support to the reports by Dr Sander and Henatsch.

46. DZA II, Rep. 77 tit. 43, no. 89, vol. 10, Report by Sander, 10.12.1910. See also ibid., Report by the Regierungspräsident at Köslin, Drews, 23.2.1912, according to which the Landrat of the Köslin district had, in his twenty years in this position, participated in a mere forty-nine cases, when the annual total was no less than 900.

47. Ibid., Report by Sander, 10.12.1910; ibid., Report by Henatsch, 8.8.1911.

48. Ibid., no. 100, Memorandum by Lentze, 1.12.1911, with an appendix giving extracts from the tax files for 1911 of Count Mirbach-Sorquitten; ibid., no.89, vol. 10, Report by Henatsch, 8.8.1911. Count Clairon d'Haussonville usually informed the estate owners that he was querying their returns on the instructions of the chairman of the Appeals Commission. He then added: 'I may comment that I myself do not find it possible to object to your returns; nor am I in a position to tell you which are the items in the calculation of agricultural income against which the queries are directed'.

49. Ibid., Report by Sander, 10.12.1910.

50. Ibid., Report by Henatsch, 8.8.1911.

wage- and salary-earners — at least as far as the annual cash income
from their labour was concerned, since this could be traced with
exactitude.

The review, which Lentze had ordered, thus fully confirmed the
long-standing suspicions of the Finance Ministry. There it had
always been felt that the *Landräte* were poorly qualified to deal
with tax assessment matters. Much more serious from a political and
legal point of view, however, were those discoveries which Sander
and Henatsch made in respect of the question of equality before the
law which all citizens were supposed to enjoy. They pointed, in a
rather convoluted prose, to the fact that the *Landräte* appeared to
'treat the returns of the larger estate owners relating to the size of
their incomes from agriculture. . . with a certain considerate reluctance'. On the other hand, this attitude was much less in evidence
when it came to the assessment of small farmers; frequently even the
opposite had been found.[51] In view of the great political significance
of their findings, the two commissioners did not dare to call a spade
a spade, i.e., that the estate owners were engaging in tax evasion
with the approval and active support of the *Landräte*.[52] Even the
Minister of Finance merely confined himself to stating that the
reports of his commissioners had revealed 'the regrettable fact' that
'the *Landräte* are lax and reserved in matters of tax assessment,
especially where the influential estate owners of their district are
concerned'.[53] Lentze, too, believed that, given the distribution of
power in Imperial Germany, he could not risk using a blunter
language, lest he might endanger his own position; for he realized
that he could not, neither at this point nor later, count on the
support of Bethmann Hollweg, the Reich Chancellor and Prussian
Minister President, when it came to the demand, however justified
on rational grounds, that the *Landräte* as tax assessors should be
replaced.[54]

To make matters worse, the Minister of the Interior, von Dall-

---

51. Ibid.; similar phrases ibid., Report by Sander, 10.12.1910.
52. Sander's report led to the reprimand and dismissal of the Landrat of the Köslin
    district, von Eisenhart-Rothe, which was accompanied by bitter recriminations;
    see ibid., vols. 10, 11. Sander's career also suffered. He was repeatedly bypassed
    in the promotions review and was rehabilitated only in the Weimar period under
    Matthias Erzberger. He then became President of the most important State
    Inland Revenue Office, Berlin-Brandenburg, but was given the less prestigious
    post as President of the Brandenburg office when the office was split up in 1921.
53. Ibid., Rep. 77, tit. 43, no. 100, vol. 1, Secret Minute for the Interior Minister
    relating to the Memorandum by Lentze, 1.12.1911.
54. Witt, *Finanzpolitik*, pp. 37ff.

witz, insisted that the *Landräte* generally had been accused of an improper treatment of agrarian tax returns, which was no doubt a correct interpretation of the two commissioners' reports. He threatened that there might be political consequences for the Minister of Finance if the charges were debated in the Prussian House of Deputies.[55] Faced with this threat, Lentze retreated even further and gave an explicit assurance that he and his commissioners had never even contemplated a reproach of this kind.[56]

Yet each of the individual reports of his commissioners contained facts which flatly contradicted Lentze's politically-motivated concessions. These reports soberly described the practices by which the estate owners evaded taxes and which had the tacit or active support of the *Landräte*.[57]

Firstly, frequent accounting errors were discovered on those estates which had a bookkeeping system. What was peculiar about these was that credit entries were regularly incomplete; debits, on the other hand, tended to be entered with a slightly exaggerated perfectionism. Advance payments on deliveries were almost never credited against sales in the fiscal year concerned; with equal regularity entries of final payments in the credit column were conveniently forgotten. In innumerable cases unpaid bills were listed as debits at the end of the fiscal year and then reappeared for a second time in the year in which they had actually been settled.[58] Depreciation claims on fixed assets, agricultural machinery and implements were invariably made in a form which violated the law: all expenditure on new equipment and replacements as well as on repairs was fully deducted in the year it had been made and further percentage deductions were then made in subsequent years for the same items.[59] Private expenditure, such as wages or payments in kind for domestic servants, private tutors and nannies, as well as the support of sons serving as civil servants or officers were listed as overheads; goods and produce for private consumption and the rent-value of the

55. *DZA* II, Rep. 77, tit. 43, no. 89, vol. 10, Dallwitz to Lentze, 4.12.1911.
56. Ibid., Lentze to Dallwitz, 29.1.1912.
57. See ibid., no. 100, vol. 1, with these reports, also for the following. To avoid an excessive number of footnotes, only the most significant cases will be mentioned.
58. Thus Fürst zu Dohna-Schlobitten declared an income of 90,000 to 130,000 marks between 1903 and 1910, while he reduced his income during this period on average by about 60,000 marks: ibid., Memorandum by Lentze, 1.12.1911, with an appendix giving extracts from the tax files of Dohna-Schlobitten.
59. Hans Count Kanitz auf Podangen, until his death in 1913 a member of the Reichstag and the Prussian Diet for the Conservatives, followed this practice and hence declared an income which was invariably underestimated by some 20,000 marks, at least from 1904, when his returns were checked: ibid.

residence were either not accounted for at all or grossly underestimated, although the law prescribed that the actual cash value was to be entered.[60] Amortisation payments on mortgages were declared as expenditure. Interest payments from the amortisation fund, on the other hand, were not credited as income.[61] The peculiar methods of Count Julius Mirbach-Sorquitten deserve a special mention. He regularly deducted some 4,000–5,000 marks from his taxable income and accounted for this sum as a salary for the management of his estates. Accordingly, this sum was inaccessible to any taxation. [62] Even if they owned land to the value of millions of marks, many estate owners claimed to have no capital assets and hence also no income from interest.[63]

Secondly, the law permitted the estimation of income where there existed no accounts. Interest payments on debts could be deducted; the value of goods consumed and of accomodation in one's own property, on the other hand, had to be added to the income estimate. Obviously, this procedure was most vulnerable to manipulation; for, in practice it was virtually impossible to check it. This is why this system enjoyed great popularity even with owners of estates of several hundred hectares. In fact many of them never even pretended that their returns bore any relation to their actual income situation. Year after year they simply declared the same income from their property. This income estimate was arrived at by multiplying the single or multiple figure of net income from rent with the number of hectares they owned. Neither they nor the *Landräte* who were bound to scrutinise all figures were bothered by the fact that such returns lacked credibility.[64]

Thirdly, there were marked discrepancies between incomes from self-managed estates and from leased properties. Income estimates based on leases would be three, four, frequently even six times

60. See the candid remarks by H. von Gerlach, *Erinnerungen eines Junkers*, Berlin, 1925, p. 27.
61. However, this procedure was significant for tax purposes only in the case of Landschaft debts which could be amortised. See the decisions of the Preussische Oberverwaltungsgericht, vol. 13, pp. 95–8.
62. DZA II, Rep. 151 II, no. 2299, fols. 68ff., extracts from the tax files of Count Julius Mirbach-Sorquitten.
63. Ibid.: up to the fiscal year 1908, Mirbach maintained that he had no capital assets although his landed property was valued at about 4.5m marks. Dohna-Schlobitten's real estate was valued at over 8m marks; he, too, pretended to have no income from capital assets, although he was able to pay considerable deposits for his purchases of further estates; See n. 58 above.
64. On this point, see DZA II, Rep. 151 II, no. 117, Memorandum by Heinke, 5.11.1918.

above the income earned through self-management. Even if we assume that the landlord generally did not take too seriously his obligation to maintain buildings during the leasing period, the discrepancy is nevertheless striking. After all, the tenant was also expecting to have an income and did not intend to live on his losses.[65]

Finally, there were frequent and quite remarkable inconsistencies between the agricultural income returned and the growth of income from capital assets, with the latter being easily controllable where portfolios were involved. Thus the growth in capital assets, as reflected in interest receipts, frequently reached heights which vastly exceeded the sum total of all returns since the introduction of taxation on income in 1891. This figure was independent of any growth in income through inheritance or gains derived from speculation with existing capital assets; nor was it related to capital gains resulting from the sale of landed property and the acquisition of capital assets.[66]

The tax evasion practices which Lentze's commissioners had brought to light and the violations of their duties which the *Landräte* had been committing were so widespread that subjectively they were no longer seen as violations. As many statements by individual *Landräte* and tax-payers demonstrate,[67] they were regarded as correct interpretations of the law in line with what the legislature had allegedly been meaning to say. Of course, this also implied that the practices were to be reserved for a particular social stratum. Peasants who were being wooed by the Agrarian League as passive voters and crowd support naturally did not enjoy these 'privileges'.[68] 'Industry' and 'capital' were deemed even less eligible

---

65. The Landrat never queried this contradiction, which became evident in the case of estate owners who had several estates, some of which they managed themselves, while others had been leased. Evidently it was seen as a matter of course that leasing yielded higher net profits than self-management.

66. Thus the income from interest of the estate owner and Member of the Prussian Diet von Glasow rose from 5,771 marks to 24,093 marks between 1892 and 1911. If one assumes an average interest of 4%, these figures would indicate a growth in capital assets by some 430,000 marks. During these nineteen years, however, Glasow declared an income that totalled no more than 285,000 marks.

67. See *DZA* II, Rep. 77 tit. 43, no. 89, vols 10, 11, with the above-mentioned reports by Sander and Henatsch.

68. A typical case is the following, related in Bundesarchiv Koblenz, Delbrück Papers, no. 11, Karl Delbrück to Hans Delbrück, 6.3.1909, and based on the proceedings of the Assessment Commission in the Randow district. An estate-owner estimated his income to have been 18 marks per hectare, which even the Landrat thought was too low. The estimate was therefore raised to 21 marks per hectare, representing the amount which had been fixed in 1841 as the net gain

to share in these methods of taxation. Reviews of individual returns by industrialists and merchants with large incomes which were undertaken by the Prussian Finance Ministry reveal that owners of large industrial enterprises were by no means always taxed according to the letter of the law.[69] Nevertheless, they were invariably subject to tougher scrutiny by trained inspectors who saw it as their task — and this is the crucial point for our purposes — to obtain returns which were at least roughly accurate.[70]

The Minister of the Interior and the majority of his colleagues in the Prussian Ministry of State did not wish to abolish the privilege of the landowners to keep large parts of their income outside the tax net. It was a privilege which was by now considered a right and which the *Landräte* were helping them to uphold. Meanwhile Lentze became more and more insistent on replacing the *Landräte* with his own officials and the lists of tax manipulators among the estate owners increasingly also included the names of the great noble families of Prussia and of Conservative MPs in the Reichstag and the House of Deputies as well as highly-placed civil servants.[71] All this only stiffened the resistance in the Ministry of the Interior

---

for ground tax purposes. A little later peasant incomes were being assessed. One peasant from the same area and farming on soil of similar quality estimates an income of 82 marks per hectare. Karl Delbrück felt that this peasant was 'of course also cheating' and had given too low an estimate. Nevertheless, he raised these still glaring discrepancies with the estate owners sitting on the Assessment Commission. He received the following reply: 'At the time of the Separation [the Hardenberg Reforms, P.W.] the peasants had gained the fat pieces and the estate owners were left with the wasteland ['Unland']!' It required no further explanation that Delbrück was not returned to the Commission after the next elections.

69. See *DZA* II, Rep. 151 II, no. 1867, with the tax files of the brothers Robert and Eduard Röchling of Saarbrücken.

70. As early as 1909 tax assessment was in the hands of special commissars in some forty-five of the 111 towns in Prussia which were independent of the Kreise (kreisfrei); by the beginning of 1914 this number had risen to sixty-three and by November 1918 to eighty-two.

71. See the list of 4.12.1911 in *DZA* II, Rep. 77 tit. 43, no. 100, vol.1, with the following names: Carl von Elern, a Reichstag MP representing the Conservatives; Lieutenant-General Count zu Eulenburg-Wicken; von Glasow-Balga, Conservative member of the Prussian Diet; Ernst von Heydebrand und der Lasa, Reichstag MP and member of the Prussian Diet as leader of the Conservatives; Hans Count von Kanitz-Podangen, Reichstag MP representing the Conservatives; Ludwig von Massow-Parnehmen, Conservative Reichstag MP, Freiherr von Mirbach-Cremitten; Julius Count Mirbach-Sorquitten, Member of the Prussian Upper House and chairman of the Association of Economic and Tax Reformers; Hans von Rautter, Reichstag MP for the Conservatives; Joachim Count von der Schulenburg; Hans Count von Schwerin-Tamsel; Wilhelm von Wedel, Minister to the Royal Household ret.; von Zitzewitz-Quakenburg. This list could be easily expanded on the basis of the remaining materials.

as the supervisory body. Discussions with the Finance Ministry were repeatedly delayed until they ground to a complete halt in 1913. Neither Lentze nor Bethmann Hollweg were, at this point, prepared to take up the struggle against the Conservatives, which had now become inevitable if the *Landräte* were to be removed from their position as tax officials. For these Conservatives had meanwhile embarked upon a collision course with the government over the general development of domestic politics and in particular over changes in Reich taxation laws which were introduced in 1913 to raise additional funds for the Army Bill.[72] The policy of *Burgfrieden* (Sacred Peace) which was proclaimed at the start of the First World War did not permit a removal of the *Landräte* either. It was, after all, the main purpose of this policy to maintain existing social and political conditions with as little change as possible. With the exception of the Köslin district, the *Landräte* were still holding their position as tax officials in East Elbia outside the districts of Potsdam and Oppeln when the monarchy collapsed in November 1918. As one member of the agrarian ruling class once put it, they saw to it that 'the Prussian *Junker* had enough and kept as much as was necessary to preserve the inherited land (*väterliche Scholle*) for his family and to enable him to send his boys to serve the king as soldiers and civil servants'.[73]

The supreme objective of the estate owners was therefore to secure the material basis of their claims to political and social leadership. To achieve this objective, they deployed every means available, ranging from the manipulative use of a perverted notion of democracy to ruthless demagogy in order to implement an agricultural tariff programme which was designed to maintain the status position of even the most incompetent and profligate members of their class at the expense of the majority of the population; nor, finally, did they have any inhibitions about introducing direct and indirect subsidies via the system of taxation. They did not hesitate for one moment continually to violate tax regulations, if they were convinced that a loyal adherence to these laws ran counter to their interests; they certainly thought that this was the case as regards the Prussian Income Tax Act. The *Landräte* who came from the same social class as the estate owners showed no reluctance vigorously to aid and abet these practices. Of course,

72. P.-C. Witt, *Finanzpolitik*, pp. 356ff.
73. *DZA* Potsdam, Reichskanzlei, no. 951, von Klitzing (Landrat ret. and Chairman of the LWK Silesia) to Reich Chancellor Bethmann Hollweg, 3.5.1912.

they took great care — also in their general conduct as administrators which objectively favoured the estate owners — that no doubts were raised in public as to the strict and loyal adherence of the Prussian bureaucracy to the law. The *Landräte* were therefore doubly sensitive to any doubts that were uttered in this respect. In the long term, they succeeded in portraying all doubts about the competence and integrity of the civil service as vicious party-political propaganda designed to undermine the exemplary political system of Imperial Germany.[74] The lasting effectiveness of this notion and the caste mentality behind it emerged after 1918. It was in February 1921 that August Lentze who, as Prussian Minister of Finance, had himself unmasked the system of political corruption operated by one section of the old civil service, i.e. the *Landräte*, praised the advantages of a prewar civil service which was 'unpolitical', dutiful and only working to uphold the law.[75] By then, of course, he found himself engaged in the struggle against the parliamentary system of Weimar and its methods of civil service selection.

74. See the campaign of the Agrarian League and the Conservatives against Delbrück's charges during the debates on the Finance Reform of 1909, in A. Thimme, *Hans Delbrück als Kritiker der Wilhelminischen Epoche*, Düsseldorf, 1955, pp. 26ff.
75. Archiv der sozialen Demokratie, Bonn, Severing Papers, M. 85, Lentze to Severing, 1.2.1921.

VOLKER R. BERGHAHN

On the Societal Function of Wilhelmine Armaments Policy

Stabilising Structures of Domination by Means of Internal Power Politics

An argument which has been advanced many times is that armaments are a typical outgrowth of capitalism.* Modern peace and conflict researchers, sceptical of the exclusiveness of this hypothesis, have tended to emphasise that armaments must be seen in the broader context of the preservation and stabilisation of established systems of domination.[1] For this reason they point to the function of armaments and large military machines in socialist countries. Prussia-Germany provides a good example for studying the relationship between armaments and a system of domination which was hardly a fully-fledged capitalism. In the second half of the nineteenth century, the country — it is true — was affected by a rapid process of capitalist industrialisation. But there was no commensurate political change by which the industrial bourgeoisie might have gained a control of the political system in any way comparable to their economic power and importance. Industrial capitalism slowly overtook agriculture in economic importance without this having a decisive effect upon the distribution of political power. Politically and socially the country continued to be dominated by an agrarian elite.

*Publ. orig. in V. Berghahn, *Rüstung und Machtpolitik. Zur Anatomie des "Kalten Krieges" vor 1914*, Droste Verlag, Düsseldorf, 1973, pp. 12–35. The author would like to thank the publishers for permission to prepare and use this translation.
    1. D. Senghaas, *Rüstung und Militarismus*, Frankfurt, 1972, pp. 322ff.

155

The Reich Constitution of 1871 may be taken as a starting-point for examining these German peculiarities. Its most striking features are the quasi-absolutist powers with which the Kaiser and the federal princes were invested. As organs of the Constitution they had the power to nominate and dismiss ministers at will and without any checks on them. The Kaiser was charged with the exclusive conduct of the country's foreign policy and acted as supreme commander of the armed forces. He was empowered to take the most important decision with which any society can be faced — whether to go to war or to stay at peace. The Kaiser and the federal princes also had the right to dissolve the representative assemblies and to call fresh elections. Compared with these far-reaching, constitutionally guaranteed powers in the hands of the monarchical authorities, those held by the assemblies were very limited indeed. They had a restricted say in the fixing of the levels of taxation and expenditure and generally participated in the legislative process. All in all it may be said that at the time of the founding of the German Empire the bourgeoisie had failed again to secure for itself the classic prerogatives of parliamentarism. The constitution-ally fixed preponderance of monarchical power was reinforced by an alliance of the federal princes with the agrarian upper class which continued to dominate large parts of the countryside economically and politically and which occupied the key positions within the bureaucracy and the army. Without going into the intricacies of the quite complex mechanisms of the Prusso-German system of domination,[2] it may be said that a congruence was lacking between the economic and the political power structure similar to that which had begun to emerge in Britain. There was no 'synchronisation' between state and society, and Wilhelm Liebknecht's dictum is not too extreme when he called the Empire of 1871 'a princely insurance company against democracy'.

Thus Prussia-Germany was led politically by a relatively small group of people whose economic power base was rooted in large-scale agriculture. Partly because of growing Russian and American competition, partly because of the increasing predominance of industry over agriculture in the national economy, the grain-

2. See E.-W. Böckenförde, 'Der deutsche Typ der konstitutionellen Monarchie im
   19. Jahrhundert', in W. Conze (ed.), *Beiträge zur deutschen und belgischen
   Verfassungsgeschichte im 19. Jahrhundert*, Stuttgart, 1967; H. Boldt, 'Deutscher
   Konstitutionalismus und Bismarckreich', in M. Stürmer (ed.), *Das Kaiserliche
   Deutschland*, Düsseldorf, 1970.

growing estates from the mid-1870s onwards had become afflicted by a deep crisis. From the 1880s it was clear that one day agriculture would be pushed to one side by industrialism. But it was precisely this prospect which caused the agrarian elites to fight all the more fervently for the preservation of their dominant position within the political system and to use the state apparatus to give generous support and to keep them afloat with the help of legislative, fiscal and administrative measures.[3]

Conversely it was to be expected that the new social groups which industrialisation had produced and strengthened would try to undermine the firm hold of the princes and the agrarians and to make at least partial inroads into vital areas of the political power structure. One aspect of this was the attempt to advance the process of a further parliamentarisation of the Constitution, resulting in more extensive budgetary and legislative powers, the establishment of ministerial responsibility to the elected representatives and in the subordination of the armed forces and of foreign policy to a government which had emerged from Parliament and was independent of the Crown. These demands were promoted with particular vigour by the industrial working class inasmuch as it was influenced by Social Democracy. The Social Democrats and parts of the trade union movement saw a parliamentarisation and democratisation of the new political system as a prerequisite of the transition to a socialist economy and society. It was these long-term objectives which seemed to threaten not merely the existing monarchical order, but were indirectly also worrying to the industrial and commercial bourgeoisie. If these latter strata therefore began to move towards the right and into the arms of the conservative agrarian elites, the perception of a threat from the left no doubt played a major part in it. Their fear of the 'red revolution' tended to make important middle class sections more prepared to reduce the pressure for extended parliamentary co-government and control and to support the constitutional status quo. In return for their willingness to compromise, the monarchy was to undertake to use its superior political power in order to secure the economic positions of the bourgeoisie against the pressure from an anticapitalist proletariat. Faced with this pressure, business in particular became less and less concerned about whether it operated under a monarchi-

---

3. See H. Rosenberg, *Grosse Depression und Bismarckzeit*, Berlin, 1967; H.-U. Wehler, *Bismarck und der Imperialismus*, Cologne, 1969.

cal or a parliamentary system of government. The most important thing was that this system created conditions which were favourable to industrial and commercial activity.

It is only against the background of these main currents in the society of Prussia-Germany and of the problems of domination that were raised by them that the armaments policy which the Empire embarked upon in the late 1890s becomes plausible. For this policy is not to be seen simply as a spontaneous defensive response to decisions by other nations to step up their armaments. Some pressure, it is true, also resulted from Germany's supposed position in a Machiavellian world. But this position was not so threatened as to require the vast programme which was adopted around the turn of the century. The decision to make large military investments is rather in the first instance to be seen against the background of the inner crisis of the Prusso-German constitutional order. From this sphere came the original impulses which set the spiral of the pre-1914 arms race in motion and which ended in the First World War. The nexus between Wilhelmine armaments policy and the country's structural crisis which the process of industrialisation had unleashed is thrown into sharper relief, however, if we also examine the ups and downs in the German economy. Soon after the founding of the Empire, that economy had become afflicted by a longer period of irregular and retarded growth which was finally overcome in the mid-1890s. Overall there was a 'moderate upward trend'[4] which secured the continued economic rise of the bourgeoisie *vis-à-vis* the agrarians. But this expansion was marred by considerable sectoral variations which left a widespread feeling among the business community of being subjected to a 'prolonged period of economic bad weather'.[5]

This pessimism found expression in constant complaints about 'low prices' and 'impertinent workers'. Above all, it strengthened the desire to seek a rapprochement with those who had command of the state machinery. Business became prepared to support Bismarck's conservative law-and-order policies, if the 'state' offered them protection against the vicissitudes of a depressed capitalist economy. This is not the place to analyse by what means the great compromise between the industrial bourgeoisie and the agrarian conservatives was forged after 1875.[6] The important point in our

4. Rosenberg, *Grosse Depression*, p. 42.
5. Wehler, *Bismarck*, p. 48.
6. See also K. W. Hardach, *Die Bedeutung wirtschaftlicher Faktoren bei der*

context is that the interest aggregates that Bismarck deployed (protective tariffs, anti-Socialist repression, colonial agitation) were not strong enough to facilitate a rallying of all forces of conservatism against social and political change. Even the reassuring tariff policies succeeded in keeping the alliance of rye and iron together only for as long as German industry was still too weak to face international competition and believed it required protective walls for its own survival and reinvigoration. The agrarian–industrial bloc began to disintegrate when in the early 1890s the international economy picked up and German entrepreneurs set out to participate in this boom. They were looking for favourable trade agreements with other nations and pressed for abandoning not only industrial protectionism, but also for scrapping agricultural tariffs in aid of the still 'ailing' agrarians.[7] It was partly the disintegration of a long-established alliance and partly the prolonged 'crisis of government'[8] which resulted from Bismarck's dismissal that caused the existing system of domination to lapse into a state of confusion which, for the first time since 1871, looked quite dangerous as regards its prospects of survival. It seemed essential to attempt to initiate a policy of restabilisation. Otherwise the now open domestic conflict threatened to rent asunder the constitutional order of Prussia-Germany.

There were two peculiarities of the Constitution which turned the possibility of disintegration into something more real than a nightmarish figment of conservative minds: the fact that the Reichstag was elected on the basis of universal manhood suffrage and was involved in the scrutiny of Reich expenditure and taxation. When he abandoned the hitherto very restricted voting system, Bismarck — as was later explained — had been guided by the assumption 'that the masses could be governed with the help of the universal suffrage roughly like Napoleon III had attempted it'.[9] Yet instead of voting for the existing order and the parties supporting it, the masses gave their support increasingly to parties which were either not reliable protagonists of the status quo or even stood in sharp opposition to the Monarchy. This opposition remained relatively harmless as long as it did not possess a majority in the Reichstag. However, if

Einführung der Eisen- und Getreidezölle in Deutschland 1879, Berlin, 1967; D. Stegmann, *Bismarcks Erben*, Cologne, 1970.
7. See J. A. Nicholls, *Germany after Bismarck*, Cambridge, Mass., 1958.
8. J. C. G. Röhl, *Germany without Bismarck*, London, 1966.
9. Thus the State Secretary in the Reich Office of the Interior in January 1904, quoted in V. R. Berghahn, *Der Tirpitz-Plan*, Düsseldorf, 1971, p. 274n.

election results shifted the balance more and more towards such parties, the government would find it increasingly difficult to obtain secure majorities in Parliament. The refusal to approve legislation which the monarchical government deemed necessary, above all to ratify the budget without major changes, could prove acutely embarrassing to that government. It looked fairly certain that such a shift in the party balance would occur simply because Germany continued to change from an agricultural to an industrial society and because the industrial proletariat grew accordingly. These latter elements of the population, as has already been mentioned, identified increasingly with organisations which demanded a change of existing social and political conditions. After the lapse of the anti-Socialist laws and with the Social Democrats capturing a growing number of parliamentary seats in the 1890s, it looked as if the erosion of popular loyalties could no longer be stopped. Sooner or later the monarchical government would lose its conservative majorities and, given its uncompromising stance *vis-à-vis* the left, face a profound constitutional crisis.

Anticipating this development, there were some conservative and military advisers of the monarch who saw a *Staatsstreich*, a *coup d'état* from above, as the only way out of the internal deadlock.[10] They proposed to revise the Constitution in a reactionary direction by dissolving the representative institutions, destroying the working-class movement and establishing a military autocracy presided over by the Kaiser. Another faction in the government opposed this drastic solution. One of its major representatives was Reich Chancellor Hohenlohe, who believed as early as 1895 that a resort to violence would only exacerbate the critical situation. He added that only once 'the fear of the Social Democrats is greater among the population than [the fear of] a reactionary policy from which one expects the abolition of civil liberties' would the government be able to rely on conservative majorities and 'a general improvement of overall political conditions' would set in.[11] In other words, the Chancellor aimed at a rallying of all anti-Socialist forces by frightening people with the spectre of 'revolution', while distracting them from their worries about a new absolutism. This was a ruling technique which Bismarck had used in his time with some, though never with lasting, success; as the first Chancellor of the

10. See the details in Röhl, *Germany*.
11. Generallandesarchiv Karlsruhe, 233/34801, Gesandtschaft Berlin, Report of 18.9.1895.

Empire had also had to learn towards the end of his career, such a purely negative strategy of political integration was in itself not enough. In the 1890s the anti-Socialist bogey was even less effective than before as the only rallying ground for the bourgeoisie. *Positive* interest aggregates were also needed. This was the function which armaments assumed when the monarchy decided to build up its defences around the turn of the century. Armaments were the key which seemed to avoid a violent solution to the internal crisis and yet was to preserve the Prusso-German military state by military means.

However, it was to be expected that such a self-induced policy of large-scale rearmament would force other nations to react. Germany already had the most powerful army on the European continent. There were hence good reasons for refraining from setting in motion an armaments spiral by a further strengthening of land forces. Russia and France, who had only recently concluded an alliance, together disposed of a larger manpower potential than the Reich. A quantitative arms race on land in the age of mass conscription could only result in Germany running out of steam. But there was also a domestic reason why it was best to let sleeping dogs lie. An expansion of the army would have required more officers and men, yet an increase in the number of officers would have undermined the homogeneity of the officer corps, and large numbers of fresh recruits among the rank-and-file threatened to destroy the reliability of the army should it have to cope with inner disturbances. After all, armies in this period were not just instruments of external war, but also of civil war. As Germany did not have a professional army, the regime, even without an arms race on land, was confronted with the problem of having to train the sons of industrial workers, whose number was growing due to the continued process of industrialisation and demographic change. The question was how far these increasing numbers could be relied upon when it came to dealing with strikes or internal unrest. It was not certain whether or not they would disobey orders or even turn their bayonets against the existing order. It was clear that the army, as the *ultima ratio regum*, had to remain at the direct disposal of the Kaiser for the monarchy to be defended against major changes in the power structure even with the force of arms.[12] The fact that the existing system of domination was being challenged on a broad

12. See, e.g., W. Deist, 'Die Armee in Staat und Gesellschaft', in Stürmer (ed.), *Deutschland*, pp. 312ff.; Berghahn, *Tirpitz-Plan*, pp. 249ff.

front, made it all the more urgent to retain the army intact as an instrument to threaten and discipline the left. Such considerations ultimately blocked an expansion of the army and even resulted in the size of the Prusso-German army being 'frozen' just before the turn of the century. There was as yet no air force which might have acted as a substitute interest aggregate; but there was the navy which possessed an excellent potential for fulfilling this task and for being deployed within the context of a strategy of integration and stabilisation as envisaged by Hohenlohe and others. This was so for the following reasons:

(1) the fleet was useless for the conduct of civil war. Its size was, therefore, not subjected to the considerations underlying the 'freeze' of the army;

(2) the navy was a highly technological military instrument and hence of interest to many branches of industry. Moreover, the plan was to build large battleships which would prove more lucrative to industry than the equipment of recruits with uniforms and rifles;

(3) the Imperial Navy was relatively small in the late 1890s. Provided its expansion occurred in stages, it was less likely to lead to an immediate response by other powers — a danger to which the Kaiser and his advisers were not oblivious;

(4) it was not too difficult to find popular slogans for the need to build up the battle-fleet.

Stabilising Structures of Domination by Means of External Power Politics

As already indicated, Wilhelmine armaments policy was primarily, though not exclusively self-induced. However, the decision to expand the Imperial Navy must also be seen in the context of the dynamic of the international system and the actual or perceived position of Germany within it. It is one of the key features of this international system that it lacks a centralised supra-national authority equipped with the means of enforcing rules of peaceful conduct among states. The 'anarchic' character of international politics furthers a number of processes which the social sciences have tried to conceptualise. Thus the unregulated state of the international system is not really capable of facilitating shifts in the status hierarchy among its members.[13] Consequently members

13. See, e.g., J. Galtung, 'A Structural Theory of Aggression', in *Journal of Peace*

frequently find themselves in a precarious situation,[14] not least because the absence of a legitimized central 'world government' tempts some members to develop expansionist policies at the expense of others.[15] Nor, in view of the peculiar structure of the international system, has it been possible to resolve the question of the coexistence of divergent systems of domination.[16] Finally, there is also to this day no instrumentarium with the help of which misperceptions of the international situation on the part of individual states might be corrected. As a result, there frequently emerge exaggerated and basically irrational perceptions of reality which in turn unleash overreactions.

If one looks at the German position in the 1890s, it is striking that all the above-mentioned peculiarities of the international system exerted a considerable influence upon it. This is particularly true of the problem of distorted perceptions as a result of the pathological nature of international politics. Considering that the dominant elites also felt threatened at home, they developed quite exaggerated views of the country's external future. To begin with, the Kaiser and his advisers were absolutely convinced that the world was about to enter into a period in which profound changes within the international status hierarchies would take place. What no doubt reinforced such ideas was a widespread Social Darwinism, which the director of the Imperial Shipyards at Kiel voiced quite blatantly in February 1898 as follows:[17]

1. The 'struggle for survival' exists between individuals, provinces, parties, states. The latter conduct the struggle either with arms or by economic means. We cannot do anything about this; hence we join in; whoever refuses to join will go under.... 2. Economic struggle is a struggle for sales, for markets. I found these [ideas] and I liked them. I can't help it.

There emerged in government circles a more specific version of this general Social Darwinism that is probably best defined as Mahanism. The term is derived from the name of American naval thinker A. T. Mahan whose books aroused considerable interest

Research, 1964, pp. 95ff.; A. F. K. Organski, *World Politics*, New York, 1958, pp. 300ff.
14. See, e.g. J. H. Herz, *Weltpolitik im Atomzeitalter*, Stuttgart, 1961.
15. See, e.g., H. J. Morgenthau, *Politics among Nations*, New York, 1948.
16. See, e.g., W. Schmiederer in *Politische Vierteljahrsschrift*, Special issue, 5, 1973.
17. Quoted in Berghahn, *Tirpitz-Plan*, p. 181n.

towards the end of the century. His most important study, entitled *The Influence of Sea Power upon History*, became a bestseller among naval officers around the world and also exerted a profound influence upon the German corps. The naval authorities thought of it as so essential a study as to organise its translation into German and to have 8,000 copies of it printed in the first impression. The Kaiser was so enthusiastic about the book that he wanted to learn it by heart.

The significance of Mahan's writings lies in the fact that he developed a naval strategy which emphasised big ships and the idea of a decisive all-out battle of the two opposing fleets on the high seas and combined it with a 'philosophy of naval warfare' derived from historical examples. In particular his books pointed to the perishability of international power positions. This was a hypothesis which immediately fascinated the Kaiser and his advisers. The reason for this fascination can be found, *inter alia*, in a memorandum by Admiral von Senden-Bibran, the chief of the Naval Cabinet. He wrote in 1899:[18] 'A redistribution of the globe will always be taking place, and one might say that another round has only just begun'. Alfred von Tirpitz, the Kaiser's Naval Minister from 1897, wrote a few months later that the end of the nineteenth century would also spell the end to an epoch 'when the history of Europe was the history of the world'.[19] The continents had moved more closely together and 'major changes in the formation of the states on this planet must follow. . . . We are just at the beginning of the redistribution of the globe which will be connected with this. The important decisions will be made in the coming century'. The same idea, put in the form of a question out of consideration for the public, was voiced by the State Secretary of the German Foreign Office, von Bülow, in November 1899:[20] 'It has been said, ladies and gentlemen, that a great confrontation, a major liquidation, occurs every century in order to redistribute influence, power and territorial possessions on the globe . . . . Are we about to enter into a fresh distribution of this kind?' The Kaiser did not display a similar cautiousness when he told the assembled notables of the Hanseatic city of Hamburg:[21] 'Let us look around us! How the face

18. Bundesarchiv-Militärarchiv (BA-MA) Freiburg, Senden Papers, N 160/3, Memo concerning Geschwaderkrieg, n.d.
19. Ibid., Tirpitz Papers, 19, Notes on the Novelle 1900, n.d.
20. B. von Bülow, *Reden*, vol. I, Leipzig 1910, pp. 98f.
21. A. E. O. Klaussmann (ed.), *Kaiserreden*, Leipzig, 1902, p. 269.

of the earth has changed within a few years! Old empires disintegrate and new ones are emerging'.

If the top leadership of the Reich shared a firm belief that nations would move up and down the international status ladder in the future just as they had done in the past, the crucial question was where Germany would find herself at the end of this period of redistribution. For Bülow it was a question of whether Germany would be 'the hammer or the anvil'.[22] Tirpitz likewise took the view that the country would either achieve a world power position or sink back into the lower ranks of the international hierarchy. As he put it in his memoirs:[23] 'If one did not wish to build the fleet and, from the 1890s onwards, take the path of retreat, we would also have had to reduce voluntarily our commerce and industry; [we would have had] to revive our emigration movement and to allow our foreign interests to linger'. This was a solution which was not unthinkable to many Old Prussian conservatives. The large-scale landowners were particularly conscious of the connection between industrialisation and naval armaments, both of which tended to undermine their traditional power positions. Otto von Völderndorff, a friend of Chancellor Hohenlohe's, put this point very succinctly when he argued in November 1897:[24]

> We must keep away from international rivalries (*Welthändel*); we must confine ourselves to securing our country against the two neighbours [France and Russia]. Greatest parsimony (except for the Army) and a rebuilding of the Reich on the only reliable estate, the rural population. Our industry is not worth much anyway. It is in the hands of Jews; its products are . . . 'cheap and bad'; it is a seedbed of Socialism . . . , Moreover, we are coming too late; all valuable overseas possessions are in the hands of others who hold on to them. We are also not wealthy enough to carry on the great power policies we have embarked upon in 1870.

Indeed, it is indicative of the unequal weight of internal over external factors determining the course of Wilhelmine armaments policy that this conservative-agrarian opposition to the 'ugly and awful fleet'[25] was directed less against 'the foreign-political dangers of *Weltpolitik* than against the social [and] domestic consequences

22. Quoted in K. Schilling, *Beiträge zu einer Geschichte des radikalen Nationalismus in der Wilhelminischen Ära*, Diss., Cologne, 1968, p. 60.
23. A. von Tirpitz, *Erinnerungen*, Leipzig, 1919, p. 57.
24. Bundesarchiv (BA) Koblenz, Hohenlohe Papers, Rep. 100, XXII, A 12, Völderndorff to Hohenlohe, 9.11.1897.
25. Thus D. Hahn of the Agrarian League.

of industrialisation, as *Weltpolitik* and naval building were seen as a function of the latter. *Weltpolitik* was rejected because in the wake of industrial development it promoted the emergence of a proletariat and undermined the existing social order'.[26] No doubt the Kaiser and his advisers were just as aware of this nexus as Völderndorff had recognised it, and yet his proposals did not offer a genuine alternative. As *Nauticus*, a naval annual close to the Reich Navy Office, put it:[27] 'Without a strong fleet Germany will be without colonies at the end of the twentieth century [!]; but without colonies she will either get choked in her [present] narrow territory or she will be squashed by the major world powers to which she will moreover have to send millions and millions of emigrants'. Clearly, the opposite conclusion from Völderndorff's had to be drawn, if the existing system of domination was not to be exposed to a revolutionary explosion. It was 'the growing number of hungry stomachs and empty hands which pushes us into industrialism, with the proletarian workers' movement following it like its shadow; it is industrialism which forces us to embark upon an economic *Weltpolitik*, [and] to appear on the world market'.[28] In view of this, the leadership of the Reich, too, believed that there was no alternative but to make an attempt to achieve the breakthrough to a world power position. The radicalism with which the choices were set out ('hammer or anvil') was less a reflection of the state of international politics at the turn of the century than of the internal crisis besetting the Prusso-German monarchy in the 1890s.

However, it was not just a sense of compulsion, inspired in the final analysis by a pessimistic view of the future, which motivated the German imperialists to compete in the international arena. Seemingly irrefutable statistics did not indicate merely that industrial Germany had to move outwards, but also that it had good prospects of success. The upswing in the national economy was so enormous in the 1890s 'that the last quinquennium of the nineteenth century must be rated among the most splendid boom periods. The period 1895–1913 may be regarded as a single great upswing which was merely interrupted by brief recessions in 1901/2 and 1908/9'.[29] During this phase industrial production and domestic consumption

26. E. Kehr, *Schlachtflottenbau und Parteipolitik*, Berlin, 1930, p. 273.
27. *Nauticus* (1900), p. 73.
28. Thus Professor E. Francke in G. Schmoller et al.(eds.), *Handels- und Machtpolitik*, Stuttgart, 1900, vol. I, pp. 94f.
29. H. Bechtel, *Wirtschafts- und Sozialgeschichte Deutschlands*, Munich, 1967, p. 379.

saw a rapid rise, and Germany became a major exporting nation. In the 1880s the protectionism of other countries had hampered German exports, but with the signing of the Caprivi tariffs, doors were once again more open for trade. Both relatively and absolutely trade attained its most impressive growth in terms of its volume on the world market.[30]

Ship-building was one of the beneficiaries of this growth. According to the Reich Navy Office, shipyards had been short of orders in 1893.[31] But in 1896, there was a 'marked increase in the use of German materials in the ship-building industry'.[32] Deliveries of merchant ships increased from 153,000 tons in 1897 to 225,000 tons in 1900.[33] The overall increase in this industry in the last three years of the nineteenth century was 38.1 per cent.[34] The German iron and steel industry experienced a similar boom. Annual production of pig iron reached 8.5m tons in 1900. Meanwhile Germany moved into second place behind the United States as far as steel production was concerned.[35] It was especially *vis-à-vis* Britain, the leading world power, that the Reich caught up very fast. In the last twenty years of the nineteenth century pig-iron production increased from 40 per cent to 78 per cent of the British figure. The performance of the steel industry is even more striking. In 1880 Germany produced less than half of the British amount; by 1900 British steel producers had been overtaken by 20 per cent. Between 1880 and 1884 the value of German exports was 65 per cent of the British figure; during the last five years of the century it was 78 per cent. Exports of machinery in the same period rose from 23 per cent to 36 per cent of the British share.[36]

Such statistics pointed towards discrepancies between economic and political power within the international system, or so it seemed. Above all, they nourished hopes among the political leadership that it would be possible to overcome these discrepancies in the course of long-term changes in the international hierarchy of nations.

30. Ibid., p. 391.
31. H. Hallmann, *Der Weg zum deutschen Schlachtflottenbau*, Stuttgart, 1933, p. 89.
32. T. Schwarz and E. von Halle (eds.), *Die Schiffbauindustrie in Deutschland und im Ausland*, Berlin, 1902, vol. II, p. 29.
33. Ibid., p. 41.
34. Ibid., p. 42.
35. J. H. Clapham, *The Economic Development of France and Germany*, Cambridge, 1936 (repr. 1955), p. 285.
36. Statistics from R. J. S. Hoffman, *Great Britain and the German Trade Rivalry*, Philadelphia, 1933, pp. 77ff.

However, the crucial point is that the removal of the gap between German economic and political power abroad was to be promoted in order to maintain a similar gap between divergent social groups at home. We shall have to deal with this domestic angle in more detail below. What is important at this point is that the expectation of changes in the international system became blended with expansionist aspirations. Ludwig Dehio was among the first to try to define the character of Wilhelmine Germany's competitive spirit more closely.[37] The Reich, he argued, did not merely hope that the international system would change, but tried to penetrate into a 'global equilibrium system' and to become a world power next to a number of others. Such objectives could not be fulfilled, however, without challenging Britain. Indeed, ultimately — so Dehio believed — they could not even be attained without armed struggle and an 'English war of succession'. However peacefully German foreign policy might conduct itself, behind it and its 'hard core, [i.e.] the naval build-up' there was a 'unique dynamic'. This dynamic endowed German armaments policy with its peculiar character 'which cannot be squeezed into the simple alternative of peace or war' and required 'the introduction of a flexible compromise term which oscillates between the poles of war and peace'. As early as 1910 Hans Delbrück had used the notion of 'dry war' to describe this peculiar condition, whereas the German Naval Attaché in London spoke of a 'latent war'. Dehio employed the term 'cold war' to this earlier period, when, writing after the Second World War, he conceived his analysis of Wilhelmine power politics.

Whoever conducts a 'cold war', so Dehio continued, aims to achieve objectives in peacetime which can normally be attained only through war, i.e. the displacement of the opponent. Such aims could never be called defensive; they were offensive, even if the hope was always that it would not be necessary to deploy the armaments generated in the meantime. In a cold war, one accepted the risk of a clash of arms, but left the decision to unleash it to the opponent. This defensive position, Dehio added, created a peculiar 'mixture of offensive and defensive elements'. Its defensive justifications notwithstanding, the building of the German fleet pursued, from the start, an offensive long-term goal. Although the intentions were those of a 'cold offensive, under the laws of the cold war they

37. See L. Dehio, *Deutschland und die Weltpolitik im 20. Jahrhundert*, Munich, 1955, pp. 76ff.

necessarily also included the risk of a hot war'. He continued:

> For in order to accelerate the desired development in a deterrent or
> threatening fashion, one's own armaments build-up is being promoted —
> but invariably in the hope that it will not be necessary to use these arms.
> They are supposed to increase the opponent's risk of war to such an
> extent that he will not dare to break out of the cold war which has been
> forced upon him and start a hot one and that he will voluntarily abandon
> his position from exhaustion.

Dehio concluded that Germany's aims had consisted 'in a new
function of German power based on the navy [and] in the quality
[of that power], both in terms of its prestige and its actual leverage,
side-by-side with other world powers in the global system of the
future'. Put differently again, Germany's aims amounted to the
'ouster of Britain from its position of supremacy which posed an
obstacle to the formation of a genuinely free world system'.

Dehio's deliberations on the aggressively competitive dimensions
of Wilhelmine *Weltpolitik* and naval armaments are supported by
the primary sources. The Kaiser and his advisers did not merely aim
to follow an international trend. Nor did they simply hope to catch
up *vis-à-vis* the strength of other second-rank naval powers. Rather
it was the first sea power, Britain, that kept appearing in their
telescope, and they thought they had developed a foolproof policy
of attrition. Writing in July 1897, Tirpitz flatly maintained that
'England is at present the most dangerous opponent at sea'.[38] The
Royal Navy was moreover 'the opponent against which we require
a certain measure of naval strength as a political power factor'. A
few weeks later, Eduard von Capelle, one of Tirpitz's closest
collaborators, summarised his superior's views as follows:[39]

> My *Chef* is of the opinion that the conflicts among economic interest
> groups inside England will grow and grow in the coming century and
> that we must be prepared for all eventualities. My *Chef* also believes that,
> once his [building] programme has been completed, we shall have a
> battle-fleet which England will be very cautious to treat as a *quantité
> négligeable*, the more so if allies must be added [on the German side] or
> England must fear their appearance on the scene.

The Chief of the Naval Cabinet von Senden perceived the dynamic

---

38. Quoted in J. Steinberg, *Yesterday's Deterrent*, London, 1965, p. 208.
39. Quoted in Berghahn, *Tirpitz-Plan*, p. 188.

behind the German rise:[40] 'Our economic and industrial development progresses at a pace which will lead to serious competition
with England. It would hence be illogical to assume that a competition in the sphere of [political and military] power has no prospect'.
As late as 1909 Tirpitz insisted on the continued validity of the
fundamental idea of his naval programme:[41] 'The question of
whether Germany will rise to the ranks of the major powers or will
decline to the position of a minor state will be fought out in this
century. But if one believes in Germany's future, a measure of naval
power will be necessary so that we will obtain "fair play" from
England'.

As its creators conceived of it, the German naval programme, as
adopted in the late 1890s, was therefore designed from the start as
an offensive, power-political lever against Britain. The German
leadership with the help of this instrument was hoping to gain a
world position, with colonial possessions commensurate with that
position. Yet on closer inspection it is possible to discover behind
the optimistic hope that these ambitions could be realised a profound sense of pessimism and insecurity. This feeling was not
merely rooted in the knowledge of the internal difficulties of the
Prusso-German system of domination, but also in an appreciation
that the Reich's strategic position was not particularly favourable
because of the policies previously adopted by Bismarck. The first
Chancellor had, after all, concentrated on consolidating the country's position as a Continental power and on deflecting conflicts
with rival powers either to the periphery of Europe or to other parts
of the globe. Rooted in a continental-agrarian tradition, Bismarck
had long resisted the idea that a rapidly industrialising Germany
needed overseas territories to secure new markets and sources of
cheap raw materials for the metropolitan area. As he put it without
much sensitivity for the dynamics of a modern industrial economy
in 1879: 'There is nothing to be discovered anymore; the globe has
been circumnavigated and we can no longer find potent customers
among the countries of any considerable size to which we can send our
exports'. Why should the Reich therefore try to acquire colonies?

Bismarck, it is true, did not adhere to this view forever. However,
after he had finally been 'converted by representatives of high
finance and Hanseatic overseas trade to seize the initiative in the

40. Ibid., p. 184.
41. Ibid., p. 183.

colonial field',[42] the other imperialist nations had already carved up most of the globe among themselves. There were but few overseas territories and bases left which Germany could acquire. Meanwhile he had promoted the accumulation of political and economic power by others and conjured up the danger of the country's relative decline. Bismarck's successors were more than ever before confronted with this danger when industry began to boom from the mid-1890s. Production was at full throttle. But in the eyes of business the situation looked far from propitious. The German economy was dependent on exports and increasingly forced to operate in markets which were politically dominated by other powers. What appeared to make the situation so worrying was that this was the period when Free Trade was evidently coming to an end. The fear was that closed blocs would be created in the wake of increasing rivalries among the industrial powers; compact empires which — surrounded by high protective tariff walls — would in the twentieth century wrestle among themselves for political and economic power around the globe. If this assumption proved correct, German industry might suffer disadvantages in overseas markets or might even be excluded from them altogether.

The Kaiser and his advisers appreciated (to put it in the words of the economist Gustav Schmoller) 'that *in extremis* the *ultima ratio regum* must be available behind our merchants [and] behind our merchant navy abroad. This is how the world ticks'.[43] *Nauticus* added that naval armaments would keep open Germany's access to the world and its markets. It was obvious that an expansion of the army could not provide such protection, quite apart from the fact that it was unwise to enlarge the land forces for the above-mentioned domestic reasons. Only a navy could do this job. This is why Tirpitz and his collaborators planned to exploit the expected continued rise of German industry to lay *simultaneously* the military foundations of a German power position overseas. Confronted with the completed build-up of the Imperial Navy, other powers, above all Britain, would be prepared to make territorial concessions and to concede to Germany a 'place in the sun'.

However, the power-political lever that was being created from 1897 onwards was useless unless it could also be deployed against Britain. Without this condition, German expansionism was likely,

---

42. Rosenberg, *Grosse Depression*, p. 271n.
43. Schmoller et al. (eds.), *Handelspolitik*, vol. I, p. 35.

directly or indirectly, to run into a British veto and the Reich's security dilemma would only be exacerbated. Clearly, the German lever had to be militarily effective against the first naval power. The completed Imperial fleet had to be powerful enough to possess a genuine chance of victory against the Royal Navy. Otherwise the projected policy of bullying would be exposed as an empty bluff. An inferior fleet would either be obliterated or be forced to retreat behind the coastal batteries.

How powerful did the Imperial Navy have to be for a decisive naval encounter? Experts were agreed at the time that it was not necessary to have numerical equality. Their view was that a 2:3 inferiority still gave the inferior power a chance of military victory, provided that there was an early all-out battle, that it had superior leadership and tactics and deployed marginally better ships. The calculations of the Reich Navy Office were based on these assumptions. The plans which were developed by Tirpitz in the late 1890s envisaged that the German fleet would comprise, at the time of its completion in 1918/20, a total of sixty big ships.[44] This implied that Britain, in accordance with the 2:3 formula, would have to build and replace some ninety ships in the same period. It was accepted that Britain's economic and fiscal muscle was strong enough and her system of recruitment sufficiently flexible to furnish such a navy.[45] However — to quote from a memo of February 1900[46] — the Reich Navy Office was also convinced

> that the enlargement of the British fleet cannot proceed at the same rate as ours because the size of their fleet requires a considerably larger number of replacements. The [attached] table ... demonstrates that England ... will have to construct and replace a fleet almost three times as large as the German one as envisaged by the Navy Law [of 1900] if she expects to have an efficient fleet ... in 1920. The inferiority in tonnage which our battle-fleet will continue to have *vis-à-vis* Britain's in 1920, shall be compensated for by a particularly good training of our personnel and better tactical manoeuvrability of large battle formations. ... The [enclosed] figures ... on the tonnage which both battle-fleets keep in service amount to a superiority of Germany. In view of the notorious difficulties in England to recruit enough personnel, it is unlikely that this favourable position will change.

44. I.e. battle ships and battle cruisers.
45. Unlike Germany, Britain had a professional navy, not a universal service navy.
46. BA-MA, Akten des Reichsmarine-Amts (RMA), PG 66040, Memo on 'Sicherung Deutschlands gegen einen englischen Angriff', (February 1900).

Just how much importance was attached to the alleged difficulties Britain would have to man her navy also emerges from a report by the German Naval Attaché in London. He had been asked in 1897 if Britain would be capable of recruiting enough men and officers for an expanded force. The Attaché reported back that personnel was about sufficient, but that there existed a widely-admitted shortage of officers in particular.[47] He did not know, therefore, where the additional personnel would come from, should the Royal Navy be expanded by 25–30 per cent.

In this way the Reich Navy Office put an upper and a lower ceiling upon the proportionate strength between Britain and Germany. Never, so the calculations demonstrated, would Germany have a more than 33 per cent inferiority.[48] If the defensive aspect of these calculations was emphasised, there was some truth in the points Tirpitz made in the summer of 1908. Arguing that he wished to make it 'bad business' for Britain to start a war against the German Empire, he referred again to the original figures of the late 1890s. However, if a 2:3 superiority was required for a British war of aggression, it followed that the defender, in turn, had a chance of victory even if there existed a 3:2 inferiority. The 2:3 formula, in other words, was like a narrow ridge where, theoretically at least and on the assumption that Britain was the attacker and Germany the defender, the two navies balanced each other out. The chances of victory could then be enhanced, if the German fleet tried marginally to improve the *quality* of its big ships.

This became Tirpitz's objective from 1898 onwards. Whether it was the question of unsinkability, of superior gunnery or smaller technical construction features, Germany tried to gain a lead over England.[49] Similar measures were taken in the areas of tactical training in battle formations and the training of men and officers.[50] This was what Tirpitz was referring to when he told the Kaiser in September 1899:[51] 'But no doubt we also have [a] good chance vis-à-vis England thanks to [our] geographical situation, system of naval service, mobilisation, torpedo boats, tactical training, systematic build-up of our organisation [and] unified command by the monarch'. The Navy Secretary was even blunter in the marginal

47. Ibid., 2221, PG 93935, Gülich to Tirpitz, 19.8.1897.
48. Ibid., 2045, PG 66081, Memorandum by Tirpitz, (Summer 1908).
49. See the details in Berghahn, *Tirpitz-Plan*, pp. 330ff.
50. Ibid.
51. BA-MA, RMA, PG 66074, Tirpitz's notes for his Audience at Rominten on 28.9.1899, n.d.

comments he made on an internal report of two books critical of his naval strategy. 'Without a victorious battle', he wrote, the Royal Navy would block the Reich's access to the open seas. ' "Victorious" is the decisive word. Hence let us concentrate upon this victory.'[52] After all, you cannot carve up the 'bear's skin before the bear has been killed'.

However crude these calculations may appear in the age of nuclear strategy with its various contingencies and scenarios, they were based on a theory of deterrence in a modern sense. As far as we know, Tirpitz did not plan to attack Britain, but he did hope to win an all-out battle should the Royal Navy steam across the North Sea in an attempt to 'Copenhagen' the Imperial Navy.[53] Such a German victory would have changed the entire military and political balance in the world at a stroke. Moreover, Germany would have found herself in a morally unassailable position. In this peculiar sense, Tirpitz's naval build-up was to act as a *military* lever against British hegemony. More important is that the political leaders of the Reich believed they had gained a *political* lever as well. They expected that the sheer size of the completed German fleet would deter a British attack and would then enable them to bully London into a recognition of Germany's aspirations as a world power. As Tirpitz explained to the Kaiser in September 1899:[54] 'Apart from the military situation which is not at all unfavourable, England will also have lost any inclinations to attack us for reasons of general politics and from the viewpoint of a sober businessman; consequently they will concede Your Majesty such a measure of naval recognition as to enable Your Majesty to conduct a great overseas policy'. Tirpitz was less precise, though still outspoken enough, when, in a conversation with Chancellor Bülow, he defined the fleet as 'the tool [which] you will need in order to build up Germany on a larger scale and on a further level'.[55] The Kaiser had certainly grasped that the navy was to be the power-political instrument of German overseas expansionism. In a telegram to Bülow following the Second Navy Law of 1900 he expressed the hope 'that I may succeed with your help soon to complete the work which is in effect beginning only now so that I

---

52. See the details in Berghahn, *Tirpitz-Plan*, pp. 190ff.
53. On this problem see J. Steinberg, 'The Copenhagen Complex', in *Journal of Contemporary History*, 3/1966, pp. 23–46.
54. BA-MA, RMA, 2044, PG 66074, Tirpitz's notes for his Audience at Rominten on 28.9.1899, n.d.
55. BA Bülow Papers, 126, Tirpitz to Bülow, 18.6.1900.

may command peace on the high seas'.[56] A little later, the monarch indicated to the French ambassador when he expected to be able to command peace:[57] first he required the fleet; later, 'after twenty years, when it is completed', he would be 'speaking a different language'.

The Link between German Domestic and Foreign Policy

Yet our analysis of the function of German armaments policy would remain incomplete if we did not try to relate these aims back to the domestic situation and the peculiarities of the Prusso-German system of domination. We have already noted that the monarchy found itself in a defensive struggle against the forces of change and parliamentarism. It is a reflection of the concern which these currents were causing that naval planning was also influenced by these worries. This is why plans were made to roll back the influence which the Reichstag wielded with regard to naval appropriations. A roll-back appeared to be all the more vital as it was to be feared that some day the then conservative majorities would be replaced by left-wing majorities keen to reduce military expenditure, declared indispensable by the monarch. In order to avoid a repetition of the Army Conflict of the 1860s, the Navy, too, was to be moved into the absolutist enclave which had been created for the Army long ago. Within this extraconstitutional zone, the fleet was to remain at the exclusive disposal of the Kaiser who would deploy it without interference from the popular assembly. The calculation was a simple one. We have seen that Tirpitz planned to build a total of sixty big ships. If this number could be reached within twenty years and a legally prescribed replacement period for these ships again be fixed at twenty years, the Reich Navy Office would have achieved an *Aeternat*, i.e. the sixty ships would be automatically replaced every twenty years and, given the peculiarities of the legislative process under the German Constitution, the Reichstag would have been powerless to reduce this number.[58] The anti-parliamentary intentions of his naval programme were formu-

---

56. Politisches Archiv des Auswärtigen Amts (PAAA) Bonn, AA Deutschland, 138 secr., vol. 5, Kaiser to Bülow, 13.6.1900.
57. Quoted in Schilling, *Geschichte*, p. 81.
58. For further details see Berghahn, *Tirpitz-Plan*, pp. 169ff.

lated by Tirpitz as follows:[59]

> Once the Reichstag has approved the formation of fresh [army] contin-
> gents, they are 'eternalised' in practice. The Reichstag cannot unilaterally
> [without the approval of the Kaiser and the princely Federal Council]
> abolish such contingents (regiments, batteries etc.). The approval of
> contingents would not have any meaning for the Navy. Simply by
> refusing to approve replacement ships, the Reichstag could 'dry out' the
> Navy. Only if replacements are prescribed by law, will the Navy achieve
> a safe position like that of the Army. This is why the Reichstag, as the
> earlier period [prior to 1897] has shown, possesses a major political lever
> *vis-à-vis* the Reich government because of its right to approve ships on
> an annual basis.

To destroy that leverage was the aim. As Tirpitz put it in 1898,
the task was 'to remove, once and for all, the disturbing influence of
the Reichstag upon Your Majesty's intentions with regard to the
development of the Navy'.[60] The automatic replacement of the
projected sixty ships was to make it impossible that the fleet would
ever become a 'fleet of parliament',[61] for such a development was
dysfunctional to the basic structure of the monarchical system. Seen
in this context and remembering the anti-British calculations of the
Reich Navy Office, it may even be said that the Tirpitz Plan was
directed against 'two parliaments',[62] the British and the German
one, and was designed to uphold the principles of monarchical
conservatism in a world in which the liberal parliamentary model
appeared to be gaining ground both at home and abroad.

It thus emerges that there is a close link between the international
and the domestic aspects of Wilhelmine armaments policy. The
naval programme was to have a calming effect on internal politics
and to rally divergent political forces on a conservative basis. The
placing of orders for big ships was to protect industry against
recession and to win it over to the naval cause. The regular building
tempo and the automatic replacement period of twenty years was
finally to end the participation of the Reichstag in the battle for
military expenditure.[63]

The agrarians who were conscious of the link between industrialisation and navalism and were at first quite unenthusiastic about

59. BA-MA, RMA, 2045, PG 66079, Memorandum by Tirpitz (November 1905).
60. Ibid., 2051, PG 66110, Tirpitz to the Kaiser, 3.2.1898.
61. Ibid., Memorandum by Knorr, 21.5.1898.
62. Formulation by K. Hildebrand.
63. See, for details, Berghahn *Tirpitz-Plan*, pp. 536ff.

Tirpitz's programme were ultimately also won over. But it was not just their own fear of the left which induced them to form a broad front with the middle classes and to allow themselves to be integrated into a military programme of status quo preservation; they also had a major economic demand fulfilled: the reintroduction of high agricultural tariffs which was finally approved in 1902 with the help of the bourgeois parties and against the vigorous opposition of the Social Democrats. They had long been arguing that only protectionism could secure their threatened position — a position vital to the preservation of the existing system of domination. In this sense the years 1898 to 1902 should be seen as an entity, a phase during which a comprehensive strategy of integration based on armaments was initiated.

This was the short-term significance of the policies of the late 1890s. But there is also a long-term perspective to official policy which is no less important. The Kaiser and his advisers also hoped to achieve a lasting stabilisation of the monarchy via *Weltpolitik* and its military back-up, the fleet. The expected acquisition of an empire in the great redistribution of the globe promised material wealth which would relieve the pressure for domestic change. After all, not just industry and the needy agrarians were to reap the benefits to be gained with the help of the Navy. The ideal was rather a monarchy, led by a glamorous 'people's Kaiser', who would enjoy the unqualified support of the large majority of the population. The masses would simply forget their demands for greater participation and leave the traditional system of domination intact. Even the industrial working class — this was the hope — would one day be part of this plebiscitarian monarchy. Bülow was one of the most indefatigable propagandists of this notion. His speeches contain many references to the economic and social calculations underlying the fleet programme. Naval expenditure and the overseas acquisitions to be gained with it would ultimately also benefit the proletariat. Its living standards would rise and this, in turn, would have a stabilising effect on domestic politics.[64] The best means of combating the Social Democrats, so Bülow proclaimed,

> is a courageous and generous policy which knows how to uphold the joy in the present character of [our] national life, a policy which mobilises national energies; a policy attracting the numerous and ever-growing *Mittelstand* which in its overwhelming majority firmly supports the

64. Ibid., p. 148.

monarchy and the state . . .; a policy which appeals to the best patriotic sentiments. The national aspect must be moved into the limelight time and again so that the national idea will never cease to move, integrate and divide the parties.[65]

He added: 'We must, unswervingly, fight for the souls of our workers; [we] must try to attract them again to the state, to the monarchy [and] keep the non-Social Democratic workers away from Social Democracy'. This would result in the isolation of the SPD and the day would approach when the unity of the nation would be achieved: 'If we fight Social Democracy, it is not in order to hit the worker, but to remove him from Social Democratic ensnarlments and to accustom him to the idea of the state.' Tirpitz made this point as early as 1895:

> In my view, Germany will, in the coming century, rapidly drop from her position as a great power unless we begin to develop our maritime interests energetically, systematically and without delay, . . . to no small degree also, because the great economic task and the benefits to be derived from it will offer a strong palliative against educated and uneducated Social Democrats.[66]

Bearing in mind such statements, the roots and functions of Wilhelmine armaments policy and of the arms race that followed may be identified with some precision. The aim was to use naval armaments as an aggregate to solve the immediate and the long-term problems of the Prusso-German monarchy at a time when it was under increasing pressure for change. Immediately it was to rally divergent forces for a distant power-political goal. And once the world power position had been achieved with the help of the fleet, foreign success would exert its stabilising effect indirectly. This is why it has been argued that Tirpitz's programme aimed to overthrow the international status quo in order to preserve the status quo at home.

65. Ibid., also for the following.
66. Von Tirpitz, *Erinnerungen*, p. 52.

HANS-ULRICH WEHLER

The German Empire

The Configuration of 1871

The German Empire of 1871 was a unique creation among the nation states of Europe.* It not only emerged from a series of three wars within the space of six years as a result of a 'revolution from above' carried out by the Prussian military, but was, moreover, founded at a time when the completion of an agrarian revolution coincided with the breakthrough of the industrial revolution in Germany. Socio-economic upheavals of profound significance coincided with the diverse ramifications at home and abroad of the appearance of a new political structure in Central Europe. It was this that was responsible for the problematical nature of this state, and not primarily the crisis of a 'latecoming' nation state which was never fully realised. Each of these developments would in itself have created major problems. Together, however, they produced extra-ordinary complications. Over seventy years ago the American sociologist Thorstein Veblen gave a penetrating analysis of the configuration of factors at this time: in a largely traditional society, only partially adapted institutionally between 1866 and 1871 and still ruled over by pre-industrial élites, the most advanced Western technology forced itself through with unprecedented speed and accelerated social change. How the representatives of that traditional society reacted to the socio-economic

* The following chapter comprises selected passages from H. –U. Wehler, *The German Empire 1871–1918* (transl. by Kim Traynor), Berg Publishers, Leamington Spa, 1985, as follows: 'The Configuration of 1871' to 'Wars for Hegemony and "Revolution from Above" ', ibid., pp. 9–13; 'Imperialism', ibid., pp. 170–81.

and political structural changes during the following fifty years forms a central theme in the history of the German Empire. Accordingly, we may proceed from Alexander Gerschenkron's general explanatory model, which postulates that the more rapid and complete the 'great spurt' forward of an industrial revolution (from an agrarian to an industrial society), the more complicated will be its effects and resultant problems. While, on the one hand, Germany certainly enjoyed some 'advantages of backwardness', being able to adopt certain features from the more advanced societies of Britain and Western Europe, on the other hand, the very success of its economic revolution involved apparently unavoidable costs in terms of uncommonly acute social problems.[1] What attempts were made to solve these problems? On whom did the costs of change fall in the long and short terms? Who profited from change? What was the significance of these problems in terms of their consequences? And how are they to be judged in retrospect?

Proceeding from this outline of the German Empire's problematical origins, we must first enquire into the most important influences at work in this period: namely, the development of the agrarian economy, of industry and of domestic politics in the new Germany under the leadership of Prussia.

The Agrarian Revolution and the Land-Owning Aristocracy

The agrarian revolution, which in Germany is usually concealed behind the misleading term 'the emancipation of the peasants' began in the latter part of the eighteenth century. It was accelerated by the legal reforms of 1807–21, and entered its final phase in the long period of economic prosperity between 1840 and 1876. It resulted in a structural transformation of the agrarian economy which, legally formalised and promoted, and encouraged by modernisation and rationalisation measures, led to an immense increase in productive efficiency. Riding on the crest of a wave at a peak in the business cycle, the self-confidence and sense of power of the land-owning aristocracy, accustomed as it was to its exercise,

---

1. T. Veblen, *Imperial Germany and the Industrial Revolution* (1915), Ann Arbor, Mich., 1966; see also Marx (MEW, vol. 23, pp.12f. — fifty years previously!); A. Gerschenkron, *Economic Backwardness in Historical Perspective*, Cambridge, Mass., 1962, 2nd imp. 1965, pp. 5–30.

was revived. Enjoying the outwardly stable economic base of a flourishing agricultural sector, it took part in the internal conflicts surrounding the German Empire's founding and thus reasserted its historical role and claim to leadership over its rival bourgeois exponents of the other revolution of this period: the industrial revolution.

Since the turn of the nineteenth century countless legal changes were made in the area of seigneurial rights from the period of a feudal power structure in the areas of land rights (for example, ownership, labour services, and taxes in kind), personal rights (serfdom and its attenuated form binding the peasant to the soil) and the arbitration of disputes (that is, judicial powers). Indeed, in some cases they were completely removed, though not to the extent that the rural population became less dependent in an informal and, hence, less oppressive sense. This prolonged process of change was determined by several aims. The immediate impetus behind the speed of these changes came from the state of emergency which resulted from the Napoleonic Wars. Reparations payments and the costs of the war made an increase in state revenue imperative. This could be achieved only by modernising the economy 'from above', which meant, in the first instance, the agricultural sector. In order to stimulate maximum output and maximise profit, agriculture was reorganised along competitive lines. The state's economic policies hoped to reap maximum benefit by releasing work energies, providing new incentives and encouraging productive efficiency. At the same time the idea gained ground that modernisation was the *sine qua non* if the German states, in particular Prussia, were to hold their own with any prospect of success in competition with other nations. From the standpoint of the most influential interest group, the land-owning aristocracy, against whose wishes the agrarian laws could never have been drawn up, the new legislation promised several benefits: the abolition of seigneurial duties concerning the legal protection of peasants, the removal of burdensome obligations and improved efficiency by the use of wage labour, but, above all, an increase in directly disposable land. Here the late-absolutist state came to the aid of its main pillar of political support on a massive scale by providing subsidised credit banks and tax benefits. The peasants, on the other hand, received no support before 1850 and had to purchase their freedom dearly. It was only through cash payments or by ceding land that they could free themselves from the legal claims of the ruling landlords, and many of them were too poor to do this. The system of large-scale agricultural enterprises which gradually arose at the expense of peasant ownership, especially east of the river Elbe (between 1811 and 1890 the area occupied by the great estates here increased by two-thirds!), and which also drew most benefit from the new methods of cultivation and rationalisation, proved able not only to provide tolerably well for a rapidly growing population, but was also increasingly capable of channelling agricultural produce into the far more lucrative export trade, particularly to England after the abolition of the Corn Laws in 1846. These export-orientated large-scale agricultural producers viewed Free Trade as the most desirable foreign trade policy. In contrast, 'protective tariffs were seen in feudal circles as a mistaken policy of the urban bourgeoisie against whom they were struggling'.[2] The prosperity which emerged in the early 1840s can be gauged not only from the pricing of agricultural produce. Land prices also rose threefold in the five decades before 1875. The quantitative effect of the changes which had taken place is also evidenced by the fact that Prussian arable land under cultivation doubled in the fifty years between 1816 and 1866 (from 26.5 per cent to 51.4 per cent of the entire land surface area). Uncultivated land shrank in the same period from 40.3 per cent to 7.1 per cent; and while the yield from increased agricultural land rose from 100 index points to 194, the population grew 'merely' from 100 to 173.[3] A surge of productivity lay behind this visible achievement in the supply and export of produce which, according to Hans Rosenberg, brought the land owners to 'the historical peak of their economic power' between 1840 and 1876. This was accompanied by an increase in their purchasing power. The agrarian market became more capable of absorbing commercial and industrial products and increased its capacity for capital saving. The accumulation of capital from export earnings directly benefited agriculture with its continual need for capital. At the same time, the agrarian sector, chiefly no doubt through its accumulation of private wealth, earnings from international trade and increased tax yields, contributed indirectly to the formation of capital for Germany's early industrial enterprises. It required only the ingenious legal device of the joint-stock

---

2. G. Schmoller, *Charakterbilder*, Munich, 1913, p. 49.
3. G. Ipsen, 'Die preussische Bauernbefreiung als Landesausbau', in *Zeitschrift für Agrargeschichte*, vol. 2, 1954, p. 47; F. Lütge, *Geschichte der deutschen Agrarverfassung vom frühen Mittelalter bis zum 19. Jh.*, Stuttgart, 1963, 2nd imp. 1967, p. 228.

company to channel these capital resources into industrial investments.

Finally, to single out one final important consequence: the qualitative changes in legal relationships (for example, the transition from
rents paid in labour to individual land-ownership, from servitude or
even hereditary serfdom to formal legal independence, from labour
services to wage labour, from the inherited legal status of tied labour
to the abolition in particular of the *Junker* right to sanction peasant
marriages) liberated an enormous demographic growth in those
strata of small tenant farmers no longer bound to the soil. This was
especially true of the north-east of Germany. Prussia's population,
for example, grew by 37 per cent between 1815 and 1840, and by 26
per cent, from 25 to 38 million, between 1840 and 1860. Because of
the negligible increase in the number of vacancies available in the
traditional occupations, together with their diminished value caused
by surplus labour, hundreds of thousands of Germans emigrated in
the years before 1850. As many as 2 million left in the years between
1850 and 1870. As well as this, many more poured into the new
industrial centres and conurbations where they formed a reservoir
of a mobile and initially unskilled labour force which the factory
system increasingly needed alongside its skilled craftsmen. Population growth, increased consumption, capital accumulation, urbanisation and internal migration were thus closely linked functionally
with the agrarian revolution. For this reason the success of this
revolution was one of the essential preconditions of the German
industrial revolution.

The loosening of the old feudal ties reached its culmination only
after the shock of the 1848 revolution. Between 1811 and 1848 some
70,000 Prussian peasants had achieved emancipation by ceding land
and a further 170,000 by cash payments. But between 1850 and 1865
as many as 640,000 bought their freedom from 6.3 million days of
service at the plough and 23.4 million days of manual work.
Whereas previously only the landowners had been able to rely on
financial help (from their own credit institutes established for the
nobility by Frederick II), new state-owned mortgage banks now
provided assistance for the peasants. However, these also increased
the mobile capital at the disposal of the great landowners, as did the
peasants' mortgage redemption payments. Since 1807 the landowners had been transformed as a result of the legal changes from 'an
hereditary nobility to an aristocracy based on the ownership of land
which could be disposed of at will, a mobile economic class of

owners of capital, estate managers and employers'. Yet the nucleus
of the old nobility within this group continued to form 'at the same
time, an exclusive feudal professional estate' which after 1849 continued to enjoy the privilege of assistance from the state. A new law
on entailed estates was introduced in 1852. In the following year the
Prussian Upper House became an aristocratic preserve, and the first
steps towards regional administrative autonomy were shelved for
what was to be the next forty years. In 1856 the landowners had
their police powers renewed. Of the 12,339 estates in that year,
whose owners were eligible to sit in local and district assemblies,
7,023 latifundia of over 5,000 hectares still belonged entirely to the
nobility.

However slowly the 'transformation of the landed aristocracy
into a modern entrepreneurial class of agricultural businessmen'
may have crept along — by 1885 only 13 per cent of East Prussian
estates had been in the same family for over fifty years — the
traditional ruling elite of the land-owning aristocracy, which was
prominently represented in the army officer corps and the civil
service, still defended its social and political privileges as vehemently and effectively as it did its economic interests. *Junker* estates
remained completely exempt from basic land taxes up until 1861,
and Free Trade was kept for agricultural exports up until 1879.[4] The
aristocracy also enjoyed direct access to the Court as one of the
formal centres of decision-making. Thanks to its unthreatened
predominance in the upper echelons of the ministerial bureaucracy,
the diplomatic service and the army, it controlled the three main
pillars of the post-1848 German state, and thus the levers of power
together with the essential instruments for its defence. Without the
economic base provided by the agrarian revolution this reassertion
of their old position as political masters would have been scarcely
conceivable. Economically successful, despite the revolutionary
upheaval of 1848, and once again socially and politically relatively
secure in the saddle, the ruling nobility went forward into the 1860s.
The successes and achievements of the Prussian military state and
Bismarck's policies were, therefore, to benefit a prospering pre-
industrial élite. Accustomed to prestige and the exercise of power,
and with the doubts raised by the 1848 revolution now suppressed,

4. Foregoing quotations from H. Rosenberg, 'Die Pseudodemokratisierung der
    Rittergutsbesitzerklasse', in his *Probleme*, pp. 33, 12, 16f.

it acceded first place to the bourgeoisie only in the sphere of the industrial economy.

The Industrial Revolution and the Urban Bourgeoisie

As in the agrarian sector, the early stages of Germany's industrialisation to some extent followed a course of natural, unchecked development. However, it was also partly a result of deliberately planned measures aimed at modernisation. These were, moreover, designed to serve the self-assertion and pursuit of success of those ruling groups which controlled the state after the hiatus of 1807–15. From the very beginning model workshops under the state's direction, together with state-aided enterprises, were to provide an important impetus, since these possessed modern machinery and received long-term commissions, underwriting guarantees and other benefits. They formed isolated islands of economic planning in a gradually expanding sea of emergent private industry. In the early 1840s industrial growth rates climbed sharply, but because of the crisis in agriculture and commerce between 1845 and 1847, the revolution of 1848–9 and the post-war depression up to 1850, the breakthrough of Germany's industrial revolution can only be dated with any degree of certainty to the beginning of the 1850s. By 'revolution' is meant, following conventional usage, a rapid, hectic and short-lived process. It does not mean a development spanning more than a hundred years, which is how the term 'industrial revolution' is often misleadingly used in popular media jargon, rather than the more precise 'industrialisation'. The question, therefore, of arriving at some form of periodisation to define an important phase in the overall development of this process becomes especially urgent. Which criteria can one employ to justify singling out 'the specific compression of industrialisation processes into periods of rapid growth' (Gerschenkron)[5] from the undeniably continuous development of the whole?

The economy is a process of social interaction. It follows therefore that social criteria determine whether the means of production are deployed and utilised in such a way as to result in the emergence of the historically specific example of industrial capitalism. The

5. Gerschenkron, p. 62.

social structure and social norms of behaviour permit modern technology and factory production methods to assert themselves. Fundamental technical advances, the replacement of human skills and manpower by machinery, improvements in the manufacture of materials by machine-made tools, and so forth, possess a latent revolutionary potential which is released only when certain social conditions prevail. These decide whether the system of political authority is reproduced in the work-place, whether unenlightened despotism may be imitated with the government's blessing and whether firms may become places purely for the pursuit of profit. They also decide whether the willingness exists to transform innovations resulting from empirical craftsmanship and scientific invention into lasting technological advances, and whether the industrial work-force can be recruited and disciplined to suit new industrial work-methods. This crucial process of creating a reservoir of trained labour, together with expanding foreign and domestic markets and encouraging capital accumulation, has never occurred anywhere without the assistance of the state functioning as part of the social structure. We can indicate these fundamental advance decisions only in passing and need not concern ourselves with details of other important, though as yet partly undefined, factors governing the pace of rapid industrialisation, for example, changes in cultural norms and the social prestige of the entrepreneur, the growth of innovation, changes in the technical processes themselves, legal privileges conferred on capital and its owners (whereas labour for a long time was not deemed a property worthy of legal protection) and the idea of risk-taking (with its reward of material gain) applied solely to capital and not to the work-place or the erosion of workers' energies. Regarding such preconditions, let it only be said here that they appear to have been sufficiently realised in Germany by the middle of the nineteenth century. Favourable social, institutional and psychological conditions were, therefore, either already in existence or were soon created to speed up decisively the process of modernisation.

If we concentrate solely on specifically economic criteria, we can take as our starting-point the existing consensus of research into economic growth and economic history. According to this, at least three phenomena lie at the core of the industrial economy (leaving aside the agrarian sector). Firstly, an abrupt increase in GNP leading to a rise in per capita income. Secondly, an extraordinary rise in the growth rates of key, or 'strategic' industries (represented in graph form as Gerschenkron's 'kink in the curve'). Thirdly, an increase in net investment in the national economy of approximately 10 to 12 per cent of the net national product.

On the basis of these preliminary factors we may conclude in the case of Germany's development that up until 1850 social changes, legal reforms, institutional changes — both natural and deliberately planned — economic growth imitating foreign models, half-hearted encouragement by the state and long-term political aims all worked together to build up the conditions which enabled the onset of the industrial revolution. The first prosperity period of this revolution asserted itself with considerable force in the years before 1857. The growth rates for industry and the economy as a whole shot upwards. The level of investment and consumer goods production doubled. Foreign trade expanded by 130 per cent. The estimated annual net rate of investment climbed to 8, then 10, and even reached 12 per cent, before levelling off in 1873. The key industries of iron, mining and engineering also showed a marked advance. The value of pig-iron production in the Prussian-led Customs Union (*Zollverein*), which grew by 250 per cent, increased from 24 million marks in 1848 to 66 million in 1857; that of coal production, which grew by 138 per cent, from 25 to 62 million, and that of iron-ore and coal-mining together went up from 45 to 135 million marks. Railway construction, too, proved to be a crucially important leading sector in Germany's industrialisation. Between 1850 and 1860 the network doubled in size from 6,000 to 11,500 kilometres. German engineering firms were already able to gain the lion's share (more than two-thirds) of contracts to supply locomotives and rolling stock. In 1858 the Berlin firm of Borsig delivered its thousandth locomotive. The knock-on effect from this leading sector pulled iron and coal production, engineering and countless other supply industries along with it. Freight traffic on the Prussian railways increased sevenfold.

From 1857 to 1859 this economic development was, however, interrupted by the first world economic crisis, which affected Germany as it did other countries. Thereafter her economy recovered and the revival continued until the brief recession of 1866. It underwent further expansion between 1866 and 1873, entering into an unprecedented prosperity period which was to end with the onset of the second world-wide economic crisis. In 1866 a million tons of pig-iron were produced. In 1870 the figure was 1.5 million, and by 1873 it had risen to 2.2 million tons. Coal production climbed between 1860 and 1870 by 114 per cent to 26 million tons, or double the volume of French output. During this decade the railway network almost doubled in size to 19,500 kilometres, then between 1870 and 1875 by as much again to 28,000 kilometres. Between 1850 and 1870 the volume of rail freight traffic increased twenty-one times over, as measured by tonnage per kilometre. This branch of the transport industry remained the most important industrial 'leading sector' and forged ahead for three decades, pulling along the development of other branches of industry by its 'backward' and 'forward linkages'.

Annual productivity measured in man-hours increased between 1850 and 1860 by 8.5 per cent, and from 1860 to 1870, owing to improved technology, by as much as 42 per cent. The increase in nominal wages in the 1850s did not, however, lead as yet to a lasting improvement in real wages. This was because of a sharp rise in the price of essential consumer items. Potatoes went up in price by 125 per cent between 1850 and 1855, rye by 150 per cent and wheat by 100 per cent! Between 1866 and 1873, however, the cost of living failed to catch up with wages, so that in terms of real wages workers' incomes eventually did show an appreciable increase.[6]

During the 1860s the new industrial labour force, continuing its older tradition of combining in associations, began to organise itself into political parties and early forms of trade unions. After a short period of rivalry Lassalle's Workers' Associations merged with Bebel's and Liebknecht's Eisenach Party to form in 1875 at Gotha the Socialist Workers' Party (*Sozialistische Arbeiterpartei*) in which Marx's theories of the class struggle and the emancipation of the working class eventually came to dominate. By the end of the industrial revolution in Germany, therefore, the workers had a political mouthpiece which sought to unite all members of the same social class for the political and social conflicts to come. A break with bourgeois liberalism had already taken place as a result of irreconcilable conflicts of interest. Helped by the upswing of the business cycle, industrial workers successfully influenced the out-

6. T. Hamerow, *Restoration, Revolution, Reaction: Economics and Politics in Germany, 1815–71*, Princeton, NJ, 1958, pp. 207, 210; A. Desai, *Real Wages in Germany, 1871–1913*, Oxford, 1968, pp. 108, 117; I. Akerman, *Theory of Industrialism*, Lund, 1960, pp. 305, 307, 309, 311, 331–80. Economic and social statistical data, unless otherwise stated, from W. G. Hoffmann *et al.*, *Das Wachstum der deutschen Wirtschaft*, Heidelberg, 1965. The figures for strikes from W. Steglich, 'Eine Streiktabelle für Deutschland, 1864-80', in *Jahrbuch für Wirtschaftsgeschichte*, 1960, vol. II, pp. 235–83.

come of industrial conflicts in their favour by the increasing use of the strike weapon. Between 1864 and 1873 there were 903 strikes; 188 took place in 1871, followed by 215 in 1872 and as many as 255 in 1873, that is, a total of 631 in the first three years of the German Empire's existence. Here, too, the pattern for modern conflicts over the distribution of the national product and efforts to realise greater equality became visible. The propertied and educated middle classes, among whom there had been talk of a 'red menace' since the period before 1848, viewed these conflicts, in the main, as the harbinger of an impending social revolution.

If one takes the British industrial revolution as the classic pioneer model, the German variant was forced to find its own home-grown solutions to emulate England's original achievements, since these could not be brought about in the same form in Germany. The large German banks which emerged in the 1850s and 1860s took on the function in Germany of supplying the wealth of capital that had been available to British industry from the City of London. From the outset they combined two activities usually separated in England: commercial banking and long-term industrial financing. As all-purpose banks (*Universalbanken*) they became, according to Gerschenkron, 'a strategic factor in Germany's industrialisation'; they mobilised investment capital by issuing stocks and channelling it into industry. They also coordinated the founding of new heavy industry and soon controlled important sectors of the economy by acting as a substitute for private economic planning. In this way they contributed to Germany overcoming its relative economic backwardness; at the same time they came together in the early phase of bank concentration to form a powerful oligarchy of high-finance. By regulating government loans via the 'Prussian consortium' of large banks, they were able to determine the general course of Germany's economic development to a considerable extent. From the early 1870s the so-called D-banks (the Disconto Gesellschaft, Deutsche Bank, Dresdener Bank and Darmstädter Bank) set the tone. These are the historical facts behind the development which gave rise to the concept of 'finance capital'.

One further factor which enabled Germany to catch up on the prolific technological development in England was created in the long term by the determined expansion of the education system. This placed human capital at the disposal of the economy on an astonishing scale. True, the German grammar schools and universities remained committed to the principles of the humanist-educated élite, a fact which scarcely prepared their *alumni* for the economic struggle of everyday life. But there soon existed a close connection between cameralist studies (i.e. economics and jurisprudence) or political science and the industrial economy. Here one need think only of names like Unruh, Hammacher, Miquel and Bamberger among others. Moreover, the larger German states had also founded educational institutes for the technical and engineering sciences as well as commercial colleges from the early 1820s onwards. Beuth's Technical Institute in Berlin dated from 1821. Following the French example, the polytechnics of Karlsruhe, Munich and Stuttgart were founded in 1825, 1827 and 1832 respectively. These were followed by the Technical College in Dresden in 1828. To these can be added the professional and vocational schools set up to transmit craft skills. Viewed *in toto*, these were the establishments that produced the experts, the technical cadres which gave further impetus to the process of industrialisation after the 1850s. Although little is known in detail about the way scientific knowledge develops to the point where it becomes an economically productive resource, or about educational investment and its effects, the systematic exploitation of scientific knowledge became so evident that, up to the watershed of the 1890s, the process of industrial economic growth, which depended on technological innovation, relied to a steadily increasing extent upon the practical application of scientific research. The lack of a national domestic market prior to 1871, which might compare with Great Britain's opportunities for foreign trade, was overcome in 1834 with the creation of the Prussian-inspired Customs Union. The significance of this 'package' of 130 bilateral and multilateral treaties, in force during the century between 1819 and 1918, has admittedly been overrated. On the other hand, it should not be regarded as unimportant, for it was an essential precondition of Germany's successful industrialisation. For its member states the Customs Union was, thanks to its rising revenue and shrinking administrative costs, a financially lucrative venture. It promoted a standardisation of law and a uniform currency by means of monetary conventions and a new commercial code. It concluded advantageous trade treaties, provided tariff protection against external competition, as well as duty-free river traffic and a low tariff area in the home market. All of these measures provided strong stimuli for long-term economic development. Prussia, as its leading member, remained undeniably the main beneficiary of this Customs Union and its policies from the 1820s onwards. As early as 1829 a French diplomat in Munich described it in grandiose terms as 'one of the most significant events since the Reformation'. In this 'gigantic system', Prussia would achieve unprecedented power. Metternich was also in no doubt that 'its decisive result' would be 'Prussia's predominance'; he added that a new 'second, smaller confederation' was emerging within the German Confederation 'which was a state within the state in the fullest sense of the term, and which would become accustomed only too soon to pursuing its own aims with its own methods'.[7] This remark hit the nail on the head. Vienna made no serious attempt to destroy this rival. Twice, however, Austria attempted to force her way in, once under Bruck and Schwarzenberg after the 1848 revolution, but with no greater result than the trade treaty of 1853 which it took a quarter of a century to achieve. Negotiations on joining dragged on until 1860. By and large, this successful stroke of Berlin's economic policy made up in full for Prussia's diplomatic reverse at Olmütz in 1850. The Franco-Prussian Treaty of 1862 confirmed Prussian supremacy before Austria's renewed approach under Rechberg between 1862 and 1865 failed once again. The Habsburg Empire lost out in this competition, and not only in terms of its trade. Since the breakthrough of the industrial revolution in Prussia had already taken place, this state also possessed an incomparable dynamism and enjoyed a superior lead over Austria in terms of industrial growth. It was not without good reason that, ten years after their failure, anti-Prussian liberals who had favoured the inclusion of Austria in a unified Germany now looked upon Prussia as the genuinely modern state of the Confederation's two rivals. One must beware, however, of drawing an inevitable and straight line between the Customs Union and the German Empire of 1871. The scope for new political and military trials of strength was still very limited. The lead that Prussia had gained as an industrial state was still precarious and not universally acknowledged. With hindsight, however, it can be seen that the industrial revolution had enabled her to make the decisive leap forward towards the continuous development of a permanently expanding economic system whose secular, long-term trend was one of sustained, albeit uneven, economic growth.

7. *Chargé* de Rumigny, 4. 4. 1829, in P. Benaerts, *Les origines de la grande industrie allemande*, Paris, 1933, p. 15.; Metternich's memorandum for the Emperor Franz, June 1833, in A. von Klinkowström (ed.), *Aus Metternichs Nachgelassenen Papieren*, vol. V, Vienna, 1882, pp. 505, 509.

Domestic Politics: Reactionaries, Liberalism and the Constitutional Conflict

Of the two social classes that promoted this development, the bourgeoisie and the working class, the bourgeoisie had
suffered defeat in its attempt in 1848 to gain a joint share of political
power. Nowhere in Germany had it tried to gain complete power
and its defeat had the effect of a lasting shock. Marx's 'third
fundamental class',[8] that is, the land-owners, particularly the aristocracy, re-asserted itself. Since, however, the masses were also on
the move — cases of unrest among journeymen revealed the demands of the newly-created proletariat — the major conservative
laws of the 1850s, designed to stabilise the political system, clearly
bore 'the stamp of victorious reactionary politics'; this is how the
conservative writer, Hermann Wagener, put it when he trium-
phantly commented on the consolidation of *Junker* rule.[9] These
laws combined with a paternalistic policy to compensate the subordinate sections of society. Driven by a sense of necessity, those
social groups performing a leadership role adopted a series of social
welfare measures to benefit the peasantry, artisans, industrial workers and their children. Another thirty years were to pass before they
would again be forced to make comparable concessions. A policy of
internal political repression and efforts by the authorities to redress
several serious social ills were the peculiarly contrasting accompani-
ments to a rapid liberalisation in the economy which released a good
deal of those energies that flowed into industry and the advance-
ment of the bourgeoisie. Following the abortive revolution of 1848,
the transition to a 'New Era' of liberal government under Kaiser
Wilhelm of Prussia was proclaimed. It was, therefore, only to be
expected that the economically successful, albeit politically hetero-
genous, industrial bourgeoisie would once more voice its political
aspirations in concert with 'progressive' businessmen, civic leaders,
artisans and civil servants — in short, middle-class groups. Although it was not brought about by design, the quarrel which began
over the Prussian army reforms grew into a conflict revolving
around the constitution. It led eventually to a new trial of strength
between bourgeois parliamentarianism and the absolutist military

8. MEW, vol. 13, pp. 639, 642. The term 'class' is understood as an analytical
   category throughout this section.
9. *Stenographische Berichte über die Verhandlungen des Preussischen Hauses der
   Abgeordneten, 1855–56*, vol. II, p. 462 (20.2. 1856).

state. And once again the bourgeoisie was defeated. That is why the 'Constitutional Conflict' marks the second great turning-point in Prussia's domestic politics and, consequently, in German history as a whole, since almost two-thirds of the German Empire was later absorbed by her. The outcome of this conflict was to seal the political impotence of the bourgeoisie up until 1918.

The confrontation took shape in 1860 when a new law was laid before the Diet to enable the already approved plans of von Roon's War Ministry to be implemented. These involved a technical reorganisation of the army; but they also contained more than this. While an increase in the strength of the peacetime army went uncontested, the proposed legal provision for a three-year term of compulsory military service for an annual intake of 63,000 recruits, as against 40,000 previously, proved to be a stumbling block. The proposal was seen as an issue involving internal social control, since it was a step towards the further militarisation of society. Secondly, the national militia (*Landwehr*) was to be weakened radically in favour of the regular army; this was tantamount to destroying the genuine citizen army of the Scharnhorst–Boyen reforms. While the Prussian Diet approved the additional expenditure involved, differences of opinion between the War Ministry and the majority faction of so-called 'Old Liberals' proved irreconcilable on the questions of length of military service and the fate of the national militia. Using skilful tactics, the military *camarilla* played up the conflict into the alternatives of an army under the control of the monarch or of the Diet. It brought about a situation in which the Crown declared the reform subject to the absolutist executive power of the 'Supreme War-lord'. Based on constitutional feudal rights and beyond the control of representative institutions, this denied the need for any form of legal control. In a quite undisguised fashion the military was to be kept free of any middle-class parliamentary influence. Henceforth, the fundamental issue of defence and, therefore, the position of the army in the state, involving the political constitution in the widest sense, stood at the centre of the debate. The military realised at an early stage the conflict of principles involved. Given the mentality of the professional soldier at the apex of the state hierarchy, they made maximum capital out of it. In the course of the controversy the 'Old Liberal' majority in the Diet collapsed. The new Prussian Progressive Party (*Deutsche Fortschrittspartei*), which now emerged, was returned in the December elections of 1861 as the largest political grouping and included in its ranks a large number of liberal civil servants. In March 1862 liberal ministers were removed from the government, which was now completely dominated by von Roon. New compromise proposals put forward by the Diet, which was anything but belligerent in its approach, failed because of the monarch's opposition, whereupon it withheld its approval of the 1863 budget. The Kaiser seriously considered abdicating at this point. His son was widely regarded as a liberal and so, for a short time, it seemed that a victory for the parliamentary majority might be possible. Now the choice suddenly appeared to be between a constitutional monarchy, on the one hand, and a quasi-dictatorship based on plebiscitary approval, on the other. In point of fact the attempt to achieve parliamentary control was prevented and the monarchy itself was to be eroded in the course of the next few decades. But the legacy of recourse to a charismatic dictator legitimised by plebiscitary approval was to remain.

In 1862 the representatives of the military state thought neither of abandoning nor of partially conceding their position. In the autumn of 1862, amid a situation of acute crisis which they had quite clearly engineered, they put forward the only candidate of the extreme conservative, ultra-royalist and outright absolutist clique for the office of Prussian Prime Minister. This was Otto von Bismarck, of whom the Prussian King had prophesied in 1848 that he was to be used only when the bayonet freely reigned. Against this background of the Constitutional Conflict, the defence of the threatened military state and the preservation of its social and political power structure, Bismarck stepped into the centre of the decision-making process of German politics as, in the words of Manfred Messerschmidt, 'the stabiliser of monarchical power'. For the next thirty years he was to fight vehemently and with staggering success on behalf of the groups that lent him support, groups representing the old Prussia and its ruling élites against the forces of social and political progress. But the consequences were to prove completely disastrous in the long run for the majority of Germany's population.

So far as an electorate, which could be mobilised for an election turn-out of at most 50 per cent, articulated political views at all, a clear majority of voters favoured liberal policies. In 1862 the Conservatives formed a small minority, but a powerful one. Above all, their government controlled 'all the instruments of organised power'.[10] Bismarck, finding himself at last in the most important

10. E. N. Anderson, *The Social and Political Conflict in Prussia, 1858–64*. Lincoln,

position in the political apparatus, was not a man who was averse to applying these in domestic and foreign policy. It is sometimes forgotten that he carried out a harsh policy of repression against the liberals in domestic politics. Imprisonment, deportation, press cen- sorship and intimidation by the courts were all devices he made good use of as the new head of government. He never underesti- mated his main opponents, the liberals. He would even have joined hands with Lassalle's Workers' Associations against the progressive liberals had the former been a real power factor. These genuine liberals were still his arch-enemies a quarter of a century later. Since they believed it was impossible to govern a state based on the rule of law without a budget approved by parliament, Bismarck's govern- ment now resorted to the 'gap' theory of the Prussian constitution. This meant, in the government's view, that in the event of failure to reach agreement on legislation, the traditional prerogative of the Crown to make the final decision allowed the government to continue to rule in accordance with the terms of the last regular budget. The ample flow of tax revenue, brought about by the rise in economic prosperity, would even permit a generous management of the economy; and while the dispute over the constitution con- tinued with unremitting bitterness, the representatives of the bourgeoisie displayed their schizophrenia in pursuing their own interests. Often in the self-same parliamentary sitting the economic policy of Bismarck's government, which was one of outright liberal Free Trade, was as unreservedly approved and sanctioned in law as its approach to domestic affairs was roundly, though ineffectually, condemned. Yet it is not certain how this conflict in internal politics would have ended had not Bismarck, while observing his maxim that 'as long as we gain respect abroad, we can get away with a great deal at home', shown also his equally dubious 'skill for running internal politics on the steam-power of foreign affairs' (Oncken). The prophecy of the conservative *Kreuzzeitung* newspaper on Bismarck's assumption to office, to the effect that he would 'over- come domestic difficulties by a bold foreign policy',[11] was soon fulfilled.

Neb., 1954, p. 441; M. Messerschmidt, 'Die Armee in Staat und Gesellschaft', in *Das Kaiserliche Deutschland*, ed. M. Stürmer, Düsseldorf, 1970, p. 95.

11. O. von Bismarck, GW, vol. XV, p. 165, cf. p. 114; H. Oncken, R. *von Bennigsen*, vol. II, Stuttgart, 1910, p. 45; G. Ritter, *Die preussischen Konservati- ven und Bismarcks deutsche Politik, 1858–76*, Heidelberg, 1913, p. 74.

Wars for Hegemony and 'Revolution from Above'

After skilful diplomatic preparations, which if viewed as a technical masterpiece can still be admired, Bismarck in 1864 involved Prussia's Habsburg rival in a combined war against Denmark over the Schleswig-Holstein question. Since 1848 the acquisition of these duchies had been an agreed aim of German nationalists from the liberals' programme right through to the political left. During the discussions concerning the only serious military engagement in the war, the storming of the fortifications at Düppel by Prussian units, Bismarck's strategy revealed itself quite clearly. For weeks the attack was the subject of argument; the commanders in the field could see no necessity for taking the fort. But Bismarck, along with von Roon, the War Minister, insisted stubbornly and in the end successfully on the attack in order to gain from the prestige which a favourable outcome would bring in the country at large. Indeed, 'the announcement of victory electrified Prussia' and inflamed nationalism to the point where it undermined 'liberal opposition to absolutism on the home front'. Even before Berlin and Vienna had established their brief condominium over the duchies, the constitutional principles of the progressive liberals began to melt away. This confirmed Lassalle's suspicion that the liberals had used the Schleswig-Holstein issue 'to divert attention from the internal situation and, under the guise of patriotism, to avoid having to solve a conflict for which they were no match'.[12]

The outcome of the bloody civil war in which Bismarck's Prussia expelled Austria from the German Confederation in 1866 at Sadowa, or Königgrätz, was by no means a foregone conclusion. Despite the meticulous planning of the General Staff under Moltke, victory for Prussia emerged only during the course of the battle itself. Bismarck was able to say without exaggeration that a defeat would have made his fall from power inevitable. Instead, this second successful war brought about the moral collapse of the progressive liberals in North Germany. Apart from those few of their number around Eugen Richter, who saw the need for a liberal-constitutional state as more necessary than ever, continued liberal insistence on its realisation was soon regarded as intransigence. A swing-round to the victorious government camp became

12. G. A. Craig, *Die preussisch-deutsche Armee, 1640–1954*, Düsseldorf, 1960, p. 214; F. Lassalle, *Gesammelte Reden und Schriften*, ed. E. Bernstein, vol. IV, Berlin, 1919, pp. 307f.

the order of the day. This is not hard to understand of a movement unaccustomed to power and responsibility, which had been defeated in 1848. But the hollow triumph of a sheer unprincipled pragmatism (*Realpolitik*), which often degenerated into an unprincipled accomodation with the power of a formerly detested opponent, broke the moral backbone of many liberals, or unsettled them to the point where they began to question the best beliefs that had guided them in the past.

Bismarck, who was shrewder than short-sighted right-wing conservatives, now agreed to make a sham concession to the liberals. He introduced an Indemnity Bill which retrospectively approved government policy since 1862. Did this, as some believed at the time and long after, solve the Constitutional Conflict? The answer must be no. Bismarck achieved only a 'procrastinatory compromise formula'[13] which concealed basic conflicts of interest for a time but did not settle the crucial issue of a modernisation of the constitution. Instead, a solution to this problem was postponed for almost sixty years. This tactically brilliant manoeuvre represented, therefore, a barely-veiled victory for the old regime. The nucleus of the authoritarian state in which the military enjoyed autonomy remained essentially intact. The newly created North German Confederation with its pseudo-parliamentary trimmings was formed around this core as the distinctly recognisable prelude to the formation of a German national state along the lines of a 'Greater Prussia'.

For a third time Bismarck succeeded 'in engineering a war at a precise juncture which suited his plans'.[14] The nervous suspicion that had been harboured in Paris for years towards the rise of Prussia was well known, especially to Bismarck, and so were the conceivable consequences. It was roused to a clumsy declaration of war by the provocative Hohenzollern candidature for the Spanish throne and Bismarck's exploitation of French mistakes of protocol. The victory over France in 1871 relieved the Chancellor of all anxieties concerning the affiliation of the South German states and, hence, the expansion of the North German Confederation into a unified Germany excluding Austria. It also removed his anxieties over a prolongation of the 'iron' army law. This law, which accounted for 95 per cent of the Confederation's expenditure and

13. Rosenberg (*Probleme*, p. 52), following C. Schmitt, *Verfassungslehre* (1928), 2nd imp., Berlin, 1957, pp. 31f., 118.
14. H. Rothfels, 'Probleme einer Bismarck-Biographie', *Deutsche Beiträge*, 1948, vol. II, p. 170 (adapted). Typically diluted in his *Bismarck*, Stuttgart, 1970, p. 20.

virtually paralysed parliamentary control, was due for renewal in December 1871. One need have no doubt that in its final phase the short-lived liberal Empire of Napoleon III diverted attention away from its own internal difficulties towards foreign policy by means of Bonapartist policies. But these ran up against the equally Bonapartist and coolly-calculated long-term policies of his Berlin counterpart. Certainly, Bismarck held several irons in the fire. He never aimed for war as the only possible course open to him; but only a peaceful solution to the problem of German unification in 1870 would have testified to 'genuine statesmanship' on his part, and no one has ever maintained that Bismarck 'applied his ingenuity to avoid war'.[15] The German Empire of 1871 emerged from this new gamble; a Prussian policy of calculated risk had paid off again. To invoke the generally accepted formula that at this time war was still a legitimate, or at least generally acceptable, means of resolving conflicts between states, and that Bismarck had merely carried out three such 'duels' in an astonishingly short space of time, does nothing to explain the crucial function of this continuation of an aggressive diplomacy by 'other means'. Quite apart from the question of whether Prussia's aims in Germany could ever have been realised without exchanging blows with its rival, two main motives have to be considered because of their effect on decisions taken within the *arcana imperii* of Berlin's policies:

(1) There is no evidence at all that these three wars for Prussian hegemony were determined strictly by economic interests. What cannot be denied easily, however, is that they were used as devices to legitimise the prevailing political system against the striving for social and political emancipation of the middle classes, or even the proletariat, a process which was partly determined by economic developments. Certainly, so far as their initiators were concerned these wars produced their desired effect. Jacob Burckhardt, whose sceptical judgement on other matters was highly regarded in Germany, recognised quite clearly, as early as 1871, that 'the three wars were waged for internal political reasons. For seven years we enjoyed and took advantage of the fact that the whole world believed that only Louis Napoleon fought wars for reasons of internal politics. Purely from the point of view of self-preservation, it was high time to wage these three wars in order to deal with internal problems'.[16] As initially proclaimed in glaring terms by the

15. G. Mann, *Deutsche Geschichte des 19. Jhs*, Frankfurt, 1958, p. 383.
16. Burckhardt to Preen, 12. 10. and 17. 3. 1871, in J. Burckhardt, *Briefe*, ed.

1848 revolution, confirmed by the constitutional conflict and underlined by the organisational success of labour, the industrial revolution had not only set society irrevocably in motion by stimulating political demands, but had begun to destroy the late-feudal power structure based on estates. It had given rise to irrepressible doubts about the system of inherited privilege and brought about a 'revolution of rising expectations'. In view of the strength of these developments the traditional strategy of 'taming' the forces in question could no longer be achieved successfully. The immediate and, even more so, the indirect consequences of the industrial revolution required the use of extraordinary methods by the groups which had traditionally held power in society. Since they possessed in Bismarck a political potential *sui generis* — and anyone who does not hold the view that 'men make history' will have to concede this — they were prepared to risk three wars as an almost desperate therapy for stabilising the monarchical system. The victorious outcome of these wars produced the desired effect. The authoritarian social and political system was once more legitimised. From then on one was able to feed on the massively prestigious success of Bismarck's diplomacy and the Prussian military. The internal crisis appeared defused. The main opponents, the National Liberals, succumbed, as desired, to the effects of this pacification carried out by the militant methods.

(2) The men of central government in Berlin, with an eye to the future, were fully aware that an expansion of Greater Prussia would fulfil the liberal bourgeoisie's desire for a unified nation state. It would also provide the best possible solution to the problem of uniting Germany while excluding Austria. The Austrian defeat in the German 'civil war' and the creation of the North German Confederation confirmed these calculations. The opinion was often enough expressed that a war fought in a common cause would soon overcome any resistance by the South German states to a Prussian-dominated Germany. It was also bound to have the effect of uniting the nation. 'To unite Germany by using force against France' was a goal which Moltke envisaged as attainable in 1866. And this is precisely what happened when during the Franco-Prussian War national passions supplied the powerful driving force behind the policy which culminated in the Empire's founding. Just as the

M. Burckhardt, vol. V, Basle, 1963, pp. 139, 152; similarly: Scrutator [M. McColl], *Who Is Responsible for the War?*, London, 1870, pp. 95, 102.

liberals had been brought to heel in the wars of 1864 and 1866, so too were the South German states by the war of 1870–1. This war, therefore, served a dual function. It was intended not only as 'a war of unification to round off the process begun by the Prussian war of secession in 1866'. It was intended, too, to cut short the fundamental political and social crisis of the Prussian military monarchy as 'a preventive war to achieve integration in internal politics'. This unification of Germany 'by the sword' and the overcoming of her internal problems by means of war had already been forecast as Prussia's mission by Clausewitz.[17] It cannot be denied that 'Bismarck's use of military force to solve the problem' of German unification was 'no less revolutionary than the liberal attempt of 1848. He broke once and for all with the old Empire's federalist tradition which had included Austria, and replaced it with a more limited nation state under Prussian hegemony and excluding Austria'.[18]

The conservative 'white revolutionary' in charge of Prussian policy was in this respect following the tradition of 'revolution from above'. He himself termed it a 'reform from above' and put it into practice using radical methods in its military phase. Shortly after the French Revolution the Prussian minister von Struensee had informed the French ambassador that 'the salutary revolution' which in France had proceeded 'from below upwards' would 'gradually develop from above downwards in Prussia'. By a policy of limited concessions the explosive revolutionary potential would be defused and a salutary transformation brought about by peaceful means. This 'revolution from above' had also been advocated in outline relatively early by Clausewitz. 'Europe cannot avoid a great general revolution', he wrote in 1809. 'Only those kings who know how to enter into the spirit of this great reformation and keep ahead of it will be able to survive.' Or, as his contemporary Gneisenau put it: 'Wise laws designed to forestall the outbreak of revolution are like detonating a mine laid under our feet from which we have removed the explosive bit by bit'. Long before Lorenz von Stein or Gustav

17. R. Stadelmann, *Moltke und der Staat*, Krefeld, 1950, p. 145; J. Becker, 'Zum Problem der Bismarckschen Politik in der spanischen Thronfrage', in HZ, no. 212, 1971, p. 603; and his 'Der Krieg mit Frankreich als Problem der kleindeutschen Einigungspolitik Bismarcks, 1866–70', in *Das Kaiserliche Deutschland*, p. 83. On Clausewitz, see Wehler, pp. 110–12.
18. W. Sauer, 'Die politische Geschichte der deutschen Armee und das Problem des Militarismus', in PVS, 6, 1965, p. 349. On the following, see also his 'Das Problem des deutschen Nationalstaats', in H.-U. Wehler (ed.), *Moderne deutsche Sozialgeschichte*, Cologne, 4th imp., 1973, pp. 407–36.

von Schmoller had popularised the idea of a 'social monarchy' the intervention of the Crown determined practice in Prussian politics. That is why Bismarck, with a self-confidence that came from many years of practising 'revolution from above', took the view that 'in Prussia only kings make revolutions'.[19] After the bureaucratic variant of this tactic had failed to defuse the mine in 1848 and the principle of compensating the bourgeoisie for its lack of political power with economic concessions had been continued during the period of reaction, the only permanently reliable guarantor of this policy in German national politics, internally and externally, was the army. In the early 1860s bourgeois liberalism again showed itself to be too weak, even if the dynamic of social developments had not lost its momentum, all traditional strategies to unify Germany without Austria had failed. It was at this point that the army, in its role of executor of Bismarck's plans and those of the traditional élites, cut through the Gordian knot of domestic and foreign affairs by unleashing three wars. Even if, in the absence of a long overdue examination of the Confederation's capacity for reform and its federalist plans, one holds to the view that Bismarck's 'blood and iron' solution was inevitable given the circumstances of the time, one can scarcely deny that, in the end, this conservative revolutionary's successes only served to exacerbate the permanent crisis of German society and politics.

After 1870 keen observers from quite diverse political camps recognised the facts of the situation only too clearly. Gustav Freytag, respected spokesman for the educated middle class of National Liberal persuasion, voiced his suspicion that 'we have achieved greatness. Now the means by which we acquired it are casting a shadow over our future. We shall all pay a price for it'. The underlying problem of whether the Greater Prussian imperial state could keep the peace better, or at least as well as, the destroyed German Confederation (for long regarded wrongly as being of secondary importance once national unity had been achieved), was also recognised by the Saxon diplomat, Alexander von Villers. Perhaps too much in the style of Metternich's intransigent attitude towards the liberals, and taking too little account of new social

19. GW, vol. V, pp. 514f.; Bismarck to Talleyrand, 13. 8. 1799, in P. Bailleu, *Preussen und Frankreich, 1795-1807. Diplomatische Correspondenzen*, Leipzig, 1881, p. 505; K. Schwartz, *Leben des Generals C. von Clausewitz*, vol. I, Berlin, 1878, p. 234 (21. 5. 1809); K. Griewank (ed.), *Gneisenau. Ein Leben in Briefen*, Leipzig, 1939, pp. 397f. (9., 14. 8. 1830); GW, vol. VIII, p. 459.

currents and driving forces within Prussia, he noted that

> the German Confederation, the last expression of statecraft in European
> diplomacy . . . had a defensive character. Within it Prussia was the
> aggressive yeast which set the well-kneaded dough in ferment. Germany
> not only lived at peace with her neighbours. She also acted as a brake
> upon every other European state that desired to break the peace interna-
> tionally. The only, albeit unavoidable, fault in this organism was the
> assumption that all its members possessed moral grandeur . . . Prussia
> had long let it be known that she would not let herself be outvoted by the
> others. On the day this was said, the Confederation should have stifled
> her for ever. But consideration was shown and, as a result, the Confeder-
> ation broke up.

In an impressive appeal to the Prussian Crown, the liberal academic
and publicist, G. G. Gervinus, who had democratic leanings, argued
movingly that

> the break-up of the German Confederation in 1866 has transformed
> two-thirds of the Empire into a state based on policies of war which is
> capable of aggression at any time. Without being an enemy of either
> Prussia or Germany, one can see in this a threat to peace in this part of
> the world and to the security of neighbouring states. . . . It is not a clever
> move to blind ourselves with patriotism to the fact that the events of 1866
> have revived and magnified to an unreasonable extent the danger to this
> part of the world and the entire epoch from a social and political order
> one had believed was dying out. After five centuries of desiring, striving,
> and hoping to outgrow the military system of earlier times . . . a power
> based on the permanent use of war has emerged with a frightening
> superiority of which the military states of previous centuries, bent on
> conquest and expansion, could never remotely have conceived. . . . This
> judgement on the situation would have been greatly scoffed at had it been
> expressed formerly. But after the experiences of 1870 one would not wish
> to question it. These events have rejuvenated this warrior state and have
> led inevitably to a rise in its self-esteem.

Was Karl Marx not also right when, after a similar analysis, he
sarcastically characterised the German Empire as 'a military despotism cloaked in parliamentary forms with a feudal ingredient and
at the same time influenced by the bourgeoisie, decked out by
bureaucrats, and safeguarded by the police'?[20]

20. Freytag (Sept. 1871) in H. Kohn, *Wege und Irrwege. Vom Geist des deutschen
    Bürgertums*, Düsseldorf, 1962, p. 178; A. von Villers, *Briefe eines Unbekannten*,
    vol. II, Leipzig, 5th imp., 1910, pp. 44f. (to A. von Warsberg, 24. 7. 1870); G. G.
    Gervinus, *Hinterlassene Schriften*, Vienna, 1872, pp. 21–3 (first memorandum
    on the peace at the beginning of 1871); Marx, *Kritik des Gothaer Programms*
    (1875), MEW, vol. 19, 1962, p. 29.

We shall return to this in more detail in connection with our analysis of the political system after 1871. What remains certain at any rate is that the policies of Bismarck's Prussia 'fled' forward in response to socio-economic and political pressures in order to stabilise and legitimise the state. As a result of three wars the Germans were given an Empire in the shape of a Greater Prussia which excluded Austria. It had been brought about by an extension of the 'revolution from above' using military means. The republican ideal of a 'people's state' appeared finally discredited. Perhaps the creation of a nation state by the liberal bourgeoisie could in fact have come about after a successful 'revolution from below'. This had been the view in the spring of 1848, not only in Germany but in England. Later, however, it became increasingly clear that the 'small leap' forward by the 'enlightened monarchical state' had led the nation without a revolution up a blind alley. In fact the administrative practice of this state, in conjunction with the idea of 'revolution from above', had for a long time 'proved sufficiently strong to compete with the avowal of human rights'. Just as 'the poison of an unresolved and protracted crisis' had circulated since 1848 in 'the body of the German people', so no original act of emancipation by Germany's political sections of the population stood at the outset of the new state. Instead, the authoritarian Prussian state expanded on the strength of its dazzling successes into the German Empire of 1871.[21] Bourgeois industrial society was expected to accomodate itself within this structure. The aristocratic forces of the military and the landowners celebrated the triumph of their aggressively waged defensive struggle against powerful contemporary trends. The history of the new German Empire began in this light. In 1914 an even more hazardous leap forward, carried out by the self-same social groups, was to lead to its downfall.

Imperialism

Western imperialism, viewed here as both the direct and indirect, formal and informal rule exercised by industrial countries over undeveloped regions by virtue of their socio-economic, technological and military superiority, is a complex phenomenon. Its

21. R. Stadelmann, 'Deutschland und die westeuropäischen Revolutionen', in his *Deutschland und Westeuropa*, Laupheim, 1948, pp. 14, 27f., 31.

prerequisite is the process of industrialisation, which forms a watershed in world history and which, despite all the undeniable elements of continuity, distinguishes imperialism from earlier forms of European colonialism. It can best be discussed within a theoritical framework which — as outlined in the introduction in general terms — enables us to analyse the central and interrelated problems raised by it.

(1) Nowadays it must obviously seem inadequate to discuss imperialism purely in terms of 'the economy' or 'industrialisation'. This is far too general an approach, leading to findings that are vague and usually inconclusive. Instead, we should try to comprehend, in terms that are as exact as possible, the significance of industrial and agricultural growth in those states which become involved in expansionist drives. It is in the historical nature of such growth that it follows an uneven pattern. The long-term secular trend of a continously prospering economy shows only one side of the picture. Periodic interruptions to growth (e.g. recessions, depressions, seasonal fluctuations), variations in the business cycle ('Kitchins' over forty months, 'Juglars' over ten to eleven years, Kuznet's twenty-year cycles, or even the long waves of 'Kondratieffs') — in short, the irregular rhythm of boom, crisis, downturn, depression, upturn is on the whole more important for contemporaries and historians than the mathematical and statistical overall trend which obscures the violent oscillations.[22]

(2) Social change is one of the preconditions of the economic processes involved; but it also accompanies them and is affected by them. It should, therefore, be examined as a specific social structure in its own right. Changes in the constellations of social forces and the problems of a nation's class structure become, therefore, the focus of analysis.

(3) This, in turn, raises the question of the political contest for the acquisition, maintenance and extension of opportunities to wield power. In other words, we must also analyse the inner dynamics of the ruling political system. At this point imperialism emerges as a strategy and means for defending and stabilising political domination, and must be seen against a background of conflict generated by attempts of either upholding or changing the system. In this respect, domestic and foreign policy become two facets of one and the same national policy. In this context the effect

22. Wehler, *Bismarck*, p. 41f., and *Krisenherde*, pp. 360f.

of ideologies such as Social Darwinism can be determined. Their impact cannot be adequately accounted for if they are seen only as quasi-autonomous factors or dealt with purely in terms of the history of ideas. The approach adopted here enables us to account for the astonishing simultaneity and similarity of the West's imperial expansion. If, on the other hand, one reduces the decisive driving forces behind imperialism to specific national 'urges', the historian's concern with the particular is turned into a dogma. It leads inevitably to a distorted picture, since it makes a comparative analysis which can elucidate problems by stressing common structural elements difficult, if not impossible.

Uneven growth and the legitimising of political domination: social imperialism If we adopt the above approach to imperialism, particular attention should be paid to two things when dealing with problems of economic growth. To begin with, the historically unprecedented dynamism of the industrial economies released forces which were widely perceived as compulsive drives emanating from the system itself. A pragmatic expansionism responded to these forces and led to the acquisition of new markets. These were secured either by informal means or by direct colonial rule over territorial possessions. There is no need to make a distinction here between the imperialism born of economic depression (up to about 1895) and that born of the trend-period of economic prosperity which followed. Nor is there any point in denying the connection between imperialism and economic development. Empirically, the genesis of modern imperialism is inseparably linked — subjectively in the consciousness of contemporaries, but also objectively for subsequent research — with the variations in the economic cycle. This is true not only of Germany's imperialist expansion but equally valid for the American, French and Belgian cases, and — allowing for its divergent historical time scale — the British example as well. But even in the period of world-wide economic boom between 1896 and 1913, the most important element common to both phases of expansion was the experience of irregular growth, i.e. the constant difficulties of arriving at a rational advance calculation of opportunities for profit. This helps explain the high expectations placed in foreign trade, which virtually became an ideology in themselves. A trend-period of prolonged prosperity never implies a continuous development free from interruptions. After 1896 the upswing was interrupted by crises and, to some extent, depressions: in 1900–01, 1907–08 and 1913. These provided painful reminders that there was no such thing as a continuous and even rise in economic development. What is historically illuminating, indeed critical, is not only the losses involved in colonial trading (felt at the time, though calculable only nowadays), but the sometimes slight, sometimes exorbitantly high profit margins of parasitical groups representing vested interests. Equally important is the fact that for those involved in the decision-making processes the undeveloped regions of the globe appeared to offer new markets and investment opportunities, as well as the possibility of stabilising the domestic economy. The pragmatic expansion referred to was, therefore, part of those actions by which an emergent state interventionism, aimed at sustaining and controlling economic prosperity, sought to contain the effects of uneven economic growth. State-sponsored export drives and the acquisition of new markets, leading to an 'informal empire' or direct colonial rule, aimed at restoring and sustaining economic prosperity in a gradually expanding domestic market whose absorptive capacity was long underestimated. The material well-being of the nation came to depend on various forms of successful expansion, including, of course, trade with countries at a similar stage of development. It was also served by a preventive imperialism which tried to secure long-term opportunities by, for example, precautionary annexations of the kind envisaged by Lord Rosebery when he spoke of 'staking out claims for the future'.

But the various economic motives behind this expansionism, however prominently they may figure in economic theories, represented only one element behind imperialism. The desire, indeed the decided aim, of legitimising the *status quo* and the political power structure by a successful imperialism was intimately bound up with the expansionist programme. The intentions behind Germany's overseas expansion, and the function it performed, served the interests of a 'social imperialism'. This amounted to a conservative 'taming' policy which sought to divert abroad reform attempts which found their expression in the emancipatory forces of liberalism and the socialist workers' movement, and endangered the system. It was a defensive strategy which aimed at the social goal of a conservative Utopia and attempted rigidly to defend traditional structures against continual change. It made use of modern propaganda techniques, but aimed at preserving the inherited pre-industrial social and political structures of the Greater Prussian

Empire, while defending the industrial and educated middle classes against the rising proletariat. Social imperialism could be applied on several fronts. It promised either real gains from overseas which could be exploited for the purposes of domestic politics, or it held out the rewards of activity — often no more than the illusory successes of activity for its own sake — which could effectively provide ideological satisfaction in terms of national prestige. It was precisely this calculation which made social imperialism an ideology of integration which could be deliberately applied from above to combat the antagonisms of German class society. It diverted the political activities of the bourgeoisie into a 'substitute sphere' and practically became 'the areas in which its accommodation . . . to the existing national state, its structures and needs' took place.[23] At the same time, the more far-sighted large-scale agrarian producers found that social imperialism offered them a new guarantee for the maintenance of their position of social and political domination in the shape of a socially reactionary *Sammlung* policy with its programme of overseas expansion.

Economic and social imperialism, as an instrument for stabilising and legitimising political domination, is associated with the birth of modern state interventionism. [. . .] In a system of state-regulated capitalism political authority is increasingly legitimised by the political leadership's efforts to ensure constant economic growth, and, in so doing, to maintain the essential conditions for social and political stability. This, together with the manipulatory technique of social imperialism, consistently formed the basis of Germany's overseas expansionist policy. At a time when the traditional or charismatic authority of the government was being challenged, Bismarck's early economic and social imperialism was designed to improve the conditions for stability on behalf of the economic interest groups and social allies of the neo-conservative 'joint protectionist' front of 1879 (Hans Rosenberg). It hoped to defuse the conflicts which had grown since 1873 over national income distribution and redirect political and psychic energies towards new and distant goals which would provide rallying-points. It would also revitalise ideas of a 'national' mission and the 'national' interest. The overall effect would be to consolidate the position of the authoritarian head of state, and with it that of the privileged social groups upholding his rule.

23. Nipperdey, *Grundzüge*, pp. 832f.

The problems caused by uneven economic growth and the need to legitimise Bismarck's Bonapartist rule coincided, and, as events were to show, made an imperialist policy appear inevitable. After the six-year-long depression up to 1879 had made way for a short-lived recovery, a further depression between 1882 and 1886 proved to be a traumatic experience in this respect (as was also the case in the USA and France). A broad ideological consensus, which had been emerging since the late 1870s, cut across pressure groups, the press, the *Reichstag* and the civil service. It was most prevalent in the 'strategic clique' (Ludz) of politicians supporting the 1879 *Sammlung*. This consensus united the growing demand for a stepping-up of foreign trade with that for fresh colonial acquisitions. Both were intended to help Germany out of the economic crisis and reduce social conflict at home. 'If regular, broad outlets are not created' to cope with 'the overproduction of German labour', ran one typical forecast, 'we shall move with giant strides towards a socialist revolution'.[24] Some liked to use the analogy of 'safety-valves', comparing Germany's internal development to an 'overheated boiler'. The President of the German Colonial Association (*Deutscher Kolonialverein*) of 1882, Prince Hermann zu Hohenlohe-Langenburg, was convinced 'that we in Germany cannot combat the danger of social democracy any more effectively' than by the acquisition of colonies. Apart from the direct economic advantages to be gained, the intensive agitation for colonies also promised 'greater security against communism' as a consequence of overseas expansion. The connection between economic prosperity and a situation of internal social stability was always present in the minds of the exponents of this ideological consensus.

It was also in Bismarck's mind when, encouraged by the favourable international situation and confident of success in view of the state of the economy, the existing ideological climate and the *Reichstag* election results of 1884, he combined his foreign trade policy, which had been building up over the years, with his methods for stabilising the domestic situation, and augmented them with a colonial policy. In a short space of time between 1884 and 1886 Germany acquired its 'protectorates' in South-West Africa, Togoland, the Cameroons, East Africa and the Pacific. Originally intended to be run by private syndicates enjoying the state's

24. E. von Weber, *4 Jahre in Afrika*, vol. II, Leipzig, 1878, p. 564; on the following, see Wehler, *Bismarck*, pp. 112–93, especially pp. 121, 163.

protection, they had almost all become Crown colonies by 1889. This was because the interested parties had balked at the initial costs involved and had expected the state to take over the expense of improving the infrastructure as well as provide protection against foreign competition. In any case, rebellions inevitably led to military interventions which involved the state. Apart from Samoa in the Pacific and Kiao-chow, with its 'protected zone', in China, little was added to the German Empire's first colonial acquisitions. Small parts of its African territories were gained later by way of concessionary agreements. Even in the 1880s the setting up of formal colonial rule would probably not have come about, had it not been for the intense competition from Germany's rivals who were advancing into the world's markets because of similar pressures. The advantages of an 'informal empire' were ever-present in Bismarck's thinking throughout his political life. In this respect, the 'Congo free-trade zone' and China's 'open door' corresponded most with his own ideas. But, caught between the pincers of internal pressures and international competition, he decided to follow a policy of establishing protectorates which soon ended up becoming colonies of the German Empire. However, by virtue of his exceptional authority, he was still in a position to stem any dangerous overflow of the drive for colonial expansion which might provoke direct conflict with Britain or France. This was shown quite clearly, for example, in his refusal to establish protectorates over certain areas and in his opposition to the idea of a Central African Empire (*Mittelafrika*), as proposed by Carl Peters and his Society for German Colonisation (*Gesellschaft für deutsche Kolonisation*) of 1882. This attitude, however, made him powerful political enemies at home who appreciably strengthened the coalition of forces which prepared the ground for his dismissal. His successors proved incapable of continuing to play the role of lion-tamer as effectively as he had done, especially when the antagonisms within Germany's class society increased and confronted them with problems for which the growth of the SPD was only the visible sign.

Wilhelmine 'world policy' as domestic policy   As events soon revealed, not only had the economic imperialism of the 1880s pointed the way for future developments to take, but the social imperialist technique of government began to determine the shape of things to come. Henceforth, imperial policy continually and deliberately fell back on the latter, once Caprivi's uphill struggle of partially adjusting economic conditions to the realities of Germany's industrial development had been thwarted by the agrarians. Miquel's *Sammlung* rested, as he himself said in 1897, on diverting 'revolutionary elements' towards imperialism, in order to turn the nation's gaze 'abroad' and bring 'its sentiments . . . on to common ground'. This functional advantage of social imperialism was also part of Holstein's thinking (from the 1880s) when he argued that 'the government of Kaiser Wilhelm II needs a tangible success abroad which will have an effect at home. This success can come about only as the result of a European war, a world historical (*weltgeschichtlich*) gamble, or else some acquisition outside Europe'.[25] Between 1897 and 1900, by acquiring Kiao-chow in the Shantung Treaty, German policy in China took account of these strategic considerations, as did the emerging naval construction programme. This sort of thinking was also clearly in evidence among the so-called 'liberal imperialists' like Friedrich Naumann, Max Weber, Ernst von Halle (Tirpitz's chief propagandist) and the political scientist, Ernst Francke, to name but a few. A successful social policy alongside an increase in parliamentary influence would make it possible to conduct a powerful *Weltpolitik* by first satisfying the workers. In this case internal reform would underpin imperialism as the main priority, for the integration of the social classes was seen as the prerequisite of strength abroad. *Weltpolitik* would, moreover, facilitate an effective social policy through tangible material consessions. Successes abroad were expected to lead to a kind of truce on the home fronts. Admittedly, these Liberals did not participate in the decision-making processes of the German monarchy; but they did lend their support to the expansionist programme to which Berlin was committed.

The true significance of Wilhelmine 'world policy' can, it seems, be appreciated only if viewed from the perspective of social imperialism. Its precipitate character should not obscure the fact that it was based on the deliberate and calculated use of foreign policy as an instrument for achieving domestic political ends. Whenever concrete economic interests were not involved, the prestige element figured even more prominently than ever. As the professor of law at

25. Miquel, in H. Böhme, *Deutschlands Weg zur Grossmacht*, Cologne, 2nd imp., 1972, p. 316; Holstein to Kiderlen, 30. 4. 1897, in Kiderlen Papers (Böhme copy); similarly to Eulenburg, 4. 12. 1894, in J. Haller (ed.), *Aus dem Leben des Fürsten P. zu Eulenburg*, Berlin, 1924, p. 173.

Freiburg University, Hermann Rehm, said with considerable fore-sight in 1900, 'only the idea of Germany as a world power is capable of dispelling the conflicts between rival economic interests in inter-nal affairs'.[26] The problem was not just one of overcoming conflicts by means of *Sammlung* policy, but as much a matter concerning rights of political participation and social equality for the workers, against whose political representatives it was easy to mobilise a 'pro-Empire' imperialism after 1884. In view of the nation's internal fragmentation into a class society and the strong tensions between, on the one hand, the authoritarian state, the ruling élite of land-owners and the feudalised bourgeoisie, and, on the other, the advancing forces of parliamentarisation and democratisation, it seemed to the Berlin politicians, operating within their own horizon of experience, that there was no alternative to the 'taming' policy of social imperialism in terms of the success it promised. From their defensive positions they no longer wanted to – nor could they – modernise Germany's social and political constitution to the extent required. It was this seeming lack of any alternative which proved to be the decisive factor, and a most unfortunate one at that; for it was not left to their free decision, as many have argued since, to exercise moderate restraints by scaling down Germany's overseas involve-ment. As a result of Germany's social and political tensions, there was a constant pressure from within the system to fall back re-peatedly on the proven technique of social imperialism. To this extent, von Waldersee hit the nail on the head when he set his hopes on 'a foreign policy' which would have 'a positive effect on internal conditions', and thought it 'a sign of malaise that we cannot help ourselves out of the situation through our domestic policy'. Surveying the situation from his position at the centre of decision-making machinery Bülow also insisted that 'only a successful fore-ign policy' could 'help, reconcile, calm, rally and unite'.[27]

All this serves to emphasise the objective function of Wilhelmine world policy's frantic and hazardous desire to be 'part of the action'. It also throws light on the avowed purpose of Germany's decision-makers and, thus, their conscious intentions. Shortly be-fore the outbreak of war in 1914, Bülow, for example, showed

26. In A. Kirchhoff (ed.), *Deutsche Universitätslehrer über die Flottenvorlage*, Berlin, 1900, p. 21.
27. Diary entry of 31. 12. 1895, in H. Mohs (ed.), *A. Graf von Waldersee in seinem militärischen Wirken*, vol. II, Berlin 1929, p. 383; Bülow to Eulenburg, 26. 12. 1897, in Röhl, *Deutschland*, p. 229.

unsurpassed candour in setting out the detailed arguments for this 'vigorous national policy' in his widely-read book, *German Policy*. *Weltpolitik* was presented as the 'true antidote against social democracy'. This amounted to an admission that the way of domestic reform was bankrupt. At the very least, it implied the abandonment of attempts to establish a modern society of freely participating citizens.[28] From the 1880s onwards, social imperialism remained embedded in German politics as a pattern of political behaviour. With the abrupt transition from Bismarck's Bonapartist rule to the polycracy of the Wilhelmine era, 'the tendency grew to neutralise' the inherited 'deep discrepancy between the social structure and a political order which had hardly taken account of the changed social situation since the industrial revolution'. This was done by 'diverting internal pressures outwards in a social imperialist fashion' which concealed 'the long overdue reform of Germany's internal structure'.[29] Can one find a more convincing interpretation than this of German 'world policy' as domestic policy? Or, to put it differently, of 'world policy' as a continuation of the defence of the domestic *status quo* in the world arena?

One thing should, nevertheless, be noted: however clearly this social imperialism represented in functional terms a conservative response to the challenge of the problems posed by a class society and its anachronistic distribution of power, it should not be reduced solely to its manipulatory element. Economic interests in a narrow sense almost always played their part and helped justify overseas expansion. While Germany's China policy after 1897 certainly provided an opportunity for brilliant moves on the chessboard of domestic politics, the Shantung Treaty, which arranged the 'lease' of Kiao-chow, also secured one of China's richest provinces for German economic penetration. It gave heavy industry and an ailing railway construction industry at home the prospect of a share in the opening-up of the massive Asian market. We cannot ignore the political aspects of the Berlin–Baghdad Railway scheme either; but it also provided tempting opportunities for specific economic interests which were always served by this kind of expansion. If the political leadership often pushed economic interests to the fore, exaggerated their importance and formally egged on businessmen

28. B. von Bülow, 'Deutsche Politik', in *Deutschland unter Kaiser Wilhelm II*, ed. S. Körte *et al.*, vol. I Berlin, 1914, pp. 97f.
29. K. D. Bracher, *Deutschland zwischen Demokratie und Diktatur*, Munich, 1964, p. 155.

into entering agreements, the state soon followed in their footsteps once they had acquired importance and influence abroad. If one narrows down the question to determining the relative importance of the different factors which motivated imperialist expansion, and attempts the same regarding the decisions that were made, the conclusion will be that the element of social imperialism was either dominant or at least of equal importance alongside economic factors prior to 1914. In the final phase of Imperial Germany's expansionist policy, namely the formulation of its war aims in the First World War, social imperialism again assumed prime importance.

Social Darwinism and pan-Germanism as imperialist ideologies   In his *Principles of Realpolitik*, published in 1853, Ludwig August von Rochau recommended contemporaries to adjust to the existing realities of the new configuration of interests in the post-revolutionary era. Nevertheless, he admitted that 'ideas . . . have always had as much power as their holders care to vest in them. Therefore, the idea that . . . inspires an entire people or epoch is the most substantial of all political forces'.[30] One such idea, often said to have possessed this power during the age of Western imperialism, was Social Darwinism: the transfer to the social and political sphere of Darwin's biological theories of 'natural selection' and 'the survival of the fittest' in 'the struggle for existence'. After the 1870s and 1880s this Social Darwinism spread throughout the Western industrialised nations where it exerted a considerable influence before reaching its apogee in the radical racialist theories of National Socialism. It provides the historian with an excellent example of the indissoluble interconnection of influential ideas with social development, and an ideological critique is particularly suitable for placing Social Darwinism into this context.

Marx and Engels grasped the connection early on. In 1862 Marx commented: 'It is noticeable that Darwin recognises among plants and animals his own English society, with its division of labour, competition, opening-up of new markets, "inventions" and the Malthusian "struggle for existence". It is Hobbes's *bellum omnium contra omnes*, and it reminds one of Hegel's *Phenomenology*, where bourgeois society figures as "spiritual animal kingdom", while with

30. A. L. von Rochau, *Grundsätze der Realpolitik*, Stuttgart, 1853, p. 28 (ed. H. -U. Wehler, Berlin, 1972, p. 40).

Darwin the animal kingdom figures as bourgeois society'. 'The whole Darwinian theory of the struggle for existence', Engels wrote in the mid-1870s, "is simply the transference from society to animate nature of Hobbes's theory of *bellum omnium contra omnes* and the bourgeois economic theory of competition, as well as the Malthusian theory of population. Once this feat has been accomplished . . . it is very easy to transfer these theories back again from natural history to the history of society, and altogether too naïve to maintain that thereby these assertions have been proved as eternal natural laws of society.' Like Nietzsche and Spengler after them, both men recognised in Social Darwinism an eminently suitable 'system for justifying bourgeois capitalism' (H. Plessner).[31] In addition, they set out a framework for its analysis which can scarcely be improved upon even today.

By reading Malthus, who as an amateur natural historian believed he had deduced his ideas from nature, both Darwin and the biologist, A. R. Wallace (whose researcher led Darwin to publish his *Origin of Species*), were inspired at a psychologically critical stage in their work into developing their own theories of evolution. It cannot be said that these evolved purely from their own findings. Darwin, who stood Malthus on his head, himself became the first Social Darwinist when he advanced the rise of the so-called 'Aryan race' in Europe and particularly the United States, as conclusive proof of the validity of his theories as applied to human society. It could even be said that he openly prepared the way for a racialist interpretation of Social Darwinism.[32] No doubt this world-view (*Weltanschauung*) based on the circular conclusions of Malthus and Darwin through to a vulgarised version of Social Darwinism, which presented itself as a summit of scientific reasoning, struck a responsive chord in providing a justification for bourgeois economic activity and the competitive capitalist system, the absolutism of the entrepreneur and national self-assertiveness. As a manifestation of

31. MEW, vol. 30, p. 249 (18. 6. 1862); pp. 20, 565 (*Dialektik der Natur*); to Lawrow, 12/17. 11. 1875; ibid., pp. 34, 170; H. Plessner, 'Zur Soziologie der modernen Forschung', in *Versuche zu einer Soziologie des Wissens*, Munich, 1924, p. 423.
32. G. Himmelfarb, *Darwin and the Darwinian Revolution*, New York, 1959, pp. 157–61, 235f., 393–6; R. M. Young, 'Malthus and the Evolutionists: The Common Context of Biological and Social Theory', in *Past and Present*, no. 43, 1969, pp. 109–45; H. -U. Wehler, "Sozialdarwinismus im expandierenden Industriestaat', in *Festschrift* for F. Fischer, Düsseldorf, 1973, pp. 133–42; C. Darwin, *The Descent of Man*, vol. I, New York, 1871, pp. 154, 173f.; and his *Life and Letters*, ed. F. Darwin, vol. I, London, 1887, pp. 69, 316.

the decline of positivism, it banished hopes for a more open society and put the fixed laws of an anti-egalitarian system of a social aristocracy in its place. Its functional significance lay in the fact that it enabled the ruling élites to appear compatible with progress, while providing a justification for the immutability of the *status quo*. At the same time, it allowed the emancipatory aspirations of the workers or colonial peoples to be dismissed as the futile protestations of inferior subjects in the struggle for existence. Vested with an aura of 'irrefutable' scientific knowledge, it was this versatility of application that gave Social Darwinism its power in its very real connection with the ruling interests. As an ideology which proved virtually ideal for justifying imperialism, it was kept alive by a host of popularisers in the industrialised nations. If one were to remove it from its specific social context, it could be evaluated as an independent factor. But this would lead only to its being seen as a mere distortion of pure science and would fail to account for its social impact.

Similarly, pan-Germanism can be seen as a variation of attempts to justify imperialist expansion, and one that drew increasingly on racialist theories for this purpose. A weed like this could only flourish in such lurid colours in a specific social environment. The processes of economic concentration and social polarisation were to some extent reflected in the 'preferantial position befitting one's own nation'. Economic progress and the subjugation of overseas territories seemed attributable to the 'special natural qualities' of the nation, 'that is, its racial characteristics'. At any rate, enormous claims were made on the basis of this belief. Racist pan-Germanism, which would 'cure' the world (Paul Rohrbach), gave rise to a pseudo-scientific 'concealed justification' for ongoing expansion. It demanded sacrifice for the sake of a 'higher common interest' — that of a Teutonic world mission. The originally circumscribed idea of the 'nation' was placed 'in the service' of these new goals as 'a propelling force', within the blurred parameters of which everyone from a banker like von der Heydt to a rabid nationalist school-teacher, from a swaggering soldier to a middle-class enthusiast of colonialism, could project his own aspirations.[33] Although it has not yet proved possible to demonstrate conclusively that pan-Germanism had a direct influence on Berlin's political decision-making machinery, it was an important factor in the public opinion

33. Hilferding, pp. 504–6; similarly Bauer, pp. 491–507.

of groups loyal to the Empire. For political reasons it was very rarely criticised by the government. It flourished mainly in the upper and middle classes who had a strong influence on public opinion and received its main backing from their militant organisations like the Pan-German League, the Navy League and the Army League. Without doubt it was one of the poisonous ingredients in that ideological mishmash which later propelled the *völkisch* nationalists and whose extremism was supposed to make good its obvious intellectual inferiority.

FRANZ J. BRÜGGEMEIER
LUTZ NIETHAMMER

Lodgers, Schnapps-Casinos and Working-Class Colonies in a Heavy-Industrial Region

Aspects of Working-Class Housing in the Ruhr prior to the First World War[*]

'Here we can see how completely erroneous and mis-placed it is to assume that the growth of industry is responsible for our poor housing conditions; the very opposite is the case.[1] Those industrial towns which have retained an efficient communal admin-istration and a pattern of construction which meets the standards of small-unit housing have developed favourably in respect of their housing question.' Thus R. Eberstadt, one of the most widely-read authors of the German housing reform movement, described the architecture of German cities in the context of a comparison of building density and building heights.[2] This statement also puts in a nutshell the predominantly blinkered way in which bourgeois

[*] Publ. orig. in J. Reulecke and W. Weber (eds.), *Fabrik — Familie — Feierabend. Beuträge zur Sozialgeschichte des Alltags im Industriezeitalter*, Peter Hammer Verlag, Wuppertal, 1978, pp. 135–75. The authors would like to thank the publishers for permission to prepare and use this translation.
1. The authors would like to thank I. Caspar and C. Liesenfeld without whom they could not have finished this article. The argument outlined here has meanwhile been further developed in F. J. Brüggemeier, *Leben vor Ort. Ruhr-bergleute und Ruhrbergbau 1889–1919*, Munich, 1984.
2. R. Eberstadt, *Handbuch des Wohnungswesens*, 2nd ed., Jena, 1910, pp. 133f. It is characteristic that he derived his view from his research into the commercial, administrative and textile towns of the Bergische Land, rather than into the Ruhr area. See also idem, *Rheinische Wohnungsverhältnisse und ihre Bedeutung für das Wohnungswesen in Deutschland*, Jena, 1903.

217

housing reformers saw the problem: attention focused upon the scandals of excessive housing densities and in particular the *Mietskasernen* (garrison-like high-rise flats) of Berlin. A comparatively spacious and low-rise pattern of construction, such as could be found in the Ruhr, was seen, by contrast, as a blessing of industry and of an efficient local government.[3] This view was influenced by the concrete exteriors of urban dwelling and their statistical reflections; it was dominated by the anonymous threat which the misery and the huge numbers of the proletariat in the cities posed to the rest of society.

By comparison, the actual housing conditions of workers in industrial regions such as the Ruhr remained abstract. The masses who lived in these regions were dispersed and remote; they were of little concern to the urban middle classes of the metropolitan centres, while they provided very little statistical data for the reformers. In other words, wherever the workers were forced to live in large industrial agglomerations isolated from close contact with an urban bourgeoisie, the housing question ceased to be an issue as far as the middle classes were concerned.

If a middle-class perspective be adopted, the above-quoted statement by Eberstadt gains in plausibility. Taking building density within a region and also within a single housing complex as indicators, figures for the Ruhr compare favourably with those for the urban centres, especially in the eastern half of the Reich; in the Ruhr, ground rents were lower and the building and housing market less well organised. Where there was little or no planning, there were few complaints about mismanagement such as were voiced in the large cities. Those who travelled through the Ruhr area would be deceived easily by the facades of idyllic villages; the underground nature of the coal industry ensured that most of the pits would remain hidden from view.

In short, it was a superficial view as far as working-class housing

3. The most important writings and discussions of the working-class housing question focused on overcrowding and mobility in the big cities. See, e.g., the work by the statistician of the Berlin city government, Engel, *Die moderne Wohnungsnoth*, Leipzig, 1873, and the proceedings of the *Verein für Sozialpolitik* (introduced by Miquel): 'Die Wohnungsnot der ärmeren Volksklassen in deutschen Großstädten, in *Schriften des Vereins für Sozialpolitik (SVSP)*, vols. 30–3, 1886f. The Ruhr is represented only by reports on the then relatively small town centres of Bochum, Dortmund and Essen: idem, vol. 31, pp. 73ff., 157ff. The availability of statistical material on big cities with their early-developed statistics departments also promoted the emphasis on the city problem. See the survey by H. Lindemann, 'Wohnungsstatistik', in *SVSP*, vol. 94, 1901, pp. 263–384.

and living conditions were concerned. Workers, it is true, lived in dwellings built to certain dimensions and equipped in a certain way; But these facts provided only limited indicators as to how these conditions were experienced. The relation between income and rent levels is important here, as is that between the place of sleeping and of work, between fluctuations in the economy and the availability of accommodation and, finally, between the length of residence and family structure.

In other words, one must enquire into the conditions which tie people to their accommodation, how far they facilitate physical and cultural contact, whether the entrepreneurs can interfere with life outside the factory, whether wives can find local employment and what class-room densities are experienced by the children. In investigating such questions, we must also bear in mind the ambivalent experiences stemming from divergent living conditions. These are aspects which contain elements of both solidarity and cooperation as well as of individual adaptation. Only if the notion of housing is related to the realities of the work-place; if it is expanded to include demography, infrastructure and the political economy of both family and community and, finally, if it transcends the sharp divide made by the bourgeoisie between the private and the public sphere,[4] will this notion provide insights into what housing meant to the working class and highlight the special conditions obtaining in the Ruhr area. This approach will also open up opportunities, however faint, of recognising behind the brick facades the contours of needs and interests, of actions and reactions by sections of the German working class.

In this article we hope to make a contribution to answering these problems. As our space is limited and the sources are incomplete, and because research into this area is only just beginning,[5] we

4. See T. Kleinspehn's Introduction to S. Reck, *Arbeiter nach der Arbeit*, Lahn-Giessen, 1977; H. Lefèbvre, *Kritik des Alltagslebens*, Munich, 1974; O. Negt and A. Kluge, *Öffentlichkeit und Erfahrung*, Frankfurt, 1972; F. Brüggemeier, 'Bedürfnisse, gesellschaftliche Erfahrung und politisches Verhalten. Das Beispiel der Ruhrbergarbeiter im nördlichen Ruhrgebiet gegen Ende des 19. Jahrhunderts', in *Sozialwissenschaftliche Informationen für Unterricht und Studium*, vol. 6, 1977, pp. 152–60.
5. See, above all: E. Lucas, *Zwei Formen des Radikalismus in der deutschen Arbeiterbewegung*, Frankfurt, 1976; D. Crew, *Town in the Ruhr*, New York, 1979; K. Tenfelde, *Sozialgeschichte der Arbeiterschaft an der Ruhr im 19. Jahrhundert*, Bonn, 1977. General background: G. Adelmann, *Die soziale Betriebsverfassung des Ruhrbergbaus vom Anfang des 19. Jahrhunderts bis zum Ersten Weltkrieg*, Bonn, 1962; W. Köllmann, *Bevölkerung in der industriellen Revolution*, Göttingen, 1974.

cannot provide much detailed evidence in support of our extended concept of housing; nor can we offer a differentiated picture of local conditions. All we can hope to do is to test its viability by giving a number of examples and by examining its salient features. This is why we focus on miners, a group of workers which was specific to the Ruhr area. We pay special attention to the repercussions of the enormous mobility within this profession and of the infrastructural weaknesses of industrial villages in relation to housing in general. Finally, in the wake of these factors, we shall be looking at the ambivalence of the *Arbeiterkolonie* (workers' 'colony'), a form of settlement which, in Germany, was widespread only in the mining and steelmaking areas. Our aim is to identify the general living conditions of the proletariat in the specific shape which they took among the Ruhr miners of Imperial Germany. This analysis will be undertaken against the backdrop of such regional comparisons which are available, but which can only be referred to here.[6] Before we begin, however, it is necessary to deal with a number of very general features of urbanisation, since these have shaped our own as well as contemporary notions of urban living. Only in this way will it be possible to describe the specific way in which the industrial agglomerations on the Ruhr developed.

Deficiencies of Urbanisation

The pre-industrial concept of the town reflects its role *vis-à-vis* the agrarian region around it.[7] It had centralising tasks, such as providing a market-place, an administration, cultural activities and processing facilities; these tasks were carried out by a middle class (merchants, artisans, officials and intellectuals) as a specific stratum; they required a compression of social space and this in turn favoured socio-political self-organisation. One of the consequences of this situation was that the contrast between a dominant class and producers typical of the countryside was less marked in the towns and was mediated by the existence of relatively broadly-based and differentiated middle strata. In this perspective, local self-government

---

6. L. Niethammer and F. Brüggemeier, 'Wie wohnten Arbeiter im Kaiserreich?', in *Archiv für Sozialgeschichte*, vol. 16, 1976, pp. 61–134.
7. On the following differentiation see in particular H. Bobek, 'Über einige funktionelle Stadttypen und ihre Beziehung zum Lande', in P. Schöller (ed.), *Allgemeine Stadtgeographie*, Darmstadt, 1969, pp. 269–88.

in the nineteenth century may be seen as a successful mobilisation of the bourgeois potential of innovation and mediation. The growth of such ancient towns in the wake of the demographic explosion, of the movement from the countryside to the towns and of industrialisation continued to secure for the urban bourgeoisie, which had until now occupied a leading position in the economic, administrative and cultural spheres, a position which was both dominant and mediating. The reason for this was that the structural consequences of the towns' centralising function grew in proportion with the expansion of industry and that white-collar employees began to take the place of erstwhile small self-employed businessmen and artisans in the social hierarchy.[8] These groups shaped life-forms and infrastructure, i.e. they furthered increasing population densities and the creation of transport networks, town planning and sanitation, the provision of water and electricity, of newspapers, schools, further education, public houses and cafés.[9] A section of the working class, especially those rooted in an artisanal tradition, participated in this urban progress. As far as their accommodation was concerned, they often lived in densely populated, but not class-specific areas inhabited by the well-to-do middle strata — even if they occupied no more than the backyard, the basement or the attic of a particular dwelling. Many of their lodgings, it is true, were extremely overcrowded and in a miserable condition,[10] however, they shared much of the surroundings, above all the urban infrastructure, with the petty bourgeoisie. It was in this milieu, especially its margins, that we can observe the emergence of the first workers' debating societies, reading clubs, trade unions and parties.

Although there also existed earlier forms of habitation in these areas, most of the industrial towns and communities in the regions of heavy industry developed differently during the nineteenth century where the social structures were not geared to a similar centralising role. Rather, these regions consisted of partly dense, partly dispersed 'conglomerations of dwellings' which were in themselves the hinterland. They lacked specifically urban forms of living and an urban infrastructure in the sense that, apart from industrialists, they

8. See W. Köllmann, *Bevölkerung*, pp. 140ff.
9. For a comprehensive analysis of 'urbanity' with specific reference to nineteenth-century London, see J. Dyos and M. Wolff (eds.), *The Victorian City*, 2 vols., London, 1973.
10. See, e.g., O. Rühle, *Illustrierte Kultur- und Sittengeschichte des Proletariats*, vol. I, 2nd ed., Frankfurt, 1971, pp. 361ff.; B. Schwan, *Die Wohnungsnot und das Wohnungselend in Deutschland*, Berlin, 1929.

attracted only that number of self-employed people and white-collar employees which could be sustained by the low living standards of a predominantly working-class population with its meagre purchasing power.[11] This was a different situation from urban centres where population growth was reflected in the expansion of the city centre under the leadership of the middle classes. In the industrial regions, such as that area known as 'the Ruhr', only production installations and work-forces were concentrated at first. Consequently urban functions and structures were a secondary development; they lacked the prerequisites and hence remained stunted, even if urban development was not blocked altogether for political reasons. The Ruhr is the outstanding example of this type of industrial conurbation; at the beginning of the twentieth century it was the largest and fastest growing zone of urbanisation in Europe, yet it was much more an industrial province than an urban region. Until as late as 1950 it was possible to see how persistent these original structures were, by working out the proportions between self-employed, white-collar employees and blue-collar workers in a number of German cities. The first two groups, which are of decisive importance for urban development, comprised about one-half of the population in cities which occupied a centralising position; in the large cities of the Ruhr area they amounted to no more than a third. Stuttgart and Frankfurt represented extreme examples of one end of the scale, with 53.1 per cent and 54.5 per cent respectively. By contrast, in a typical mining town such as Gelsenkirchen a mere 28.3 per cent belonged to the self-employed and the white-collar employees.[12] In 1907 none of the then five largest cities in the Ruhr area had even one quarter of the inhabitants falling into these two categories. (The figure for Gelsenkirchen was 16.4 per cent);[13] the percentage for the surrounding industrial communities, in which two-thirds of the Ruhr population lived, was in most cases probably between 10 per cent and 15 per cent.

Some 120 years ago, a large part of what is today the Ruhr was still agricultural land. Except for a few towns along the *Hellweg*, among them Essen, Bochum and Dortmund with a total of 30,000 inhabitants in 1852, the country was shaped by villages and hamlets, huddled around the local church. Rarely did the population total several thousands. Change, however, had already come to some

11. See H. Bobek, 'Stadttypen', pp. 273ff.
12. W. Köllmann, *Bevölkerung*, p. 160.
13. Ibid., p. 184.

areas. Industry was spreading from the south to the north. Above all it was the coal mines, and later the iron- and steel-works, which were looking for labourers; it was the mines which suffered from the acutest labour shortages. The number of their employees rose from 80,000 to about 400,000 between 1880 and 1913. This rapid increase was possible only because the new miners did not come merely from the vicinity, but, from the 1870s onwards, increasingly also from the eastern provinces of Germany. These people poured in particular into the northern zone of the Ruhr, causing a veritable explosion in the population. Hamborn, for example, had a mere 4,260 inhabitants in 1890; twenty years later the figure had risen to 102,000. As was to be expected, the villages were in no way prepared for their new role or for the newcomers. They lacked centres for social crystallisation around which constitutional and infrastructural changes towards greater urbanisation might have developed. Instead the greater density of human settlements led merely to a proliferation of private dwellings, factories and railways. The most basic infrastructural provisions followed very slowly. Some peasants, it is true, had gained unexpected wealth by selling land to the mine owners and had invested this capital in construction firms, pubs and private housing; but these investments were totally inadequate. Nor were there broad middle-class strata and hence the customary basis of an efficient free market for dwellings and also for a building pattern that mixed the social classes was lacking.[14]

The towns along the Hellweg also lacked promoters of a systematic urban development. The purchasing power of the working class was weak; demand tended to fluctuate depending on labour migrations in line with the fluctuations in the economy. The settlement of these migrants threatened to impose additional financial burdens for schools and other communal institutions. Given that the capacity of the workers to pay taxes was low, these costs would have had to be borne by the indigenous bourgeoisie. Two contemporary reports show characteristic reactions: either old buildings in the city centre were profitably filled to the roof with 'guest workers' or there was a simple denial of any responsibility for the problem.

14.   Lack of sources makes research into industrial villages very difficult. For a case study, see L. Niethammer, *Umständliche Erläuterung der seelischen Störung eines Communalbaumeisters in Preussens grösstem Industriedorf oder: die Unfähigkeit zur Stadtentwicklung*, Frankfurt, 1979. An earlier version can be found in U. Engelhardt, V. Sellin and H. Stuke (eds.), *Soziale Bewegung und politische Verfassung*, Stuttgart, 1976, pp. 432–71.

The deputy mayor of Dortmund described the situation as follows: 'In the inner city there are still a fairly large number of older, poorly-maintained dwellings with low ceilings, small rooms, deficient stairwells, small backyards and outbuildings not particularly suited for habitation; these serve as workers' accommodation'. During the years of boom following the founding of the Empire in 1871 there had been increased building activity outside the inner city. But, so the deputy mayor reported, these dwellings were jerry-built. During the depression that followed the building market began to collapse. Between 1876 and 1886 Dortmund, a town of 75,000, built no more than some 200 new houses.[15] The head of the town-planning department of Essen reported as follows:

"Neither the State, nor the local authority, nor the charities did anything towards solving the housing crisis which occurred in the 1860s as a result of the extraordinary growth of the city of Essen. There was also no reason for them to act as the crisis was a consequence of industrial prosperity and the concomitant influx of innumerable workers. It was hence seen in the first instance as a task for the owners whose factories were doing so well to provide good accommodation for the labouring masses whom they required.[16]

Yet, as entrepreneurial capital brought considerably higher returns if it was invested in new equipment, no more than a very reluctant commitment to solving the housing crisis could be expected from the employers as long as they got the workers they needed and these workers found some kind of accommodation.

In principle four different solutions to the housing question existed. Firstly, where, as in the southern parts of the Ruhr, miners had worked in this industry for a longer period, either on a full-time or part-time basis, or had received a small inheritance, they might be able to build themselves a small cottage with a vegetable garden. This traditional type of housing had never been completely abandoned, but it diminished in importance when mining saw an expansion in the second half of the nineteenth century.[17] Secondly, where

15. Arnecke, 'Die Arbeiterwohnungsfrage in Dortmund', in *SVSP*, vol. 31, 1886, p. 172.
16. Wiebe, 'Die Wohnungsverhältnisse der ärmeren Klassen in Essen a.d.R.', in ibid., pp. 192ff.
17. See the articles by H. Winkelmann and I. Lange-Kothe in *Der Anschnitt*, vol. II, 1950; M. J. Koch (*Die Bergarbeiterbewegung im Ruhrgebiet zur Zeit Wilhelm II.*, Düsseldorf, 1954, p. 16) has argued that up to 1850 every miner had his own cottage. This figure is doubtlessly too high.

industrial settlements grew up next to existing village- or town-type settlements, local property owners frequently tried to develop new land to meet fresh housing demand. As in other cities, a market for privately rented accommodation emerged. It provided housing for the majority of the workers who lived there either paying high rents or living in poorly maintained buildings, or both! Often there was no sanitation and the rooms were badly overcrowded.[18] However, this type of housing differed from that in other urban areas in that it was scattered over a wider area and avoided high-rises. There was also no separation of residential and industrial areas. As the demand came almost exclusively from highly mobile workers, speculative developers could neither plan for nor mix different social groups which, had it been possible, would normally have increased returns on investments and reduced wear and tear. However, this 'self-made' speculative housing development, undertaken rather aimlessly with limited local capital resources, could not cope with the erratic expansion of the factory work force.

The third solution was for workers to move more closely together — either several families living in one flat or individuals renting a bed with another family. This resulted in a particularly mobile form of life-style which was characteristic of about half the miners in the 1890s. Where, finally, even this solution was unavailable, the employers were forced to create accommodation in order to attract workers. Large dormitories for men (*Menagen*) were the cheapest. But it was difficult to tie the workers to the enterprise in this way on a long-term basis. Entrepreneurs who desired greater stability among their work-force had to provide family accommodation (if possible with an allotment). This type of housing emerged above all in the industrial villages of the Emscher region in the

18. See the housing index in Niethammer and Brüggemeier, 'Arbeiter', pp. 96f., 101. Our figures show that the housing structure was more favourable in Rhineland-Westphalia than in Upper Silesia, Berlin, the towns of eastern Germany or the agrarian eastern provinces. However, it was worse than in most other towns. In particular, accommodation tended to be overcrowded in boom periods. This can be gleaned from the reports by the housing inspectorate (see ibid., p. 88). See also the verdict of the Dortmund district physician, Wollenweber, *Mängel im Wohnungswesen im westfälischen Industriebezirk und ihre Bedeutung für die Ausbreitung der Infektionskrankheiten*, Berlin, 1913, p. 14: 'On the basis of one's own observations and of the statistics one must, all in all, come to the conclusion that housing conditions in the industrial district . . . are poor'. However, he did exempt company housing from this. It is probably also a short-cut to correlate housing densities with the high susceptibility to infectious disease in the Ruhr by comparison with the rural districts of Westphalia. Such correlations exclude the work- and wage-conditions of labourers as possible causes of disease.

Table 1.   *Accommodation in the Ruhr Mining Industry (%)*

	Southern region[2]	Northern region[3]
Owner-occupiers	14.77	8.02
House owners living in rented acc.[1]	1.60	1.97
Company-owned flats	2.14	1.93
Rented acc. in colonies	5.28 (7.76)[4]	9.76 (13.10)[4]
Other rented accommodation	53.94	49.47
Inhabitants of dormitories	0.79	0.77
Lodgers	21.49	28.06
Total	100.00	100.00
Absolute fig.	34,226	87,774

1. That is, individuals who owned a house in the country but had to work in the Ruhr to make a living.
2. Dortmund-Süd, Witten, Hattingen, Bochum-Süd, Essen-Süd, Werden.
3. Recklinghausen, Dortmund-Ost, Dortmund-West, Bochum-Nord, Herne, Gelsenkirchen, Wattenscheid, Essen-Ost, Essen-West, Oberhausen.
4. Fig. for 1900 in brackets.

north, where the free housing market proved insufficient. Here we find areas of dense settlement without urbanisation.

A quantitative break-down of these four types of housing (home ownership, rented accommodation, lodgings, company housing) in the mining areas is provided by Table 1 above, which is based on a careful statistical assessment for December 1893:[19]

In evaluating how these figures relate to the individual mining districts, there appears to be an ideal-typical correspondence between two sets of figures: whereas the number of miners in owner-occupier dwellings was relatively high in the older districts, the northern region presents a different picture. There the gap had to be filled by the increased building of company housing. Meanwhile provision of housing through the free market remained uniformly limited owing to the decentralised pattern of settlement. This trend continued at an increased pace after 1901.

Overcrowding remained the key problem of urban housing for the working class, both in the sense of cramped and high-rise building and of the usage of the rooms by too many people[20] — in particular the problem of large families being packed into very small

19. Calculated on the basis of O. Taeglichsbeck, *Die Belegschaft der Bergwerke im Oberbergamtsbezirk Dortmund nach der Zählung vom 16.12.1893*, vol. I, Essen/Dortmund, 1896, pp. 6–15; R. Hundt, *Bergarbeiterwohnungen im Ruhrgebiet*, Dortmund, 1902, p. 9.
20. See Niethammer and Brüggemeier, 'Arbeiter', pp. 86ff.

one- or two-room flats. As far as one can tell from the fragmentary statistics available, such problems of urban housing were particularly acute in the vicinity of large steel-works like those at Essen or Duisburg; they were also present in the Ruhr, although not on a comparable scale, since the average individual flat in that area appears to have had a size more adequate for a whole family than elsewhere. But this does not say anything about the number of occupants per flat. Rent levels — partly due to the large share of company housing — were probably also lower in the Ruhr than in many cities. High levels of occupancy therefore remained the main problem.

As can be demonstrated for most cities at the end of the nineteenth century, overcrowded flats were not the result of a shortage of accommodation. The problem was rather that proletarian families either did not have an income large enough to pay for more sizeable accommodation or that their rural origins had accustomed them to such poor housing conditions that better accommodation had a low priority in their budget. This was all the more applicable because rent was part of the fixed costs which in view of the fluctuating income had to be kept as low as possible. In the Ruhr, on the other hand, there was an actual shortage of local accommodation. Working-class housing was not profitable enough for speculative building. Above all, the market did not respond fast enough to the steady expansion of the mining industry. One indication of this is that levels of occupancy in the mining 'colonies' also shot up in the years of the largest influx. In short, overcrowding was not primarily a consequence of the limited economic resources of the tenants. Rather it resulted from the attempt to pack the population surplus into the existing accommodation despite the housing shortage.[21]

The local infrastructure responded even more slowly and inadequately to the influx of workers than the building market. In the industrial villages as well as in those larger settlements which had begun to assume urban dimensions, public and private services lagged far behind the growth of the population. There were political reasons for this, but also the economic one that the working-class

21. The population was divided into three groups on the basis of their tax assessment; each group elected one-third of the councillors. Frequently the first group comprised a mere handful, while all the workers were included in group three. This is demonstrated in action on the Sophienau Estate in Gelsenkirchen-Schalke by G. Schäfer, *Lebensstandard und Wohnungswesen der Arbeiter in der Gemeinde Schalke*, state exam. thesis, Essen, 1975, pp. 51ff.

population, which amounted to four-fifths of the total population in some communities, did not create a large and attractive demand for such businesses as shops and public houses. Politically, the peculiarities of the three-class voting system[22] frequently resulted in a situation in which four-fifths of the population (the workers) elected less than one-tenth of the local councillors. The response to these discriminations was in many cases abstention from the ballot. Consequently, the councils in the industrial villages of the Rhineland were in the hands of the ancient class of indigenous landowning peasants. These people lived like parasites on industry and its working class; but via the council they tried to keep local expenditure as low as possible. Wherever industry had established housing colonies within a particular council district, these peasants were happy to pocket exorbitant profits from the sale of land; however, they showed a marked reluctance to finance consequential costs like roads and, above all, education through higher rates and other taxes. In Westphalia the electoral law gave special privileges to the entrepreneurs.[23] Nevertheless there existed a so-called Settlement Act under which councils could demand from companies which built housing colonies the pre-financing of infrastructural costs, in particular expenditure on education. It must be left open whether there was truth in the frequently made complaint that companies were thus all the more reluctant to provide housing for their employees. It is difficult to find the statistical evidence for this. One explanation may be that the entrepreneurs held a strong position in the local councils. This would seem to have been of some influence in the negotiations between the mine-owners and the local communities.

If the electoral law provided the lever by which the propertied groups could keep public services to a minimum, the tax law formed the basis of their policies. Income tax was the most important

22. Industrial establishments also had the right to vote in local elections. Frequently the directors of the local coal mine, as the biggest single tax-payer, could pick one-third of the councillors directly. See Niethammer, *Communalbaumeister*, pp. 139f.; H. Croon, *Die gesellschaftlichen Auswirkungen des Gemeindewahlrechts in den Gemeinden und Kreisen des Rheinlandes und Westfalens im 19. Jahrhundert*, Cologne/Opladen, 1960; idem, 'Bürgertum und Verwaltung in den Städten des Ruhrgebiets im 19. Jahrhundert', in *Tradition*, vol. 9, 1964, pp. 23ff.

23. The so-called Settlement Act of 25 August 1876. See A. Born, *Das preussische Polizeirecht*, Berlin, 1902, p. 293; Schäfer, *Lebensstandard*, pp. 39ff; Hundt, *Ruhrgebiet*, pp. 40f., who adds that the mining companies of Westphalia either expanded existing collieries or built new ones in urban areas to evade a contribution to the cost of providing a communal infrastructure when the erection of colonies was adopted.

source of revenue of the communities. But the working class of the industrial districts earned too little to enable them to raise large sums. In Borbeck (near Essen) income tax revenue was 630 marks p.a. per 100 inhabitants. The comparable figures for Frankfurt and Berlin were 2,617 and 1,707 marks. Despite the low revenue, the burden in percentage terms was higher in Borbeck. There a communal charge of 220 per cent was added to the basic rate; in Berlin and Frankfurt it was respectively 100 per cent and 105 per cent. It is not surprising therefore that the local council which represented the major taxpayers should put its face against increases in these rates. Nor did other taxes provide a way out. The most important indirect tax in the hands of the councils was the 'turnover tax' which was levied on the sale or purchase of land. Two factors must be taken into account as far as the mining areas are concerned. Underground shafts were liable to cause subsidence. Land for building purposes was hence limited as well as less valuable. While in other urban areas the growing concentration of the population made land more valuable, in the mining districts the trend was in the opposite direction — to the detriment of communal revenue. Moreover, from the start, the mining companies had bought as much land as possible in order to avoid claims for damage caused to property by subsidence. Consequently, a large turnover in land holdings did not develop. The combination of these factors resulted in a drying-up of this source of communal revenue.[24] If, nevertheless, a council decided to make larger investments, further problems were likely to arise. If subsidence occurred after an area had been developed at considerable expense, no damages could be claimed from the mining companies. Furthermore, it happened frequently that, where infrastructural investments were made (gas, water, electricity), private households were the only consumers. Companies, which as big consumers would have made these services potentially profitable, tended to supply their own energy and water; the incentive to the councils was correspondingly diminished.[25]

In the industrial towns, and above all those of the Emscher region, most of the community budget went to education.[26] Class-

24. H. Lücker, 'Die Entwicklung und die Probleme des Gemeindeabgabenwesens in den Städten und grossen Landgemeinden der preussischen Industriebezirke', in *SVSP*, vol. 127, 1910, pp. 33ff; W. Gerloff, *Die Finanz- und Zollpolitik des Deutschen Reiches nebst ihren Beziehungen zu Bund- und Gemeindefinanzen*, Jena, 1913.
25. Ibid., p. 6.
26. See R. Gräfin von Schmettow, *Schulpolitik und Schulpraxis in Borbeck 1850–*

room rolls were high and in this respect, too, the working-class population was therefore permanently disadvantaged in its access to training and culture.[27] In view of the majorities which, as we have seen, obtained in the local councils, it was not entirely a question of funding. There existed but few channels to wield an influence in environmental matters and to establish something like a policy of town-planning.[28] To this day, the Ruhr is shaped by the manifestations of a Social Darwinist pattern of growth: houses, factories, roads, railroads and waterways form a veritable maze. Housing estates are surrounded or cut in half by factories and transport links; in between we find industrial wastelands or a few small fields, punctuated by hamlets and the ubiquitous large industrial installations.

In order to obtain better planning and higher expenditure, many mayors tried to gain for their community the recognised status of a town. This would have carried with it the introduction of the three-class voting system, and this — incomprehensible as it may seem to us today — appeared to these mayors as a progressive, even utopian step. The communal administrations would, in this way and by allying themselves with the largely insignificant and numerically weak petty bourgeoisie, have achieved a greater independence from the local farmers and industrialists; higher taxes could have been imposed on the latter to finance infrastructural planning and improvements and thus to attract more middle-class people. They would also have escaped from the clutches of the Prussian *Landrat* (local administrator), under whose authority they were now forced to operate. But it was precisely for this latter reason that their aspirations came to nought. A letter by the *Regierungspräsident* (regional administrator) at Düsseldorf of 1898 provides a good insight into the considerations of the higher authorities, when they were confronted with an application by the Altenessen council. This council was reputed to be in the vanguard of the movement to become elevated to the status of a town among the 'Rhinish-Westphalian industrial communities between Oberhausen and Hamm'.

The *Regierungspräsident* replied that Altenessen was no more than a conglomerate of widely scattered pits, workers' colonies and

---

    1915, Diplomarbeit, Essen, 1976, esp. pp. 47f.
27. Ibid., p. 100.
28. For details see Niethammer, *Communalbaumeister*.

individual houses. There was no middle class from which the payment of higher taxes could be expected. All in all, he argued, the workers' communities resembled 'everything rather than that which one commonly associates with the notion of a town'. Above all, there were political reasons which spoke against a change of status: 'The disadvantage of having ultramontane [Catholic] majorities in the town councils would be exacerbated by the existence of urban police forces which would be detached from the supervision of the *Landräte*'. He therefore felt bound to reject the notion of elevating Ruhr communities to the status of towns 'on grounds of principle', particularly bearing in mind the consequences of a situation which excluded 'firm supervision by the State', which might have to be upheld in times of 'economic crisis and political ferment in the most densely populated industrial region of the Prussian State'.[29]

A few of the huge industrial villages, it is true, ultimately managed to gain recognition as towns. This happened in some cases after the number of inhabitants had risen to over 100,000 and the inequities had reached scandalous proportions; and after the 1906 reorganisation of the police forces under central control had given the state powers which extended beyond the towns and cities. The elevation to city status might have been advantageous for the building of schools and parks or for the provision of roads. Basically the decision came too late. The pattern of development had been fixed long beforehand; factories, colonies and communications could no longer be changed; the destruction of the environment was already taking place. The regional planning which was undertaken after the First World War could do no more than preserve and rationalise what was already there. The mass of industrial villages continued to grow without much control, until they were absorbed as suburbs by the cities which were looking for land for the settlement of factories and people.

For the labouring population this made little difference because the deficient urbanisation of their environment continued in the new suburban context. As far as the larger cities of the Ruhr are concerned, absorption of surrounding industrial villages invariably involved a step towards a position of centrality. This in turn led to the formation of secondary city centres away from the housing areas. There public and private services were concentrated and, in

---

29. Landesarchiv Koblenz, 403, no. 13885, Regierungspräsident Düsseldorf to Prussian Interior Minister, 16.8.1898.

view of the low purchasing power of the surrounding working population, developed only slowly.

Mobility as a Way of Life

The sense of being sedentary has been lost completely in recent years. . . . No inhabitant of the suburbs feels secure on his 'plot', in his street, within his four walls from one quarter to the next. Nor does the inhabitant of the inner city know in what distance from, and in what part of, the sprawling city he will rest his tired limbs during the next six months. It is therefore hardly possible to speak of accommodation; at most there are temporary abodes, tents made out of brick which constantly change hands. Nobody can glory in or enjoy a 'home'; nobody can dare to select and furnish his accommodation with a view to a future expansion of his family. Thus a trace of unrest and anxiety affects the entire population; the ephemeral life of a nomad replaces a quiet sedate bourgeois existence; and the metropolis now houses within its walls a population which is permanently on the move and is pushing and shoving its members.[30]

Although this is a description of mid-nineteenth-century Vienna, it very neatly reflects the conditions which obtained also in German cities in the second half of the century. For this reason it was always cited approvingly by bourgeois reformers in Germany. Above all, the quotation mirrors the anxieties of the bourgeoisie. It feared that this 'pushing and shoving' doom-spelling mass 'must, full of anger about the insecurity in their housing condition, increasingly lose its feeling of attachment to the soil as well as a healthy sense of law and order'.[31]

Similarly, the compiler of the housing statistics for Essen was reminded in 1900 of 'conditions which dated back to the period before all settlement and culture'.[32] The figures which he collected would seem to support these anxieties. As is reflected in Table 2, about one half of all of Essen's households had moved in the two

30. B. Friedmann, *Die Wohnungsnot in Wien*, Vienna, 1857, quoted in Engel, *Wohnungsnoth*, p. 6. Best survey on mobility: D. Langewiesche, 'Wanderungsbewegungen in der Hochindustrialisierungsperiode', in *Vierteljahrsschrift für Sozial- und Wirtschaftsgeschichte*, vol. 64, 1977, pp. 1–40. A more detailed discussion of the following arguments may be found in Niethammer and Brüggemeier, 'Arbeiter', pp. 83ff. 109ff.; Brüggemeier, *Leben vor Ort*, pp. 52ff.
31. B. Friedmann, in Engel, *Wohnungsnoth*, p. 6.
32. Wiedfeldt, 'Das Aftermietwesen in der Stadt Essen nach der Aufnahme vom 1. Dezember 1900', in *Beiträge zur Statistik der Stadt Essen*, no. 7, Essen, 1902, p. 50.

Table 2. *Household size, sub-tenants and duration of accomodation*
To show % of 100 households who, 1.12.1900, have occupied their flats since:

No. in house-hold		1900				Total					Total
		1.10.	1.7.	1.4.	1.1.	1–4	1899	1898	1897	1896	5+6
		1	2	3	4	5	6	7	8	9	10
2	a*	19.0	10.4	11.6	4.4	45.4	15.8	8.2	4.4	3.1	61.2
	b*	17.4	10.9	7.6	—	—	15.2	10.9	4.4	3.3	—
3	a	14.8	8.3	10.6	4.2	37.9	20.5	10.7	5.5	3.6	58.4
	b	13.4	10.3	11.3	6.5	41.5	16.4	12.0	5.8	4.1	57.9
4	a	12.9	7.1	8.7	3.5	32.2	18.0	12.4	7.9	5.3	40.2
	b	14.0	6.9	13.6	4.3	38.8	17.7	10.8	8.9	3.5	56.5
5	a	11.5	7.4	8.2	3.4	30.5	16.3	11.9	7.1	6.1	46.8
	b	14.0	9.1	13.0	4.8	40.9	15.9	12.2	6.2	3.8	56.8
6	a	10.0	7.3	7.2	2.9	27.4	16.8	10.8	7.9	5.2	44.2
	b	12.0	8.1	10.6	4.8	35.5	17.1	12.7	9.4	6.7	52.6
7	a	10.6	6.8	6.6	2.8	26.8	15.5	10.6	7.9	5.9	32.7
	b	9.6	8.7	10.2	4.9	33.4	19.8	10.4	6.4	6.2	53.2
8	a	11.8	7.4	7.0	3.0	29.2	14.2	8.9	7.5	5.7	43.4
	b	10.7	9.6	9.0	4.0	33.3	20.3	11.5	8.1	3.8	53.6
9	a	9.5	4.1	5.1	2.4	21.1	12.8	9.2	6.1	7.0	33.9
	b	10.0	6.2	9.4	5.6	31.2	15.6	14.3	8.7	5.0	46.8
10	a	11.3	5.0	6.3	3.6	26.2	10.9	9.1	7.1	6.3	37.1
	b	12.8	7.2	5.1	3.8	28.9	20.4	10.6	7.7	7.2	49.3

*a = without subtenants
*b = with subtenants
Source: Wieldfeldt, 'Das Aftermietwesen in der Stadt Essen nach der Aufnahme vom 1. Dezember 1900', in *Beiträge zur Statistik der Stadt Essen*, vol. 7, p. 52.

years prior to the collection of data; between 21 per cent and 45 per cent had moved during the previous year and a sizeable proportion (up to 19 per cent) had done so within the previous two months. The data also revealed that mobility was not confined just to young single workers, but affected also families, some of whom had a large number of children and who were apparently forced frequently to change their accommodation. Thus some 30 per cent of families with eight members had moved in the course of 1900.

The most important reason for this high degree of mobility emerges from Table 3. It shows that on average more than half of the work-force in the firms listed had been taken on or had left the

Table 3. *Mobility of labour within the iron, coal and steel industries,*
1896–1908 (%)

	Krupp*		Bochumer Verein ı		Zechen im Ruhrgebiet		Bergrevier Duisburg*	
	(a)[1]	(b)[2]	(a)	(b)	(a)	(b)	(a)	(b)
1896	36	25	60	40	49	50	—	—
1897	47	32	58	52	59	45	87	52
1898	49	39	62	51	59	49	83	60
1899	52	44	63	59	63	51	—	—
1900	45	45	58	65	68	52	96	74
1901	24	33	23	40	54	47	—	—
1902	14	21	18	26	48	44	98	73
1903	31	23	47	40	58	48	86	69
1904	54	35	45	40	54	48	78	62
1905	59	40	66	56	38	34	61	48
1906	48	45	79	64	57	49	82	68
1907	34	44	82	69	71	56	86	70
1908	36	33	41	60	63	58	72	67

(a)[1] = joining   (b)[2] = leaving
*Krupp has been chosen as the example of a company with low mobility;
Bergrevier Duisburg, because of its rapid expansion, shows a rapid fluctu-
ation.

Source: R. Ehrenberg, 'Schwäche und Stärke neuzeitlicher Arbeitsgemeinschaf-
ten', in *Archiv für exakte Wirtschaftsforschung* (Thünen Archiv), Jg. 3,
1911, p. 450.

company in the course of a year. The figures for Krupp are a bit
lower, but are nevertheless very high by present-day standards.
Similar figures have been collected for other regions and cities of the
German Empire. It is important to remember that there was no
commuter transport in those days or, where it existed, it was too
expensive for a worker. Changes of the work-place therefore frequently led to a change of address, except in those cases where
accommodation was already in the vicinity of the new work-place.
Renting a flat was invariably of a temporary nature and this, in turn,
influenced to a high degree the pattern of living. Whoever was
constantly on the move, found himself in a new environment and
was forced to forge new contacts and relationships, lived necessarily
more 'open'. He could not retreat to his house and turn it into a
haven of *Gemütlichkeit* and seclusion from the outside world.
Accommodation was something temporary; he could not strike
roots there and make a home for the rest of his life.

This loose relationship with one's abode, which it is difficult to relive today, was reinforced in many families by the existence of sub-tenants (*Aftermieter*) and overnight lodgers (*Schlafgänger*), who shared the flat and frequently even the bed.[33] The sub-tenants were almost exclusively made up of single young men who had left the parental home in search of employment opportunities, but could not afford to rent their own accommodation, not even a bedsitter, and hence had to move in as sub-tenants. Single women who had left their parents and moved into the city worked primarily as domestic servants and hence lived in the house of their employers. Areas with a high proportion of female factory labour were the exception, such as the centres of the textile industry (e.g. Mönchengladbach); there were even female overnight lodgers in such areas.

Many newcomers were probably used to living away from their own family, in a strange household. This was even more true of those who had grown up in the country, where it was customary that the children of day-labourers, farm-hands and impoverished peasants would leave their parents at a very early age. They would find work on a farm and sleep with other servants in the servants' quarter — often no more than a partitioned-off corner in the stables. Or they had perhaps grown up in a household which had lodgers. Between 10 per cent and 20 per cent of all households in Imperial Germany took lodgers and in working-class families the proportion was certainly higher. A decline occurred only after the turn of the century. These figures, however, can provide only limited information as to the actual extent of sub-tenancies. The percentage of families that took lodgers at some stage was certainly higher. Often lodgers were accepted in times of crisis; the additional income could be vital, above all if the father's income ceased or became reduced through illness, accident or long-term unemployment; or else if family expenditure rose due to child-bearing. Children meant additional costs and reduced income because the wife could no longer remain in full-time employment. In 1900, for example, around 70 per cent of Essen's households with sub-tenants also had children. The figures for other cities are similar.[34]

33. Lodgers rented a bed or part of a bed; *Zimmermieter* had a claim to a separate room. The difference was more apparent than real, however. It was the outcome of a fear of the Housing Police from which one attempted to escape by resorting to such practices.
34. Wiedfeldt, 'Aftermietwesen', p. 33.

Once the children grew older and began to earn their own money or once the father had recuperated, there was no economic need to continue a lodging arrangement. Within the life-cycle of a family there were therefore crisis situations which were overcome by sub-tenancies. Consequently, no more than 10 to 20 per cent of households had overnight lodgers at any one time, although looked at over a longer period, the percentage was higher. This at least temporary opening-up of a family may best be defined as a 'half-open family structure'. It was a structure which not only facilitated the acceptance of strangers, but also eased the mobility of the families themselves.

The lodgers, too, were motivated primarily by economic considerations when they accepted a bed in a family, but it was also important for them that they were able to avoid social isolation in this way. They could establish social contact, adapt quickly to new circumstances and even feel 'at home'. Moreover, the women in the family looked after the washing and mending of clothes and did occasional shopping for them, with or without an extra charge.

We cannot determine with certainty the actual relationship between overnight lodgers and "their" families. Disputes and tensions are likely to have been a recurrent phenomenon. After all, these were adults who, though they lived under the same roof, did not know each other and probably found adjustment to each other difficult. If the writings of bourgeois reformers are to be believed, it was Sodom and Gomorrha everywhere and culture went by the board. But from what can be gleaned from autobiographies, reports and interviews, this type of coexistence appears to have been possible without insuperable problems.[35]

The combination of frequent moves and sub-tenancy was not a phenomenon restricted specifically to the Ruhr; it was also to be found in other parts of the Reich.[36] In the region between the Emscher and Lippe Rivers living patterns, especially among the miners, assumed particular features, owing to (a) the occupational structure; (b) the social structure of the neighbourhood and (c) the type of newcomer to the area. These three factors led to a greater degree of homogeneity and a relatively untroubled coexistence.

35. Niethammer and Brüggemeier, 'Arbeiter', pp. 109ff.
36. There are historical precedents for the lodging tradition and open family structures, e.g. in the crafts professions where journeymen were part of the master's household. What was new was that families became open to members of their own class and that the practice reached such major proportions.

In the iron and steel industries the range of skilled occupations was wider and their practice frequently required a training in a particular craft.[37] Workers who had had such a training were much in demand in the period of rapid expansion prior to the First World War. In a market situation which favoured them in this way they tended to change their work-place frequently in pursuit of higher wages, but also of better working conditions. Next to these skilled workers were the large numbers of unskilled newcomers. The best they could hope for was to learn specific skills without, however, being able to gain genuine qualifications. Consequently their income levels remained low. By changing their work-place frequently they sought to improve their situation and to attain a measure of material security which their lack of training was unable to provide. Their mobility was marked by economic pressures and great insecurity. Conditions in the mining industry were different. There were mainly two groups: hewers and hauliers. They made up respectively 50 per cent and 20 per cent of the total work-force and hence comprised a larger proportion of the underground workers. It is possible to differentiate these two groups further in terms of their work, but these differences were not particularly significant because the Ruhr mining companies expected a miner to be able to do all mining jobs. Until after the end of the First World War there was no formal training; newcomers worked as hauliers at first; later they became trainee hewers and finally hewers. From trainee hewer level onwards, if not before, they would work in a gang (*Gedinge*) of four to six men who would provide the necessary training. As can be seen from the high proportion of the two groups among the total work-force, most newcomers eventually became hewers, thus skilled labourers. Their rise to this position varied, but normally took about four to five years. It was only in mining that this avenue to skilled worker status existed.

Another special feature of mining-work were the forms of organisation underground: the *Gedinge*. This was a group of miners which worked quite autonomously and hence determined its own pace and division of labour. They were paid jointly and in the Ruhr were exposed to hardly any supervision.[38] This form of organisation

37. There are very few detailed studies on work processes and their connection with company structure. General references in R. Ehrenberg, 'Krupp Studien III. Die Frühzeit der Krupp'schen Arbeiterschaft', in Thünen-Archiv, III, 1911; Crew, *Town*, pp. 205ff.; Tenfelde, *Sozialgeschichte*, pp. 219ff. On the relation between skills and mobility, See Langewiesche, *Wanderungsbewegungen*, pp. 29ff.
38. Most of the available literature stresses the hierarchical structures of the mining

and remuneration generated a sense of togetherness which was
reinforced by the dangerous work the miners were involved in. The
homogeneity and the mechanisms of integration which existed in
the production sphere also obtained in the sphere of reproduction,
and in particular in the sphere of accommodation. Miners, more
often than other workers, kept to themselves. This was true of
single industry areas like Bottrop, but has also been demonstrated
for Bochum, for example.[39] This homogeneity was reinforced by
the building of miners' colonies. As early as 1901 some 21 per cent
of all miners lived in company-owned housing; by 1914 this figure
had risen to 35 per cent and by 1919 even to 40 per cent. Another
factor was the taking of lodgers. The mining companies approved of
this because the construction of houses could not keep up with the
influx of people. In their campaigns to recruit new miners, the
companies explicitly drew attention to the fact that lodgers provided an additional source of income: 'As four lodgers can be put up
in a room, rent per month will be reduced by four marks, quite
apart from the income to be gained by the family for food. If a
family has four rooms, it would have to pay 4 × 4 = 16 marks per
month. If it takes four lodgers, rent would be no more than 12
marks'.[40] In 1901 every other dwelling owned by a mining company
had — at least in terms of the statistical average — one overnight
lodger. The percentage of lodgers among miners was 21 per cent in
1893. This percentage probably remained about the same up to the
First World War. This means that in 1914 there were some 80,000
overnight lodgers in the mining industry alone.[41]

It was also important where the newcomers came from. The early
waves arrived from the locality or region. But as early as the 1870s

---

industry. The implicit assumption is that controls were very far-reaching and
intensive. However, such notions are based on complaints etc. and do not
include an analysis of work-processes. See, e.g., *Die Verhandlungen und Untersuchungen der Preussischen Stein- und Kohlenfallkommission*, Berlin, 1906;
Brüggemeier, *Leben vor Ort*, pp. 92ff.

39. See Crew, *Town*, p. 332; O. Stoltenberg, *Herkunftsgebiet und Zuwanderung
Bottroper Zechenbelegschaften am Ende des 19. Jahrhunderts*, state exam. thesis,
Bochum, 1970.

40. Thus the leaflet distributed by one agent, repr. in L. Fischer-Eckert, *Die
wirtschaftliche und soziale Lage der Frauen im modernen Industrieort Hamborn
im Rheinland*, Ph.D. thesis, Tübingen, 1913, p. 60.

41. See H. Münz, *Die Lage der Bergarbeiter im Ruhrrevier*, Essen, 1909, p. 136. For
comparison purposes, some percentages of accommodation with lodgers in a
number of towns of the Ruhr area: Recklinghausen (18); Castrop (19); Bochum
(9.8); Wattenscheid (15.1); Herne (15.3). See *Ergebnisse der Wohnungsauf-
nahme in den westfälischen Städten vom 1. Dezember 1905*, pt. 1, Münster
1907/09, passim.

fresh waves arrived from the eastern provinces of Prussia, some of whom had been recruited by agents sent there. It frequently happened that whole groups from one or more villages moved to the Ruhr and stayed and lived together. Once settled, they would ask relatives and friends who had stayed behind to join them. Others came of their own accord and at first would move in with people they already knew. As a result of these mechanisms, there emerged areas of concentration. Gelsenkirchen, for instance, became a gathering place for Masurians. Almost half of the newcomers working for the Prosper Colliery in Bottrop originated from two districts in Silesia, Rybnik and Ratibor. The mining companies attracted workers with the explicit assurance they would not even notice that they had left their homeland:

> Masurians! The main objective of the mining company is to recruit modest and decent families for this brand new colony. If possible, this colony is to be made up exclusively of Masurian families. In this way, the Masurians will remain completely among themselves and will have nothing to do with Poles, East Prussians etc. Everyone may think he were still in his Masurian homeland.[42]

The immigrant and family centres which emerged in this way, eased the move to the Ruhr area. But they also facilitated mobility within the region itself. The 'half-open' family structure with its conditions and mechanisms which were mediated via the spheres of production and reproduction provided additional help. It is not possible to evaluate all these different factors and the life-styles resulting from them in detail. There were undoubtedly problems and tensions; nevertheless it can be said that without these it would not have been possible to meet the difficulties which resulted from move and mobility, low wages and shortage of accommodation.[43]

However, such considerations were alien to the authorities and to the bourgeois reformers. They remained blinkered by their own moral values. How prejudiced the authorities were may be seen in a report by Freiherr von Berlepsch, the *Regierungspräsident* of Düsseldorf and later Prussian Minister of Trade, who was reputed to be liberal and progressive. He started from the assumption that housing needs were 'more flexible and elastic' than 'nutritional

42. See Fischer-Eckert, *Soziale Lage*, p. 61; Stoltenberg, *Herkunftsgebiet*, p. 45.
43. A similar argument in J.K. Modell and T.K. Hareven, 'Urbanization and the Malleable Household. An Examination of Boarding and Lodging in American Families', in *Journal of Marriage and Family*, vol. 35, 1973, pp. 467–79.

needs'. Poor housing conditions were therefore the fault of the workers, who reduced their requirements in this area 'firstly and mostly'. Workers, Belepsch believed, preferred to live in 'poor and unhealthy' accommodation rather than 'saving a bit on food or even drink'.[44] Workers themselves saw the situation rather differently, as can be seen from documents relating to their income. Their earnings were so low that they were barely sufficient to keep above the poverty line; it was not possible to save on food; the only way out was to move into an even smaller flat and/or to take lodgers.

Official ignorance is reflected above all in the authorities policies, which consisted in the main of bans and prescriptive decrees. Lodgers, for example, were only allowed if a separate room was available. This was totally unrealistic and hence was not enforced. The main complaint, however, was that the police did not do enough. Police intervention was seen as an effective instrument, in particular in that area which caused special anxiety, that of morals.

For example, brickmakers from Lippe-Detmold who worked in the Düsseldorf district during the summer often had no more than a bale of straw to sleep on. Their hovels were barely protected against wind and rain, often consisting of a single room in which to accommodate the entire family. To the authorities this did not appear to be too bad a situation. They started from the assumption that the

> brick-makers spend no more than the short summer nights in the brick huts; they work in the open in daytime and are hence hardened by the weather. No serious damage to health has up to now therefore resulted from the poor condition of the brick huts. On the other hand, this accommodation is more worrying from the moral view-point as there is no adequate separation of sleeping facilities according to sexes.[45]

Obsessed by such ideas, the authorities resorted almost exclusively to repressive measures which interfered deeply with the private sphere of the working class. Such measures may have given

44. See Hauptstaatsarchiv Düsseldorf, Regierung Düsseldorf, 24781, Denkschrift des Regierungspräsidenten, 'Geben die Wohnungsverhältnisse der arbeitenden Bevölkerung des Bezirks zu Bedenken Veranlassung und wie können dieselben evtl. durch polizeiliche Vorschriften und Massnahmen verbessert werden?', 8.6.1887. In view of the very inadequate pensions and and the lacking or poorly-paid jobs for women, taking a lodger was frequently the only chance of survival for widows. They were the people to suffer most from police activities.
45. Ibid., also for the following.

them a greater degree of self-satisfaction and contributed to many a burgher remaining undisturbed in his sleep. But the poor housing conditions were not changed by such policies. This latter point did not escape the authorities of (for example) the Essen rural district. Their report to von Berlepsch came to the conclusion that 'a combating of existing conditions and violations by the police' would be impossible 'until housing was constructed on a larger scale'.

Self-Help and Intervention

The housing sphere had thus seen the emergence of structures and mechanisms of self-help among which the 'half-open' family was the most important. These patterns cushioned and mitigated the initial problems of integration and adaptation and helped to bridge economic crisis situations. However important the role of the family was in these respects, it was of no more than limited use as an instrument for solving structural deficiencies. A solution of these deficiencies would have required a collective effort. But the state failed its citizens here. Nor was it possible to solve these tasks via the free market. The working class could not dispose of sufficient money to secure a profit for the entrepreneurs, while providing the workers with their requirements. Consequently there was no improvement in the insufficient provision in the cultural and social sphere (play-groups, schools, hospitals). Indeed, this deficiency persists to some extent to this day. In one small area it was, however, possible to remove existing deficiencies through self-help in the formation of book clubs (*Lesezirkel*), cooperative societies and building societies.[46] In the Ruhr there developed moreover a special form of cooperative organisation: the 'schnapps-casino'. This institution aimed to deal with a particular problem — the shortage of public houses.

The Ruhr and the industrial communities of the area in particular were among those parts of the German Empire with the lowest density of public houses (see Table 4). That part of German communities which was least provided for in this respect was situated, up to two-thirds, in the industrial provinces of Silesia, Westphalia

---

46. See G. Huck, in J. Reulecke and W. Weber (eds.), *Fabrik — Familie — Feierabend*, Wuppertal, 1978, pp. 215–45.

Table 4. *Correlation between public house and inhabitants in selected German towns, 1898*

	Berlin	Münster	Bochum	Recklinghausen	Dortmund
Inhabitants per pub	135	160	275	317	329

	Borbeck	Gelsenkirchen	Essen	Altenessen	Schalke	Ueckendorf
Inhabitants per pub	329	367	457	495	511	594

Source: G. Tenius 'Die Gast-und Schankwirtschaften in den deutschen Gemeinden mit mehr als 15,000 Einwohnern nach dem Stande vom November 1898', in *Mitteilungen des Statistischen Amtes der Stadt Dortmund*, vol. 3, Dortmund, 1901.

and the Rhineland. Of all the places in the Ruhr appearing in the statistics some eighteen, amounting to 78 per cent, belonged to this category. The ratio became even worse in subsequent years. The authorities granted few if any licenses, while the influx of people continued. In 1900 Hamborn had a pub for every 545 inhabitants; in 1910 the ratio was 1:764. Such figures by themselves do not give a sufficient impression of the dimensions of the problem. We must also take into account the sprawling building pattern. The industrial villages tended to cover large areas over which colonies, terraces and single houses were distributed. The distance to the next pub was considerably greater than in the densely-populated traditional urban centres.

On the other hand, it was very important to have access to pubs. They offered a rare possibility of escape from the cramped conditions of the flats, to meet after work, to exchange information and to talk about things. Often the rooms were used for meetings organised by the trade unions or by the Social Democrats; there were also celebrations by clubs and associations. In short, pubs were an indispensable part of working-class life, and yet their use was systematically denied to the inhabitants of the Ruhr area and of the colonies in particular.[47] The problem was not just the locating of

47. On the importance of these pubs, see Reck, *Arbeiter*. However, he rather simplistically divides workers into three groups according to the (supposed) frequency of their pub-going: (1) family-orientated workers; (2) very frequent customers (Dauergast); (3) workers between family and public houses. The analysis of schnapps-casinos is largely based on the files in Staatsarchiv Münster, OBA Dortmund, 1834.

a pub. Many workers could not even go. Whoever worked on the midday shift would not return home until 11 p.m.; by then pubs would be closed. Night-shift workers had similar problems and they, too, were excluded from a fundamental part of communal life.

The establishment of schnapps-casinos appeared to be an improvement on this situation. These were closed societies founded for the purpose of buying beer and spirits cheaply and of selling them to their members at a reasonable price. The societies would rent a number of rooms, often in the vicinity of the pits. Schnapps-casinos emerged towards the end of the 1880s and soon gained a large membership. Thus no less than five of these societies were founded in the small town of Castrop between 1890 and 1892, with a total membership of 550. According to a report by the *Oberbergamt* Dortmund, there were some 110 schnapps-casinos in the Ruhr area in 1894 with 16,640 members. They were concentrated in the northern parts around Dortmund, Recklinghausen and Oberhausen, and their membership consisted mainly of miners.[48]

The statutes, often copied from each other, specified as the societies' objectives, the purchase of beer and spirits in order to sell them to the members as well as providing social club facilities. The societies were not registered; their legal form was that of a cooperative as this was the only form of organisation that was allowed to trade with alcoholic beverages. Being cooperatives, they formed closed societies, so that they did not have to observe licensing hours. Nor could they be controlled as the police had no access to their meeting places. In spite — or perhaps because — of this lack of controls, the authorities were convinced that the schnapps-casinos were 'breeding grounds for Social Democratic and insurgent movements'. The members, 'mainly Social Democrats', were assumed 'to be sitting until the small hours drinking large quantities of schnapps which is cheaper here than in pubs [half the price] and conducting politics'.[49] It was especially this last point which appears to have caused the authorities frequent nightmares; and to some extent these worries were justified, as the casinos were also a response to the official machinery of control. The SPD complained frequently that it experienced great difficulties in finding assembly rooms for

48. See ibid., Denkschrift des OBA Dortmund, November 1894. See also Stadtarchiv Castrop, Amt Castrop, 17. Schnapps-casinos were not restricted to the Ruhr; they also emerged on the Saar and in Upper Silesia where conditions were similar, as well as Saxony and Hesse-Nassau. However, they were most widespread in the Ruhr region.
49. Ibid., Report by Bergrevier Dortmund-West, n.d.

its meetings, since 'publicans who. . .make their rooms available
to Social Democratic meetings' had to put up with 'disadvantages
imposed by the authorities'.[50] The result was that the schnapps-
casinos put their rooms at the disposal of the SPD. It is also
significant that some casinos, especially in the area of Dortmund,
employed miners who had been dismissed because of their involve-
ment in the 1889 strike as *Kastellane* (stewards). Here again we are
dealing less with a party-political strategy than with a response by
ordinary workers. The SPD did little to promote the schnapps-
casinos, probably because it did not wish to endanger its own
'honourable' cooperatives, which were geared to the provision of
groceries.[51] Thus the *Rheinisch-Westfälische Arbeiterzeitung* of 20
December 1894 bemoaned the closing down of casinos not so much
as a matter of principle, but rather because of its timing, and
wondered: 'Did this action, which deprives a number of family
fathers of their livelihood, have to be taken just before Christmas?'

At the beginning, however, the founding of schnapps-casinos was
not a political act, but was based on pragmatic considerations. They
are enumerated in a letter which the *Zur Guten Hoffnung* (Good
Hope) Society of Castrop wrote on 11 July 1894:

As is well-known and can, if necessary, easily be ascertained, it is very
hot in the pits of the *Graf Schwerin* colliery. The miners working there
are bathed in sweat at all times of the year. The midday shift starts at 2
p.m. and finishes at about 11 p.m. Many miners live at a fair distance
from the colliery, [in some cases] up to one hour. If these miners in their
state of heavy perspiration return from their work and have to walk back
to their houses, especially in wet or cold weather, above all during the
winter in snow and freezing temperatures, their health is obviously very
highly endangered, unless they can suitably refresh themselves beforehand and dry their clothes. The house of widow Swift is very close to the
colliery at the intersection of the streets [and is] hence the most appropriate place in the area. The pubs are closed at the times mentioned [above]
for people to warm up. And even if they were open, the publican would
not like to see people who are so drenched as to soil the furniture to dry
their clothes. The Society's rooms, on the other hand, are to be kept
warm by day and by night during winter-time. They will be open to
members irrespective of whether they are in wet or black and dirty
clothes. The purpose of the Society is in no way to pander to human
passions, but to protect the health of its members against harm in every
possible way.[52]

50. *Rheinisch-Westfälische Arbeiterzeitung*, 20.12.1894.
51. See Stenographische Berichte über die Verhandlungen des Reichstags, IX. Leg.
    Per., IV Session, 1895/97, vol. II, pp. 1273ff.; ibid., vol. IV, pp. 2505ff.
52. Stadtarchiv Castrop, Amt Castrop, 17.

The authorities were not prepared to accept such arguments. According to a report by the *Oberbergamt* Dortmund, schnapps-casinos were 'the actual seedbeds of drunkenness, sloth, brutalisation, of domestic instability and the destitution of families; [they] damage the public weal to the highest degree'.[53] Consequently they pursued only one aim — to ban these places of mischief. In this no effort was too big and no move devious enough.

The *Landrat* at Hörde, for example, issued a decree stipulating that half a square metre of space had to be provided per member. He knew well that this was the end of large workers' societies. They would not be able to rent facilities of this size. Middle-class societies, on the other hand, were not affected by such stipulations. The casinos did not give up so easily. They went to court. The lower court sided with the *Landrat*. But they appealed and ultimately even won before the *Kammergericht* at Berlin. There were many court cases of this kind and the outcomes differed. Some casinos were prosecuted because it was alleged that non-members had obtained alcoholic drinks. Penalties in such cases were draconian, varying from 20 to 50 marks. This must be compared with annual rents. Thus the Unity Society at Huckarde paid 170 marks per annum for its rooms. Faced with such high penalties, several casinos stopped trading. Others continued, however, and charged a very small entry fee of 20 pfennigs. The membership list was left in the rooms so that everybody could be quickly entered just before the arrival of the police. Alternatively, where a spontaneous entry was no longer possible, those present were nominated honorary members. Some societies in fact had more honorary than ordinary members.

The casinos could thus not be curbed by means of administrative measures or through the courts. Moreover, the verdict in some cases was not always to the authorities' liking. Above all, in many cases, their repressive policies led to a highly undesirable result, as the report of the *Oberbergamt* Dortmund admitted: 'The [casinos'] organisation was at first very informal; it has assumed a more stable form, in line with legal requirements, in the wake of the conflict with the regional police authorities'.[54]

Effective measures were possible only after the law had been changed by the Reichstag majority. Thereafter cooperatives were required to have a licence if they wished to serve alcoholic drinks.

Such licences were never granted, of course, so that all casinos were closed down within a short period.[55]

Thus the authorities also blocked this particular attempt to find cooperative solutions to infrastructural deficiencies. However, the idea of self-help remained alive and was practised through the founding of associations in other fields. It remained relatively easy for clubs to obtain permission for organising celebrations, in fact, many clubs were founded for the sole purpose of organising an event and went into liquidation once it had been held. The authorities knew this; the meeting of mayors from the Essen *Landkreis*, in discussing this phenomenon, admitted defeat and saw no possibility of banning it. Instead they resolved, on 18 October 1910: 'It does not appear to be objectionable to permit dance festivals (*Tänzlustbarkeiten*) for individual resorts (*Ausflugsorte*); in fact [it is] even desirable [to grant such permissions] in consideration of the easy alternative to circumvent a ban on dancing by organising an alleged club event (*Vereinsfest*)'.[56] Of course, this did not protect individual groups — above all Poles and Social Democrats — who time and again suffered from police intervention and bans. Family celebrations, such as baptisms and weddings, offered another opportunity for a tax free and unsupervised get-together. However, it was impossible to escape control by the authorities completely. The police kept a watchful eye on whether it was really only family members and invited guests who attended an event for which an extension of the licence had been granted. If a family was discovered to be in breach of these rules, or if the guests paid a contribution to the costs, an entertainment tax (*Lustbarkeitssteuer*) would be levied.

Consequently there were limits to the attempts to circumvent the strict regulations governing clubs and associations. Almost everywhere in the Ruhr area there existed a ban on celebrating in public on pay day or on the day when a down payment (*Abschlagszahlung*) was made, i.e. on every first and third weekend of the month. There was complete agreement between employers and authorities as to the introduction and enforcement of this regulation. Both complained that workers would spend all their money on those two days and — worse — miss work on the following day. There is nothing surprising about this kind of absenteeism. There was no paid leave before the First World War and almost the only way of

55. The bill, involving a revision of the Gewerbeordnung, was ratified after its third reading on 10.6.1896.
56. Stadtarchiv Essen, Landkreis Essen, 114, 12.

having a free day was simply not to turn up.[57]

Two celebrations were considered a particular nuisance by employers and local bureaucrats: the annual spring and autumn fairs which were of peasant origin, but which continued as a tradition and became the great events of every community. Supported by the regional administrators (*Regierungspräsidenten*), the local administration tried time and again to abolish these fairs or to permit a 'defused' version of them. In Hamborn this alliance between employers and authorities was ultimately successful. There the fairs were replaced by a general popular festival which was intended to provide an opportunity for individual clubs and in particular for the young 'publicly to demonstrate their skills in the most varied fields, such as singing, games and sport as well as during a splendid parade'.[58] The working class, however, showed no particular enthusiasm for such events. Even the chance of offering three cheers to the Kaiser failed to inspire them. Elsewhere it worked to the advantage of the workers that the local peasants held the majority in the local councils. The mayors vehemently advocated a ban on fairs, the councillors, however, were not to be convinced. Not only did they like the events themselves, they had an economic interest in them: the fairs were traditionally also markets and there was a fear that the abolition of fairs would lead to an end of the markets. It was to no avail that — as happened in Bottrop — the mayor asked the mining companies to submit documentation on the number of work days lost during fairs. He even went so far as to have the police observe which children spent more than 50 pfennigs. He then placed a list before the local council, arguing that the children could only have acquired such sums illegally; but even the 'appalling' observation that an older boy had snatched a ball from a little one could not convince the obstinate councillors that fairs were immoral. However, the boy's name was given to his teacher who 'set disciplinary measures in train'.[59]

57. J. Reilecke, 'Vom blauen Montag zum Arbeiterurlaub', in *Archiv für Sozialgeschichte*, vol. 16, 1976, pp. 205–48.
58. Verwaltungsbericht Hamborn 1910, 5, 70; see also Lucas, *Radikalismus*, pp. 103ff.
59. Stadtarchiv Bottrop, BOT AV 7, 3.

Functional Change in Mining Colonies

'Enjoy what you have been granted. Stay with your kith and kin after a day's work, [stay] with your parents, your wife and children and think about household and family. Let this be your aim and you will enjoy many pleasant moments.' Thus Alfred Krupp, the apostle of company housing in Germany, said to 'his' workers in 1877. It was, indeed, an entrepreneurial alternative programme to the living conditions of the proletariat.[60] He had the vision of an industrial empire in the sense that he aimed to attach a 'large workers' city' to his works — 'an animated part of the factory'[61] situated like a colony in the forefield of his enterprise. It was to be a sphere in which even the private life of the workers would be shaped by the company and subjected to industrial discipline.

Such aspirations played a major role in the contributions which the factory owners made to the debate on the question of working-class housing in the last decades of the nineteenth century. To be sure, in most cases it was the more moderate version of this idea that was being mooted and which one entrepreneur described as follows in 1865: 'The workers to whom one can offer good accommodation are mostly the ones on whom one can rely more'.[62] Up to the First World War, company housing played a very insignificant part in Germany in quantitative terms. This was because capital invested in it yielded lower interest than investment in production. Moreover, the police 'whip' was easily available in the Wilhelmine state, and most entrepreneurs thought therefore that no more than token investments were necessary as 'carrots'. Social welfare policy at

---

60. W. Berdrow (ed.), *Alfred Krupps Briefe, 1826–1887*, Berlin, 1928, p. 93.
61. Historisches Archiv der Friedr. Krupp AG, Essen, Alfred Krupp to his Company, 25.11.1872. However, the housing programme of the company did not originate in visionary ideas, but in the need to accommodate the workers, when the town of Essen made no effort to deal with this problem. Accordingly, Nissen huts and barrack-like buildings were at first erected. Model settlements which were inspired by the British example were built only from the 1880s. On the Krupp settlements, see R. Günter, 'Krupp und Essen', in M. Warnke(ed.), *Das Kunstwerk zwischen Wissenschaft und Weltanschauung*, Gütersloh, 1970, pp. 128ff.; J. Schlandt, 'Die Krupp-Siedlungen — Wohnungsbau im Interesse eines Industriekonzerns', in H. G. Helms and J. Janssen (eds.), *Kapitalistischer Städtebau*, 2nd ed., Neuwied/Berlin, 1971, pp. 95ff.; H. Sturm, *Fabrikarchitektur, Villa, Arbeitersiedlung*, Munich, 1977, pp. 133ff.
62. Quoted in L. Puppke, *Sozialpolitik und soziale Anschauungen frühindustrieller Unternehmer in Westfalen*, Cologne, 1966, p. 183. This study also includes further material on the motives behind company housing, especially in the textile and metal industries.

factory level remained an academic question for the mass of the German working class.

In these circumstances it is most unlikely that it was the arguments of the participants in the debates on social policy which persuaded the Ruhr industrialists, and in particular the mine owners, to provide funds for the construction of company housing and colonies. Around 1890 it was only in the mining areas that over one-tenth of the workers and their families were in company accommodation. Thereafter there was a steep rise: a further 10 per cent was added in each decade and after the First World War some 40 per cent of the miners lived in this type of housing. As the total number of miners also rose by leaps and bounds, the absolute figures for dwellings in the hands of the mine owners is even more impressive. In 1873 there were a mere 5,500, rising to 10,525 in 1893. By 1901 the figure had reached 26,547, climbing to 82,816 in 1914 and to 124,859 in 1920. They housed 173,854 mining employees which implies that between 500,000 and 750,000 people were actually living in these houses.[63]

In the northern parts of the Ruhr, where the infrastructure was particularly backward, one half to two-thirds of the mining-employees lived in company-owned housing colonies as early as the pre-1914 period: Hamm = 68.2 per cent; Duisburg = 66.6 per cent; Recklinghausen-Ost = 53.8 per cent; Essen-West = 52.6 per cent (and if the Westphalian areas including Bottrop are added = 51.2 per cent: Recklinghausen-West = 44.6 per cent. In the traditional settlement areas to the south around Witten, Hattingen or Wattenscheid, on the other hand, no more than 10 per cent lived in colonies.[64] This contrast alone would seem to make it unlikely that the directors of the mines were much concerned for the welfare needs of the population or had a particular strategy of social control in mind.

Rather we must differentiate between two motivations. On the one hand we must ask what forced the mining companies to build

63. Figures for 1873: J. Hiltrop, 'Beiträge zur Statistik des Oberbergamtsbezirks Dortmund mit besonderer Berücksichtigung der Ansiedlungsbestrebungen der Grubenbesitzer für die Belegschaft ihrer Werke', in *Zeitschrift des Königlich-Preussischen Statistischen Bureaus*, 1875, pp. 245ff.; for 1893: Taeglichsbeck, *Belegschaft*, vol. II, pp. 6ff.; for 1901: Hundt, *Ruhrgebiet*, pp. 16ff; for 1914 and 1920: Staatsarchiv Münster, OBA Dortmund, 1837. Estimates for the following decade were for an additional requirement of 120,000 dwellings. But only another 28,000 were in fact completed. See *10 Jahre Treuhandstelle für Bergmannswohnstätten im rhein.-westf. Steinkohlenbezirk*, Essen, 1930, pp. 22f.; also the brief survey by I. Lange-Kothe, '100 Jahre Bergarbeiterwohnungen', in *Der Anschnitt*, vol. II, 1950, pp. 7ff.
64. Figures for 1914: Staatsarchiv Münster, OBA Dortmund, 1837.

accommodation for their own workers; on the other, the question is: what were the additional aims which they pursued more or less vigorously once the provision of housing was seen to be unavoidable? These two questions do not raise the problem of the actual consequences of their policies, and these will be discussed separately. The economic pressure exerted upon the mine owners was the initial problem of recruiting labour, followed by the need to deploy a skilled work-force in the immediate vicinity of the pits in a situation of immobile production locations and deficient urbanisation. In the southern parts of the Ruhr these pressures might result, during the Bismarckian period, in the provision of company-owned housing for foremen at the colliery gates, of a row of cottages for families and a dormitory for young newcomers. Smaller or medium-sized companies in the north might have started similar schemes at this time. But these were traditional practices which must be seen against the background of the fact that the older mines, formerly run by the respective sovereign as a source of revenue (*fiskalische Bergwerke*), had long housed some miners in their own purpose-built accommodation.[65]

It was only in the face of the very rapid expansion of the mining industry after 1890 and in particular after the turn of the century that the problem appeared in a completely new light. This becomes even more evident, if one looks more closely at the absolute figures rather than the percentage rates of growth. The work-forces of the Ruhr mines increased by some 20,000 to 30,000 men per annum during the peak years of expansion. Even the annual average for the years 1890–1913 was almost 15,000 new miners. If one adds to these figures the family members and basic support services, the mining industry alone year after year drew into the Ruhr a population the size of a huge industrial village or of a medium-sized town. The whole problem was thus not merely one of housing construction, but also one of town planning. It was particularly acute in the northern Emscher River region with its large collieries. But it was precisely in this region that village burgermasters and rural interme-

---

65. See Tenfelde, *Sozialgeschichte*, pp. 321ff. For the other mining areas, see O. Taeglichsbeck, 'Die Wohnungsverhältnisse der Berg- und Salinenarbeiter im Oberbergamtsbezirk Halle', in *Zeitschrift für das Berg-, Hütten- und Salinenwesen im dem Preussischen Staate*, vol. 40, 1892, pp. 1ff.; idem, 'Die Beförderung der Ansiedlung von Arbeitern der Staatsberg-, Hütten- und Salzwerke . . .', in *Schriften der Zentralstelle für Arbeiterwohlfahrtseinrichtungen*, 1, 1892, pp. 98ff.; K. Seidl, *Das Arbeiterwohnungswesen in der Oberschlesischen Montanindustrie*, Kattowitz, 1913.

diate groups played an important role in local politics. Accordingly, the potential for finding a solution to the housing problem was most inadequate. The mining companies had to expand and systematise their earlier housing schemes tremendously if they wanted to be able to accommodate the workers they required. '

There was another problem which has already been mentioned: the continuous movement of miners between companies, especially during an upswing in the economy. This mobility was evidently due to a desire on the part of the workers to use the demand for labour to improve their wages. As a result administrative costs for the companies increased; calculation and planning became more difficult; there was competition for workers, in addition to the need to train people all the time, leading to reduced productivity and increased accident rates. Having analysed mobility rates of the work-forces and compared them with those of workers living in colonies, a report by the Association of Mining Interests came to the following conclusion:

> The construction of good accommodation is the best and only means for the Ruhr mining industry to settle the worker [and] to restrict the very frequent job-changes with their economically and socially detrimental consequences. The low rate of return on capital is merely an apparent one; in effect the higher productivity of a stable work-force which is familiar with conditions in the pits will soon more than make good the loss in interest earnings on capital; the construction of good accommodation will therefore be no less to the economic advantage of the employers than it is to the benefit of the workers.[66]

The reasons for the reduction in mobility rates which thenceforth began among the inhabitants of colonies can be found on two levels. On the one hand, living in company-owned accommodation amounted to a material gain: it was less expensive than a similarly large dwelling on the free market (if it could be found); moreover, it usually had a garden and hence facilitated the growing of vegetables; it was also located in the immediate vicinity of the work-place; commuting over long distances was unnecessary and hence in practice reduced work hours. This, in turn, made the colonies

---

66. Hundt, *Ruhrgebiet*, p. 39; an analysis of the reasons, motives and conquences of company housing programmes in A. F. Heinrich, *Die Wohnungsnot und die Wohnungsfürsorge privater Arbeitgeber in Deutschland*, Ph.D. thesis, Marburg, 1970, pp. 134ff.; and, with particular reference to the colonies in the Ruhr area, M. Weisser, 'Arbeiterkolonien', in J. Petsch (ed.), *Architektur und Städtebau im 20. Jahrhundert*, vol. II, Berlin, 1975, pp. 7ff.

attractive to lodgers and enabled the miner's wife to earn some money. On the other hand, these privileges constituted a restriction: the rent agreement was tied to the work contract. Consequently wives and families tended to press the worker not to exploit the competition between the companies for skilled workers and to refrain from strike action. The colony, which occasionally included a public house, was supervised by the mine owner. It was clearly advisable to be well-behaved politically as well as in other respects. The significance of the link lay more in the latent threat it posed rather than in an actual danger. The owners, faced with a shortage of labour and with great working-class solidarity, were often left with no choice but to re-employ strikers once a strike was over; otherwise they would have been left without any miners.

If mining companies tried to achieve both objectives (both attracting and restricting workers), their collective growth virtually forced them into adopting a housing policy of their own. Soon nothing was to be gained any more from the provision of dormitories. Settlements had to be constructed because they offered greater economic as well as ecological advantages. Several factors came together to facilitate this development, that is, the opportunity to construct the larger parts of the colonies as well-laid-out estates with small and medium-sized dwellings, each housing from two to eight flats, including garden flats, and at relatively cheap rents. The most important factor was that the mining companies held large plots of land which could not be sold or built upon because of the danger of subsidence. It was also important that the construction of a large number of houses provided scope for rationalisation and cost reduction. In order to avoid developmental mistakes and to make further savings, the architectural design was frequently that developed by the housing reform movement. The work of this movement was also reflected in the layout of some colonies, however few in number, which used models of the garden city movement or of philanthropic pioneer settlements (*Pionierwerksiedlungen*) (See Fig. 1).[67]

That the academic discussions of the reformers gradually turned into a practical policy based on economic calculations was probably

67. See Sturn, *Fabrikarchitektur*, pp. 126ff. For a valuable morphological-historical survey of Dortmund see the catalogue by F. Bolerey and K. Hartmann, *Wohnen im Revier. 99 Beispiele aus Dortmund*, Munich, 1975. An analysis is to be found in idem, 'Wohnen im Revier', in *Stadtbauwelt*, 46, 1975, pp. 85ff. See also the examples in Landeskonservator Rheinland (ed.), *Arbeitersiedlungen*, I, 2nd ed., Cologne, 1975; W. Hartmann and J. Kirschbaum, *Arbeitersiedlungen*, II, 2nd ed., Cologne, 1975.

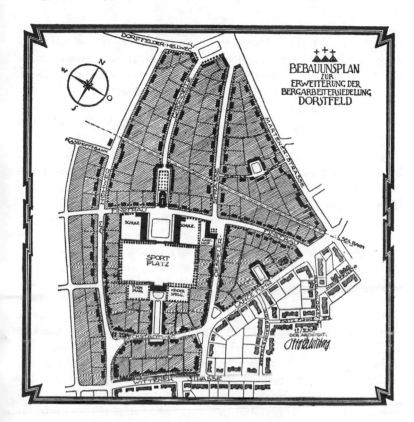

Fig. 1. *Dorstfeld: an example of a model settlement with a structured street system and houses strung out around a 'village' centre.*

also due to the creation of new credit facilities at low rates of interest, above all through second mortgages which were normally rather dear. From the 1890s onwards, the regional insurance associations (*Landesversicherungsanstalten*) set up under the new national pensions scheme used the saved-up contributions to provide loans at low interest rates of between 2.0 per cent and 4.75 per cent to building cooperatives engaged in the construction of working-class housing on a non-profit basis. But private enterprises were also eligible and they all had to build their accommodation to a certain standard. Some enterprises even went so far as to undertake their housing programme via the building cooperatives. They made land available to these cooperatives and thus retained the ultimate ownership. As in such cases workers frequently gave a hand in the construction of these houses and the cooperatives were able to count on low-interest credit from the regional insurance associations, capital costs were reduced even further. Owing to a lack of research, it is difficult to give a reliable estimate of the individual impact of these loans (which the workers had raised themselves) upon housing policy. Considerable sums were involved, overall. Up to 1916 loans amounted to some 530m marks for the whole of Germany. One-third of this sum (over 90m marks) was lent to building cooperatives and non-profit making associations in the provinces of Rhineland and Westphalia alone. Meanwhile the building costs per unit were below 4,000 marks, and not all of this was provided through outside finance. Only a relatively small part of all these sums was made directly available to the construction of company-owned housing, with the only reliable figure being some 21m marks lent out by the Bochum Miners' Insurance Association (*Knappschaftsverein*). Nor do we know at this point the percentage of company-owned dwellings constructed by building cooperatives. We can say only that the nominal capital of company-owned housing construction for miners between 1890 and 1914, totalling some 280m marks, was for the most part raised by the companies themselves. But in real terms it was considerably lower due to the use of land already in the companies' possession and the deployment of an existing work-force. There was also the reliance on mortgages from the regional insurance associations whose interest rates were mostly below the returns from rents. Obviously, all this made the financing of these ventures much easier.[68]

The colonies, which developed after the turn of the century from earlier models and from various rudimentary experiments and which now became the dominant form of settlement in most mining communities in the northern parts of the Ruhr, infused an element

68. These considerations are based on the material presented by Schmohl, 'Der Arbeitgeber', and Rusch, 'Die Förderung der Kleinwohnungsproduktion durch Reich, Staat und Gemeinden', in C. J. Fuchs (ed.), *Die Wohnungs-und Siedlungsfrage nach dem Kriege*, Stuttgart, 1918, pp. 263ff., 312ff. See also Rusch, 'Die Leistungen der Landesversicherungsanstalten auf dem Gebiet des Arbeiterwohnungsbaus', in *Sonderbeilage zum Reichs-Arbeitsblatt*, no. 6, June 1916, pp. 21ff., esp. pp. 24f. See also C. Schmidt, *Die Aufgaben und die Tätigkeit der deutschen Invalidenversicherungsanstalten in der Arbeiterwohnungsfrage*, Cologne, 1905; A. Bosse, *Die Förderung des Arbeiterwohnungswesens durch die Landesversicherungsanstalten*, Jena, 1907; E. Dösseler, 'Die Entwicklung des sozialen Wohnungsbaus', in *Tradition*, vol. 13, 1968, pp. 133ff., for the development in Westphalia.

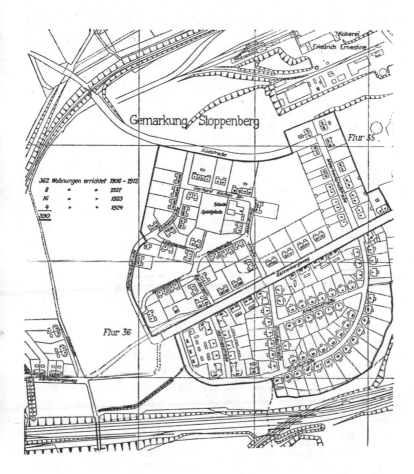

Fig. 2. *Essen: the Stinnes housing scheme. Within the unstructured industrial environment of streets, railway tracks and mine buildings the colony appears as an isolated cell of purposeful design.*

of private planning into the public planlessness of industrial villages which had grown into shapeless agglomerations. Here the architecture was regular and standardised. At first the house fronts formed a straight line and were strung together in terraces, until after the turn of the century when, influenced by the garden city movement, there

69. See the maps and the architectural-historical periodisation in Bollerey and Hartmann, *Dortmund*, pp. xiiff. See also Fig. 2.

Table 5. *Company flats and work-force mobility, 1900*

Mine	No. of flats	Invest- ment cost per flat (in M)	% increase of equiv. flat on free market	Work-force mobility % of total work- force	% of population of colony
Neu-Essen	509	1,842	20	49.9	3.0
Kölner					
Bergwerks-Verein	385	5,000*	100	58.2	12.0
Prosper	643	2,651	20	101.9	10.5
Concordia	222	3,515	30	72.3	5.0
GHH-Bergbau:					
Hugo	32	9,000	10		nil
Osterfeld	230	3,653	60	78.2	1.57
Oberhausen					
Schacht I, II, III	77	3,298	40–50		nil
Deutscher Kaiser	1,507	4,476	100	77.9	5.0

Source: G. Adelmann, *Quellensammlung zur Geschichte der sozialen Betriebs-verfassung*, vol. 2, Bonn, 1965, p. 66.

was an increasing number of round villages or estates built around a common.[69] During the large waves of immigration, multi-storey blocks were erected also. But the dominant pattern reflected the desire to copy the architecture of detached rural dwellings which, although several flats had been squeezed into them, nevertheless, by virtue of separate front-door entrances, preserved a semblance of individuality. It was the aim of this housing pattern to provide a structural seclusion for the families of an expanded permanent work-force and to tie them to the colony; to isolate them from the temptations of the city and of politics and to promote, on these islands of a planned agrarian romanticism, a perception of the environment which counteracted proletarian class formation.

But in one way it should be said that the host had made his calculations without consulting the guest. Even if the colonies grew into fully-fledged villages and suburbs, they never completely succeeded in obscuring reality; they were dominated by the pithead rather than the church spire. During the pre-1914 boom years there was a decline in the mobility rate of tenants in these colonies, but the rest of the work-force fluctuated all the more markedly (see Table 5). The most mobile among them (young single men) found accommodation as overnight lodgers in these colonies in considerable numbers. The half-open family structure continued as a class-based institution of socialisation and communication, which declined in importance only slowly.

The colonies in particular provided opportunities to develop structures of solidarity which replaced the older ones. They petrified that structuring that urbanisation in Germany had produced very much less often than urbanisation in Britain had done, that is, housing areas that were homogeneous in terms of class and even of occupation, united in their dependency upon a single enterprise.[70] The architectural layout chosen also contributed to the creation of a family structure which was open to communication and communal life. There was the joint garden work, the semi-public, semi-private path between house and outbuildings; there was the afforded protection of the private sphere with the help of a closely-knit community of neighbours. In the long term, the colonies generated the opposite of what the industrial patriarchs had intended:[71] their inhabitants appropriated them to themselves instead of allowing their consciousness to be expropriated. They seized the opportunities of forming class-based communities; they profited from cheap rents, nearness to the work-place and to the garden; by developing a high degree of internal communication and organisation in clubs, they erected counterweights to the deficiencies of a cultural infrastructure prevalent within the agglomeration.[72] Just how far the appropriation of the colonies transcended the aims of their owners

70. This tendency increased considerably, especially in the 1930s and became almost a general experience of the mining communities, which standardised in a unique way their daily experience in production and reproduction. During that decade miners' housing grew by 150,000 units, while the total work-force in the mines fell to under 300,000, in parts well below this figure. With male children and lodgers being included, this would indicate that considerably more than two-thirds of the miners lived at times in company-owned housing, of these some 80 per cent in colonies.

71. This is also true in a political sense. There are many indications that the colonies became centres of activity and resistance for the working-class movement during strikes, during the period of the Councils in 1918/19, during the Ruhr Occupation of 1923, at elections during the Weimar period in support of the Communist Party and, finally, in generating solidarity under Fascism. For Hamborn, see Lucas, *Radikalismus*, pp. 155ff.; for Bottrop: H.T. Breuer and R. Lindner, 'Sind doch nicht alles Beckenbauers', in *Aesthetik und Kommunikation*, vol. 24, 1976, pp. 9ff. For an election analysis of Essen North-East, an area shaped by miners' colonies, see H. Kühr, *Parteien und Wahlen im Stadt- und Landkreis Essen in der Zeit der Weimarer Republik*, Düsseldorf 1973.

72. This has been demonstrated by reference to the oldest colony of Oberhausen in J. Boström and R. Günter, *Rettet Eisenheim*, 2nd ed., Berlin, 1973.

can be gauged today by studying the independence and persistence with which these islands of cheap housing promoting a community spirit are defended against bulldozers and the heirs to the mining fortunes. It was this struggle position that generated the first large movement of local citizens' initiatives that German workers organised in the field of housing.[73]

73. See J. Boström and R. Günter (eds.), *Arbeiterinitiativen im Ruhrgebiet*, Berlin, 1976.

KARIN HAUSEN

Technical Progress and Women's Labour in the Nineteenth Century

The Social History of the Sewing Machine

That modest piece of equipment, the sewing machine, is clearly much too insignificant for it to have played any substantial part in industrial development.* That at least is the impression given in surveys of nineteenth- and twentieth-century social and economic history, where the sewing machine is mentioned only in passing. An exception to this is a contribution made by David Landes in 1965 to the *Cambridge Economic History*, in which he emphasises the technical, and economic and social importance of the sewing machine, which he describes as the most significant innovation in the production of consumer goods since the invention of the mechanical loom.[1] On closer inspection it is indeed apparent that the change in production techniques was by no means the only effect of the transition in the second half of the nineteenth century from sewing by hand to the use of a machine. This development affected the whole labour and market structure of the clothing industry, which was at that time moving away from production by

* Publ. orig. in *Geschichte und Gesellschaft*, 4, (1978), pp. 148–69. Transl. by Michael Davenport. The author would like to thank the publishers for permission to prepare and use this translation.
1. See D. Landes, *The Unbound Prometheus*, Cambridge, 1970), pp. 294–5.

hand on demand towards capitalistic market-orientated production. In addition, production of sewing machines in factories from the 1850s onwards gave fresh impetus to the future construction of machines and machine tools. Finally, the widespread distribution of the sewing machine both as a means of production and as a consumer item unleashed a dynamic process which gave effect to the mechanisms of the capitalist goods and labour market, even in the very homes of the various classes and strata of society. Karl Marx understood the emergence of this 'revolutionary machine' as a 'key' and used it to illustrate the development of the capitalist market and of capitalist production.[2] In what follows I want to pick up where he left off in the hope that in concentrating on this small machine, which played a relatively insignificant part in the industrialisation process, we will be able to analyse the development of and structural relationship between industry and society. However, unlike Marx, I have not chosen the sewing machine as an arbitrary example. My interest in the sewing machine as the starting point of a social analysis derives from its being at once both a household object and a means of production, making it impossible to draw any clear dividing line between the domestic and the commercial economy, something which is so commonly done in nineteenth-century history.

Even in the form it took in the late nineteenth century machine sewing was above all the preserve of women and this female labour ran through the whole gamut of different types, from private to organised labour. In reality this female labour cannot be included in the usual economic categories, which tend to separate consumption from production, productive from unproductive labour and which make it difficult to establish any link between piece payments and family earnings and between family businesses and industry. It appears to me that a better understanding of social reality at the apogee of capitalism can be arrived at by paying more attention than hitherto to the theoretical and factual no-man's-land between the private household and the capitalist agricultural and industrial economy. That then is the framework for a social history of the sewing machine. In what follows I shall, using Germany in the period leading up to the First World War as an example, discuss technical, economic and socio-historical aspects of the sewing machine's history. Condensing such a wide subject into a few pages is cer-

---

2. K. Marx, *Das Kapital*, vol. 1, chap. 13 (MEW, vol. 23) pp. 494–6.

tainly not without its difficulties. A concise outline of the subject and its problems will possibly be more useful for putting forward information and interpretations for discussion and for stimulating further thought than a minutely detailed case-study.

I

Between 1850 and 1855 knowledge in Germany of the first workable American-built sewing machines spread extremely fast. Meyer's *Encyclopaedia*, which in 1852 made no mention of the sewing machine, compensated for this by giving it comprehensive treatment in a supplementary volume in 1854. In 1855 the *Kleine Brockhaus* itself called the sewing machine 'one of the most recent American inventions, improved in Germany and in widespread use, able only to produce the so-called straight stitch, but with almost unbelievable regularity and speed. Only one operator is needed to guide the material towards the seam marked for the purpose and to thread the needles'.[3] Ever since the Great Exhibition of 1851 in London various trade journals[4] had carried reports on newly registered sewing machine patents for the benefit of technical experts and manufacturers. In 1854 the first 'iron seamstresses' imported from the United States were shown to an astonished public at trade fairs, in shop windows and at travelling fairs, where an entrance fee was payable.[5] But people did not only stand and stare! In the 1850s German craftsmen were already constructing their own sewing machines, having learnt how they worked from carrying out repair work.[6] The real boom in Germany dates from the 1860s, when the first sewing machine factories grew up and American firms, with the Singer Company in the vanguard, conquered the German market.[7]

A glance at the sewing machine's history may provide an explanation for the extraordinary interest shown in it right from the start.[8] Elias Howe is regarded as the inventor of the sewing machine.

3. *Kleineres Brockhaus'sches Conversations-Lexikon für den Handgebrauch*, vol. 3, Leipzig, 1855, p. 700.
4. Cf. e.g. Dingler's *Polytechnisches Journal* (*PJ*); *Der Arbeitgeber* (ed. by M. Wirth).
5. See R. Herzberg, *Die Nähmaschinen-Industrie in Deutschland*, Berlin, 1863, pp. 5ff.
6. See W. Köhler, *Die deutsche Nähmaschinen-Industrie*, Leipzig, 1913, pp. 21–7.
7. Köhler, *Nähmaschine*, pp. 28ff.
8. On the invention, see G. R. Cooper, *The Invention of the Sewing Machine*,

He patented his model in the United States in 1846, but was only able to establish his first patent after lengthy disputes with the wealthier sewing machine manufacturers who were springing up everywhere around 1850. While we can be justified in regarding Howe as the father of the sewing machine in that it was his machine that brought the breakthrough to machine sewing, this is nevertheless an oversimplification. As with all inventions, numerous precursors of the sewing machine since the turn of the century had cleared the way forward from the initially futile attempts at imitating hand sewing to the successful production of a seam by machine. The most important stages in this development were shifting the eye of the needle to the tip and removing the need for short-length thread by no longer pulling the thread all the way through the material at each stitch, but instead making loops underneath the material which were then knotted either by a succeeding loop or by a second thread underneath the material. Further technical problems, involving feeding in the material and the tension on the thread, were solved by several intervening innovations. Nor was Howe's sewing machine in any sense the final product, but rather the basis for a whole range of improvements and additions which were themselves patented in order to free production from the fetters of Howe's restrictions. Not least, use of the sewing machine was dependent on the development of a thread which met the increased demands of machine sewing. Suitable cotton machine thread only came onto the market at the beginning of the 1860s.[9] It should also be noted that the sewing machine quickly became all-important in the production of leather goods as well as of textiles and even made inroads in the sphere of bookbinding. This in turn encouraged the development of a number of specialised machines and opened up good prospects for further innovation.[10]

The development from hand to machine sewing was a process which involved much more than just solving existing technical problems. The idea of a machine to do the job had been mooted ever since the turn of the century and had preoccupied inventors increasingly since the 1830s.[11] It is hardly surprising that there was a

---

Washington, 1968. H. W. Lind gives a very detailed description of the problems which had to be solved in idem, *Das Buch von der Nähmaschine* 1, Berlin, 1891.

9. Cooper, *Invention*, p. 64.
10. It would be intriguing to carry out a comparative analysis of the socio-economic consequences of technical progress, taking the invention of the sewing machine and its application in the leather and textile industries as a starting point.
11. Sewing machines were invented separately in England, France, Austria and the

climate favourable to innovation: whereas productivity in spinning and weaving had greatly increased since the eighteenth century, the final stage of textile manufacture had lagged behind and was still dependent on time-consuming manual labour. The productivity barrier became even more noticeable when in the 1820s and 1830s the market became more organised, not only for second-hand clothes but also increasingly for new material and quality products. New stores for clothes and linen captured first the provincial, then the overall home market for ready-to-wear clothes and finally conquered the overseas market. In the long term this development made excessive demands on tailors and seamstresses, whether working at home or elsewhere, and helped the clothing industry to achieve its breakthrough.

In the German clothing industry[12] the capitalist production of goods really took off when first the retailers and then the wholesalers became dissatisfied with dealing solely in finished products and material and went over to the production of ready-to-wear clothes or at least to commissioning them from other sources. In the manufacture of clothes the linen trade was usually the starting point. Even in the 1820s customers were evidently already interested in commissioning their linen from a shop rather than doing the sewing themselves at home. The items produced were at first produced in so-called 'sewing schools'[13] and later by seamstresses employed directly by a small business, but mostly working at home. To begin with products were made to measure, but the trade very soon started to produce standardised goods and to specialise in

---

United States — see Cooper, *Invention*, pp. 4–16. The only one to be used was, however, the chain-stitch machine patented by the Frenchman, B. Thimonnier, in 1830. The eighty Thimonnier machines, used for making uniforms after 1841, fell victim to machine-breakers. Shortage of money and the 1848 Revolution prevented the inventor from making further use of his patent before the better American machines conquered the market. See ibid., pp. 37ff.

12. G. Schmoller, *Zur Geschichte der deutschen Kleingewerbe im 19. Jahrhundert. Statistische u. national-ökonomische Untersuchungen*, Halle, 1870/Hildesheim, 1975, pp. 642–52; L. Baar, *Die Berliner Industrie in der industriellen Revolution*, Berlin, 1966, pp. 73–85, taking Berlin as an example, provides an excellent study of the rise of capitalist production. For the history of the clothing industry in Berlin see, among others, J. Feig, *Hausgewerbe u. Fabrikbetrieb in der Berliner Wäsche-Industrie*, Leipzig, 1896, pp. 1–8; H. Grandke, 'Berliner Kleiderkonfektion', in *Schriften des Vereins für Sozialpolitik (SVSP)*, vol. 85, 1899, pp. 129–389, esp. pp. 132f.; E. Wittkowski, *Die Berliner Damenkonfektion*, diss., Berlin/Leipzig, 1928, pp. 3–8; B. Maurer, *Die deutsche Herrenkonfektion*, Jena, 1922, pp. 12–14; P. Ardnt (ed.), *Die Heimarbeit im rheinmainischen Wirtschaftsgebiet*, vol. 3, Frankfurt, 1913, pt. 1, passim.

13. The sewing schools followed on from the weaving schools of the eighteenth century and were not so much schools as factories.

particular garments. Nevertheless, it was not until the 1860s that such garments were being produced on a large scale. Berlin's industrial success is an illustration of the development of the clothing industry. Berlin was not simply a pioneer in the trade, but retained a position of preeminence into the twentieth century. The first area to be developed was that of ladies' coats. This was made possible by drapers' stores and fashion bazaars beginning in the 1830s to follow the trend and produce and sell shawls, scarves and capes. In the decades that followed the range of ladies' clothing was continually extended. Coats were followed by jackets and thick undergarments and then in the 1860s by blouses and aprons and at the end of the century by suits and dresses. Similarly, men's and children's clothing also developed in stages. As early as the 1870s Berlin had an efficient, export-conscious clothing industry. The centralised system for tailoring uniforms, with division of labour, employment of unskilled workers and standard sizes and patterns, paved the way for the abandonment of individual tailoring.[14] The clothing industry did not, however, really take off until the guilds had abandoned their restrictive practices, thus creating a free market for goods and labour. Increasingly, the clothing industry sought its market amongst all classes of society. There were cheap standard products for the urban and rural working class and exclusive, well-tailored garments for the well-to-do. All in all the attitude of the consumer and the supply of goods by the manufacturer seem to have had a stimulating influence on each other. The increased demand may perhaps have been due less to the factory girls' much ridiculed obsession with 'dolling themselves up' than to the growing desire at all levels of society to dress more expensively and more fashionably.[15] The cheaper standard goods were assured of a constant market inasmuch as such garments, made at breakneck speed from low-quality materials, had only a short life expectancy.

The developing clothing industry, run on capitalist lines and bent on securing cheap labour, provided the basis for the invention and rapid distribution of an efficient sewing machine. In view of the advanced state of development of the clothing trade in the European capitals[16] and in New York, what is surprising is that it was not

14. This aspect is emphasised by J. Krengel in *Die Berliner Bekleidungsindustrie vor dem 1. Weltkrieg*, thesis, Berlin, 1975, pp. 6–15.
15. An item from Breslau in *Der Arbeitgeber*, 1857, p. 220, illustrates this: 'There is such a senseless profusion of embroidery, undergarments, nightdresses, petticoats and handkerchiefs that the shops can hardly satisfy the demand'.
16. For the situation in London, see: E. P. Thompson and E. Yeo (eds.), *The

possible to develop a technically satisfactory sewing machine before 1850.[17] The introduction of a machine was justifiably expected to speed up the sewing process enormously. Even Howe's sewing machines, with their 300 stitches a minute, proved faster in a sewing contest than five practised seamstresses.[18] By the 1850s the more advanced, foot-operated machines were reaching speeds of 600 to 1,000 stitches a minute, equivalent to ten or twenty times faster than a single seamstress. By the 1880s, with the use of steam power, the maximum speed was increased to as many as 3,500 stitches a minute.[19] Numerous additional inventions during the first twenty years brought onto the market on the one hand more manageable machines, easier to operate and providing increased precision, and on the other hand multi-purpose, specialised and industrial machines and machines designed for home use. American production figures give us the clearest impression of the rapid distribution of the sewing machine. The leading manufacturers, J. M. Singer & Co., Wheeler and Wilson, Groover and Baker, were founded in the United States in 1850, 1851 and 1852 respectively. Up to 1853 2,509 sewing machines had been produced. By 1859 it was already 104,000. Annual production had reached 55,000 by 1860 and 464,254 by 1870.[20] The only country able to compete with the American concerns in the period up to the First World War was Germany, and there it was not until the 1860s that production took off to any great extent. In the absence of precise production figures we are dependent on indications that individual factories were continually expanding production. The same leading firms which had had twenty to thirty employees in the 1860s had by the 1870s developed into large concerns with more than a hundred employees.[21] By 1907

Unknown Mayhew. Selections from the Morning Chronicle 1849-1850, London, 1971, pp. 116–227; J. G. Eccarius, *Die Schneider in London oder der Kampf des Grossen u. des Kleinen Kapitals*, Leipzig, 1876. More recent studies: H. A. Cobrin, *The Men's Clothing Industry, Colonial through Modern Times*, New York, 1970; J. Thomas, *History of the Leeds Clothing Industry*, Leeds, 1955; C. H. Johnson, 'Economic Change and Artisan Discontent. The Tailor's History 1800–1848', in R. Price (ed.), *Revolution and Reaction*, London, 1975, pp. 87–114.

17. The reasons for this are connected with the small amount of capital in the clothing industry and with the surplus of extremely cheap labour.
18. See *PJ*, vol. 130, 1853, p. 235; E. Lüth, *Die Nähmaschinenfabrikation*, Leipzig, 1936, p. 8 (for the Pfaff company).
19. On the speed of sewing, see Lind, *Nähmaschine*, 2, p. 4.
20. For figures, see Cooper, *Invention*, p. 19: in 1870 the Singer Manufacturing Co. produced 127,833 machines. Figures are not restricted to textile sewing machines only.
21. See Köhler, *Nähmaschine*, pp. 55–9. The manufacture of sewing machines in

trade statistics show that out of 232 factories involved in the manufacture of sewing machines sixteen had more than 500 employees. Output in Germany for 1890 is estimated at 500,000 machines, equivalent to about one-third of world production, and by 1907 this had risen to 1.1m, higher than the Singer Company in the United States and still one-third of world production.[22]

So far, in showing that the sewing machine was able to spread very fast on account of the increased demand in the clothing industry, we have left unanswered the question decisive for *social* history — exactly how this was brought about. The nature of industrial sewing machine manufacture provides us with part of the answer. In the United States the sewing machine was the first non-military piece of equipment to be produced in series and with replaceable component parts. The use of improved machine tools provided the basis for this increasingly efficient method of production.[23] Aggressive American competition from the 1860s onwards forced German factories to free themselves from the fetters of manual production.[24] In the 1870s and 1880s German firms probably acted as forerunners for American production techniques and precision tools.[25] Series production had the advantage over traditional methods, not only of considerably reducing production

Altenburgs began in 1871. Annual production figures were: 1871 = 20; 1881 = 16,630; 1891 = 32,353; 1901 = 122,547; 1907 = 199,747. See F. Sagel, *Die Altenburger Nähmaschinen-Industrie*, PhD diss., Jena/Altenburg, 1910, pp. 8f. Pfaff started production in 1862 with two employees; in 1872 thirty employees produced 1,000 machines and in 1891 590 employees produced 25,000 machines (Lüth, *Fabrikation*, pp. 12ff.; *Pfaff 1862–1962*, jubilee sp. issue, June 1962, p. 13). H. Richard (*Die Nähmaschine, Ihre geschichtliche Entwicklung, Construction u. ihr jetziger Standpunkt*, Hanover, 1876, p. 47) is perhaps exaggerating when he claims that the Fa. Cl. Müller of Dresden produced 18,000 machines in 1872 and up to 80,000 in 1875.

22. Lind, *Nähmaschine*, 2, p. 3; Meyer's *Grosses Konversationslexikon* vol. 14, 6th ed., Leipzig, 1908, p. 390. Köhler, *Nähmaschine*, p. 261, gives the following export figures for German sewing machines: weight index, 1885 = 100, 1911 = 365; value index, 1885 = 100, 1911 = 476.

23. See N. Rosenberg, 'Technischer Fortschritt in der Werkzeugmaschinenindustrie 1840–1910', in K. Hausen and R. Rürup (eds.), *Moderne Technikgeschichte*, Cologne, 1975, pp. 216–42.

24. This happened as early as the end of the 1860s in the case of the Berlin sewing machine manufacturers, Frister & Rossmann and L. Loewe: see Baar, *Industrie*, p. 121. The parallel development in Berlin of the sewing machine and clothing industries may also be observed in the choice of location: J. Thienel, *Städtewachstum im Industrialisierungsprozess des 19. Jahrhunderts. Das Berliner Beispiel*, Berlin, 1973, pp. 68, 77.

25. In the case of Pfaff the switch to American machines took place after a two-year visit to the United States by Pfaff's eldest son — see *Pfaff 1862–1962*, p. 13. The following announcement in *Der Arbeitgeber* for 1865 (p. 4537) is particularly revealing: 'It is well-recognised that the manufacture of sewing machines in

costs,[26] but of facilitating repairs, since component parts could quickly and easily be replaced.[27] Series production is only profitable where certainty of demand makes high-cost investment worthwhile. The sewing machine was excellently suited to mass production from the outset, since it took up very little space, was operated by hand or by foot-pedal, consequently had no motor and was ready for immediate use. The cheap, easily repairable machines produced in the United States in the 1850s for use in the home were the first mass-produced machines to flood the market. When bicycles appeared in the 1890s it was no accident that sewing machine manufacturers were attracted by the similar requirements in production and sales and decided to diversify into bicycle manufacture.[28]

The triumph of the sewing machine as a mass-produced article was due at the outset both to its price and to the sales techniques employed.[29] From 1850 onwards the pioneer in this respect was Isaac Merrit Singer[30], who was not only the first to introduce series production, but also developed extremely effective new sales techniques. He managed to appeal to a whole cross-section, from the industrialist to the private individual, from the bourgeois housewife to the working woman on her subsistence budget. Not only did Singer build up his firm's own sales and repair network, he also managed to sell his machines to the poorest of customers by a system of hire purchase which proved to be decisive in the sewing

---

Germany is not so technically advanced as in America. Our imports are striking proof of this. The main reason is that in America *the component parts of the sewing machine are machine-made. We are now able to deliver many of the machine-tools used in the production of sewing machines in America. We deliver machines for screw-cutting, planing, milling, drilling, hole-punching, all at factory prices'.*

26. Singer offered his first family sewing machine for sale in 1858 for $100 and was able to reduce that to $75 within a year. In Germany the first straight-stitch machines were on sale for 350 talers, whilst similar machines were on sale in America at half that price.

27. Lind, *Nähmaschine*, 2, pp. 13ff., emphasises that German as opposed to American manufacturers still produced individual machine-made parts to measure, which made them less readily interchangeable and hindered smooth running. Lüth, *Fabrikation*, pp. 18–20, states that Pfaff did not implement the American system of production, which required less qualified operators, until after the turn of the century.

28. In Germany Duerkopp/Bielefeld was the most well-known manufacturer of both sewing machines and bicycles. For this, on technological convergence see Rosenberg, 'Technischer', pp. 224ff.

29. G. von Viebahn, *Statistik des zollvereinten u. nördlichen Deutschland*, Berlin, 1868, p. 669, refers to the 'immensely wide distribution in the trade and in the home in all parts of Germany'.

30. See R. Brandon, *Singer and the Sewing Machine: A Capitalist Romance*, New York, 1977.

machine becoming a product for the masses. Nevertheless, in Germany in the 1860s a home straight-stitch sewing machine cost 200 to 300 marks. Even when the price had eventually been cut by half the purchase of a sewing machine remained an expensive business for most people.[31] Following Singer's example, the German sewing machine business also found ways and means of reaching more and more customers.[32] Apart from price lists sent by post and advertisements in newspapers it was the travelling salesman who proved most effective. In addition to cash payments in shops the hire-purchase system began to flourish in Germany as well.[33] Hire purchase made the buying of a machine considerably more expensive but was often the only means by which a customer could acquire a piece of equipment that was urgently needed. A hire-purchase contract was, however, not entirely without its dangers. Until the rules governing such contracts were laid down by law in 1894 the impecunious customer who defaulted on only one payment was threatened not only with the loss of the sewing machine but also with the loss of all payments made to that date.[34]

II

So who were the people who bought sewing machines and what importance did they attach to them? David Landes' explanation for the sewing machine becoming a sales hit is that 'women found in it liberation from an old bondage'.[35] In emphasis-

31. Various examples in *PJ*, vol. 152, 1859, pp. 313f.; Herzberg, *Nämaschinen-Industrie*, pp 22f.; Köhler, *Nähmaschine*, p. 43; Lüth, *Fabrikation* p. 29; *SVSP*, vol. 65, Leipzig, 1895, p. 148.
32. Lind, *Nähmaschine*, 2, pp. 8–12; Köhler, *Nähmaschine*, pp. 220–57.
33. Some examples: in Elberfeld in 1887 the hire purchase price was 150 per cent of the normal value. The seamstress would pay 125 marks for a machine bought from the factory for 57 marks (Sten. Ber. d. Reichstages, 7. Leg., 2. Sess., 1887, documents to vol. 1, file 83, p. 714). In 1895 a machine priced at between 90 and 120 marks would cost between 140 and 160 marks on hire purchase (*SVSP*, vol. 67, Leipzig, 1895, pp. 16f.). In 1907 a seamstress in the Frankfurt area earned 140 marks per annum (Arndt (ed.), *Heimarbeit*, p. 191).
34. See V. Mataja, 'Abzahlungsgeschäfte', in *Handwörterbuch der Staatswissen-schaften*, 3rd ed., vol. 1, Jena, 1909, pp. 13–20.
35. Landes, *Prometheus* p. 296. This claim is made the more remarkable by the further comment that the exploitation and the sweatshop system were intensified, whereas the tedium of sewing with a needle and thread had ended. Landes is simply following in the footsteps of that active propagandist, A. Daul, who wrote in *Das Buch von der Amerikanischen Nähmaschine*, Hamburg, 1864, p. 73, of 'the invention of the sewing machine, which is truly cosmopolitan, humane and good in every way'! Similarly, M. St Parker and D. J. Reid, *The*

ing the emancipating effect of the sewing machine Landes was rather missing the point in the same way as those who make similar claims for the typewriter.[36] While it is obvious that the only way to judge a new invention is to analyse the way in which it is applied, this is often overlooked in the tendency to idealise technical progress. The intention in what follows is to examine the true repercussions of the sewing machine for different social groups, especially for women.

For the benefit of the middle classes the sewing machine was extolled as a work-saver which enabled mothers to devote themselves to bringing up their children and wives to improving their education, all of which fitted in neatly with the bourgeois conception of the family. In 1852 the Berlin women's journal *Bazar*, indicating how ideally suited the sewing machine was to enhance the idyllic quality of bourgeois family life, went so far as to write: 'Nobody can deny that the sewing machine makes work seem like a joyful pastime and pleasure rather than a pressing burden'.[37] German manufacturers, however, had not managed to emulate the cunning with which the more elevated social circles were successfully wooed in the United States. Nevertheless, similar efforts in Germany did not go unrewarded.[38] Ideology apart, there is some evidence that in middle-income and well-to-do families the sewing

---

British Revolution 1750–1970: A Social and Economic History, London, 1972, p. 162; 'The crippling dependence on the hand-worked needle was reduced, with great gains in human happiness'.

36. See also the polemic of G. H. Daniels, 'Hauptfragen der amerikanischen Technikgeschichte', in Hausen and Rürup (eds.), *Technikgeschichte*, pp. 48f.

37. A. Daul, 'Die Nähmaschine. Zum Gebrauche in Familien', in *Handwerkstätten der Näherinnen u. in der Industrie*, Hamburg, 1865, p. 38; ibid., p. 36; similarly in Herzberg, *Nahmaschinen-Industrie*, p. 21. On the 'idyll' of leisure, see B. Duden, 'Das schöne Eigentum. Zur Herausbildung des bürgerlichen Frauenbildes an der Wende vom 18. zum 19. Jahrhundert', in *Kursbuch 47*, 1977, pp. 125–40, esp. pp. 132f.

38. See Cooper, *Invention*, pp. 2, 32, for descriptions of the lavish sales salons of Wheeler & Wilson and J. M. Singer & Co. Daul (*Das Buch*, pp. 57–60), describes this luxurious American advertising. In 1858/9 Singer made the claim that his family sewing machine was 'decorated in the best style of art, so as to make a beautiful ornament in the parlour or boudoir' (Cooper, *Invention*, p. 35). A German 'lady', on the other hand, was still regarded in 1859 as doing something outrageous in buying a sewing machine: 'One lady who was amongst the first to try out the innovation in Berlin gave me a description of what happened. . . . For some time she stared enquiringly at the new tool through the shop-window, then, full of apprehension, she bought it with her own savings at her own risk. For a long time she did not dare to admit that she had a sewing machine and in the shop was embarrassed by having to ask for machine thread. People came to understand only slowly how the machine worked. At first people would ask "So you have a sewing machine? Do you have to be at home when it is sewing?" After a while, however, she was suddenly inundated with

machine, like the arrival of ready-to-wear clothing, had the effect not so much of saving the housewife work as of saving or reducing the amount of money spent on employing a tailor or a seamstress. More decisive, therefore, was the recommendation that middle-class daughters should be taught to use a sewing machine rather than to play the piano. The sewing machine was regarded as being useful in all circumstances and as providing a woman with the chance to earn a living if she were widowed, divorced or abandoned by her husband.[39] This is the crucial point: the sewing machine appealed to the lower-middle classes not just because it was needed in the home, but also because it was perfectly suited to the needs of a cottage industry independent of the big factories. Unlike work in factories, work in the home was regarded by the lower-middle classes as entirely respectable, particularly if it was a traditional woman's activity. Sewing by machine was thus advertised as an 'activity entirely suitable for women'.[40] Machine sewing seemed to solve the problem of supplementing the family income and at the same time performing the 'duties of a wife and mother',[41] so it was given special emphasis in private schools for middle-class girls. It was even more common for the daughter of a minor official or manual labourer to become apprenticed to an 'intermediary master' in the clothing industry, where she worked without pay for as long as a year and perhaps continued to work there until marriage, assuming no better-paid sewing job was offered her.[42] Whilst girls from this group could regard their earnings as supplementary income, since they continued to be provided for by their parents, the financial situation for other middle-class women was very much more precarious. Schmoller found that in 1870 it was by no means only working-class women who were working in the clothing industry:[43] 'Countless daughters of shopkeepers, craftsmen and clerks, not yet having reached the desired haven of a comfortable marriage, are, along with

---

people thirsty for knowledge. Now the spell is fully broken and many people are buying sewing machines. The manufacturer fully appreciated her pioneering work and gave her the improved version for only a small additional payment and presented her with the final version without any charge at all', article by L. von Benda, in *SVSP*, vol. 85, Leipzig, 1899, pp. 53ff., esp. n. 3.

39. So Daul, *Das Buch*, p. 79; M. Pinoff, *Reform der wiebliehen Erziehung*, Breslau, 1867, p. 106.
40. Herzberg, *Nähmaschinen-Industrie*, p. 18.
41. Ibid., p. 21.
42. There are numerous indications of this in *Reichstag 1887*, file 83, esp. pp. 700, 707, 711–13, 745.
43. Schmoller, *Geschichte*, pp. 648f.

a good many widows, only too happy to find such employment'. These observations continued to hold true for the rest of the century. Women in this category who depended for their livelihood on their sewing were trapped in a hopeless battle for survival in the same way as working-class women.

For the working classes the purchase of a sewing machine served a purely economic purpose and the machine remained primarily the women's preserve. One reason for this is to be found in the development of the clothing trade itself. Traditionally, women were taught to sew for their household needs but were barred from membership of the guilds until restrictions were lifted. For a long time unqualified seamstresses were able to earn a living only by going to work in other people's homes. The guilds' relaxation of restrictions merely had the effect up until the 1850s of enabling women to work in their own homes and to produce articles for stores selling clothes and linen. Whereas the unqualified seamstress had always had a monopoly on linen goods (at least in so far as the consumer did not make them in the home), the clothing industry developed in direct competition with trained ladies' and gentlemen's tailors. The move of workers away from the traditional clothes trade filled the new workshops and at the same time enabled increasing numbers of journeymen to set themselves up independently and on the basis of a division of labour to give employment to more and more almost totally unqualified women.[44] In the 1870s the rapid development of the trade had the consequence of restricting trained tailors to the production of new patterns and made-to-measure clothing. Most of the sewing was now done by untrained seamstresses. It was typical of the decentralised mass-production in the clothing industry[45] that all that was done in the 'factory' itself, apart from the buying and selling, was that patterns were made up and the finishing touches put to the garments themselves. The sewing was either passed on directly to seamstresses working in

44. See also: Baar, Industrie, p. 74; J. Bergmann, *Das Berliner Handwerk in den Frühphasen der Industrialisierung*, Berlin, 1973. Other reports in 'Untersuchungen über die Lage des Handwerks in Deutschland mit bes. Rücksicht auf seine Konkurrenzfähigkeit gegenüber der Grossindustrie', in *SVSP*, vols. 62–6, Leipzig, 1895–6.
45. For the organisation of production see W. Sombart, 'Verlagssystem', in *Handwörterbuch der Staatswissenschenschaften*, 3rd ed., vol. 8, Jena, 1911, pp. 238f.; *Zusammenstellung der Ergebnisse der Ermittlungen über die Arbeitsverhältnisse in der Kleider-u. WäscheKonfektion* (Drucksachen der Kommission für Arbeiterstatistik Erhebung no. 10), Berlin, 1896, p. 8–14; also: Feig, *Hausgewerbe*; Grandke, 'Kleider-Konfektion'; Maurer, Herrenkonfektion; Wittkowski, *Damenkonfektion*.

their own homes or it was delegated to an 'intermediary', who in turn employed women either in his workshop or at home. This network of intermediaries, also known as the 'sweating system', became notorious for the appalling working conditions which prevailed. The same room served simultaneously as a workshop and a living-room and was extremely cramped, particularly during the busy periods when the number of seamstresses was increased and the working day extended.[46] In the clothing trade the intermediary was usually either a master tailor or a journeyman who was responsible for cutting. In the production of linen, however, where the division of labour was most complete, the intermediary no longer even had to be a qualified tailor. The intermediaries were almost exclusively men — many of them had been trained in a different field and now acted in a purely managerial capacity.[47] Centralised production made early headway in the production of collars, cuffs, dickeys and similar items, which in addition to the sewing involved had to be marked, washed, starched and pressed, all of which were labour-intensive but increasingly mechanised operations. In other areas larger, more specialised machines and faster, electrically-powered sewing machines were introduced only gradually.[48] As long as there was enough cheap labour in the form of seamstresses working either at home or in a workshop, the anticipated increase in

46. Grandke gives the following examples: a flat consisting of two rooms and a kitchen, the workshop taking up the kitchen and one of the rooms, where altogether seven seamstresses worked, five sewing by machine and two by hand, together with one ironer, the intermediary as manager and his wife sewing button-holes. Also, a flat consisting of three rooms and a kitchen, of which two rooms were taken up by the workshop, in which ten seamstresses worked, seven sewing by machine and three by hand, together with two ironers and the intermediary and his wife (idem, 'Kleiderkonfektion', pp. 202f.). O. Olberg, *Das Elend in der Hausindustrie der Konfektion*, Leipzig, 1896, thus (p. 54): 'The intermediaries' workshops are no better. There is one, for example on the fifth floor of an old house in the town centre of Leipzig, where in the peak period five girls work for one intermediary producing ladies clothing. Both the manager and his wife are fully trained and both of them work, cut to size and do the ironing in the same room, which is 2.45m high, 3.6m wide and 4.3m long, although one of the side walls slopes in, so that there is much less room than the measurements indicate.
47. See Grandke, 'Kleiderkonfektion', pp. 167f.; Arndt (ed.), *Heimarbeit*, p. 197. In the production of linen goods it was more common for women to be workshop managers: B. A. Lehr, 'Die Hausindustrie in der Stadt Leipzig u. ihrer Umgebung', in *SVSP*, vol. 48, Leipzig, 1891, pp. 84f., 88–90; von Stülpnagel, 'Uber Hausindustrie in den Berlin u. den nächstgelegenen Kreisen', in ibid., vol. 42, Leipzig, 1890, p. 15.
48. In 1900 the main such areas were workers' clothes and summer clothes (Elberfeld-Barmen, München-Gladback) and starched linen (Bielefeld): see *Zusammenstellung*, 1896, pp. 8f. Such large machines included button-holing machines. Eight or nine electric sewing machines produced the equivalent of fifteen treadle (foot-pedal) machines: see Maurer, *Herrenkonfektion* pp. 26f.

productivity was still offset, at least for a seasonal trade, by the higher cost of premises and machinery.

The fact that less training was needed to do the work is only part of the reason why the clothing trade had no difficulty in finding the cheap labour it required. The pre-1914 annual incomes, particularly of privately-employed seamstresses, hardly enabled them to scrape together the most meagre existence.[49] The almost endless army of women competing with one another for jobs clearly had a disastrous effect on earnings. But how did this army come into being and why was it that the competition had no positive spin-offs for these women? There were clearly several factors which contributed to women either being available for this kind of employment or to their being forced into it.

The labour-intensive clothing industry, which is only profitable when wages are kept low, developed very rapidly from the 1850s onwards, chiefly in the big towns.[50] In 1899 Alfred Weber established for the first time a connection between the development of the clothing industry and the simultaneous processes of urbanisation and accelerated industrial centralisation. These last two developments altered the economic foundation of the family and contributed to the emergence of women's cottage industries. Farm labourers, craftsmen and small traders, who had traditionally worked in or near their homes, now went out to work in factories. Factory work, which was a typical feature of the second half of the nineteenth century, was mainly left to the men. The new industries, apart from the textiles industry, were certainly dominated by men. The same was true of the building trade, which grew apace in the wake of increasing urbanisation. Nevertheless, if the husband's income was insufficient his wife and children were forced to try and supplement it and with heavy rent increases this was even true for the lower grade of government officials.[51] The fact that parents and children were no longer working together to earn the family in-

---

49.　The starvation wages paid in the clothing trade gave rise to numerous investigations after 1885, the year in which a planned increase in the price of yarn provoked a public outcry (seamstresses usually had to pay for needles, machine oil and yarn themselves). One aspect on which some attention was focused was whether seamstresses were forced onto the streets as prostitutes, as the contemptuous term 'Nähmamsell' would seem to suggest.

50.　A. Weber, 'Die Entwicklungsgrundlage der grossstädtischen Frauenhausindustrie', in *SVSP*, vol. 85, Leipzig, 1899, pp. xiii–lx.

51.　On the need to earn a supplementary income, see L. Schneider, *Der Arbeiterhaushalt im 18. u. 19. Jahrhundert. Dargestellt am Beispiel des Heim-u. Fabrikarbeiters*, Berlin, 1967, pp. 98–100.

come, but were thrown individually onto the labour market, seems
to me to have been just as important for working-class families in
the late nineteenth century as the separation of home and work-
place, which is more commonly emphasised. This separation affected single and married men and also single women, but not
married women and particularly not women who had small children. Historians, who even today tend to give special emphasis to
this separation of home and workplace,[52] ignore the fact that
working-class women who were unable to go out to work because
they had children to look after continued to work at home in the
time-honoured way. The one difference, however, was that the
mother was now almost exclusively responsible both for bringing
up the children and for the housekeeping. This state of affairs was
particularly exacerbated in the big cities, where there was no opportunity to earn additional money by gardening or looking after
the animals, so that women were forced to take on extra work at
home in order to contribute to the family budget. Until the First
World War, however, urban jobs for women were either not very
appealing or very few and far between; such vacancies as there were
mainly for domestics, who endured appalling working conditions
and who, for obvious reasons, had to be unmarried. This situation
was exploited by the clothing trade. In order to escape the horrors
of being a household servant adolescent girls and unmarried women
from working-class or lower-middle-class families would work for
a pittance either in the shops and factories or for an intermediary.
Married women on the other hand formed the army of even more
poorly-paid seamstresses working at home.[53] The industry profited
from the fact that women were still paid at rates applicable to
supplementary work. All contemporary observers agreed that a
single woman was only able to make ends meet if parents or
relations provided cheap accommodation and food.

The sewing machine was of decisive importance in this kind of
labour market, dominated as it was by the clothing trade. In
Germany it was only the more specialised machines, such as those
for button-holes, which were paid for centrally. It was not the

52. See W. Conze's remarks, in H. Aubin and W. Zorn (eds.), *Handbuck der
Deutschen Wirtschafts- u. Sozialgeschichte*, vol. 2, Stuttgart, 1976, pp. 632f; the
questions of supplementary incomes and the 'dual burden' are dealt with in
ibid., p. 621.

53. Married women and those with children were distributed very differently
between home, workshops and factories from single women. Figures apply to
Berlin:

clothing manufacturers but the seamstresses and intermediaries who financed the increasing mechanisation of production by purchasing their own sewing machines. Interestingly, contemporaries commented with astonishment in the 1850s and 1860s that 'the guilds' master tailors, who complained so bitterly about the shortage of labour, allowed themselves to be overtaken in the use of modern machinery by the seamstresses'.[54] The tendency for untrained seamstresses to be more innovative was a direct result of their meagre wages. The labour market for women being what it was meant that machine-sewing as opposed to hand-sewing was essential if women were to earn any more than a bare minimum.[55] Seamstresses with machines, as long as they were competing with women sewing by hand, were potentially able to earn enough to invest a proportion of their earnings in new machines, so as to be able to employ other women working in a larger flat. The contention made in 1863 by one observer[56] that 50 per cent of all sewing

			single (%)	married (%)	widowed (%)	divorced (%)
Clothing industry[a]	236	workshop women	56.8	26.3	15.3	1.3
	138	home workers	25.4	55.8	18.1	—
Linen industry[b]	239	home workers	30.8	54.7	9.6	4.9
Linen industry[c]	47	factory workers	85.0	15.0	—	—

[a]*Grandke, 'Kleiderkonfektion', p.* 267
[b]Dyhrenfurth, *Arbeiterinnen*, pp. 20–2 (see n. 60, below).
[c]Feig, *Hausgewerbe*, pp. 146ff.

For the wage gap between factory and the home see *Reichstag 1887*, p. 748 (on high wages generally); in Hamburg women working in factories were earning an average of 10 marks per week for 9½ hrs of actual work: in workshops, 9 marks for 10–10½ hrs; at home, only 5 marks. For a similar analysis of the wage gap, see Grandke, 'Kleiderkonfection', p. 253.

54. *Arbeitgeber*, 1858, p. 899, for Würtemberg; ibid., for Trier; See also Herzberg, *Nähmaschinen-Industrie*, p. 12, for 1863; *Arbeitgeber*, 1865, p. 4713; Viebahn, *Statistik*, p. 669. Apparently the first tailor in Erlangen to possess a sewing machine employed others to use it (1860). By 1865 the sewing machine was spreading very quickly; See *SVSP*, vol. 64, Leipzig, 1895, pp. 401f.
55. See Herzberg, Nähmaschinen-Industrie, p. 20; L. Otto, *Das Recht der Frauen auf Erwerb. Blicke auf das Frauenleben der Gegenwart*, Hamburg, 1866, p. 22, according to whom the high cost of a sewing machine 'placed thousands of poor seamstresses in the same position as hand spinners with the onset of machines ... the machine is looked upon as the seamstresses' enemy — it provides them with competition'.
56. Herzberg, *Nähmaschinen-Industrie*, p. 4.

machines were owned by the working classes leads us to conclude that not only journeyman tailors but also other workers were investing in sewing machines, either so that their wives and daughters could work at home or in order to open up their own workshop. The greater productivity which could be achieved by using a sewing machine very rapidly became the norm. By 1869 the sewing machine was an 'absolutely essential requirement for profitability in the clothing industry'.[57] Long-serving seamstresses noted that wages for piecework fell continuously in the 1880s and 1890s, a result no doubt of the competition for jobs at this generally higher level of productivity once again depressing wages.[58] It was certainly primarily for want of any other work that women continued to accept these low wages. Nevertheless, even investing in a sewing machine could become a financial millstone. A woman with small children had no prospects of earning very much without a sewing machine, whilst its ownership seemed to provide a certain financial security. Thus, more and more people were prepared to pay the sales representative a small sum and enter into a hire-purchase arrangement. However this system worked, the mobility of the urban proletariat represented a decided risk for the seller, since an impecunious buyer could simply abscond with the machine before it was paid for; compensatory profit margins and security precautions were therefore necessary to prop up the hire-purchase system. One effective form of insurance was for the factory owner to stand surety with the sewing machine dealer for his permanent employees in order to enable them to carry on working for him at home after a full day in his factory.[59] Not infrequently the purchase of a sewing machine started off a vicious circle for the impecunious seamstress — the instalments of between 50 pfennigs and 1.50 marks had to be paid off weekly. In order to get a clear idea of the financial burden involved it is worthwhile looking at the results of the first empirical study, carried out in the 1890s by G. Dyhrenfurth[60] and based on the evidence of 200 seamstresses working in Berlin producing

57. *Vierteljahresschrift für höhere Töchterschulen 3.*, 1869, pp. 158f.
58. Feig, *Hausgewerbe*, pp. 51f., 60, 62, reports a decrease in the piece payments in Berlin between 1880 and 1895 of one-third to one-half. For complaints about cheap labour in the Berlin clothing industry and the drop in wages in Bavaria and Vogtland, see *Reichstag 1887*, pp. 717f. This may provide an explanation for the increasing importance of the intermediaries between 1882 and 1907, whilst work in the home lagged behind over the same period.
59. Example from Freig, *Hausgewerbe*, p. 79.
60. G. Dyhrenfurth, *Die hausindustriellen Arbeiterinnen in der Berliner Blusen-, Unterrock-, Schürzen- u. Tricotkonfektion*, Leipzig, 1898, pp. 48f., 56.

blouses, underwear and aprons. The most suitable sewing machine for this particular purpose was the Singer, which cost 135 marks on hire purchase. It had a two-year guarantee and, with continuous use, a life expectancy of five years. At a weekly rate of 1.50 marks a seamstress was able to pay off the price over two years, provided that she was in a position to pay the instalments every week. Out of her gross earnings she had to pay not only the instalments together with interest, but also 1 mark for machine oil and yarn, not to mention repairs, rent, lighting and heating. Dyhrenfurth worked out the net weekly income for 80 seamstresses working at home by deducting production costs and converting piece payments into a ten-hour day six days a week. She concluded that the net weekly income exceeded 7 marks per week in only 23.7 per cent of cases. No account was taken of seasonal variations,[61] including the two- to five-month period with very few orders or no orders at all. With these earnings a seamstress was barely able to purchase a sewing machine, since the 7 marks net income had to cover the minimum 6.35 marks expenses of a single woman — any meat or clothing was an additional luxury. For a working family of limited means investment in a sewing machine was out of all proportion to the profits to be made.[62] The same held true for the intermediaries.

Nevertheless, women continued to shoulder the burden of paying for the machines themselves, chiefly because the sewing machine was so well suited to home production. This was the backbone of the clothing trade's prosperity. By contrast, the 'poor seamstress'[63] continued to live in utter destitution. When single or married women became dependent on earning a fixed weekly wage they had no choice during the season but to work more efficiently for even

61. The workload remained most constant in the production of linen; in men's and boy's clothing there were usually three quiet months and in ladies' clothing five, from April to June and November to December; See Grandke, 'Kleiderkonfektion,' pp. 142–54; Lehr, 'Hausindustrie', pp. 75, 80; Stülpnagel, 'Hausindustrie', pp. 14, 16.
62. See Dyhrenfurth, *Arbeiterinnen* p. 59: 62 per cent of her married home workers had husbands earning less than 21 marks per week, which was insufficient to pay the rent (p. 33); see also Grandke, 'Kleiderkonfektion', pp. 142f., 146f., where he looks at women's earnings in the context of family income; and again, Schneider, *Arbeiterhaushalt*, p. 118, for his overview of the amount and distribution of workers' weekly earnings for 1890.
63. Cf. *Reichstag 1887*, passim; *Zusammenstellung*, 1896, which glosses over the problems; the Heimarbeit exhibition of 1906 reported individual cases of poverty — see C. Heiss and A. Koppel (eds.), *Heimarbeit u. Hausindustrie in Deutschland. Ihre Lohn- u. Arbeitsverhältnisse*, Berlin, 1906, pp. 58–79, 180–205 (for women's weekly wages). This was published for the exhibition by the Bureau für Sozialpolitik.

longer hours. As long as there was work to be done they had to work until they dropped, trying as far as possible to ignore what needed to be seen to in the way of family and household chores. The situation was not much better in the notorious sweatshops run by the intermediaries. Several machines were often in use at the same time in flats which were far too small, and in the season the employees and even the intermediary's own family would be driven to breaking point, so that the hours worked often considerably exceeded the statutory maximum. Dyhrenfurth's description of the attempt to reconcile the duties of a mother with earning a living and of the separation of home and workplace was probably familiar to many women:[64]

> One mother of several children, all of whom worked, slept, played, bawled and fell ill in one single room in Berlin with only one window, found the monotonous regularity of work in the factory, where she used to be employed, a relief from the chaos and noise at home. At the end of a day's work she could hardly bring herself to return home. The baby had, however, been over-fed by the other children, so that it was always ill, forcing her to give up her job in the factory. She now makes blouses at home and, despite working much longer hours, earns considerably less. She finds herself hopelessly torn between the desire to earn enough to live on and the need to look after the children, whose requirements she is now made constantly aware of. Infuriated by every little interruption and yet tormented by the state of the family and household whenever she looks up from her sewing, she finds herself repeatedly forced to neglect one thing for another. Life becomes a series of small irritations — 'Sometimes I think to myself in the morning, How can I get up and start another day like that?'

Thus on closer inspection the emancipation which is supposed to have resulted from the introduction of the sewing machine assumes a different hue. A correct evaluation of the situation already described would only be possible if the precise extent of female labour in the clothing industry were known. Unfortunately there are no exact statistics available which show the numbers of women working as seamstresses in the clothing industry, whether in factories, workshops or in their own homes. In any survey the distinctions between the various trades and professions are blurred and there is a considerable measure of uncertainty since the conditions of employment in decentralised production were particularly confused.

64. Dyhrehfurth, *Arbeiterinnen*, pp. 67ff.

Other factors which made any statistical assessment more difficult were the tendency to engage people for seasonal work, the inclusion of unascertainable family workers and the 'secret' work done by middle-class women anxious that their social standing might be adversely affected if it became known that they were working. Without discussing the available statistics in detail it may nevertheless be of some use to give a few of the more important findings.[65] In 1895 there were about 1.5m women employed in trade and industry, most of whom came into the category of 'worker' even if they were self-employed or working at home. A third of the women were working as seamstresses or dressmakers or in some other capacity in the clothing industry. Included in this group are the not so numerous custom dressmakers and the many home seamstresses, who satisfied mainly local demand. The majority of these women probably worked more or less exclusively for the clothing industry. In 1907 this particular group comprised 940,000 women. In terms of the clothing trade, in 1895 496,831 women and by 1907 584,783 women were working to produce 'linen, clothing, millinery and finery'. The vast majority of these were employed as seamstresses. This was certainly true of those working at home, of whom 110,000 were registered in 1907, although it is generally agreed that there were many more than that. However imprecise this information may be, it at least conveys an impression of the extent to which the lives of women in the German Empire were changed or even shaped by the development of hand and machine sewing.

There seems to have been no notable improvement in the conditions prevailing in the clothing industry in the period up to the First World War. Apart from the surplus of labour on the market, the decentralised organisation of the industry was an important contributory factor. Up to 1914 it was only the production of linen which benefited from the increased centralisation brought about by the twin processes of electrification and rationalisation. Women working for the clothing industry either in workshops or in their own homes were not covered by the protective factory legislation, by insurance against sickness and accident or by pension arrangements. The state of the labour market and the decentralised nature of

---

65. The 1882 census was not included since it took no account of members of the family who also worked. For details, see *Statistik des Deutschen Reiches*, vol. 207; idem, vol. 211, p. 57; idem, vol. 213, pp. 260ff.; idem, vols. 220/1, suppl., pp. 118f. For a good account of the statistical information, see R. Wilbrandt, *Die Frauenarbeit. Ein Problem des Kapitalismus*, Leipzig, 1906, p. 94.

production meant that demands for higher pay were almost pointless.[66] The survival of labour such as this, situated as it was half-way between the traditional cottage industry and the modern factory, seemed for various reasons to be assured. Between the manufacturer on the one hand and the seamstress on the other the intermediary was himself part wage-earner, part entrepreneur. The supplementary earnings of middle-class girls and the 'secret' work done by middle-class women were both effective in keeping down labour costs, though both served in individual cases either to maintain respectability or, less frequently, to keep earnings at subsistence level. Finally, it was extremely difficult to organise protest activities since employers were widely dispersed and the women, particularly those working from home, were worked so hard that they had neither the time nor the energy for anything else. Until 1907 the German combination laws in any case prevented any such joint action.[67] In the clothing industry the mechanisation of sewing had the effect more of consolidating than of improving the miserable working conditions which prevailed. This was a direct consequence of the sewing machine being used by people in their homes. To maintain that the private household was relieved of the burden of production is simply to give currency to a much-vaunted cliché which is too much of an over-simplification to contribute to a sound interpretation of the changes. In reality the parallel development of the clothing and sewing machine industries led to a very complicated process which affected different types of household in very different ways. It is bordering on cynicism to attribute any such beneficial effects to the flourishing clothing industry when one realises that a significant percentage of goods was produced by underpaid working-class and lower-middle-class women at home on their own sewing machines. Any attempt at an assessment of the position of these seamstresses takes us on to the as yet unsolved problem[68] of differentiating correctly between the various types of female labour: work done for the family and household, paid work done at home and work in workshops and factories. There is still

66. See Grandke, 'Kleiderkonfektion', pp. 341–78, for his account of the 1896 strike of the Berlin clothing workers.
67. In 1904 there were only 4,186 women members of the free Christian trade unions in the clothing trade — see Wilbrandt, *Frauenarbeit*, pp. 127f. For obstacles put in the way of union organisation by the police, see A. Berger, *Die zwanzigjährige Arbeiterinnenbewegung Berlins u. ihr Ergebnis*, Berlin, 1889, pp. 24–52.
68. Despite preliminary studies by, for example, J. Scott and L. A. Tilly, 'Women's Work and the Family in 19th-Century Europe', in *Comparative Studies in*

more which remains to be discovered about this area of work, which has tended to be overlooked in the widespread concentration on big industry. Only then will a true understanding emerge of the degree to which in the nineteenth century the various forms of labour, paid and unpaid and for organisations both large and small, however recruited, were interrelated and interconnected. The introduction of the sewing machine was certainly a step forward from the technical and economic viewpoint. However, the claim that this was accompanied by social progress should not be made without some qualification.

Social History, 17, 1975, pp. 36–64; P. Branca, 'A New Perspective on Women's Work. A Comparative Typology', in *Journal of Social History*, 9, 1975/6, pp. 129–53; E. Plech, 'Two Worlds in One. Work and Family', in ibid., 10, 1976, pp. 178–95.

KLAUS TENFELDE

The Herne Riots of 1899

Towards the end of the nineteenth century the Ruhr mining industry was approaching the peak of an economic boom which had set in from about 1895 onwards.* The depression, which had begun in the 1870s and had, with ups and downs and at generally very low price levels, continued in the 1880s, had first given way to a forceful upswing between 1888 and 1891. It was a change which affected both the mining industry and the iron-and-steel-producers. Coal production experienced a brief reduction in 1892; but thereafter, from 1895 up to the turn of the century, annual growth rates averaged between 5.3 per cent and 9.1 per cent in the Ruhr mining district. By 1900 output totalled almost 60m tons per annum. This meant that annual production was roughly double that of 1887. Prices had risen by about 15 per cent in comparison with those of the 1880s and had remained stable. These were growth rates which so far had, for a brief period and admittedly starting from a lower plateau, only been achieved during the period 1871 to 1873 at the time of the *Gründerjahre* boom. As early as 1888 the number of miners had more than doubled to 105,445, in comparison with the figure for 1870. It doubled again in the 1890s and reached 226,902 in 1900. The average annual recruitment rates even surpassed the annual production rates owing to a decline in productivity per worker from 1888 onwards. In 1897 the work-force grew by 8.8 per cent in comparison with the previous year. Calculated on the same basis it increased by a further 8.9 per cent in 1898, by 6.9 per cent in

*   Publ. orig. in *Internationale Wissenschaftliche Korrespondenz*, 15 (1979), pp. 71–101. The author would like to thank the publishers for permission to prepare and use this translation.

1899 and by 10.6 per cent in 1900.[1] The annual quantitative growth
of the work-force was hence roughly as large as the figure for the
entire Ruhr mining industry in the mid-1850s.

However, in comparison with previous decades, shifts had
occurred in the regions where the growth of the mining industry
took place. The social composition of the miners also experienced a
profound change in terms of the backgrounds of those who arrived
as newcomers. The growth in production and work-forces had been
borne by the collieries of the middle generation, i.e. those pits
which had been developed in the 1840s and 1850s. These collieries
were situated along the Hellweg and had employees numbering
between 500 and 1,000. From the 1890s the main region of growth
was further along the Emscher River. Here and under the influence
of the *Gründerjahre* boom very large enterprises emerged which
frequently employed more than 2,000 miners.[2] The different quality
of the coal mined in this region significantly improved the market
opportunities of the Ruhr mining industry. With the formation of
the coal syndicate in 1893,[3] it had also been possible to stabilise sales
and prices on a long-term basis. This made it possible to mitigate the
repercussions of temporary downturns which invariably deeply
affected wage- and price-structures.

The social composition of the miners also saw a fundamental
change in the period up to the First World War by comparison with
the situation during the first phase of growth in the middle of the
nineteenth century: during the latter period, newcomers had mi-
grated predominantly from the regions in the immediate vicinity
and from the neighbouring provinces and states. From the 1880s
onwards, the eastern provinces of Prussia became the main recruit-

1. Calculated on the basis of the figures compiled in C. L. Holtfrerich, *Quantitative Wirtschaftsgeschichte des Ruhrkohlenbergbaus im 19. Jahrhundert. Eine
   Führungssektoranalyse*, Dortmund, 1973, pp. 17f., 23f., 52, 68 (for production
   and work-forces); also P. Wiel, *Wirtschaftsgeschichte des Ruhrgebiets. Tatsa-
   chen und Zahlen*, Essen, 1970 (for population and economic development);
   R. Spree, *Die Wachstumszyklen der deutschen Wirtschaft von 1840–1880, mit
   einem konjunkturstatistischen Anhang*, Berlin, 1977, pp. 166–178.
2. For the growth regions of the Ruhr area, see in particular O. Quelle, *Industrie-
   geographie der Rheinlande*, Bonn, 1926; also W. Brepohl, *Der Aufbau des
   Ruhrvolkes im Zuge der Ost-West-Wanderung*, Recklinghausen, 1948; idem,
   *Industrievolk im Wandel von der agraren zur industriellen Daseinsform,
   dargestellt am Ruhrgebiet*, Tübingen, 1957. See also the quantifications in
   F. Bierhaus, *Die Ausbreitungs- und Wanderungsbewegungen des Steinkohlen-
   bergbaus im niederrheinisch-westfälischen Industriegebiet*, PhD. thesis, Bonn,
   1952, esp. pp. 41–67, 61, 73.
3. See, e.g., V. Muthesius, *Ruhrkohle, 1893–1943*, Essen, 1943, and the survey by
   F. Schunder, *Tradition und Fortschritt. Hundert Jahre Gemeinschaftsarbeit im
   Ruhrkohlenbergbau*, Stuttgart, 1959, pp. 215–25.

ing grounds. This resulted in a rapid increase of the proportion of the non-German speaking citizens of Prussia among the mining population, especially in the fast-expanding northern industrial zone. As early as 1893 pits in the Herne mining area and the neighbouring districts had between 35 per cent and 45 per cent of newcomers from the eastern provinces of Prussia, and between 25 per cent and 30 per cent of this work-force did not speak German as their first language.[4] The authorities tended to see little difference between Prussian nationals who were Masurians and those of Polish origin. Among the towns of the Ruhr, it was Herne who had the largest proportion of Poles (15.2 per cent) among its inhabitants as early as 1890.[5] By the end of 1897 the number of Polish-speaking miners was 34,361, i.e. 18.6 per cent of the total work-force and double the figure for 1893. By the end of 1899, 33.9 per cent of the Ruhr miners came from the eastern provinces of Prussia.[6] Of these 70,000 or so workers 9 per cent had arrived from Upper Silesia, 35.5 per cent from Poznan, 11.4 per cent from West Prussia and 44.1 per cent from Masuria. Between 1893 and 1899 the total number of miners grew by 58,666, but between the end of 1893 to the end of 1899 some 34,549 labourers from the eastern provinces joined the Ruhr mines. In other words, almost 59 per cent of the total growth in the work-force was sustained by migrants from the East. The new miners were scattered over sixteen Ruhr mining districts, with diminishing density from north to south. In 1899 their share of the total work-force in the Ruhr River valley (Werden, Hattingen, Süd-Dortmund, Oberhausen, Süd-Essen, Witten) was between 5 per cent and 21 per cent; in the northern districts of Gelsenkirchen, Herne and Recklinghausen, by contrast, it was as high as from 48.2

---

4. Based on the statistics provided in O. Taeglichsbeck, *Die Belegschaft der Bergwerke und Salinen im Oberbergamtsbezirk Dortmund nach der Zählung vom 16. Dezember 1896*, 2 vols., Dortmund 1895/6, esp. vol. I, pp. 6–15, vol. II, pp. xxi.
5. See L. Maaß, 'Deutsche Binnenwanderung mit besonderer Berücksichtigung des deutschen Westens', in *Staat und Volkstum. Bücher des Deutschtums*, 2 vols., Berlin, 1926, esp. vol. II, pp. 353–62; also F. Schulze, *Die polnische Zuwanderung im Ruhrgebiet und ihre Wirkungen*, PhD. thesis, Münster, 1909, pp. 29f.; M. Broesike, 'Die Polen im westlichen Preussen 1905', in *Zeitschrift des Königlich-Preussischen Statistischen Landesamts*, vol. 48, 1906, pp. 251–74, 252. See also the discussion of the statistical problems in H. U. Wehler, 'Die Polen im Ruhrgebiet bis 1918', in idem (ed.), *Moderne deutsche Sozialgeschichte*, 3rd ed., Cologne/Berlin, 1970, pp. 437–55, esp. 441f. Of fundamental importance is C. Klessmann, *Polnische Bergarbeiter im Ruhrgebiet, 1870–1945*, Göttingen, 1978.
6. Calculated on the basis of Taeglichsbeck, *Bergwerke*, vol. I, pp. 6–19, and L. Pieper, *Die Lage der Bergarbeiter im Ruhrrevier*, Stuttgart/Berlin 1903, pp. 17–22, also for the following.

per cent to 57.4 per cent. Of all the newcomers from the eastern provinces who arrived between 1893 and 1899 some 31 per cent moved to these three areas alone. When between the end of 1893 and the end of 1899 the mining work-force in these three districts rose from 37,485 to 50,891, 80 per cent of the increase had been recruited from the eastern provinces. Most of them had Polish as their native tongue. Around the turn of the century, there existed nineteen so-called *Polenzechen* ('Poles' pits') where the proportion of miners using foreign languages or a mixture of these with German was over 50 per cent. The percentage breakdown by colliery was as follows at the end of 1897:[7]

Gelsenkirchen district	
Pluto	74.7
Unser Fritz	54.6
Konsolidation	55.3
Hibernia	50.1
Wilhelmine Viktoria	52.2
Recklinghausen district	
König Ludwig	61.9
Ewald	85.0
Graf Bismarck	71.0
Herne district	
Viktor	51.2
Friedrich der Grosse	62.5
von der Heydt	57.5
Julia	52.5

Following the influx of the 1880s and at the turn to the 1890s, the economic upswing from around 1895 was accompanied by the second major wave of immigrants to the northern Ruhr area, most of whom did not have German as their native tongue. The composition of the work-force at those collieries which were at the centre of the riots in the early summer of 1899 changed dramatically from one year to the next. Group relations formed at the work-place, such as had existed in the Ruhr mining industry for a long time in the shape of underground work teams were almost daily thrown into disarray because of the high rate of work-force fluctuation at collieries with a high percentage of new miners. Workers came and

7. Ibid., p. 20; Klessmann, *Bergarbeiter*, p. 208, n. 12; further information in K. Murzynowska, *Die polnischen Erwerbsauswanderer im Ruhrgebiet während der Jahre 1880–1914*, Dortmund, 1979.

left. The establishment of social contact was impeded in particular by sizeable linguistic barriers which separated the skilled from the unskilled and those who had lived there for a longer time from those newcomers who had no roots and no ties. There was also the gap between the majority of older and married miners and the young ones. Also certain technical and organisational changes underground contributed to the dissolution of the erstwhile work teams because, increasingly, the room-and-pillar system of mining was being replaced by the long-wall system, in which dozens of hewers worked either individually or with the support of hauliers.

The details of the work-place changes cannot be discussed here. Nor is it possible to examine the situation of this fragmented work-force outside the pits in their families, households, accommodation, neighbourhood or sprawling industrial community; this all the more so as research in this area is insufficient. In particular we are lacking careful histories of individual collieries and their work-forces based on the archives of the large mining companies in the northern Ruhr area. Indeed the social history of the Ruhr region during the period of intensive industrialisation up to the First World War is marked by many gaps, and on the basis of the available literature it is still barely perceptible.[8]

Nevertheless, a few pieces of information can be provided here. It is clearly discernible that the joint impact of an economic boom and a shortage of labour at the end of the 1890s resulted in a rapid increase of nominal wages. According to the calculations of various authors, the wage levels of the *Gründerjahre* of the early 1870s were reached again for the first time in 1896. The upward trend continued until 1900.[9] However, food prices and, above all, rents rose steeply

8. Older or more recent short biographies of entrepreneurs, company histories and Festschriften as well as other local and regional accounts are mostly of little value for a careful social history of the Ruhr area during the period of advanced industrialisation. The social history of the Hellweg zone is better known. Among recent studies see W. Fischer, *Herz des Reviers*, Essen 1965, 251–96; G. Adelmann (ed.), *Quellensammlung zur Geschichte der sozialen Betriebsverfassung*, 3 vols. (inc. *Index*), Bonn 1960–68, esp. vol. II; also L. Rothert, *Umwelt und Arbeitsverhältnisse von Ruhrbergleuten in der 2. Hälfte des 19. Jahrhunderts*, Münster, 1976; G. Steinberg, *Sozialräumliche Entwicklung und Gliederung des Ruhrgebiets*, Bad Godesberg, 1967; H. Hilbert, *Die Zusammensetzung der Grubenbelegschaft des Ruhrkohlengebietes um die Jahrhundertwende und ihre Probleme*, PhD. thesis, Cologne, 1955.
9. Thanks to records kept by the authorities, firm data on wages, though not perfect, are available. They are differentiated according to wage levels, mining areas and pension rights and were regularly published at the time. See, e.g., the journal *Glückauf*, vol. 26, 1890, p. 381; also the data collected in K. Tenfelde, *Sozialgeschichte der Bergarbeiterschaft an der Ruhr im 19. Jahrhundert*, 2nd ed.,

during this period, particularly in the northern regions where there developed a desperate housing shortage. It is therefore questionable as to whether real incomes did actually increase everywhere. In this respect it must be taken into account that there were differentiations within the region. There were zones, especially in the south, where food prices and wages were relatively low; in other regions wage levels were very high, but prices kept closely behind. In this respect, differences between town and country continued to be relevant, as did the local market situation. Supplementation of income through agricultural production remained insignificant among the newcomers. On the other hand, they could expect to achieve top wages in the northern region. Attaining the wages of hauliers after a brief training period, the Polish labourers in particular proved to be a match for their German colleagues as far as their productivity was concerned. The charge could be heard even in trade union circles that these Polish workers had a depressing effect on wage levels and that the desire to get a job at all cost disturbed the team-work patterns of the older German-speaking workers.[10] But this was true at most during the first weeks of adaptation. The shortage of labour and the fluctuations among the Poles, the 'migratory birds' of the Ruhr, demonstrated that these prejudices were without foundation and were more likely the result of resentments between the two groups of workers.

It has been reported that the Poles, the retention of their peculiar habits of dress notwithstanding, soon adjusted their life-style to that of the indigenous working-class population.[11] Differences in household conduct and family-life still require investigation. Over and above all this it must be borne in mind that a majority of the newcomers were youthful and unmarried labourers. This is also

---

Bonn, 1981, p. 296; Holtfrerich, *Wirtschaftsgeschichte*, pp. 54–6; also the discussion of the contemporary debate concerning the interpretation of the data on wage levels in M. Saitzew, *Steinkohlenpreise und Dampfkraftkosten*, Munich/Leipzig 1914, esp. pp. 70ff.; W. Retzlaff, *Das Lohngefüge im deutschen Steinkohlenbergbau von 1886–1956*, PhD. thesis, Freiburg, 1958. On the north–south wage differentials see, e.g., W. H. Fischer, *Die Entwicklung des Ruhrtalbergbaus und seine Existenzbedingungen*, PhD. thesis, Heidelberg, 1925, pp. 172f.

10. See Hilbert, *Grubenbelegschaft*, p. 51f.; E. Franke, 'Die polnische Volksgruppe im Ruhrgebiet, 1870–1940', in *Jahrbuch des Arbeitswissenschaftlichen Instituts der DAF*, vol. II, 1940/1, pp. 319–404; Klessmann, *Bergarbeiter*, pp. 36, 50.

11. See J. V. Bredt, *Die Polenfrage im Ruhrgebiet*, Leipzig, 1909, p. 73. Unfortunately the recent book by R. C. Murphy, *Guestworkers in the German Reich: A Polish Community in Wilhelmian Germany*, Boulder, Col./New York, 1983 (German transl. 1982) does not pay attention to this fundamental question.

reflected in housing patterns.[12] The large collieries in the north were
forced to take some action about the housing shortage and fluctuations in the work-force by adopting an extensive construction
programme. This at least put a curb on price rises for private
accommodation. However, extensive families and the taking-in of
lodgers led to increasing housing densities. These conditions still
constitute one of the darkest chapters of the history of industrialisation. Moreover, by deliberately settling the Polish newcomers in
overcrowded housing 'colonies' on the fringe of, or at a distance
from, the town (where the German workers tended to ostracise
them), the lack of accommodation was turned into a virtue, albeit a
dubious one: such isolation perpetuated the rifts within the collieries between newcomers and indigenous miners and extended them
beyond the colliery gates; it incited resentments and latent conflict
between the groups, and it cemented differences in customs, religious denomination and language which were coloured by the
higher rates of illiteracy among the newcomers. Finally, it reinforced the diaspora situation of innumerable families, producing a
result which was decisive for the general social climate: the disposition of workers and management to engage in conflicts which were
in fact produced by the system was masked and loyalties which
were dysfunctional to the company's interest or to the system were
undermined. This situation 'guided' the growth of consciousness
and the articulation of interests through the promotion of group
fragmentation.[13]

These observations can be backed up with further evidence, if we
look at the tradition of conflict in the Ruhr mining industry and at
the degree of interest organisation which had meanwhile been
achieved. As far as the development of modern forms of interest
organisation is concerned, the most important impulses which
touched off structural changes were given by the reform of mining
law and the industry's expansion during the decade after 1850. The
experience of liberal-capitalist forms of organising production
which climaxed during the period from 1867 to 1872 resulted in
collective learning processes. In the course of these processes the
miners began to depart from traditional forms of conflict regulation
under the guidance of the public supervisory authorities of the
mining industry. They no longer lodged complaints, petitions or

---

12. See the article by F. Brüggemeier and L. Niethammer in this volume and the
    literature on housing cited there.
13. See, e.g., Pieper, *Bergarbeiter*, p. 205; Klessmann, *Bergarbeiter*, pp. 48f., 93f.

appeals with the sovereign. Rather they adopted modern forms of conflict; they resorted to mass action in the shape of rallies, to organisational work through clubs, to relatively institutionalised work-place confrontations and to early forms of permanent association. It was a period of transition, in the wake of which followed the refusal of the state to allow permanent trade union organisations; it was a transition which was impeded and temporarily even totally blocked by persistent counter-measures on the part of the public authorities and the entrepreneurs.[14] These conditions were an outgrowth of the fact that after the 1848 Revolution the mine-owners made their peace with the Prusso-German constitutional order and the conservative-monarchical forces supporting it. They did so having become mesmerised by a prosperous economy and impressed by the successful reform of mining legislation in Prussia up to 1865. Another contributing factor was that as early as 1858 the Ruhr mining companies had begun to develop their own organisation, the Association of Mining Interests in the District of the *Oberbergamt* Dortmund,[15] which turned out to be quite effective in legal, commercial and general questions of economic policy. It was also an organisation which was later, and especially after the founding of the Empire in 1871, complemented by other organisations of heavy industry, among them regional cartels and limited sales syndicates.

Starting with the strikes at Essen in 1872, there developed a continuous chain of conflicts. However, these actions, including those in the Dortmund region towards the end of the 1870s, were sustained by an older generation of miners. Most of them were either natives to the area or had lived there for a long time or they

14. For details, see K. Tenfelde, 'Konflikt und Organisation in einigen deutschen Bergbaugebieten, 1867–1872', in *Geschichte und Gesellschaft*, vol. III, 1977, pp. 211–35, esp. p. 234f.
15. On the Bergbauverein see, e.g., H. Meis, *Der Ruhrbergbau im Wechsel der Zeiten*, Essen, 1933; Schunder, *Tradition*, pp. 32–54; and on the early history of the Association, E. Kroker, 'Industrialisierung und bergbauliche Verbandspolitik in der zweiten Hälfte des 19. Jahrhunderts', in *Der Anschnitt*, vol. 25, 1977, pp. 110–20. On the Ausstandssicherungs-Verband which, having been formed in 1890 in the wake of the 1889 strike, operated side by side with the Bergbauverein, was absorbed by the Zechenverband in 1908 and with an initial membership of 100 mining companies comprised about 90 per cent of Ruhr coal production, see esp. E. Jüngst, *Festschrift zur Feier des fünfzigjährigen Bestehens des Vereins für die bergbaulichen Interessen*, Essen, 1908, p. 151; P. Osthold, *Die Geschichte des Zechenverbandes, 1908–1933*, Berlin, 1934, 25–9; G. Kessler, *Die Deutschen Arbeitgeberverbände*, Leipzig, 1907, p. 291; a more recent study is H. G. Kirchhoff, *Die staatliche Sozialpolitik im Ruhrbergbau, 1871–1914*, Cologne/Opladen, 1958, pp. 116f., 160–7.

were newcomers from the surrounding region with similar ethnic background. Then, from the 1880s, as we have seen, a fundamental shift occurred in the social composition of the mining population. This shift also changed the preconditions of an institutionalisation of conflict which had always been curtailed by the repressive authoritarianism of the mine-owners. It was only the massive miners' strike of May 1889[16] which created the organisational forms of future action and this, in turn, created new conditions for the way in which conflicts were carried out in the industry.

This development is partly related to the way in which the state at least temporarily perceived its role in the handling of industrial conflicts. This new role became visible after the promulgation of the Mining Industry Court Bill (*Berggewerbegerichtsgesetz*) and in particular after the revision of the General Mining Law of 1892. Even if these developments were partially eroded later on, this was the beginning of a policy of formulating a specific legal framework for the regulation of industrial conflicts which had long been recognised as being inevitable.[17] It was a policy which can be traced in the revival of the debate on nationalisation, in the controversy over workers' committees and their introduction, for the time being on a voluntary basis, in conjunction with the Mining Industry Courts. These developments were vigorously fought by the mine-owners. They held a strong political position through their associations and used their influence in the parliamentary bodies decidedly in opposition to any reforms. This buttressed the *Herr-im-Hause* authoritarianism which was continually fed by the peculiar forms of company organisation and had not arisen from a traditional patriarchal outlook.[18] Nor should we overlook the hostile anti-working-class and anti-reformist predisposition of large and crucial groups within the Prusso-German political leadership. From the

16. See W. Köllmann and A. Gladen (eds.), *Der Bergarbeiterstreik von 1889 und die Gründung des 'Alten Verbandes' in ausgewählten Dokumenten der Zeit*, Bochum, 1969; A. Gladen, 'Der Ruhrbergarbeiterstreik von 1889. Ein sozialer Konflikt aus konservativer Motivation', in O. Neuloh (ed.), *Soziale Innovation und sozialer Konflikt*, Göttingen, 1977, pp. 149–201; see also the edition of documents by G. Seeber and W. Wittwer (eds.), 'Friedrich Hammachers Aufzeichnungen über den Bergarbeiterstreik von 1889', in *Jahrbuch für Geschichte*, vol. 16, 1977, pp. 403–58.
17. See esp. Kirchhoff, *Sozialpolitik*, passim; K. A. Hückinghaus, *Die Verstaatlichung der Steinkohlenbergwerke*, Jena, 1892; also K. E. Born, *Staat und Sozialpolitik seit dem Sturz Bismarcks, 1890–1914*, Wiesbaden, 1954; H. J. Teuteberg, *Geschichte der industriellen Mitbestimmung in Deutschland*, Tübingen, 1961, pp. 410ff.; C. Medalen, 'State Monopoly Capitalism in Germany: the Hibernia Affair', in *Past and Present*, vol. 78, 1978, pp. 82, 112, esp. 93–100.
18. See Tenfelde, *Bergarbeiterschaft*, pp. 336f.

1890s, the recently formed miners' associations were confronted with this powerful opposition, with the result that they constantly lived on the verge of a legality whose preservation or destruction was dependent on the opposition. They also had to wrestle with the legacy of the period of corporatist organisation and in particular with the separatist consciousness of large groups of miners who continued to uphold long-past privileges and peculiarities.

However, the heaviest burden with which they had to cope was the fragmentation of the miners. This fragmentation developed well before they had begun to organise and was exacerbated in subsequent years by well-nigh insuperable denominational and political differences. The earliest organisational efforts had been marked by this burden. When, in the autumn of 1889, the *Alte Verband* was established which was based on the principle of free trade unionism it promptly faced a counterpart wedded to the idea of a Christian unionism, the *Glückauf* Association. Even though the latter did not survive the crisis years that followed, the seeds had nevertheless been sown for the Christian counter-association which actually emerged in 1894. It also did not help that the *Alte Verband*, experiencing a massive influx of members during the early years of its life in the wake of the 1889 strike,[19] overestimated and probably misjudged its possibilities for organised activity as well as the durability of the sense of solidarity which had only just been generated. As a result it all too unthinkingly advanced radical demands and organised confrontations which were planned without regard to the economic climate and the market situation and which ended in failure.[20] This in turn led to a decline in its membership which continued until 1896 and threatened its survival. While the national association saw a renewed growth in membership from 1895, its chapters in the Ruhr area revived only in 1897. But this revival was accompanied by the growth of the Christian Miners' Union. This development was due to a policy of moderation and

19. Membership figures in J. Fritsch, *Eindringen und Ausbreitung des Revisionismus im deutschen Bergarbeiterverband*, Leipzig, 1967, pp. 109–11; see also G. A. Ritter, *Arbeiterbewegung, Parteien und Parlamentarismus*, Göttingen, 1976, pp. 95–101.
20. The sources on these strikes are rich. For an all too brief treatment, see M. J. Koch, *Die Bergarbeiterbewegung im Ruhrgebiet zur Zeit Wilhelms II., 1889–1914*, Düsseldorf, 1954, pp. 53f.; also H. Imbusch, *Arbeitsverhältnis und Arbeiterorganisationen im deutschen Bergbau*, Essen, 1908; Otto Hue, *Die Bergarbeiter*, 2 vols., Stuttgart, 1910–13, esp. vol. II; a good survey is S. Hickey, 'The Shaping of the German Labour Movement: Miners in the Ruhr', in R. J. Evans (ed.), *Society and Politics in Wilhelmine Germany*, London, 1978, pp. 215–40.

reformism which emphasised the political neutrality of trade unionism[21] and benefited from the renewed economic boom. It was a policy formulated above all under the influence of Otto Hue, and it asserted itself against strong opposition.

In surveying the organisations of the movement of Ruhr miners at the end of the 1890s it is important to bear in mind that in 1899 the *Alte Verband* had 18,606 members and the Christian Miners' Union some 22,000. Both unions therefore comprised almost 20 per cent of all Ruhr miners.[22] On the other hand, these figures do not include the small association of *Hirsch-Dunckersche Gewerkvereine* which had its supporters also among the miners. Moreover, there were the even more important Protestant and Catholic workers' associations which partly represented a form of unionism, even though denominational affiliation and clergical influences predominated.

This leads us to a brief discussion of an area which has been largely neglected by research, the miners' clubs, which experienced a renewed prosperity from the 1890s onwards.[23] Side-by-side with the denominationally based clubs they were formed for a variety of purposes which frequently appeared to be unpolitical. The older denominational and 'free' *Knappenvereine* had anticipated the function of the trade unions as institutions of financial assistance. They had promoted networks of partly formal communication among those who had experienced the same organisation of industrial work. In some of these clubs the boundaries towards a trade unionist type of interest articulation continued to be fluid. We should not underestimate their importance as institutions in which patterns of regulated communal life were learned and the rituals of democratic assembly and organisation could be internalised. They also offered opportunities for the unimpeded enjoyment of social

---

21. See esp. Fritsch, *Eindringen*, passim; also O. Hue, *Neutrale oder parteiische Gewerkschaften*, Bochum, 1900. On Hue: N. Osterroth, *Otto Hue*, Bochum, 1922.
22. See n. 19 above. The figures for the Alte Verband are for the Ruhr area, with its total supra-regional membership being 33,170 in 1899. I had only supra-regional figures for the Christian Gewerkverein; the actual degree of organisation would therefore indeed appear to be lower. However, the proliferation movement of the Christian miners was still in its early stages towards the end of the nineteenth century.
23. See K. Tenfelde, 'Bergmännisches Vereinswesen im Ruhrgebiet während der Industrialisierung', in J. Reulecke and W. Weber (eds.), *Fabrik—Familie—Feierabend*, Wuppertal, 1978, pp. 315–44; also E. Lucas, *Zwei Formen des Radikalismus in der deutschen Arbeiterbewegung*, Frankfurt, 1976, pp. 94–6. On the Polish clubs, see Klessmann, *Bergarbeiter*, pp. 94–6.

needs beyond the pressures imposed by the work-process. This was particularly applicable to the Poles. The Germans, despite their 'clubbishness' (*Vereinsmeierei*), were 'hopelessly backward' (*reine Waisenknaben*) in comparison with the Poles.[24] The early club formations of the latter, founded in the 1880s, had operated relatively free from interference. They could subsequently have played a significant role in helping to integrate the newcomers from the East, if the authorities had not taken a particular interest in them after the promulgation of Bismarck's anti-Polish repression (*Polenpolitik*). As early as 1885 Catholic circles in the Ruhr began to ask themselves why the 'fear of the Poles' dominated the 'delirious fantasies of the officials' (*Delirien der Offiziösen*): 'Is it blind hatred of the suffering Polish nation that drives them into such an exorbitant misapprehension of the most harmless and simplest matters, of the most ordinary ways of earning a living?'[25] To be sure, the national Catholicism of the Poles also promoted the process of alienation, especially after 1890, which was accelerated by the daily problems of pastoral care within the community. But the policy towards ethnic minorities no doubt assumed grotesque proportions when one looks at police surveillance of the mushrooming clubs and meetings of the Polish community and remembers that these clubs were sustained by the determined efforts of Polish clergymen. It was the ban on the use of the Polish language at public meetings which plagued the authorities long after the turn of the century. Later this ban led the Poles to 'articulate' their protest by holding silent meetings.[26] They tended to react to the expressions of mistrust and continuous bans on the part of the authorities with a 'shyness which grew to the point of pusillanimity (*Ängstlichkeit*)'.[27] This was the official extension of the isolation of the Poles at social and company level. It became encapsulated in the Mining Policing Decree (*Bergpolizeiverordnung*) of the *Oberbergamt* Dortmund at the beginning of 1899, which contained a stipulation that foreign-language workers had to have a minimal knowledge of German.[28] It is therefore hardly surprising that the activities of the clubs which

---

24. O. Mückeley, *Die Ost- und Westpreussen-Bewegung im rheinisch-westfälischen Industriebezirk*, Gelsenkirchen, 1926, p. 17.
25. *Tremonia*, no. 122, 2.6.1885.
26. Archival sources for the 1880s and 1890s, inter alia, in Staatsarchiv Münster, Oberpräsidium, 2748, I–II; ibid., Regierung Münster, VII 23, I–II; Hauptstaatsarchiv Düsseldorf, Regierung Düsseldorf, Pr 867; ibid., 8856.
27. Frank, 'Volksgruppe', p. 360.
28. See Wehler, 'Ruhrgebiet', pp. 452f.; Klessmann, *Bergarbeiter*, pp. 63f.

had been founded in the early 1890s to look after denominational and pastoral concerns soon also assumed undertones of Polish nationalism.

Bochum became the centre of Polish agitation in the Ruhr area and the surveillance of the Polish population in the region was coordinated by the police headquarters of the city. The year 1890 saw the publication of *Wiarus Polski* as the joint organ of the Polish population which was regularly translated into German for the information of the authorities. In 1894 Bochum also became the founding-place of the Association of Poles in Germany.[29] It acted as a blanket organisation for the Polish clubs, of which more than 100 had come into existence by 1890. As this blanket organisation which wielded little influence deliberately avoided taking up a Social Democratic stance, the *Alte Verband* tried, from 1898 onwards, to win over Polish miners with a Polish-language publication of its own. It was called *Górnik*, but was not particularly successful.

The growing network of denominational or professional Polish clubs devoted to choir-singing, athletics and leisure activities provided important points of orientation and indirectly helped to integrate newcomers into an industrial environment which was completely different from the rural world from which they came. However, the associations lacked trade-unionist objectives. The problems to which the newcomers saw themselves exposed were of a different order, at least for the time being. A trade union emerged only in 1902 in the shape of the Polish *Berufsvereinigung*.[30] The lack of organisational experience to guide political action became particularly evident during the riot-like events at Herne during the early summer of 1899. These events will now be described in detail and interpreted against the background of the above analysis.[31]

On Friday 23 June 1899, sixty-nine miners, all of them young

29. See Wehler, 'Ruhrgebiet', p. 447; Bredt, *Polenfrage*, pp. 62–5; C. Klessmann, 'Wiarus Polski', in *Beiträge zur Geschichte Dortmunds und der Grafschaft Mark*, vol. 71, 1974, pp. 383–97, esp. p. 388.
30. See esp. C. Klessmann, 'Klassensolidarität und nationales Bewusstsein', in *Internationale Wissenschaftliche Korrespondenz*, vol. 10, 1974, pp. 149–78; ibid., pp. 110–25.
31. Most important archival sources in Staatsarchiv Münster, Oberpräsidium Münster, 2847 VI, 2847a and 2847c; ibid., Regierung Arnsberg, I, 41, 42 and 43; ibid., Regierung Münster, 718; ibid. Bergamt Herne, A 8, 16 and 27, with newspaper accounts. See also O. Hue, 'Die Krawalle von Herne', in *Die Neue Zeit*, vol. 17, 1899, pp. 534–40; also Bredt, *Polenfrage*, pp. 84f.; Hue, *Gewerkschaften*, pp. 528f.; Hilbert; *Grubenbelegschaft*, pp. 93–5; Kirchoff, *Sozialpolitik*, p. 124; Hickey, 'Miners', pp. 227, 230f.; V. -M. Stefanski, *Zum Prozess der Emanzipation und Integration von Aussenseitern. Polnische Arbeitsmigranten im Ruhrgebiet*, Dortmund, 1984, pp. 135–9.

Polish hauliers and horse-handlers, stopped work at the Von der Heydt colliery. On Saturday the strike spread to the neighbouring Julia colliery, where thirty miners walked out. These had been the two days when the wages of the previous month after the deduction of advances had been paid out. The justification for the strike was said to be that the increase in *Knappschaft* insurance contributions for workers below the grade of hewer, which had just been decreed, should either be revoked or be compensated for by a commensurate wage rise. Soon demands focused on a twenty-five to thirty per cent wage claim. The increase in *Knappschaft* contributions derived from a change in the statutes of the Bochum *Knappschaftsverein* which had taken effect on 1 April. With the active support of the miners' representatives in the *Knappschaft*, this change had removed an injustice of the existing system. *Unständige* miners (those below the grade of hewer) paid lower contributions than their skilled comrades, the hewers, but the period of these payments was not counted as service years to be included in the subsequent calculation of pensions. Now the change of statutes which the workers' representatives in the *Knappschaft* had advocated had resulted in increased contributions of well over 100 per cent: from 1.50 marks per month to 0.80 marks per week. The resultant reduction in their wages had the initial effect of agitating the hauliers and horse-handlers; their dissatisfaction exploded when this reduction became manifest, on pay day. This, incidentally, was a response which had been typical of a mode of interest assertion practiced well back in the past.[32]

The tendency of young miners to resort to impulsive action was nothing new in the Ruhr area, which is why the authorities at first did not pay much attention to the walk-outs. This changed very quickly when a miners' rally which had been called in Herne for Sunday 25 June was dissolved.[33] According to the police, the assembly room, which had seats for 148 persons, was overcrowded long before the beginning of the meeting. Figures are imprecise and vary between 300 and 500. Numerous miners were pushing and shoving in the corridors of the public house in question. Hundreds are reported to have been waiting outside in the street and in a state of growing agitation. When the dissolution was announced, the miners noisily voiced their anger. At this point police reinforcements tried to disperse the crowds and made the first arrests.

---

32. Tenfelde, *Sozialgeschichte*, p. 401, and passim, inter alia on the unrest in the 1850s.
33. See the *Versammlungsaufruf zum 25. Juni 1899*, repr. in the appendix of the German original of this article.

The hasty dissolution was later privately admitted to have been a mistake by the authorities.[34] This measure directed the demonstrators against the authorities and provided the spark which ignited several days of rioting in areas which were vital to the communal life of the miners: the unrest occurred in the streets and backyards of the housing colonies whose size had just been doubled by new construction.[35] The families who lived there were all recent arrivals. It was these neighbourhoods that turned into foci of uncoordinated excitement.[36] It spread to the pit heads on the following day after the miners had agreed on their tactics before their arrival there. This behaviour, too, was in line with a practice which had been tried out in previous decades and which was furthered by the way the shift changes were organised.[37] It had been one of the great achievements of unionisation that the process of interest articulation was put on a rational footing by the regulated procedures of opinion formation. The behaviour of the mostly youthful Polish workers, who were joined by older German hewers only after the dissolution of the Sunday rally, signalled a clear step in a backward direction. The miners expressed their displeasure by throwing stones and by noisily resorting to similarly aggressive behaviour against their superiors and colliery installations. But they were unable to formulate the objectives of their strike and to find a practicable way of reaching their aims, for example by electing delegates. Consequently the movement continued to spread beyond the Von der Heydt and Julia collieries to others in the vicinity of Herne, namely Friedrich der Grosse, Konstantin der Grosse II/IV, Shamrock I/II and Mont Cenis. The total work-force of these collieries was 9,610 prior to the beginning of the strike.[38] However, in none of these

34. It is not clear from the files whether it was Landrat Spude, who was present, or the police officer in charge who was responsible for the dissolution order. Spude would have had good reason, given the repercussions of that order, to conceal his responsibility in the internal correspondence.
35. See Staatsarchiv Münster, Bergamt Herne, A 8, 27, with a report that company-owned dwellings had risen from 510 in 1898 to 1,008 in 1899. At the Shamrock colliery, these new estates were already known as 'Polenwinkel' ('Poles' corners'). See ibid., Regierung Arnsberg, I, 41, Report by the Arnsberg Regierungspräsident on the strike (draft), 27.6.1899.
36. See *Deutsche Berg- und Hüttenarbeiter-Zeitung (verbunden mit Glückauf, Bochum)*, vol. 11, no. 26, 8.7.1899, repr. in the appendix of the German original of this article. See also *Rheinisch-Westfälische Zeitung*, 29.6.1899. All papers reported that the colonies were centres of unrest at night, with noise, shots fired and an increased consumption of alcohol.
37. See Tenfelde, *Sozialgeschichte*, pp. 418–21.
38. On the strength of the work-force prior to the strike, see Staatsarchiv Münster, Regierung Arnsberg, I, 42. There are gaps and contradictions in the evidence, but the basic outlines can be reconstructed.

cases was the strike joined at any stage by all the miners employed there. Rather it was typical of the movement that only a few hundred stayed away from the morning shift. The midday shifts made extensive use of the opportunity of staging their protest before the start of the shift, as this seemed more easily feasible. As a result, the midday shift failed to turn up *en bloc*.

This pattern explains why unrest reached its climax in the afternoons and evenings when the early shifts had finished working and the midday shifts stayed out. Having demonstrated at the colliery gates, partly by resorting to violence against strike-breakers, the miners went noisily through the streets. It was not possible to discover a purposeful organisation of events. On Tuesday 27 June many whose curiosity had been aroused gathered with numerous strikers in the main street of Herne. The police moved in and made two arrests. In the course of the ensuing upheaval shots were fired. Sixteen people were injured, two of whom died shortly thereafter.[39] This Battle of *Bahnhofstrasse* as it came to be called in the regional press, led the Kaiser to issue an order to the Commanding General at Münster, General von Mikusch. He was told personally to supervise an 'immediate and energetic restoration of order'.[40] On Wednesday evening two battalions of infantry from Wesel and a squadron of Münster curassiers moved into Herne. In short, some 2,000 foot-soldiers and 150 cavalry appeared on the scene. The soldiers bivouacked in or near the collieries concerned up to company strength.[41] They supervised shifts and provided escorts and protection for strike-breakers on their way to their work-place. In addition the Herne local council, sitting late into the evening of 27 June, and following a well-tried tradition,[42]speedily decided to set up so-called 'pit militias'. These were protective contingents made up of colliery employees or, more rarely, loyal miners who were

39. Ibid., Constable Warnecke to Oberwachtmeister Britt, 7.7.1899, repr. in the appendix of the German original of this article. The files do not make clear whether it was the police or the Mayor of Herne, Schäfer, who gave the order to fire. The latter is made responsible in H. Sicburg, 'Der Aufstieg des Ruhrlandes vom Agrargebiet zum Industrieschwerpunkt Deutschlands im Spiegel der Entwicklung Hernes vom Dorf zur Stadt, 1850–1914', MS, n.d., pp. 17f. (in the Herne Stadtarchiv).
40. Telegrams in Staatsarchiv Münster, Regierung Arnsberg, I, 41.
41. Accounts on provisions in Stadtarchiv Herne, VI, 26. In the Recklinghausen area expenses were paid by the mining companies: see Stadtarchiv Recklinghausen, Altes Amts-Archiv, 1963.
42. K. Tenfelde, 'Gewalt und Konfliktregelung in den Arbeitskämpfen der Ruhrbergleute bis 1918', in F. Engel-Janosi et al. (eds.), *Gewalt und Gewaltlosigkeit*, Vienna, 1977, pp. 185–236, 217f.

sworn in as auxiliary policemen. They wore a cap and an armband
and were issued with a pistol. Their task was to restore law and
order inside the collieries under the direction of the management.
On Wednesday, before the arrival of the troops, the strike movement reached its climax. Some 1,749 miners from the six collieries
affected so far were by now involved. By Friday the whole movement had largely crumbled, partly because of the appearance of the
troops, but probably also because a Catholic holiday — Peter and
Paul — intervened. The Poles were warned against violence from
the pulpit during services on that day. The miners' associations also
began to exert a moderating influence, which we will discuss below.
On the other hand, the holiday also provided an opportunity for
carrying the strike to neighbouring areas where preparations for
protest meetings were started. Some twenty hauliers had stopped
work at the König Ludwig colliery as early as Monday. They were
joined on Tuesday by fifty-one men at the Shamrock III/IV colliery near Gelsenkirchen. By Friday the strike movement had
spread north to König Ludwig, General Blumenthal and Ewald in
the Recklinghausen district; Shamrock III/IV and Pluto (Wilhelm
pit) in the western parts of the Gelsenkirchen district has also been
affected. All five collieries had employed a total of 8,344 men before
the beginning of the strike. By Friday 1,773 of them were on strike;
on the following day it was still 1,360 men. The movement was less
successful at the Kaiserstuhl, Borussia, Hannibal, Alma and Unser
Fritz collieries, where only a few Polish hauliers struck. Quick
police reinforcements and the army, however, succeeded in con-
taining the further spread of the movement. By Monday 3 July the
authorities were able to report, in inimitable bureaucratic German,
that the midday shift had 'passed extraordinarily satisfactorily at all
collieries'.[43] No less satisfactory was the outcome of a meeting, held
on 4 July, between the *Oberpräsident* of Münster and *Landräte*
from Bochum, Gelsenkirchen and Dortmund, the police commissioners of the districts concerned and the Mayor of Herne,
Schäfer. By Wednesday the strike was deemed to be 'extinct'. The
military began to withdraw on the following day.

As the *Landrat* of the Gelsenkirchen district put it in August
1899, the Herne movement had 'less the character of an organised
economic wage-conflict than of a trial of strength which had been

43. Telegram in Staatsarchiv Münster, Regierung Arnsberg, I, 41.

deliberately brought about'.[44] And indeed, at no point did a discernible and clear organisation of the conflict, definite forms of decision delegation and a formulation of aims materialise. This was because the miners' associations condemned the strike and because Polish efforts to get organised had not yet reached a degree which would have permitted the Poles clearly to concentrate on their interests. Nevertheless, the riots did not develop 'spontaneously', either in the sense that they were completely unexpected, or in the sense that the movement did not even evolve embryonic forms of conflict organisation. This also applies to other incidents which are in many ways comparable to the events in Herne and which represent early forms of collective protest by the German labour movement: the machine breakers, the uprisings of the weavers, the bread riots, the violent revolts of the pre-1848 period and the decades thereafter were all more than 'spontaneous' outbursts of conflict potentials.[45] Conflicts will be internalised or conducted on an individual basis for as long as institutionalised forms of conflict regulation are lacking and opportunities for establishing ties and relationships between those equally affected are missing. There are certain preconditions of violent collective action short of organised procedures. These are marked by an identity of interest which is felt, rather than recognised, by a minimum of collective consciousness and by a common horizon of communication. Viewed from this perspective, the Herne Riots did not signal the beginning of conflicts initiated by Polish workers which bore a relation to their interest; rather they reflected the degree of consciousness which they had reached on their way towards this goal.[46]

In several respects the disposition of the Polish miners on the Ruhr to engage in confrontations had evolved towards a climax in the months before the riots. The feeling of living in a familial diaspora and of being discriminated against at their work-place and

---

44. Ibid., Landrat to Regierung Arnsberg, 15.8.1899; quote in ibid., report by the Regierungspräsident (draft), 22.8.1899.
45. See, e.g., G. Puchta and E. Wolfgramm, 'Spontaneität und Keimformen der Bewusstheit in der Frühzeit der deutschen Arbeiterbewegung', in *Wissenschaftliche Zeitschrift der Universität Leipzig (gesellschaftswissenschaftliche Reihe)*, 1956/7, pp. 673–81; L. Uhen, *Gruppenbewusstsein und informelle Gruppenbildung bei deutschen Arbeitern im Jahrhundert der Industrialisierung*, Berlin 1964; E. J. Hobsbawm, *Labouring Men*, London, 1964, pp. 5–22.
46. See, e.g., A. Mitscherlich, 'Aggression — Spontaneität — Gehorsam', in idem (ed.), *Ist die menschliche Aggression unbefriedbar?*, Munich, 1969, pp. 66–103; M. Olson, 'Rapides Wachstum als Destabilisierungsfaktor', in K. von Beyme (ed.), *Empirische Revolutionsforschung*, Opladen, 1973, pp. 205–222; n. 89 below.

in society had reached danger-point in view of the gigantic influx of people during the recent boom. One indication of this was the sharp increase of crime, particularly crimes of violence and theft, in the Ruhr area during the 1890s. In the 1880s the district of the Higher Court (*Oberlandesgericht*) for Rhineland-Westphalia was at the bottom of the statistical league. There were no more than 658 convicted persons per 100,000 adults. By 1901 the district had moved up to sixth place with 1,154 convicted persons. Two developments had caused this change. To begin with, adolescent crime rose from 1,316 to 2,605 convicted persons in the Düsseldorf *Regierungsbezirk* and from 764 to 1,705 in the Arnsberg *Regierungsbezirk*. Secondly, as a comparison between the eastern judicial districts, which had a large Polish population, and the rest of the Ruhr area shows, a considerable percentage in the rise of crime rate may be reduced to the newcomers.[47] Thenceforth there were regular reports concerning rioting and violence by Polish-speaking, mostly young miners, among which the 'Polish battle of Jordan' at the end of August 1897 on the occasion of the anniversary celebrations of one of the Polish clubs in Dortmund-Kirchlinde[48] gained a special notoriety. But to these conflicts others were added at the beginning of 1899 when tensions increased after the promulgation of the above-mentioned language decree by the *Oberbergamt* and the ratification of the revised miners' pension statute. Finally, at the end of May, the Penitentiary Bill (*Zuchthausvorlage*) was introduced into the Reichstag, which abolished § 153 of the *Gewerbeordnung* and imposed heavy penalties on closed shops and picketing.[49] As early as the summer of 1898 the Polish community had established in Herne a local branch of the Polish Social Democratic Party which had recently been founded. It was named *Przedsvit* (Dawn) and its chairman, the typesetter Szcotkowski, also took on the translating and editing for the journal *Górnik*. However, this association found it just as difficult to gain influence in the Herne

47. See P. Frauenstädt, 'Die preussischen Ostprovinzen in kriminalgeographischer Beleuchtung', in *Zeitschrift für Sozialwissenschaft*, vol. 9, 1906, pp. 570–83. Critical perspective in: Hilbert, *Grubenbelegschaft*, pp. 90–3; Klessman, *Bergarbeiter*, pp. 80f.
48. See A. Mämpel, '"Fremdarbeiter" — Probleme um 1900', in *Der Märker*, vol. 20, 1971, pp. 102–6.
49. Text of the Bill in *Stenographische Berichte über die Verhandlungen des Reichstages*, 10/I., 1898/1900, no. 347, 26.5.1899; also Staatsarchiv Münster, Regierung Arnsberg, I, 41, Polizeikommissar Bochum to Regierung Arnsberg, 11.7.1899, with the prehistory and the usual anti-Socialist stereotypes current among the bureaucracy.

region as the branches of the Christian trade union movement or the *Alte Verband*. The number of members remained small, at least for the time being. On the other hand, meetings were held from December 1898, and the records show that, at least at the meetings on 1 June and 11 June, strong opposition was voiced against the pension statute and the Penitentiary Bill under the leadership of Adamski, a miner. The meeting on 11 June even passed a resolution to that effect. The meeting on 25 June had been prepared on the previous day in conjunction with the *Alte Verband*.[50]

Such embryonic forms of interest articulation indicated at least a growing feeling of solidarity among Polish workers. If during the riots they were not canalised under clear leadership, the inexperience of the Polish labour leaders would appear to be one reason for this. Another was the explicit retreat of the *Alte Verband* from all responsibility for the strike. Thenceforth the action could in fact no longer be called a strike. The exchange of experience and opinion formation among the participants remained confined to processes of communication that were dictated by circumstances. One further reason for this was that many of the newcomers were either totally or almost illiterate. Hence communication remained restricted to the collieries, the streets and housing estates. Having only themselves to rely on and barely familiar with local industrial and communal conditions, the Polish leaders did not get beyond sending agitators into the region on bicycles and issuing, on a minor scale, instruction leaflets.[51] As the strikers were not led towards specific objectives, their solidarity found expression in rioting, vandalism, attacks on non-strikers, in stone-throwing and night-time firing of pistols. The role of rumour was typical of the partially formal channels of communication among the Polish population during the riots. Thus the authorities tried, with their usual thoroughness, to find both victim and perpetrator of an incident in which someone's ear had apparently been bitten off.[52]

Like the working-class press in the Ruhr region and the Social Democrats,[53] the two miners' unions spoke in unison against a

---

50. There had been thirty-five Polish workers at this preliminary meeting. Using the equipment of the *Alte Verband*, leaflets calling for the rally were printed then.
51. Staatsarchiv Münster, Regierung Arnsberg, I, 42, Bekanntmachung, 29.6.1899, repr. in the appendix of the German original of this article.
52. Ibid., report by Landrat Spude, 5.7.1899.
53. 'Social Democratic Appeal to the Miners', in *Rheinisch-Westfälische Arbeiterzeitung*, no. 149, 29.6.1899, repr. in the appendix of the German original of this article.

general walk-out, even if the tone of their statements was marked by different nuances. Soon after the news of the incidents had spread and in the wake of the dissolution of the rally, the unions dispatched August Brust, Otto Hue and other leading figures into the strike area. The riots provided an occasion to exchange traditional criticisms between the two unions. Moreover, the *Alte Verband*, in particular, tried to turn the victims of the excessive police actions into martyrs of the working-class cause.[54] On the other hand, their refutation of the strikers was unequivocal. Even the authorities went so far as to concede this much in their correspondence. Both unions had been caught unawares by the unrest.[55] The riots came at a most inopportune moment for the *Alte Verband*, as it had just begun to agitate among the Poles and knew of the very meagre initial success of this agitation.[56] It was an aspect of a pragmatism among the unions which became stronger from the mid-1890s onwards. For them building up an organisation was conceivable only through determined action under the chief executive. Now this approach turned out to be an impediment to success, and the question must be asked as to whether the work among the Poles had not been more successful in the long run, if one had taken the bull by the horns and, in exploiting the favourable market situation and the notorious labour shortage,[57] had claimed the leadership of the embryonic movement. There is also the question as to how the situation had become bogged down because the protest also involved a controversial clause in the pension statute to which the *Alte Verband* had given its support.

In view of all this, the leaders of the *Verband* did not have an alternative to their policy of appeasement and of using the events, where possible, for a consolidation of their organisation. Certainly

54. *Deutsche Berg- und Hüttenarbeiter-Zeitung (verbunden mit Glückauf)*, vol. 11, no. 26, 8.7.1899, repr. in the appendix of the German original of this article.
55. See the claim by Otto Hue that the union was totally surprised by the unrest and considered it an outgrowth of the immigrant workers' ignorance in *Rheinisch-Westfälische Zeitung*, no. 485, 29.6.1899. According to Kirchhoff (*Sozialpolitik*, p. 124), the union leadership, wishing to end the strike as soon as possible, did not even recoil from a police offer to provide intelligence information.
56. Of the ninety members of the Herne branch of the *Alte Verband* some thirty were Poles. The miners had three delegates on the cartel of unions at Herne, among them the Pole Adamski: see Staatsarchiv Münster, Regierung Arnsberg, I, 41, report by Regierungsrat Müller (copy), 3.7.1899.
57. See ibid., Oberpräsidium Münster, 2847c, Circular of the Verein für die bergbaulichen Interessen im Oberbergamtsbezirk Dortmund to its members, 28.6.1899, repr. in the appendix of the German original of this article; ibid., report of the Obergamt, 28.9.1899.

the unions' public statements show a remarkable insight into the causes and the failure of the strike. Their dilemma was that they expected to have a decisive say in the regulation of conflict in the industry, yet at the same time they found it impossible actually to fulfill this role. In this respect it proved decisive for the unions that the more experienced German workers participated only temporarily in the strike movement when provoked by police violence. This division may in the first instance have been the result of the fragmentation of the working class which occurred with the expansion of the work-force and which was more or less openly promoted by the employers.[58] It was also a minority problem, a problem of religious and ethnic discrimination in the pits and outside the colliery gates. Nevertheless, two observations must be made in this context: on the one hand, the divergent responses to the strike reflected a generational conflict which had manifested itself before and for the first time apparently during the 1877 strike movement,[59] when no one even faintly thought of Polish immigrants. As early as 1889 the argument could be heard that, if the barely 20-year-old hauliers and horse-handlers had not yet taken the lead, they nevertheless had formed 'something like the vanguard of the agitation which had been instigated'.[60] Indeed the phenomemon of a strike by the hauliers henceforth accompanied all struggles of the Ruhr miners, including, for example, the major miners' strike of 1905.[61] August Brust, still president of the Christian *Gewerkverein*, summed up his impressions of the strike by dubbing it an 'adolescent prank' (*Dummenjungenstreich*).[62]

Indeed one will have to look for a partial explanation of the 'eruptions'[63] in the socialisation processes experienced by city children within the family and community which detailed empirical work still has to bring out. We may also surmise that step-by-step

---

58. The working-class press repeatedly talked of the 'truly affectionate preference' of the entrepreneurs for the Polish workers. How far this was a deliberate strategy on the part of the employers, requires further investigation. That it was, has been demonstrated by the references to the Georg Fischer AG by R. Vetterli, *Industriearbeit, Arbeiterbewusstsein und gewerkschaftliche Organisation*, Göttingen, 1978, 184, passim.
59. See Tenfelde, *Sozialgeschichte*, p. 507.
60. Stadtarchiv Duisburg, 13/419, report of Mayor of Beeck to the Landrat in Mülheim (draft), 28.9.1889.
61. Hauptstaatsarchiv Düsseldorf, Regierung Düsseldorf, 15933 and 15934, with several reports to this effect; Hickey, 'Miners', p. 230.
62. Staatsarchiv Münster, Oberpräsidium, 2847c, report on a meeting of the Gewerkverein christlicher Bergleute at Herne on 30.7.1899, n.d.
63. Lucas, *Zwei Formen*, p. 126.

there emerged in this phase of industrialisation and urbanisation an indigenous urban youth culture. The reactions of the older German-speaking workers by contrast had long been conditioned by the experience within the factory, by their familial and communal ties with their neighbourhood, their parish and their social clubs. Finally there was the memory of the corporate past of the Ruhr miners. All these factors had led them to recognize that strike actions against the well-organised phalanx of Ruhr mine-owners required an extraordinary discipline — a discipline which one had adhered to during the strikes of 1872 and 1889. It had been in these and other strikes that the miners had still conformed to traditional patterns of company-based decision-making and delegation which dated back to the days of the *Stände* (estates). In other words, they had formally elected delegates from among their colleagues (normally three) and vested them with a limited mandate to negotiate with the management. This pattern of conflict regulation was even adopted by the older work-codes, of course in characteristic connection with formal complaint procedures designed to channel expressions of dissatisfaction. Thus we read in one of these codes that 'no more than three participants' could put forward justified complaints by a number of workers.[64] In 1889 this form of grass-roots organisation collided with the claims of the *Knappenvereine* to lead the strike movement, just as more generally it turned out to be the more radical variant of interest articulation among miners. Above all, this organisation remained intact as a body of effective opinion formation in the 1890s and even after the turn of the century, at a time when the associations began to monopolise the modes of conflict regulation in the mining industry by alternative principles of decision-making outside the work-place. They did so in clubs operating a free mandate, through regulated financing and by developing a clear strategy relating to the labour market.[65] Workers' councils, which first emerged on a voluntary basis and became obligatory from 1905, and shop stewards (*Sicherheitsmänner*) should also be seen against the background of this grass-roots organ-

64. Thus §26 of the Work Code of Shamrock I/II of 1892, which was in force at the time of the strike and which was modelled on a code of the 1860s (copy in Staatsarchiv Münster, Regierung Arnsberg, I, 41).
65. See the references to the 1891 strike at Langenbrahm colliery and the 1892 strike at the Ludwig colliery in Stadtarchiv Essen, 120/4; ibid., 120/5, for a strike meeting in Recklinghausen in 1905; Hauptstaatsarchiv Düsseldorf, Regierung Düsseldorf, 15924, Regierungspräsident to the Interior Minister (copy), 5.12.1904, relating to the 1904 disturbances at the Bruchstrasse colliery.

isation, without it being an 'alternative' labour movement, as E. Brockhaus has argued.[66]

This tradition of grass-roots activity, which had been a matter of course in earlier times (whatever its usefulness to the successful conclusion of a labour conflict may have been) was not accessible to the young or the Polish miners. They were without such path-finding aids and without determined leadership; they had no self-confidence nor a sense of identity which had grown out of communal ties and relations. As a result, the hauliers and horse-handlers were pushed into a planless aggressiveness, and their movement was doomed to failure from the start. As was repeatedly stated in the trade union press, their actions served nobody any good except the 'hardliners' (*Scharfmacher*) on the employers' side.[67]

This was to become clearer in the weeks following the end of the strike. As usual, preventive measures were taken by the authorities even before the days of unrest were over.[68] Up to the end of the first week of July, two of the Polish miners had been killed and at least thirty had been injured. Up to Sunday 2 July, some fifty people had been arrested. Attempts by the miners to hold open-air meetings were prevented by the police and by the military with bayonets (*mit blanker Waffe*).[69] The events aroused considerable public attention, and it is not surprising that vastly exaggerated estimates of the extent of the strike movement were circulating in the press.[70] Considering that the total work-force of the collieries concerned was 18,000 and that subsequent attempts at spreading the strike were unsuccessful, the overall number of strikers of about 3,500 looks rather meagre; the more so, if one remembers that participation never exceeded 1,800 on any one day. Moreover there occurred a brief regional shift in activities after the 29 June holiday. Some 192 miners, i.e. some five to six per cent of the strikers, were disciplined by the management. The composition of this group reflected the basic features of the unrest. Some 171 of those disciplined were under twenty-five; among them 157 were of Polish origin, five were

66. E. Brockhaus, *Zusammensetzung und Neustrukturierung der Arbeiterklasse vor dem ersten Weltkrieg*, Munich, 1975, pp. 98–130; for critical comments see, e.g., B. Rabe, *Der sozialdemokratische Charakter*, Frankfurt, 1978, pp. 24ff., 31.
67. *Deutsche Berg- und Hüttenarbeiter-Zeitung (verbunden mit Glückauf)*, vol. 11, no. 26, 8.7.1899, repr. in the appendix of the German original of this article.
68. See the 'Bekanntmachung des Landrats Spude anlässlich der Unruhen', in *Rheinisch-Westfälische Arbeiterzeitung*, no. 149, 30.6.1899, repr. in the appendix of the German original of this article.
69. *Tremonia*, no. 270, 2.7.1899.
70. *Westfälische Volkszeitung*, no. 149, 4.7.1899, mentioned 6,000–7,000 miners.

Masurians, twenty-nine were Germans and one was Austrian. After the end of the strike the military and police authorities mutually heaped upon each other their 'unconditional praise' (*rückhaltlose Anerkennung*) for their courageous actions and referred to proposals for future decorations.[71] The participating police officers were given high 'gratifications', amounting up to 100 marks per person, which were apparently paid predominantly by the mine-owners.[72]

In the following weeks draconian sentences (if we take into account what they had actually done) were meted out to those arrested miners who had been committed for trial. Neither for the first nor the last time, the judiciary applied to the miners what can only be described as unmitigated class justice.[73] While the mine-owners now generally insisted on a clause in their work codes which stipulated that up to six days of wages could be withheld in the case of a breach of contract,[74] the courts dealt with all conceivable kinds of prosecutions, such as resistance against the authority of the state (§ 133f. of the Criminal Code), riotous assembly (§ 115), breach of the peace (§ 123), grievous bodily harm (§ 223), intimidation (§ 240), threatening behaviour (§ 241) and incitement to disobedience against the law (§ 110). Sentences were also passed based on the Association Law of 1850 and on the notorious § 153 of the Reich *Gewerbeordnung*.[75] It is impossible to be precise about the total number of sentences, because some cases took a long time to reach the courts and because of appeals. But there were certainly dozens of people who were put behind bars for months for the most minor offences. Thus Johann Iwan, a miner, went to goal for five months because he had threatened working miners with a stick in his hand and with the words: 'You just wait until night time'. The miner Ludkowski was given eight months for trying to talk a working colleague into joining the strike. The miner Fürkötter was given a 'mere' six months for a similar offence in view of his young age.

71. Report of the Arnsberg Regierungspräsident, 17.7.1899, repr. in the appendix of the German original of this article.
72. *Tremonia*, no. 306, 25.6.1899; additional material in Stadtarchiv Herne, VI, 26 and Stadtarchiv Recklinghausen, Altes Amtsarchiv, 1963. The Herne Riots led to a tightening-up of the regulations relating to the possession of fire-arms in Prussia in 1901.
73. See K. Saul, *Staat, Industrie, Arbeiterbewegung im Kaiserreich*, Düsseldorf, 1974, pp. 188ff.
74. See §6 of the Work Code of the Shamrock I/II colliery (also n. 64 above).
75. Staatsarchiv Münster, Oberpräsidium, 2847c, report of the President of the Landgericht at Bochum to the Oberpräsident at Münster, 15.8.1899; ibid., Generalstaatsanwaltschaft Hamm, I, 12; numerous press cuttings in ibid., Regierung Arnsberg, I, 42 and 43.

There was also a court case involving Dr Reismann-Grone, the former secretary of the Mine-Owners' Association (*Bergbauverein*) and now editor of the *Rheinisch-Westfälische Zeitung*.[76] Its outcome was, however, typical of the situation in the Ruhr area. Reismann had personally gone to the area of unrest. He had, it was said, mingled with Social Democrats while looking for witnesses. On one of these occasions he had been temporarily arrested, much to everybody's embarrassment, by colliery security guards (*Zechenwehr*). The editor had of course not followed events out of sympathy with the workers' cause; rather he was hoping to prove how totally incompetent the civilian authorities were in handling industrial conflicts, such as appeared to threaten almost daily in the Ruhr region. Under Reismann's editorship the *Rheinisch-Westfälische Zeitung*, which was widely read in the Ruhr region, had resorted to chauvinist agitation in the spirit of a folkish antisemitism. It had also appeared in the front-line of the Pan-German naval propaganda. Now Reismann began to criticise sharply the 'sloth of paunchy police constabularies' (*wohlbeleibte 'Gendarmeriewirtschaft'*).[77] In his view the only salvation against working-class unrest was to be found in a speedy use of the army. The paper also criticised the regional authorities, situated at Arnsberg, as too remote, unfamiliar with conditions in the Ruhr area and in case of an emergency not available quickly enough for reasons of transport and telegraphic communication.[78] These arguments were in line with views which bourgeois circles in the Ruhr region had held for some time and continued to adhere to. As a matter of fact, the administrative divisions within the Ruhr region, which have been upheld to this day, can more easily be explained in terms of bureaucratic inertia and bear little relation to criteria of efficient government. Reismann promptly incurred the wrath of the head of the Arnsberg district who initiated criminal proceedings against him. He was not even distracted in his determination to bring the eager editor to court by intercessions made in Berlin on behalf of the latter. But the end result of these pleas was that they helped to produce a mild sentence.

76. For the following, see the material in ibid., Regierung Arnsberg, I, 41. On the Reismann case, see K. W. Schmidt, 'Die "Rheinisch-Westfälische Zeitung" und ihr Verleger Reismann-Grone', in *Beiträge zur Geschichte Dortmunds und der Grafschaft Mark*, vol. 69, 1974, pp. 241–382.
77. See the criticisms of the insufficient strength of the security contingent in *Rheinisch-Westfälische Zeitung*, no. 916, 5.12.1899.
78. Criticisms, ibid.

Papers like the *Rheinisch-Westfälische Zeitung* were prominently involved in building up an image of the Poles which the Herne Riots glaringly seemed to illustrate. It was an image which henceforth affected even working-class circles. Thus we read: 'The Herne Riots have once again highlighted the brutality of the Poles who subvert our working population. For those who know these sly and brawling fellows the unrest was nothing new; for the Poles they presented a welcome opportunity to give free rein to their coarseness and blood-thirst by which a number of them are presumably in fact possessed'.[79] Also in the middle and lower echelons of the bureaucracy the incidents were seen as a new 'chapter in the statistics on brutalities'. The *Landrat* at Bochum wrote of the 'full rage of the Polish scum (*Pöbel*)' and its 'nationalist vanity'. He also spoke of 'Slavic race conceit'.[80] At Arnsberg the talk was about the 'terrorism' of the 'Polish masses which had been fanaticized to the outmost'.[81] Finally the Dortmund *Oberbergamt* reported on the 'irrationality and brutality of the workers living in the Herne area'.[82] All this, as well as the 'irreverance and relaxed stupidity' of the Polish workers was seen as a new variant of the Polish Question.[83] In Berlin one felt no inhibitions in using, as far as possible, the knowledge gained from the Herne Riots and began systematically to collect material for presentation in the parliamentary deliberations relating to the Penitentiary Bill.[84]

As is testified by the comments in its press,[85] the working-class movement recognised the causes of the Polish riots at Herne and the dangers which such incidents posed, for instance in relation to the Penitentiary Bill. Without falling for the stereotypes about the Poles that were spreading, the movement also correctly sized up these dangers. What was not appreciated was that a new phenomenon concerning conflicts in the mining industry had suddenly erupted to the surface. This was the fragmentation of the working class, their division into groups with divergent interests and loyalties or at least

79. Ibid., no. 489, 30.6.1899.
80. Staatarchiv Münster, Regierung Arnsberg, I, 41, report, 11.7.1899.
81. Ibid., report of the Regierungspräsident at Arnsberg, 17.7.1899.
82. Ibid. report of the Berghauptmann, 19.7.1899; also ibid., Oberpräsidium, 2847c, Report of the Berghauptmann, 8.9.1899.
83. *Kölnische Zeitung*, no. 510, 2.7.1899.
84. Staatsarchiv Münster, Regierung Arnsberg, I, 41, letter by the Minister of Trade, 13.7.1899, to submit a detailed report; ibid., Oberpräsidium, 2847c, with the material submitted to the Oberpräsident by the subordinate authorities.
85. See *Deutsche Berg- und Hüttenarbeiter-Zeitung (verbunden mit Glückauf)*, vol. 11, no. 26, 8.7.1899, repr. in the appendix to the German original of this article.

with different priorities in the articulation of their interests. Henceforth the unions found themselves confronted with this new phenomenon.

The events in Herne demonstrated that conflicts within the working class could not, at this stage in the industrialisation process, be exclusively reduced to conflicts of alienation and domination which were inherent in the social and economic organisation of capitalism. Other dispositions of conflict which had surfaced within the working class before now moved into the foreground. These were contradictions resulting from ethnic and denominational differences; they were conflicts of generation and were related to questions of length of residence, of skills and of hierarchies within the work-force which, faced with the strengthened power of the employers who no longer operated their policies of conflict pacification at company level, led to divergent perceptions of interest. The unions also had to include in their planning and strategic calculations factors such as ties outside the work-place which were determined by the urban environment of industrial communities, by the type of dwelling, family and neighbour relationships, by leisure organisations and increasingly also in the area of daily consumption habits. Conditions of proletarian solidarity which had just been created, broke down again under the impact of social change. It is therefore questionable that the strike weapon, which had been developed in previous decades, took adequate account of the new conflict situations.

The trade unions were in the first place concerned to preserve and to strengthen their organisational structures. As a result they barely perceived the consequences of the renewed radical changes which occurred at a technological and managerial level and affected their members and potential recruiting grounds in wider fields in the mining industry. In subsequent years this was to become abundantly clear when one looks at the impact of changing methods of coal production and the introduction of new machinery underground. Meanwhile the unions were primarily preoccupied with problems of illness and invalidity resulting from work in the pits. They often yielded to an unwarranted degree to pressures for the protection of the best organised, skilled German-speaking workers in the face of the problems raised by the massive influx of immigrants from the East. The polemical argument that the Polish newcomers had a depressing effect on wages was one manifestation of this tendency. Thus the unions failed to respond to the changes

that took place, especially among the hauliers, in the wake of the
waves of immigration and technical as well as organisational re-
structuring.

On the other hand, it is difficult to imagine, even with the benefit
of hindsight, how much these manifestations of uneven development with its manifold tensions and contradictions (*spannungsge-
ladener Ungleichzeitigkeit*) irritated both workers and union
leaders. It was these manifestations which promoted the events at
Herne and which continued to be typical of conflict situations in the
age of advanced industrialisation. A brief excursus and glance at
comparable developments at Königshütte in 1871 may serve to
elaborate this argument, which we have first raised in the context of
the pre-1848 protest movements. In 1869 a strike by German miners
in the Waldenburg area of Lower Silesia, which still bore the district
marks of the corporatist tradition of the mining industry, had failed.
It resulted, surrounded by considerable public attention, in the
decline of the liberal trade union movement which had only just
emerged.[86] Two years later, in 1871, disturbances occurred in the
Royal Mines at Königshütte which anticipated the Herne events in
several respects.[87] Faced with the introduction of *Markenkontrolle*,
an innovation which, like that at Herne, was in the miners' interest,
a large number of hauliers, having gathered at their assembly point
on the way to the pits, walked out. There were tumultuous scenes.
Ethnic and denominational tensions had been stored up for a long
time between the skilled German-speaking miners and their younger
Polish colleagues. Outside the pits the situation of the workers
had been affected by a very rapid growth of Königshütte; but no
urban community had been formed. The strikers did succeed in
formulating their demands; but their refusal to work did not lead to
the emergence of clear forms of organisation and decision-making.[88]
The organisation of clubs among the Polish workers was still
rudimentary and trade union objectives therefore played but a
subordinate role. Violent attacks against persons and property
resulted in the appearance of a strong army detachment on the scene
which 'cleared up' the situation in its own violent way within a

86. See U. Engelhardt, *Nur vereinigt sind wir stark*, 2 vols., Stuttgart, 1977, esp. vol.
     II, pp. 1071ff.
87. See Hue, *Gewerkschaften*, pp. 299–304; also a brief reference in L. Schofer, *The
     Formation of a Modern Labor Force: Upper Silesia, 1865–1914*, Berkeley, Calif.,
     1975, 146; detailed analysis of the strike in L. Machtan, *Streiks im frühen
     deutschen Kaiserreich*, Frankfurt, 1983, pp. 44ff.
88. Ibid., for the text.

short time. They left behind several dead and many injured civilians.

By comparing the two cases it is possible to look at the mentality of a working population with its mechanisms of socialisation, its familial and neighbourly relations and its ethnic peculiarities, which had barely adapted itself to industrial living and working conditions, and by doing so we are also provided with clues to explain the events at Herne. Our findings are at the same time a call to concentrate historical research into social conflict upon behaviour patterns outside the work-place. The insufficient integration of large groups of workers (and not just those of foreign origin) during the period of advanced industrialisation signifies the new structural conditions which have been described above with the help of the notion of *Ungleichzeitigkeit*. Of course this is a phenomenon which must be explained through a number of other variables, in particular with differences in regional and sectoral growth patterns and the divergencies in the degree of modernisation (*Modernisierungsgefälle*) resulting from this. At least the evidence would seem to be insufficient that a lag in socialisation and acculturation within the framework of an industrial society caused by structural change and the ups and downs in the economy with their stabilising and destabilising consequences was levelled out within the working class. The development of the Polish *Berufsvereinigung* after the turn of the century proceeded along its own specific path.

Nor is it sufficient to use the term 'radicalisation' when trying to interpret working-class protests and, in the final analysis, the policies of their organisations, against the background of non-German-speaking immigration and its consequences.[89] This view may be tenable, if one subsumes under this concept the external forms of conducting conflict. However the notion requires further testing, that the miners of most mining areas, inside Germany and without, were relatively prone to resort to strike action and hence represented the vanguard of the struggling proletariat. These tests should be undertaken not merely in statistical terms, they also require detailed investigations of smaller strikes and daily conflicts inside and outside the collieries.[90] They should be conducted away

89. See esp. Brepohl, *Industrievolk*, p. 165; also D. Crew, 'Regionale Mobilität und Arbeiterklasse', in *Geschichte und Gesellschaft*, vol. I, 1975, pp. 99–121, with references to recent American research on mobility and strike propensity; Hickey, 'Miners', p. 233: 'There was no close relationship between industrial militancy and political radicalism'.

90. J. Kuczynski, 'Streikende Bergarbeiter', in *Beiträge zur Geschichte des Bergbaus und Hüttenwesens*, vol. 7, Leipzig, 1969, pp. 39–48; also the comparative study

from the major conflicts[91] which commanded national attention, and they should take account of the peculiarities of the miners' existence. Among the peculiarities would be those of work conditions in the pits and of managerial structures; one would also have to include the development of local ties in the wake of massive agglomerations of people. Research should also move in this direction in respect of disputes in other industries. The task is to complement the results of the analysis of strike statistics in the decades prior to 1914[92] with detailed regional and sectoral studies of various conflicts (and not just of strikes). Only in this way will it be possible to reinforce (or to refute) the statistical findings.

It appears that actions like that by the Herne miners in 1899 are more easily described as social protests and hence to be linked to a type of historical conflict research which is barely developed.[93] They are less accurately described as strikes in the sense of a relatively controlled form of regulated conflict — a form which had been developed over the previous decades. The crucial point here is that renewed industrial change fundamentally called into question once again the modes of channelling and regulating industrial conflicts — that outstanding cultural achievement of the working-class movement — at a time when these modes had barely begun to establish themselves and before they had gained general acceptability.

---

by G. V. Rimlinger, 'International Differences in the Strike Propensity of Coal Miners: Industrial and Labor Experience in Four Countries', in *Industrial and Labor Relations Review*, vol. 12, 1959, pp. 389–405.

91. A. Gladen, 'Die Streiks der Bergarbeiter im Ruhrgebiet in den Jahren 1889, 1095 und 1912', in J. Reulecke (ed.), *Arbeiterbewegung an Rhein und Ruhr*, Wuppertal, 1974, pp. 111–48.

92. See esp. H. Kaelble and H. Volkmann, 'Konjunktur und Streik während des Übergangs zum Organisierten Kapitalismus in Deutschland', in *Zeitschrift für Wirtschafts- und Sozialwissenschaften*, vol. 92, 1972, pp. 513–44; H. Volkmann, 'Modernisierung des Arbeitskampfs?', in H. Kaelble et al., *Probleme der Modernisierung in Deutschland*, Opladen, 1978, pp. 110–70; K. Tenfelde and H. Volkmann (eds.), *Streik*, Munich, 1981.

93. See C., L. and R. H. Tilly, *The Rebellious Century, 1830–1930*, London, 1975, with R. H. Tilly's study on social protest in Germany ibid., pp. 191–238. Against the all too ideal-typical juxtaposition of forms of social protest (traditional, preindustrial, backward vs. modern, industrial, progressive) recent research has emphasized the contemporaneity of different stages of development, as evidenced at Herne in 1899 in comparison with Königshütte in 1871. See also: P. N. Stearns, 'Measuring the Evolution of Strike Movements', in *International Review of Social History*, vol. 19, 1974, pp. 1–26; R. J. Holton, 'The Crowd in History', in *Social History*, vol. III, 1978, pp. 219–33 (a critique of crowd research).

About the Contributors

Volker R. Berghahn, born 1938. Professor of History, University of Warwick. His published works include *Der Tirpitz-Plan. Genesis und Verfall einer innenpolitischen Krisenstrategie unter Wilhelm II,* (1971); *Germany: The Approach of War in 1914* (1973); *Militarism: The History of an International Debate* (1982); and *The Americanisation of West German Industry, 1945–1973* (forthcoming in 1986).

Franz J. Brüggemeier, born 1951. Assistant Professor at Open University, Hagen. His publications include *Leben vor Ort. Ruhrbergleute und Ruhrbergbau 1889–1919* (2nd ed., 1984).

Werner Conze, born 1910. Professor Emeritus at the University of Heidelberg and a long-time director of the Working Circle for Social and Economic History in Heidelberg. Early writings on the history of the Baltic region; extensive postwar writings on the socio-political history of Germany, including the history of labour and of the family.

Karin Hausen, born 1938. Professor at the Technical University of Berlin. Her writings include *Deutsche Kolonialherrschaft in Afrika. Wirtschaftsinteressen und Kolonialverwaltung vor 1914* (1970), as well as studies in the social history of women and the role of gender during the period of industrialisation.

Georg Iggers, born 1926. Professor at the State University of New York at Buffalo. Emigrated to America from Germany during the Nazi period. His writings include *The German Conception of History* (1968, 2nd rev. ed., 1983); and *New Directions in European Historiography* (1975, 2nd rev. ed., 1984).

Jürgen Kocka, born 1941. Professor at the University of Bielefeld. His writings include *White-Collar Workers in America 1890–1940. A Social and Political History in International Perspective* (1980); and *Facing Total War: German Society 1914–1918* (1984). Founder and co-editor of *Kritische Studien zur Geschichtswissenschaft* and of the journal *Geschichte und Gesellschaft.*

Lutz Niethammer, born 1939. Professor of Modern History, Open University, Hagen. Published work includes *Die Mitläuferfabrik. Die Entnazifierung am Beispiel Bayerns* (1982); (ed.), *Wohner im Wandel* (1979); and *Lebensfahrung und Kollektives Gedachtnis. Die Praxis der Oral History* (1980, rev. ed., 1984).

Hans Rosenberg, born 1904. Professor Emeritus at the University of California at Berkeley and Honorary Professor at Freiburg University. Emigrated to America during the Nazi period. His writings include *Bureaucracy, Aristocracy, Autocracy. The Prussian Experience 1600–1815* (1958); and *Probleme de deutschen Sozialgeschichte* (1969).

Klaus Tenfelde, born 1944. *Dozent* at the University of Munich. His writings include *Sozialgeschichte der Bergarbeiterschaft and der Ruhr im 19. Jahrhundert* (1977), and work on working-class culture, particularly of miners.

Hans-Ulrich Wehler, born 1931. Professor at the University of Bielefeld. His works include *Bismarck und der deutsche Imperialismus* (1969); and *The German Empire 1870–1918* (1985). Co-editor and founder of the *Kritische Studien zur Geschichtwissenschaft* and of the journal *Geschichte und Gesellschaft*.

Peter-Christian Witt, born 1943. Professor, Gesamt Hochschule Kassel. Author of *Die Finanzpolitik des Deutsches Reiches von 1903 bis 1913* (1970); co-editor of *Arbeiterfamilien im Kaiserreich* (1983).